Livelihood
and Resistance

Livelihood and Resistance

**Peasants and the Politics
of Land in Peru**

Gavin Smith

University of California Press
Berkeley/Los Angeles/Oxford

University of California Press
Berkeley and Los Angeles, California

University of California Press, Ltd.
Oxford, England

Library of Congress Cataloging-in-Publication Data

Smith, Gavin.
  Livelihood and resistance: peasants and the politics
of land in Peru / Gavin Smith.
     p.   cm.
  Bibliography: p.
  ISBN 0–520–06365–1
  1. Peasantry—Peru—Huasicancha.   2. Land
tenure—Peru—Huasicancha.   3. Land reform—
Peru—Huasicancha.   4. Haciendas—Peru—
Huasicancha.   I. Title.
HD1531.P4S55   1989   305.5′63   dc19   88–17499

Printed in the United States of America

1   2   3   4   5   6   7   8   9

To Winnie and to Coryn, Laura, and David

Contents

Preface

In one of the first anthropology books I read, as the 1960s were drawing to a close and before "anthropology" meant much more to me than the name of a Charlie Parker tune, Claude Levi-Strauss mulled over a conundrum: drawn to sail unknown seas to unknown soils by the criticism they feel for their own society, anthropologists are then constrained from criticizing the ways of life of the people they study. To observe with critical awareness, not necessarily criticism, seemed to me at the time what gave Levi-Strauss his *raison d'être*. Yet, in those same days, before I thought of becoming a professional anthropologist, I was much influenced by the account of a young journalist sent by *Life* magazine to write a story on the destitute sharecroppers of the American South. In the book he produced later, James Agee wrote with some bitterness of simply observing and recording for its own sake, and his discomfort has stayed with me in my wanderings, like a stone in my boot.

> It seems to me curious, not to say obscene and thoroughly terrifying, that it could occur to an association of human beings . . . to pry into the lives of an undefended and appallingly damaged group of human beings . . . for the purpose of parading the nakedness, disadvantage and humiliation of these lives before another group of human beings, in the name of science, of "honest journalism" (whatever that paradox may mean), of humanity, of social fearlessness, for money, and for a reputation for crusading and unbias which, when skillfully enough qualified, is exchangeable at any bank for money. (1966: 7)

I have no doubt that Levi-Strauss's writings are motivated by a desire to present the dignity and profundity of the powerless and disappearing people whose worlds he has so painstakingly analyzed, and, despite his self-loathing, Agee did add a greater historical purpose to the lives of those sharecroppers than would have occurred without him. Nevertheless, for me whose prose would never match theirs, the reflections of these two observers made me want to seek out ways in which such disadvantaged people might find from within their differences from me, the resources to resist, however minimally, the ravages wrought upon them from the moment, centuries past, when Europeans like myself set off on their wanderings. It was this desire which drew me, with the encouragement of Norman Chance and Don Attwood, to anthropology and gave me the opportunity to see how teaching, in the hands of John Janzen at McGill and Freddie Bailey at Sussex, could be simultaneously critical and constructive. But in this book on the Huasicanchinos, my greatest and first debt is to a rather shy, tall man who twenty years ago sat with me and a few students in a Montreal apartment listening to jazz records he had brought from Cuba. Since then Eric Hobsbawm's deeply felt commitment to help such people make their own history has always remained a model, and though I know there will be disappointments and disagreements for him in this book, I hope it is some small return for what I have received from his writings and his long-standing personal encouragement. It was he who, hearing that I wanted to live with peasant rebels less primitive than his, told me of Huasicancha and introduced me to Bryan Roberts and Norman Long, who were working in the Mantaro Valley. To these old friends and mentors I can offer my thanks with no apology for those parts of this curate's egg that are not so excellent: after all they have long known the length of my stride and should be happy enough that the stepping stones were set no wider apart.

I worked my passage to Peru on the *S. S. Cotopaxi,* out of Liverpool just after Christmas 1971 and once in Huancayo, Bryan and Susan Roberts saw me through more downs than ups, as well they will remember. For their hospitality and that of Rensje and Hans Oosterkamp, I owe many thanks as I do also to the Mayer family in Huancayo: if they kept a plaque of passing friends to whom they offered sustenance it would be the biggest monument in the city. Other colleagues in Peru whose friendship mattered so much were Anick and Julian Laite, Giovanni Mitrovic and Carmen Checa, Margarita Giesecke, and Marcial Rubio as well of course as "Diablo," "Zapo," Carlos Eduardo Aramburu, and Charles de Weck. In Lima too, I owe a special thanks to Juan Martinez-Alier for his astringent advice and guidance in working with archives.

I left Peru a week before Chile's last democratic government fell in September 1973, and I could not have left without the help of Jorge Dandler who may well remember the circumstances. I am grateful to him for that and many other moments. In all, my time was divided so that just over half was spent in Huasicancha and the rest in Lima and Huancayo. Throughout that period my constant companion and aid was Pedro Cano Hinostrosa who brought me to the village and taught me dimensions of friendship I had not known. To Pedro, to my comadre, Paulina, and to Ramiro, my ahijado, I hope this book will be some small reminder of that first, little Ramiro, my ahijado too, and I hope it will be of some value to all the Cano children. In Huasicancha my debts are so widespread as to make me hesitate to mention names, but even so special thanks are due to Grimaldo and Guillermina Pomayay and to Liberato Pomayay and also to Don Victor Hinostrosa and Don Martín Ramos. Don Angelino Cano gave me his house for a year, and for that I owe him much thanks. In Huancayo Herminio Zarate gave me much help, Teodoro too. In Lima, again there are so many, but I should mention especially Eulogio, Tomas, and Mauro. They will know which ones I mean.

For support during fieldwork carried out in Peru in 1972 and 1973 I am grateful to the Social Sciences and Humanities Research Council of Canada (SSHRCC) and to the Ministry of Education of the Government of Quebec. I returned to Huasicancha and to the barriadas again in 1981, thanks to financial support found for me by Richard Webb and a grant in aid from the SSHRCC. Then I was able to answer questions left hanging and acquire a greater longitudinal dimension to my fieldwork. It goes without saying that my debt to the Huasicanchinos is enormous. I hope this book will repay them. Indeed, even as they may disagree with this and that in it, I feel sure that the excitement of old debates thus renewed will be some reward. Finally, I would like to remember Don Sabino Jacinto who died within a week of so painfully sharing his memories with me.

The agrarian reform carried out by the Velasco government after 1969 involved the collection of all the available documents from the expropriated haciendas, and these provided an excellent starting point for historical materials on Hacienda Tucle and Huasicancha. There were other archival materials in Lima and in Huancayo that I used, as well as the materials available in the communal office of Huasicancha itself and a few odd items left in the abandoned hacienda buildings. A number of Huasicanchinos made available to me their "diaries," or exercise books, in which important information was kept rather haphazardly but was of great value to me. Among the non-Huasicanchinos I interviewed were Sr. Bernuy Gomez, onetime lawyer for the community, and Sr. Jesus Veliz Lizarraga, Tacunan's right-hand man for many years. I also interviewed people involved in the running of Hacienda Tucle and of the Cercapuquio Mine.

I administered a questionnaire to roughly a third of the households in Huasicancha. In virtually all cases husband and wife were present where applicable, and the part of the questionnaire in which informants became most involved was the life-history grids, a technique originally worked out by Jorge Balan, I believe, and which I adapted with the help of Bryan Roberts. Essentially it covered the years and informant's age down the page, and then various entries across the page, such as births, migrations, material acquisitions, and other items. Besides life-history material much household economic data were gathered in the questionnaire and subsequently verified over the course of the field work. In Lima just over a hundred similar questionnaires were administered.

From these data I selected out case studies. The selection was supposed to take into account differences in wealth, migration experience, age of head of household and, as I began to understand social relations better, households with different kinds of extra-household linkages. In fact the balance of cases was greatly influenced by my ease of entry vis à vis the groups concerned. But the case study technique was very successful and allowed me to spend extensive periods of time with each group both participating in a wide variety of activities and carrying out detailed inquiries. Indeed it is hard to say precisely how many cases were covered since, once begun, an initial case spread out to cover others, so that a "household case" soon became a "group case." The cases presented in this book represent a very small proportion of those studied but have been chosen for the insight they provide in each instance.

Besides these techniques, the usual general activities of fieldwork were undertaken, working in pastoral herding and arable farming in Huasicancha, standing with people at the market stalls in Huancayo, and walking the streets with ambulant vendors in Lima. In addition to the usual informal interviews and participating in general conversations (and community assemblies), I began to encourage group sessions, either at my house or at the municipal building (or in Huancayo or Lima at somebody else's house). These took place in the evening and would begin with a particular topic and then carry on at their own momentum. Such sessions were extremely fruitful and turned out to be a source of great enjoyment for participants, if somewhat of a strain for the anthropologist trying to take notes. (I occasionally used a taperecorder but soon found that transcribing took up the major part of fieldwork!) The collection of oral histories was obviously a major occupation, and again the life-history grid was of great use in matching up one incident with another in an informant's life. When I returned in 1981, I followed up on every questionnaire administered in Huasicancha, except when the entire family was defunct. In Lima, I was able to follow up on just under 50 percent.

For helping me to work through some of the ideas contained in this book (as well as others not here included) I would like to thank Jonathon Barker, Malcolm Blincow, Terry Byers, Jane Collins, Harriet Friedmann, Colin Harding, Olivia Harris, Joel Kahn, Temma Kaplan, David Lehmann, Winnie Lem, Josep Llobera, Florencia Mallon, Jay O'Brien, Tristan Platt, Bill Roseberry, Teodor Shanin, Robert Shenton, Gerald Sider, Carol Smith, Joan Vincent, Christine Whitehead, Eric Wolf, and Kate Young. Those I have mentioned will no doubt remark on how little I have remembered of what they advised me. Those not mentioned will be equally aware of my poor memory.

Introduction: The World of the Huasicanchinos

People of Huasicancha

    Though this study addresses general questions of how peasants make a living and how they engage in political resistance, it focuses on one group of people to make its argument. First then, we should meet these people: the people of Huasicancha (pronounced Wăsəcăncha; hence Wăsəcănchēnōs).

    The settlement of Huasicancha lies today on the edge of a long flat plateau that falls back for four miles to a point where it rises to form dense mountains (see Map 2).[1] Until very recently the pasture land of this plateau and mountains was controlled by a large livestock ranch—a *hacienda* (large farm or ranch run on traditional lines*). Through a campaign lasting over a hundred years, these people have conducted a long war of attrition against this and neighboring haciendas. The struggle ended in 1972 with the collapse of the hacienda and legal recognition of what was by then de facto possession of over 30,000 hectares of land by the Huasicanchinos.

    The village itself lies at an altitude of 12,400 feet (3,780 meters) above sea level, in the high pasture lands of the Peruvian central sierras (see Map 1). The Huasicanchinos include the 403 families (1,934 inhabitants) residing in the village, as well as 400 other families who have migrated to the provincial town of Huancayo, the mining towns around La Oroya to the north, and the national capital, Lima. This study focuses on all those people who refer to themselves as Huasicanchinos.

    Geographically Peru is divided into three zones which run roughly from northwest to southeast. In the west is a long coastal strip of desert broken by

---

*Foreign words are italicized on the first instance of their usage only. A glossary can be found on page 257.

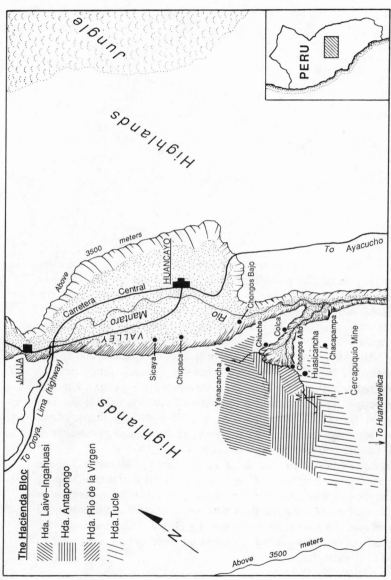

Map 1. The map shows a part of the mountainous spine that runs northwest to southeast through Peru. To the west of the map, the high mountainour land gives way to low coastal desert. To the east, the mountains fall back on to the high jungle (the ceta de selba). This high Andean puna is broken up by the wide and fertile inter-Andean valley of the Mantaro River, on which Huancayo is situated. A smaller tributary valley breaks through the Mantaro Gorge in the south, toward Huasicancha and the "Hacienda Bloc." This is the Canipaco River, whose name is sometimes used to refer to the area. The Hacienda Bloc is highlighted by cross-shading.

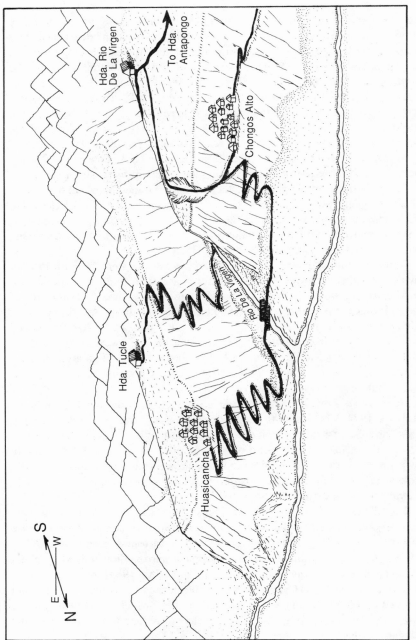

Map 2. *Diagram showing relative position of Huasicancha and Tucle.*

the short, spasmodic rivers that drain into the Pacific, along which are many
of the country's largest settlements. Running like a backbone down the center
of the country is the high mountain range of the Andes. Varying from the
uninhabitable heights of the permanently snow-covered summits, through the
puna grazing lands between 13,500 and 12,000 feet, to the inter-Andean valleys that descend to 10,000 feet, this is the zone of Peru's traditional peasantry. Moving eastward, the mountains descend steeply to the Amazonian
jungle, the third and most easterly of the zones. These easterly slopes of the
Andes are referred to as the *ceja de selba* or the "eyebrow of the jungle."

Sugar, rice, cotton, and fruit plantations have long been concentrated along
the coast, and more recently strip mining has taken on increasing importance
in the southern desert. Copper and other metals are mined in the central sierra,
where for many years arable and livestock haciendas have existed alongside
small peasant farms, while in the large inter-Andean valley of the Mantaro
River, commercial farmers exist alongside small manufacturing and commercial enterprises (see Long and Roberts 1978, 1984).

Lima lies almost exactly halfway down the coast of Peru. The twelfth de-
gree of latitude runs directly through the city, as it does through the provincial
town of Huancayo in the heart of the Mantaro Valley, directly to the east of
Lima. Huancayo is the capital of both the department (Junin) and the province
(Huancayo) in which Huasicancha is found. It is reached by a 200-mile paved
road and railway from Lima, which pass over the high western spine of the
Andes and descend to the Mantaro Valley through the smelting town of La
Oroya, long associated with the Cerro de Pasco Company (once American
owned but now nationalized).

Huancayo is a relatively recently developed and vigorous commercial town
(Roberts 1974*b*) of 120,000 people located at a communications crossing
point for west-east traffic from the coast to the jungle and north-south traffic
moving down toward Ayacucho or Huancavelica. It has also been a supply
town for the various mining operations of the central sierras. More recently
growth has been linked to its position as administrative center for a variety
of branches of government.

The Mantaro Valley itself was the locus of the Huanca (or Wanka) peoples
who were dominated by the Incas prior to the Spanish conquest, and whose
influence extended into the high pasture lands surrounding the valley. The
valley retained a dominant influence over the surrounding upland dwellers
until well after the conquest (Samaniego 1974; Mallon 1983), but in the south-
western area, known as Canipaco, where Huasicancha is located, the growing
importance of the Huancavelica mercury mines, which were next only to
Potosi in their value to the Spaniards, acted to reduce the influence of the
Mantaro Valley.

Surrounding the Mantaro Valley are high mountainous pasture lands historically dominated by livestock haciendas on the edge of which were Indian communities far less commercially developed than the settlements of the Mantaro Valley. Huasicancha is one such community, lying at the edge of the Hacienda Tucle, itself part of a geographically consolidated block of haciendas bordering on one another. By reference to map 1 it is possible to see that these haciendas—Tucle-Rio de la Virgen, Antapongo, and Laive-Ingahuasi—form an almost perfect rectangle that is cut into by the River Canipaco, a tributary of the Mantaro. The communities of Colca, Chicche, Chongos Alto, and Huasicancha lie on the edge of this valley, with the haciendas controlling the pasture right up to the edge of the communities and, to all intents and purposes, restricting the villagers to the steep hillsides, known as the *faldas* or skirts, running down to the river.

It is important to get a sense of the road connections that make Huasicancha and the hacienda buildings of Hacienda Tucle especially remote. For many years the only road link to the Mantaro Valley ran from Chupaca, through Yanacancha, to the Hacienda Laive-Ingahuasi; the road was subject to the hazards of the climate and was frequently impassable. Huasicancha could only be reached thus: by passing first Hacienda Antapongo, then Hacienda Rio de la Virgen, skirting not far from the buildings of Hacienda Tucle, and arriving eventually, via the *pampa,* at the village. For villagers, of course, this route was never taken. Instead mules, llamas, and donkeys were driven down the pass of the Canipaco and Mantaro. Another line of communication for them was southwest up the Rio de la Virgen into Huancavelica, thence to the town itself or branching west to descend to the coast via the Cañete River.

This relative isolation contrasts with even the neighboring community of Chongos Alto, which remained closely linked to the Mantaro Valley center of gravity, as did the other villages marked on the map. The remoteness of Huasicancha and Hacienda Tucle is reflected too in administrative boundaries, for these lands lie on the edge of three departments: Lima, Huancavelica, and Junin.

In the 1930s this remoteness was greatly reduced when the Cercapuquio Mine, bordering on Hacienda Rio de la Virgen, built a road with government assistance that climbed up from the south of the Mantaro Valley and then ran around the edge of the Canipaco Valley through Colca and Chicche to Chongos Alto and the mine. From here, once more, Huasicancha or Hacienda Tucle could be reached by crossing the Rio de la Virgen near the mine and climbing up to the high pampa (see Map 2). Vehicles taking this route could be seen from Huasicancha the moment they broke out into the Canipaco Valley above Chicche, some six or seven hours before they could reach the community. For the villagers, on the other hand, access to the Mantaro Valley via this road was facilitated by descending the steep hills opposite Chongos Alto, fording the river, and then climbing up into that village. This fortress quality of Huasicancha was greatly reduced soon after the major land invasions of the mid 1960s when the government built a bridge directly from Chongos Alto to Huasicancha.

As can be seen from map 2, the community lies just over the lip of a spectacularly flat four-mile plateau that forms the northeasterly edge of extensive pasture land going back into the mountains into the Province of Huancavelica. Along the steep sides of the slopes that run down to the de la Virgen and Canipaco, lie the community's arable plots. The climate at this high altitude varies from rainy temperate days from October to April, to hot dry days and freezing cold nights from May through to September. These sheltered slopes offer the most suitable microclimate for potatoes, wheat, barley, and broad beans, as well as the peculiarly Andean crops of *mashua* and *quinua*.

Sections of the pastureland to the southeast reach up to well over 16,000 feet and the edge of vegetation growth. On the lower levels strong, highland breed double-purpose cattle can be raised, although the harsh conditions make calving especially hazardous. Sheep are well suited to these ecological conditions and at one time provided the basis of the hacienda economy. Water scarcity during the winter months gives special value to catchment areas in the high zones, but beyond a certain point altitude restricts sheep pasture and defines the limits of the haciendas. The haciendas' lack of interest in such high altitude pasture gave a special impetus to the continued raising of lamoids (llamas and alpacas) by the local population, thus allowing some to remain pastoralists despite the expansion of the haciendas.[2]

The people of Huasicancha, which means house (*huasi*) and corral (*cancha*), consider themselves to be descendents of the Huancas. They continue to speak Huanca which, they argue, is different from imperial Quechua. Although all men and women below the age of forty speak Spanish too, the language within the household remains Huanca.

Huasicancha is at the same time a municipality, a district within the Peruvian administrative breakdown of the country into departments, provinces, districts and annexes and, most importantly, a legally recognized peasant community (*comunidad campesina*). As a Municipality, Huasicancha has an *alcalde* whose job relates to the running of the physical unit of the town: the recording of births, marriages, and deaths; the upkeep of public buildings and roads; the administration of municipal revenue; and the control of the town market. All households are obliged to contribute labor toward municipal work teams (*faenas*) devoted to public works. By initiating public works of lasting value alcaldes try to establish something of a lasting reputation in the town. Thus one is remembered for his construction of a football field, another for the bullring, and a third for the roof on the boys' school.

Historically districts, or *distritos,* have been formed out of a series of breakaways by *anexos* from the distritos that dominated them. Thus in 1906 Huasicancha and Chongos Alto had broken away from the Distrito of Colca (see Map 1) and Chongos Alto had received recognition as a Distrito, with Huasicancha as its Anexo. Then in 1930 the same process occurred again, this time with Huasicancha setting up as a distrito with anexos in two small hamlets or *caserios,* San Miguel and Pachacayo, the latter of which became the focal point for incursions onto hacienda land in the 1930s.

The *gobernador* of the distrito is theoretically appointed in Huancayo, but is in fact chosen in the general assembly in Huasicancha and then sent to Huancayo to receive recognition. He is supposedly the state's representative in the village and, as such he acts as the local sheriff in solving minor conflicts in the village. Since the *guardia civil* post was besieged by Huasicanchinos in 1959 and thereafter removed, the gobernador fulfills most policing functions. But in practice, in Huasicancha the gobernador has often arbitrated conflicts with outsiders and is seen specifically as the *pueblo's* representative to the world outside rather than the other way around. He has no control over policy in the village but is in charge of seeing to it that policies legislated by the municipality or the community are observed.

The gobernador has a *teniente* (lieutenant) for each of the anexos and a body of deputies numbering from six to twelve to help maintain the peace in the village.[3] These men are used for controlling the meetings of the general assembly, collecting fines (for nonattendance at faenas and for damage to crops by animals), and for arresting wrongdoers who are usually punished summarily by the gobernador but in extreme cases may be taken to the guardia civil post in Chongos Alto. The position requires firmness and tact as well as the cooperation of the village as a whole. As such it is usually reserved for an older and respected man in the village.

For the people themselves, however, it is to Huasicancha as a "community" that they have the greatest emotional ties. While such may not be the case for the towns of the Mantaro Valley or even for highland villages with less successful histories of political mobilization, here it is certainly the case that people feel that Huasicancha would be a community whether or not it received legal recognition as such by the national government. All children of Huasicanchinos are regarded as *comuneros* once they acquire their own household, and since there is very little marrying out of the community, the comuneros form a fairly clear-cut group. People who do marry into the community may petition for membership after a few years and, if residing in the village, will acquire it. (A person marrying in but not taking up residence would not be accepted.) Once comuneros, those who migrate remain comuneros with all their rights (e.g., to community lands) and obligations (e.g., to perform in community faenas).

These then are principles felt to be in place regardless of whether Huasicancha is designated a legally recognized *comunidad indigena* or *comunidad campesina*. Nevertheless, this latter dimension of being a community—containing its own rules regarding rights and obligations—is also of great importance to Huasicanchinos, and the two dimensions run over into each other. In fact, the national government's recognition of "indigenous communities" was itself expressed as the rediscovery of a de facto past. Before going further into the Huasicanchino community, I need to review the background to this important rediscovery.

In decrees of 1824 and 1825 Bolivar had made ownership by individuals the only form of property and thus legitimized the private accumulation of property within what were previously taken to be—legally at any rate—communal villages, and also strengthened the power of the expanding haciendas who were able to buy or lease land from individuals. The constitution of 1919 began to reverse these decrees by outlining a program for the recognition of "indigenous communities" that would then own land as corporate bodies from whom alienation through sale or otherwise would be illegal. Communities were urged to register any legal title they may have had to lands during that year, and sales thereafter were declared illegal. Huasicancha rushed to register its deed in the same year.

Throughout the 1920s and 1930s the notion of a truly Peruvian socialism based on the indigenous communities grew among a wide range of intellectuals and aspiring politicians, notably Mariategui (1928), Castro Pozo (1936), and Haya de la Torre (1936), and after 1933 communities were required to register as such with the *Sección de Asuntos Indígenas*. It was estimated that some 5,000 communities existed, but the costs of going through the red tape and the difficulty of finding legitimate-looking documents meant that only those able to use recognition as a means toward the settlement of land disputes came forward. By the census of 1940 only 1,472 had actually registered. Huasicancha did so in 1936.

The *personero* was the supreme authority in the legally recognized community, and his authority extended to all communal lands, which in principle meant arable plots farmed by households as well as the open pasture. Some arable land was held by the community and farmed by the faenas, and a small flock of communal sheep was kept also to cover various community costs. In practice, however, there was very little communal pasture, since the haciendas had taken control of most of it, and the arable plots were actually passed on from one generation to the next with little reference to the personero, though sales of land between families were not recognized and sales to outsiders expressly prohibited.

When the military government headed by General Velasco overthrew the

government of Belaunde in 1969, it soon placed great emphasis on reinvigo-
rating the indigenous communities (now redesignated peasant communities),
inspired by the writings of the 1920s and 1930s. The personero was replaced
by a president of administration and a president of vigilance, and the community was to be used as the basis for the setting up of production cooperatives.[4]
Though elected in the General Assembly of the community, these officers had
to be approved by the authorities in Huancayo. Development aid was only
available to communities proceeding along the road from precooperative to
recognized cooperative, but the formation of the cooperative itself depended
upon the reduction of wide differences in the size of herds using communal
land and an insistence on residence in the village as a prerequisite for membership. Inasmuch as the community was eventually to merge into the cooperative, this meant that migrants would no longer be able to be comuneros,
nor would the better-off pastoralists. At the same time the unequivocal position of the personero as the representative of the comuneros was now undercut
by the need for the new authorities to be recognized by the military in Huancayo. During the time of fieldwork these factors gave rise to an ongoing
tension and reinterpretation of the indigenous versus the legal versions of
"community."

Historically the people of Huasicancha were first and foremost pastoralists
who engaged also in arable farming, muleteering, and a variety of artisan
activities. Nevertheless, today migration has become so thoroughly a part of
life that at least half the Huasicanchinos now make their livelihood from
activities concentrated in Huancayo, La Oroya, and Lima. In Lima, for example, Huasicanchinos can be found both in the inner-city slums known as
coralones and the shanty towns around the edge of the city, known as *barriadas*. They make their living by selling fruit on the streets of the city and
they supplement this activity by a variety of other occupations, so that each
household is in fact a multioccupational enterprise. Meanwhile in the village
many men and women leave the highlands in the slack agricultural season
from January to April and journey to Lima where they lodge with friends or
relatives. Many of these villagers will sell strawberries in the suburbs of the
city.

Most villagers, then, are familiar with the life of their colleagues in the
city, and the migrants, for their part, maintain their status as comuneros, returning to the village when the opportunity presents itself and in many cases
keeping livestock on the community pasture. It would thus be impossible to
comprehend the life of the people of Huasicancha if we confined ourselves
to the village alone. In this book, therefore, when I refer to "the Huasicanchinos" I include migrants and villagers alike. When I wish to refer only to
the villagers, I make this clear. It must still be remembered that being a
Huasicanchino has not always been so divorced from geographical locality.

1

Forms of Struggle

I realised that reality isn't just the police that kill people, but also everything that forms part of the life of the common people. All of this must be incorporated.

—Gabriel García Marquez

Livelihood and Resistance

The way peasants make a living and their contribution to rebellion and revolution are both themes to be found in studies of the peasantry. Oddly though, between the two there is a blind spot. Those who focus on the development problems associated with improving peasants' livelihood discount the role of their political initiatives, and because those who focus on peasant rebellion concern themselves overmuch with peasants' revolutionary potential, they are unable to see how resistance is interlinked with development and development policies (Walton 1984:3–4).

Yet for Peru in the 1960s there was a clear connection between the political initiative of peasants and development policy—to such an extent that these initiatives provoked the collapse of one government and instigated its replacement by another with a more aggressive development policy. Early in that decade, between 100 and 350 incidents occurred in which small farmers and landless rural people marched on to the land of large ranches, called haciendas, and refused to budge (Cotler and Portocarrero 1969; Paige 974:166). In many cases there was violence and in some cases these *reivindicaciones* (reclaiming of lands said to be unjustly in the hands of others) were accompanied by other forceful methods. Failure to resolve this problem resulted in the downfall of the first Belaunde government in 1968 and its replacement by the Velasco regime that put in motion a radically different development plan.

This widespread rural initiative was neither the result of well-synchronized guerrilla units manned by cadres brought up in the middle-class suburbs, possessing degrees in sociology or political theory and trained in Moscow or

Havana, nor of peasant leagues well-organized for the coordination of political activity. Instead this mobilization, which one writer describes as "unquestionably one of the largest peasant movements in Latin American history" (Handelman 1975:121; see also Hobsbawm 1973:10), was made up of a series of local initiatives lacking a centralized leadership or organizational structure. In the following pages I hope to suggest that the essentially local initiatives exhibited in this form of resistance are an important component in our understanding of contemporary political movements. And I want to do this by studying in some depth one group, the people of Huasicancha, who were part of these so-called spontaneous actions when a hitherto apparently passive peasantry hit the headlines. In the course of the study it will become clear that such passivity was more apparent than real and that this appearance resulted precisely from the blind spot in the paradigms just mentioned. Looked at more closely, there was nothing new about resistance for the Huasicanchinos: it had become an essential part of their daily lives. Put another way, not only did they have a long history of intense *political* struggle but also their experience of those spectacular moments is inseparable from their *daily* struggle for a livelihood.

This is not merely to turn convention upside down and suggest that peasants are not as passive as we thought but are resisting all the time, or to suggest that *all* local political initiatives *contribute* to rather than hinder political consciousness and hence class formation. I do not for a moment wish to deny the exceptional nature of the Huasicanchinos' culture as one that derived so much of its vitality from being "in resistance" or oppositional. Indeed the entire purpose of this book is directed toward understanding that specificity.[1] And so one focus of attention will be on the role of local historical experience (what might quite properly be referred to as one element of "the local culture") in determining the form political resistance takes.

When the Huasicanchinos, in the words of a local newspaper, "broke their pact and invaded Hacienda Tucle" in April 1964 and then persisted in their campaign for the subsequent eight years, they were drawing on a long experience. Indeed, as the newspaper suggests, they were at last breaking a pact that had kept up an uneasy truce since their last offensive, seventeen years earlier. At that time, Huasicancha in its entirety had "entered" hacienda land. As though in some communal exercise of will to redraw the lines of history, everybody, indeed every living thing, had been removed from the village on to the hacienda-controlled land. Villagers abandoned their houses and took with them every pig, chicken, and guinea pig. And once installed, they built small stone huts and thatched them with old straw to give them the appearance of permanence. They set up a school for their children and quickly set about the reestablishment of their daily routines. The reivindicación of 1948 led to an out-of-court settlement with the hacienda that gave the villagers a small piece of land but which was so disappointing that many left the rural setting to seek their livelihoods in the cities. And we shall have cause again and again to return to the impact of that disappointing settlement of 1948.

Even then there was nothing new under the sun. Back in the 1930s the haciendas Tucle and Rio de la Virgen found themselves "invaded" by Huasicanchinos and made a truce with Sabino Jacinto who claimed to be leading that particular incursion. He himself had a personal history of banditry and rustling and had been imprisoned in 1910 in connection with a previous confrontation over land. Sabino had been born in the 1880s, a time of much contentiousness—when Huasicancha had been the center of a guerrilla campaign one of whose leaders subsequently, "after cross examination confessed to having sacked the haciendas Tucle, Laive, and Ingahuasi whose produce had been divided up among his men," according to the national newspaper *El Commercio,* in 1884. The expropriation of these haciendas lasted nearly ten years and ended in terrible retribution. But its occurrence became a vivid part of the Huasicanchinos' history, an event whose telling and retelling themselves became events in their own right. Nor do those years signal the beginning of resistance, for we find even in the earliest documents that make mention of such a place as Huasicancha that assertion, defeat, counterassertion, alliance, and betrayal are intricately woven into the fabric of what constitutes endurance for the Huasicanchinos.

Nevertheless, once having discovered, with the case of the Huasicanchinos, that the passivity of peasants is not as ubiquitous as might have been thought, it would be a mistake to dwell exclusively on their *political* struggle. If occasionally these struggles were sufficiently spectacular as to reach the national press, this was not the central concern of the Huasicanchinos themselves. So we must begin in a less spectacular place, before the sun rises, as the blankets are thrown off in the cold morning and, in the dark, a man and a woman grope for hat and shawl to face the day. This daily task of piecing together a living influences the form a people's political struggle takes, just as much as does the specificity of their historical experience. The Huasicanchinos make a living primarily through the operation of domestic enterprises: the developmental trajectories of these enterprises, their logics of reproduction, therefore play a major role in their experience of history and in our understanding of their political resistance.

In turning to the other arm of struggle—the quotidian one of making a living—variation in both *the structure of enterprises* and the labor process *in a broader arena,* must be scrutinized. Half the people who call themselves "Huasicanchino" do not live in Huasicancha but have migrated to work centers, in the provincial capital of Huancayo, the smelting town of La Oroya, or the national capital, Lima. Hence the links between Huasicanchinos, not just within the rural area but between the various work centers both rural and urban, play a major part in how people achieve their identity as Huasicanchinos. Because ambulant fruitsellers on the streets of Lima and marketstall operators in Huancayo joined livestock herders and arable farmers in Huasi-cancha to struggle against the haciendas for land, we must be wary of speak-ing specifically of "peasant" resistance. Nevertheless what is common to all Huasicanchinos is that their living derives from a domestic enterprise, be it a farm or a nonagricultural operation in Lima or Huancayo.

Huasicanchinos have organized their livelihoods around such domestic units for a long time, but the *form* of these units has changed radically. De-spite their persistence, these domestic units are by no means uniform in their composition. They vary enormously from one Huasicanchino household to another, which provides a clue to the complexity of Huasicancha's political history. These production units share another characteristic today as in the past: they are, and always have been, subordinated to the imperatives of larger economic and political units. Once again, however, the degree and form of this subordination varies from one unit to another today as it varied in the past. This situation means that an analysis of both domestic production in all its variation and the differing forms of its integration into a larger social economy *through history* is a prerequisite for our understanding of the way in which Huasicanchinos perceive their own identity as social actors and the way in which they engage in political struggles.

In focusing on the structure of domestic enterprises, it is important not to lose sight of the very general nature of the labor process we are dealing with here. If the Huasicanchinos derived their income uniquely through wage labor on a factory floor, we might be able to delineate reasonably clearly the parameters of that labor process (cf., Burawoy 1985). But in the case of petty production, while the omnipresence of the labor process is an undeniable in-fluence on people's political interests, it is not an experience that is institution-ally or normatively isolated from the entire experience of social relations. The "rationality of production" represented by the activities of the domestic unit is also the "rationality of social reproduction" represented by all the social relations pertinent to the continued survival of this form of livelihood. These include specific personal networks of kin, friends, and neighbors as well as investment in the cultural apparatus that defines them as such. All these are essential to domestic production and in effect expand the notion of "labor process" to the broader arena of culture as a whole. Once this connection is understood, however, the notion of the labor process as one further perception of culture to be added to that of "historical experience" already mentioned, has the advantage of drawing attention to culture as an ever incomplete con-tinuing process, as opposed to an integrated system or completed tradition.

Moreover, in being common to both, the labor process provides a useful bridge between our notion of culture and class. If the Huasicanchinos made their living from domestic enterprises in relative isolation, we might be able to talk of the construction of culture without reference to culture's opposi-tional characteristics. Seen in terms of a labor process, however, cultural activities include, on an almost daily basis, perpetual reminders of the threats to livelihood represented by the loss of land, livestock, market position, and so on. And these give to cultural expression an oppositional and political dimension. This aspect of culture then provides the link between the relations of production so narrowly defined as to be bereft of any political component, and what Gramsci would call "political will." It is precisely because on the one hand the labor process is such a broad one, while on the other hand the form of dominance and exploitation is so clearly a threat to the reproduction of livelihood that the forms of unity and opposition take on the *cultural* expression they do in specific political struggles: land occupations, strikes, rustling and trespassing, market resistance, and others.

Yet it would be a mistake then to see local expressions of "culture" as in some way resisting the expression of conflict in terms of class. Rather we must be sensitive to the ways in which political resistance is expressed either through oppositional culture or through class consciousness. For example, the characteristics of a class relationship in which social reproduction requires simultaneously relationships of interdependence and conflict are present in this case too but expressed in different form. First, while there may be *general* propositions applicable to the wage relationship of simultaneous conflict and interdependence between capital and labor, the relationships within domestic enterprises and between those enterprises and contemporary institutions of expropriation and dominance (such as the hacienda) do not represent a radical break with preceding institutions and must therefore be situated in a quite *specific* history. I will discuss modern social relations as transformations of the past in chapter 2. Second, in recent times linkages have not been limited to those between contracting individuals and the hacienda but have included the linkages between domestic enterprises and a variety of *sectors of the economy*. Yet capitalist expansion has been uneven. Huasicanchino enterprises distributed through various regions and sectors of the economy, therefore, are differentially affected as one sector develops while another contracts. This leads to heterogeneity among enterprises that gives a specific character to developing social relations among Huasicanchinos themselves. In chapter 5 the extent of these variations is explored through the use of case studies.

Third, we cannot limit ourselves to the effect of domestic enterprises on the form of political struggle; rather, we must remember too that the political struggles of Huasicanchinos have themselves had conditioning effects on those domestic enterprises. Forms of association with others and the social investment in existing institutions, to mention only two examples, are not just a function of livelihood requirements. They also reflect the requirements of political struggles in the past and political potential for the future. Social relations reflect not just the production of a livelihood but the political protection of the conditions seen to be necessary for its continued reproduction. This question is addressed in both chapters 3 and 7.

The concern of this book then, is to understand the Huasicanchinos' political resistance in terms of the *interconnected* facets of the dynamic properties inherent in the production relations they engage in to earn a living over time, and the historical experience, especially of past political engagement, which forms an essential part of their contemporary subjectivity.[2] I attempt, throughout the book, not to lose sight of the interconnection between these two facets. I wish to see a present that is thoroughly infused with the past and an intentional political praxis that is dialectically related to the historical unfolding of social relations of production. That means I want to stress that certain social relations engaged in over time have a dynamic property that perpetually escapes conscious experience.[3]

It is this emphasis on the dynamic property of structured relationships that has allowed a number of writers to extend the precision of Marx's analysis of the capitalist mode of production to gain insights into petty commodity production. While Marx, however, wished to stress the revolutionary rupture characteristic of large-scale capitalist social relations, the social relations of petty commodity production emphatically do not represent a radical break with the past. Rather they are grafted on to preexisting social relations thereby modifying them in the process. An understanding of contemporary social relations is unattainable without setting them within the specificity of this historical process. This assumption has important implications for understanding the relationship between existing social relations of production and the way people experience those social relations. The effect of this process of grafting is to modify the relationship between the dynamic properties inherent in certain social relationships and the meanings people attach to the terms used to describe those social relationships. A modification in the exercise of a social relationship based on reciprocity, for example, undermines the principle embraced by its accepted meaning, and this interplay between practice and meaning forms a perpetual dynamic of interpretation and reinterpretation, linking the dynamics inherent in certain social relationships continually engaged in with the agency of actors working within that changing web.

This is the way in which the structured relationships of the past relate to the present: "their present as a rearrangement of their past, and their past as a determinant of their present" (Wolf 1956 [1971]:53). There is a history at the same time, though, of directly experienced practice, in which people have consciously grasped the reins of history to resist the conditions of their existence. This need by no means be exclusively political, but in the case of the Huasicanchinos such political agency has been so potent a force in their history that it has the effect of focusing their attention when talking of the past.

I have tried to write the history of the Huasicanchinos by preserving this uneasy tension between conditions and will: the conditions (albeit dynamic) of their existence and the will to restructure those conditions. Throughout the book then, I have tried to relate the ordinary, daily experience of life for the

Huasicanchinos to the more spectacular political events that have colored their lives. For the purposes of clarity, I have had to make breaks and distinctions that run the risk of delineating elements which in reality cannot be so clearly drawn. Thus with care and caution, I have highlighted the *daily struggle* for livelihood among the Huasicanchinos, which appears to be characterized by a monotonous continuity resembling incremental changes at best and stasis at worst, and the outburst of *political struggle* seen as a moment in which these people attempt to take the reins in their own hands to change history.

And once we suppress this distinction between one kind of struggle and another, we must necessarily rethink a number of other distinctions. Our ideas of political struggle must not be associated too closely with sudden spasmodic outbursts of activity. It is important, of course, not to go too far in the other direction and minimize the historical significance of concerted and intentional mobilization by suggesting that, in the study of resistance, uprisings are the exceptions rather than the rule. They are, after all, important exceptions.[4] But we must be careful to keep the exceptions and the mundane routine closely linked—moving together like a river flowing over fissured limestone, the water traveling beneath the surface for long stretches and then bursting to the surface through those fissures, flowing briefly there and then returning to its subterranean depths.

Of course if, as I am suggesting, concerted and intentional acts of political struggle are thoroughly intertwined with daily affairs around the hearth, in the street, or behind the oxen, then as the form of this concerted political action emerges from the parameters of that daily life, so political action itself conditions that daily life in its turn. As the institutions, practices, and identity of people in daily life are used during concerted political action, so the resulting modification in their function serves to reformulate the institutions, practices, and identity of people as they come to bear once more on their daily lives.

Political and cultural elements then are brought into play from the beginning to set the process of production in motion and to maintain its reproduction. This is the case, whether we are talking about petty commodity production units, the contemporary hacienda, or the older production relations of the past.[5] And it leads us away from production relations, narrowly defined, to the entire array of the production and reproduction of culture, which includes the political struggles necessary for that continued reproduction, political struggles, moreover, whose form is conditioned by the specificity of the cultures they arise to protect and advance.

In this book I shall also be concerned, however, to show that once resistance is expressed openly and in concert, the imperatives of that intense political activity take on a momentum of their own. Failure to note this creative property of political experience results in relegating all experience to a thing of the past, something remembered rather than something actively engaged in at the moment. In the case of the Huasicanchinos, it is quite clear not only that political engagement forced a reexamination of many taken-for-granted assumptions but also that this very intense internal dialogue among participants gave momentum to the political struggle itself.

Cross-Disciplinary Studies of the Peasantry

Study of the peasantry has always benefited from the interaction between disciplines. And recently each of those disciplines has itself benefited from its exposure to the cross-fertilization occurring in "peasant studies." Social anthropologists have become more historical, just as historians have become more anthropological (see Medick 1987). Economists concerned with the peasantry have had to become more sociological, while for Marxists generally, peasant studies have always been a provocation and an inspiration. It would be not too much of an exaggeration to suggest that even postmodernism itself has been much influenced by perceptions of the peasantry (see Kahn 1985). Although I have presented the foregoing discussion with minimal reference to these various writings, the book that follows owes much to cross-disciplinary investigations.[6]

The title of the book contains the word, "peasant." While this usage makes for something of a problem, it provides us with a useful point of departure. Although the term is used generally by many writers to refer to the poorer members of the rural population, in anthropology its use is intended to draw attention to a definitional feature of the peasantry: their partial integration into the larger society. "An intermediate place is occupied by the peasantry. Peasants are definitely rural yet live in relation to market towns; they form a class segment of a larger population which usually contains also urban centers, sometimes metropolitan capitals" (Kroeber 1948:284 [first edition, 1923]). Many subsequent writers have been at pains to distance themselves from Kroeber's original observation that peasants, "constitute part-societies with part-cultures" (1948) yet, while laying emphasis respectively on culture, economy (as defined by neoclassical economists) and power relationships, Redfield (1941, 1947), Firth (1958), and Wolf (1956, 1966) have essentially acknowledged, in one way or another, this Janus-faced propensity of peasants to relate both to the characteristics of the larger society and to those of the local, face-to-face community. Thus, a caveat: even though it is important to be aware of its use in the above senses, many of the people I shall be referring to are not rural dwellers at all but live in the slums and shantytowns of large cities.

But there is another reason that makes scholars wary of Kroeber's emphasis: in stressing the shared cultural features of the peasantry he focused on their homogeneity and thus ran the risk of drawing attention away from the differences among them. And, once the term "peasant" could be applied both to an independent, yeoman farmer as well as to an impoverished allot-ment-holder, then was it not likely that such different kinds of people might have different views of the world, possibly even different "cultures" or at least different perspectives on and interpretations of the same culture?

Once socioeconomic differentiation was seen to be a common feature of the peasantry, it drew attention away from the integrity of their shared culture by focusing on a different characteristic of the peasantry. Shanin (1973) using the writing of Chayanov (1966) and students of the peasantry influenced by Chayanov's work (see for example, Thorner 1966; Kerblay 1971; and Galeski 1972) stressed the need to focus special attention on the distinctive charac-teristics of the peasant enterprise itself. Chayanov had noted especially the implications of the close identity of the family and the farm in peasant econ-omies. A useful point of departure in beginning the study of peasant economy was to analyze the farm qua enterprise, which satisfied simultaneously the consumption needs of the family and the given number of family members for the enterprise's labor needs.

Interest in the particularities of Chayanov's views of the cyclical properties of the family farm that results from rigid application of this model (Shanin 1972; Deere and de Janvry 1981) have tended to obscure a more important development: renewed interest in Chayanov served, above all else, to focus attention on the need to understand the workings of the farm enterprise. While much ink was spilled in taking sides in the supposed incompatible hostilities of Lenin's (1974 [1899]) study of the Russian peasantry at the turn of the century and Chayanov's studies after the revolution, the game could only be played so long as the original protagonists were given a dogmatic rigidity in-compatible with the very practical goals they were both trying to achieve (Lehmann 1986a). True, Lenin stressed the primary importance of capitalist penetration of the peasantry in explaining their differentiation, a process he felt likely to be cumulative; true too that Chayanov stressed the importance of the logical properties of the peasant economy itself in explaining differen-tiation, a process he felt likely to be cyclical as the family passes through its various stages. And Lenin is most commonly criticized from the point of view that empirically the peasantry have often persisted by in some way resisting the cumulative effects of differentiation, and Chayanov from the point of view that the imperatives of capitalism, combined with the effects of commodity penetration into peasant social relations, have seriously modified the "givens" in his model. But what was most fruitful in both studies was the focus on the logical imperatives of *forms of production* on the one hand and the contextual determinations of *a larger social formation* on the other—what Harriet Fried-mann has termed nicely "the double specification of this kind of production" (1980:160). Thus, while the term *peasant* can be useful when employed in a general sense, it is important to recognize that, by definition, it embraces both socioeconomically differentiated groups and heterogeneous enterprises. That is to say, the so-called partial integration of the peasantry into the larger society, which we have seen to be its essential defining characteristic, inevitably brings with it differentiation and heterogeneity. We shall have occasion to stress this fact time and again throughout the study.

While the difficulty in making a theoretically precise statement about "the peasantry" led some to reject use of the term entirely (Ennew, Tribe, and Hirst 1977), Shanin (1979) argued for its continued use precisely because of the provocativeness of the empirical differences found among peasants throughout history. With appropriate caution something *can* be gained, I argue in this book; by being quite precise about the logical properties required in the reproduction of a particular kind of enterprise, for we can then explore the developmental implications of such variation. Increasing sophistication in our understanding of these implications came with the concept of simple commodity production (see Bernstein 1979; Kahn 1980; Friedmann 1980; Chevalier 1983).

Although Roger Bartra (1974) and Bernstein (1979) initially used the term to refer to the peasantry generally, Friedmann introduced greater precision by distinguishing between simple commodity production and peasant economy. Under simple commodity production all the factors needed by the enterprise and produced by it are commodified, that is to say, they are bought and sold at market prices that reflect their exchange value.[7] All, that is, except one: that being labor, which is provided by the family. Such a farm seeks to reproduce its various capital needs and provision the family, rather than extend reproduction in an ever-expanding cycle, but the farm must operate in a capitalist economy because it is through its dynamic interaction with the capitalist market that it ensures its reproduction. By contrast, argues Friedmann, while producing to greater or lesser extent for the market, peasants do so through social relationships unmediated by the commodity form. The personal ties of kin and community are a significant part of such an economy, which means (among other things) that peasants do not have the kind of straightforward convertibility and mobility of factors that comes with the pure commodity form.

As a result, faced with competition, the two enterprises respond differently: while the simple commodity producer is compelled to improve the productivity of his/her labor by investing in the means of production (a process which, Bernstein notes, tends to increase their indebtedness and lead to a "simple commodity production squeeze"), the peasant, by contrast, can only increase his/her overall drudgery and seek to make further use of personal ties. The self-exploitation of household members referred to by Chayanov occurs in both cases, but in different forms.[8] For simple commodity production, exploitation increases by simultaneously working more *and* improving the techniques and equipment by which labor can be better exploited. For peasant economy, the lack of unfettered exchangeability associated with commodity relations means that only by working more (and persuading kin and neighbors to do likewise) can the enterprise face heightened competition.[9] Faced with the same conditions, the two types of enterprises respond differently.

In chapter 6, I make clear that there are factors that mitigate the strict application of theoretically derived concepts. Even so I find it useful to be precise about the structural imperatives highlighted by writers like Bernstein and Friedmann. Empirical observation insufficiently sensitive to the structural imperatives of social relationships once entered into can be misleading; it can leave us with classifications that do not help to pinpoint the forces of historical change. Despite their empirical richness recent studies of the central sierras have not been rigorous in this respect. Writers faced with what appear to be almost identical empirical data on the Mantaro region draw opposite conclusions about the state of class formation there. Mallon (1986:148) summarizes the state of play as follows:

> Representing the Chayanovian position, several anthropologists and sociologists who have done research in the Mantaro Valley emphasize the survival of the peasant economy and of household production, denying the existence of a "pure" proletariat in the region (Long and Roberts, 1978; Laite, 1981). In the Leninist corner, I have found through historical study of agrarian transformation in the Mantaro and Yanamarca Valleys that the areas' peasantry is divided into an agrarian bourgeoisie and a rural proletariat and that this is now the primary class contradiction in the central sierra. As has been the case in previous debates, the bone of contention is the significance that should be attributed to household production. The Chayanovians maintain that household production is important enough to halt class transformation, whereas I argue that it now serves exclusively to help reproduce a wage labor force for agrarian and urban capital. (Mallon 1983)

Here then, in the region close to Huasicancha, the different priority given to particular historical forces determining the class formation of the peasantry is seen to derive from the mutually exclusive character of Lenin's and Chayanov's positions, which I have argued is heuristically unhelpful. Mallon wishes to suggest that those who focus on the dynamic properties of small-scale enterprises in the Mantaro region, such as Long and Roberts (1978) have done, should be firmly placed in the Chayanovian camp, and those, like herself, who stress the thoroughgoing capitalist penetration of the area are to be placed in the Leninist camp.

First, without getting into the difficult question of how one can prove that any institution serves exclusively to perform a certain function for the reproduction of capitalism, it has to be said that Mallon's is an unusual reading of Chayanov. Roger Bartra (1974) for example has argued that it is precisely the Chayanovian propensity of the peasantry to self-exploitation that makes them *un*dynamic, while others (e.g., Vergopoulos 1978) have argued that it is this Chayanovian character of the peasantry's enterprises that makes them so especially *functional* to capital.

Ironically both Mallon (1983) and Long and Roberts (1978:297–325; 1984: 1–24, 235–257), describe a similar situation in the Mantaro region though occurring at somewhat different times, one in which a dynamic class of entrepreneurial farmers have come into existence together with an increasingly proletarianized class of wage workers both in the mines and refineries and in the agricultural sector. They interpret these facts differently. In essence, however, the problem with both Mallon's position and Long and Robert's position is their empirically-derived conceptual tools.

Mallon argues that "the bone of contention is the significance that should be attributed to household production," and goes on, "I argue that [household production] now serves exclusively to help reproduce a wage labour force." And yet she neither refines the concept of "household production" nor produces a thoroughgoing analysis of the dynamics of "household production" in the Mantaro region. Had she done so, she might have shown that ironically it is only the Chayanovian kind of household that is primarily concerned with the production of "labor units" (sold to capital as the commodity—labor power). Yet it is a fact (that both Mallon and I show) that throughout the variety of these household forms, other commodities are produced, but they are not produced exclusively to reduce the cost of labor power to capital, either as an intended or unintended consequence. In fact there are occasions where petty producers compete with largescale capital in the production of certain commodities (MacEwen Scott 1979) and occasions too where they are aided in this competition precisely by the quality and price of inputs they derive from that sector (Schneider 1987). Household production, narrowly defined—i.e., as unpaid labor within the household for auto-provisioning of the household—is, almost by definition, a means for reducing the cost of reproducing labor. But it is only one of a number of strategies, and these strategies have to be explored in all their complexity.

This is what Long and Roberts do at great length in their studies, yet their lack of theoretical rigor makes it hard to draw conclusions from their work about the developmental properties of different kinds of enterprises. Rather than using the distinctions suggested by Friedmann and others, discussed above, Long and Roberts talk of peasant capitalists. Certainly the extent to which these people use extensive networks of interpersonal ties for the viability of their enterprises brings them closer to the peasantry proposed by Friedmann, yet Long and Roberts appear to be eager to stress Friedmann's other kind of enterprise when they then refer to precisely these same operators as "independent farmers." Without a clearer theoretical framework such as the one worked out by theorists of simple commodity production, it is hard to see what is to be gained by referring to operators so thoroughly tied into extended networks as *independent* farmers. Precisely the kind of tensions that are revealed by Long and Roberts's otherwise confusing use of terms like "peasant capitalist" and "independent farmer," as well as by Mallon's insistence on there being "a primary class contradiction" in the region, can be better understood by examining the hidden implications of certain social relationships engaged in over time.

But there is a second difficulty with the prevailing literature on the Mantaro. I have argued earlier that daily livelihood priorities cannot be separated from the *political* conditions for reproduction. The two go hand in hand. Once political imperatives highlighted Huasicancha as a community, for example, then just as the community served as a collective means for protecting the conditions for reproduction, so the extensive arena of noncommodified relations that went along with "community" became simultaneously a source with which to meet the daily economic needs of the household enterprise. Mallon is thus right to insist as she does throughout her book on the role of class *conflict* in the historical development of the peasantry in the central sierra, but both she and others (cf., Tullis 1971; Alberti and Sanchez 1974), separate the political dimension from the dimension of economic reproduction. Moreover the argument of Long and Roberts that the reproduction of these household enterprises did not serve solely the purpose of providing cheap labor for agrarian and urban capital but also competed with it is insufficient at least in the case of the Huasicanchinos, for the very rationality of their enterprises, *from the beginning,* cannot be understood without reference to the conditions for their political reproduction.[10]

Despite the variety of conclusions reached by these and other studies that attempt to relate characteristics of the domestic enterprise to class position without considering any significant component of political struggle (for other regions of Peru, see Deere and León de Leal 1981, Collins 1986; for Mexico, see Young 1978, Crummet 1987), they all have in common the notion that capitalism advances inexorably and that the noncapitalist components of the peasantry respond. Although this response is seen to be variable (as is the way in which capitalism expands), it is confined to economic features or to other economically related characteristics. There is a persistent failure to interlace thoroughly from the beginning the economic *and* the political. Partly as a result of this strict confinement to the basement of economics, faced with empirical evidence one is never quite clear whether it is class position that determines the structure of each household or, conversely, the structure of each household that provides the conditions for entry into certain (capitalist) class positions—worker, petty commodity seller, or others.

Considering many other factors of a more global nature, however, the rapidity or sloth in capitalist advance is directly a result of an ongoing history of accommodation and resistance to that advance on the part of a variety of factions of the peasantry (in addition to other classes engaged in the struggle, like merchants and landlords). While there is no question that this political dimension is taken up forcefully in the historical and descriptive parts of studies of the peasantry (especially in the case of Mallon 1983), there is far less evidence in the more abstract theoretical exegeses that this dimension is incorporated thoroughly into the discussion of the dialectical relationship between forms of the peasant enterprise (and the forms of the interrelationship between those enterprises) and capitalism. It is my intention in this study to offer a more thoroughgoing dialectic between primarily economically-informed models of forms of production and the political determinations of their existence (see Warman 1980; C. Smith 1986)[11]

The reproduction of the household enterprise is dependent simultaneously on the economic relations of production and on the political relations necessary to protect those relations. In an initial article (1976), "Agrarian class structure and economic development in pre-industrial Europe," which subsequently gave rise to "the Brenner Debate" (Aston and Philpin 1985), Robert Brenner was at great pains to retain the historical unity of these two elements of class structure, arguing that it was the level of class struggle that ultimately determined the degree of surplus extraction from the peasantry. In chapter 2 I superimpose different historical periods on one another in order to stress the long history of interplay between dependency and conflict, between the peasantry and those who exploit them. And subsequently, throughout the book, I intertwine the labor process with conflictive relations over control of direct labor and land. It is for this reason that I find Brenner's article useful. But in the concluding chapter I shall suggest that Brenner takes a somewhat too rigidly structural view of class. For him, one *begins* with the fundamental classes in a society defined by the property relationship and then one sifts through history to find those groups whose struggles express that class structure. It seems to me that the experience of conflict itself has been a major factor in the Huasicanchinos' sense of class. And in this, I find myself closer to the views of E. P. Thompson (1968), who has emphasized the role of historical experience in class formation. The effect of so entirely cutting class analysis loose from the structural imperatives of the property/direct-labor relationship, however, is that Thompson appears to take class formation and class consciousness as the same thing, which severely handicaps his notion of class (cf., Johnson 1979; Anderson 1980).

But once having stepped into the spotlight of "consciousness" we have returned, very nearly, to a point raised at the beginning of this section: we want to ascribe to peasants a distinct culture but at the same time to retain a sense of distinctiveness *among* peasants. Indeed it was Edward Thompson (1961) who criticized Raymond Williams (1961) for seeing culture as "a whole way of life," pointing out that no way of life is without its struggles and confrontation between opposed "ways of life." The question of the heterogeneity of peasants thoroughly informs this study and thus influences my approach to two other factors concering the peasantry: rebellion and distinctive peasant culture.

Acknowledging the differentiation of the peasantry either within a single village or between one better-off region and another poorer region has had a great influence on the study of peasant rebellions, leading some writers to stress the greater propensity of certain strata to rebel or certain geographically placed peasants to rebel (e.g., Wolf 1969), or of peasants engaged in certain sectors of the agricultural economy to rebel (Paige 1975). Other students of peasant rebellion have stressed the importance of leadership (e.g., Hobsbawm 1959) or of peasants' shared belief that certain customary agreements have been broken (Scott 1976). This study is more modest in scope. I am not asking why peasants rebel or which peasants rebel but rather *how* the rebellion is put together.

My approach has further implications for scholars who seek to make the distinguishing characteristic of the peasantry their strangeness and thus render them exotic. Studies that counterpoint the peasantry to modern society have great difficulty in dealing with the peasants' heterogeneity whether they are sophisticated anthropological studies or more widely accepted accounts of peasant behavior. Taussig (1980), on the one hand, suggests that the confusion peasants suffer in trying to comprehend our commonsense belief that capital generates value (and thus has organic properties of growth *sui generis*) is in fact inherently a critique of capitalism. Gose (1986), on the other hand, using data gathered in the southern Peruvian Andes, makes similar claims concerning peasant sacrifices, though drawing the opposite conclusion. Faced by the characteristic of capitalism to rend apart individuals from the organic unity of their community and values from the very bodies that produced them, sacrifice offers no resistance but only the promise of a radical reuniting in fire and death, as it were. Although anthropological and Marxist terminology separates Taussig and Gose from Vargas Llosa's more popular but supposedly factual "Story of a Massacre" (1983) that claims to deal with a peasant assassination of journalists in the central Andes, the underlying assumptions are the same. Peasants share a common set of cultural beliefs, and they live in a world apart from our own, even though we share the same soil. Though, unlike these writers who exoticize the peasantry, James Scott (1976) shares their assumption of a uniform set of beliefs. Still, all of these interpretations seek to understand experience, the experience of others as we look from here over there. But what is seen over there is a completed experience, an integral culture of the past and not a lived culture of the present. And so the word *experience* means the past, a past of tradition, of custom, and of anything but experience as we ourselves know it to be.

These propositions—that we are not dealing with a homogeneous peasantry and that culture is an engagement with the present mediated by the

past—oblige us to look at both peasant rebellion and peasant culture somewhat differently. The Huasicanchinos, hailing as they did from the shantytowns of Lima, the marketstalls of Huancayo, the arable plots of the village,
or the remote estancias of the mountains, were a heterogeneous lot, but when
it came to confronting a large ranch, the police, the army, and the proclama-
tions of the president of the republic, they presented a common front. What
does such behavior mean for studies of peasant rebellion on the one hand and
for the exotic culture of the peasantry on the other? The evidence suggests
that intense conflict with outsiders over a resource essential to daily life (land)
had the effect of intensifying discussion internally among participants. Conflict obliged them to reexamine not only what constituted membership in the
community but also what "community" itself meant. This throws a certain
light on how cultural identity is forged (or not forged) out of these conflicts
over land—so ubiquitous to the peasantry the world over. Heightened discourse engaged people intensively in "the production of culture" and insofar
as membership and meaning were not just abstract notions vaguely linked to
identity but rather were essential to the continuation of livelihood, participants
were intensely committed to the outcome of this debate.

The dynamic intensification of internal interaction that went along with external political resistance took the form of exchanges over the *formal meaning*
of words referring to key factors in daily life (community, property, advance-
ment, etc.) and the variations in their daily, *instrumental usage* by individual
Huasicanchinos. Words of this kind, what Raymond Williams has called
"keywords" (1976) contain a multitude of meanings, but ironically the value
of their currency lies in a shared belief that their formal, orthodox meaning
is in some way fixed—in the case of Huasicancha if not in a dictionary, then
in some vaguely acknowledged reference to culturally accepted practice: the
unchanging component of the enduring memory (Zonabend 1984). On the one
hand the ultimate, fixed, and unarguable definition of such words can never
be finally agreed upon and, on the other hand, there is continual negotiation
of their significances from day to day. They are two sides of the same coin.

Williams himself favors the use of "hegemony" in this context, though in
his hands, as with Gramsci's original usage, hegemony refers to an ongoing
process in which the establishment of agreed upon meanings is part of the
mastery of both daily life and history. The bourgeoisie's ability to embrace
ever greater areas of expression and make them part of the dominant ideology
for the purposes of social control is not itself hegemony but merely one expression, one endproduct of the process of hegemony. And by the same token
the public political language of the Huasicanchinos contained in banners and
in "statements to the press" as well as the act of marching onto the land of
the hacienda are the external moments of an internal hegemonic process occurring among the Huasicanchinos.

What happens *among* the Huasicanchinos when they rebel is actually an extension of what happens in their confrontations with others: the prevailing definitions of reality are thrown into question. This, however, does not appear to mean that the Huasicanchinos need to have very precise definitions. It means rather a rejection of hegemonic definitions *and* the rejection of their nonnegotiable fixity (Marcuse 1969).[12] And aspiring leaders in Huasicancha learned quickly that the fastest way to lose favor was to attempt to impose their own hegemonic rigidity on the significance of keywords such as "community," "ownership," "responsibility," and so on, and thus fix their orthodoxy in terms so finite and prescriptive as to be beyond dispute.

Hence, when I said earlier that once resistance is expressed openly and in concert, the imperatives of such intense political activity take on a momentum of their own, it is a process of hegemonic formation at all levels. Moreover it was this process "which defined the terms in which oppression was understood, and it was what provided the vision of an alternative" (Jones 1983:95). It is by studying this process for what it is and not for what we expect it to look like when completed that we might begin to understand the historical, always-incomplete production of culture among peasants.

The production of culture is especially relevant for our understanding of the peasantry for two reasons. First, this approach suggests that far from seeing peasant culture as at first pristine and then invaded from without, we should see it *from the beginning* as the assertion (or failure) of will and identity under conditions of domination and resistance (Muratorio 1987). Second, heterogeneity—be it in terms of socioeconomic differentiation, the form of domestic enterprise, or engagement in geographically dispersed sectors of the economy—is a basic part of the definition of peasantry. It is therefore useless to discuss peasant culture as something derived from "tradition," from a past when peasants were hypothetically homogeneous in some sense or other, or to interpret their potential political engagement in terms of a failure to attain a lost homogeneity.

This new view of culture has implications too for studies of peasant resistance, for it suggests that we should at least rethink the role of leadership and the role of unity, notions closely related to our understanding of peasant rebellion. It is likely that the importance of charismatic leadership (often by outsiders) has been exaggerated largely because of the requirements of post hoc account-giving, which tends to conform to the structural requirements of narrative over and above the structural requirements of the movement being described. Whether or not peasant rebels actually require charismatic leaders may depend on many factors; the fact remains, however, that good narrative does indeed so require at least some such equivalent of the hero. Fieldwork done during rather than after resistance provides an opportunity to make such an observation.

Too often unity and solidarity in political resistance are diametrically opposed to, and made to be exclusive of, individualism. Unity is seen to rest on homogeneity, and homogeneity is seen to depend on the suppression of individual differences in favor of submission to group uniformity (Scott 1986). In many cases too, individualism is confused with *possessive* individualism. Peasants are thereby given the Hobson's choice of no individualism at all or individualism of the kind specifically associated with the rise and establishment of western capitalism. By contrast, the evidence presented here suggests that solidarity in the height of struggle was greatly a result of outspoken individuality and the continual working and reworking of heterogeneity. Because the struggle was over a vital material resource that could not be given up without loss of livelihood, participants were simultaneously committed to participation in the struggle and committed to asserting exactly what they saw the struggle to be about—the means and ends. This process of negotiating meaning, identity, and membership is the ongoing, always-incomplete, production of culture.

2

Domination and Disguise Transformations in Community Institutions

[I]n order to oppress a class, certain conditions must be assured to it under which it can, at least, continue its slavish existence.
—Marx and Engels, *The Communist Manifesto*.

People continue to think of themselves as Huasicanchinos despite the varied places in which they live today. But the character of being "a Huasicanchino" has changed over time as a number of institutions essential to Huasicanchinos have both survived and been transformed. Seeing Huasicancha in this broader historical development helps us understand how the community is integrated into a dominant culture while still manifesting a culture in opposition to that hegemony. Historically direct producers have been exploited through the preservation and manipulation of existing local institutions. As a result, those institutions have become simultaneously the means for *inserting* Huasicancha into a larger economy and society and means for expressing a local identity in *contradistinction* to that economy and society.

There are two interconnected reasons why common identity of sufficient strength has persisted to make Huasicanchinos a significant political force at particular historical moments. In the first place the social relations of production among Huasicanchinos have been dependent upon the continuity of community membership and institutions over time. Hence a consequence of continual engagement in those social relations is the apparent permanence of the institutions of community. In the second place, the insertion of these local social relations into the dominant society has, through time, had the effect of transforming them. History has witnessed a common enough theme in societies where the peasantry has persisted: a dominant bloc maintains the rural production system in order to subvert it, the better to exploit it. As a result, a perpetual contradiction exists: in each historical period community institutions are used to extract surplus from community members, while the social relations underlying those community institutions are themselves based on an ideology of shared reciprocity. Attempts to resolve this contradiction lead to continual transformations in the functioning of community institutions.

Nevertheless, it is important to note that the process of exploitation itself is based upon general acceptance of the orthodox view of community institutions. Inasmuch as the prevailing social relations of production are important for their survival, both "master" (the power bloc) and "slave" (the peasants) rely on the continued idiom of "community," and both collude in maintaining the orthodox essence of community institutions, though for each their instrumental feature is different. The long-term effect is one in which a slippage occurs between accepted meaning and actual practice.

Referring specifically to key words, Raymond Williams (1976) captures the dialectic between survival and change by stressing the masking role played by the nominal continuity of a word. The meaning of a word in its specific context arises from the interplay of the "traditions" of that word (what people often call its "proper usage") with the contemporary conditions to which the word refers:

> The dictionaries most of us use, the defining dictionaries, will in proportion to their merit as dictionaries, list a range of meanings, all of them current, and it will be the range that matters. Then, when we go beyond these to the historical dictionaries, and to essays in historical and contemporary semantics, we are quite beyond the range of the proper meaning. We find a history and complexity of meanings; conscious changes . . . or changes which are masked by a nominal continuity so that words which seem to have been there for centuries, with continuous general meanings, have come in fact to express radically different or radically variable, yet sometimes hardly noticed, meanings and implications of meaning. (1976:15)

A particularly potent word in our culture, for example, is the word *individual,* but its earlier meaning of "being indivisible from the group, identified with the whole," is hardly what we take the word to mean today.

While Williams is referring to a general historical process affecting the meaning of words, I emphasize a process that arises quite specifically from the particular features of communal social relations on the one hand, and the way they are inserted into a dominant social formation (for the purposes of exploitation) on the other. Much of the effectiveness of the direct, interpersonal relations underlying communal institutions derives from the interplay of traditional (orthodox) meaning and contemporary (instrumental) practice. This is because the practice of an institution depends upon assumptions about its continuity through time (its tradition), so that to acknowledge a distinction between traditional meaning and contemporary practice would be to devalue the currency of reciprocity itself.

But the effect of interaction with a dominant bloc intent on extraction is to twist this essential link. Institutions, like the communal work on village commons called the faena or like the exchange of labor between households called *uyay*, are based on the exchange of equivalents over time. As such they have an appearance of permanence, a nominal continuity, which must mask any changes that occur to them. In this they concur with those beyond the community whose purpose is to use local institutions for extraction. But as time goes on an institution is made to serve slightly different functions, and as these differences become manifest, so they are open to interpretation. Participants themselves thus disagree about the *essential* character of an institution. Even so the word that characterizes the institution in question—faena or uyay—is used on the assumption that everyone knows what constitutes the set of activities to which it refers. It is a shorthand way of referring to a body of activities, relationships, and ideas. And its constant usage means that the identity of the word with the instituted practice becomes taken for granted, only questioned at moments of crisis (in function) or conflict (between participants).

It is within the context of this process that the past becomes relevant for an understanding of the present. And it can best be seen by starting with a description of contemporary institutions and then revealing their genealogy by following their transformation through successive historical periods, from the Pre-Colombian, through the colony, to the early republic. So we begin our history in the present.

Community Institutions in Huasicancha, 1960–1972

Institutions in Huasicancha can best be understood by examining the interrelationship between categories of land and the organization of production in the community. All land is held by the community as a corporate body representing its comuneros. This land is divided into three categories:

> *pasto comunal* (communal pasture)
> *chacra comunal* (communal arable land)
> *chacra particular* (household arable plot)

The *pasto comunal* is the land on which all comuneros graze their household livestock. There are a small number of animals held by the community as a whole that are also grazed here, but by 1960 Huasicancha had lost so much of this pasture to the neighboring hacienda that communal pasture could support few community livestock. Instead, what little land existed was allocated to individual households by the community representatives, headed by the personero.

The *chacra comunal* is divided into three parts, each representing the three *barrios* (divisions) of the community: Rauracancha in the East, Chaupimarka in the center, and Huasallco in the West. In principle, produce from these fields is used to fund the *fiestas* of the respective patron saints, Santa Rosa and San Cristobal for the East and West and Santa Barbara for the central barrio and for Huasicancha as a whole. In practice the chacra comunal is farmed by communal work teams (faenas) drawn from the entire village, and all funds derived from these fields were administered by the personero for any community expenses of which fiestas were just one part. While acknowledging that these fields do have a special place in the community and are indeed associated with their respective barrios and, by extension with the patron saints who represent them, villagers strongly deny that these fields have ever "belonged to the church." Widows and other needy villagers are permitted to go through the stubble after a day's harvest and gather lost ears of wheat or barley. They are also sold the straw at a nominal price to dispose of for their own benefit.

But by far the greatest part of Huasicancha's arable land—over 80 percent—is farmed as household plots. Originally there had been some link between the location of these plots and the barrio in which each household was found, but by 1960 they presented a patchwork quilt of tiny fields spread out over the steep hillsides around the village or in any of the small valleys and inclines to the East and West, often as much as two hours' walk away. Villagers use the expression, *Esa chacra pertenece a fulano de tal* ("That chacra pertains to so-and-so") and households do regard their chacras as belonging more to them than to the community. Nevertheless this land cannot be sold or rented to noncommunity members. Indeed, when talking in general terms (rather than in reference to their own land) villagers argue that when a man or woman dies childless, their chacra reverts to the community, though in practice such land is quickly reassigned to the deceased's siblings "as though he or she had never lived."

The interrelationship between these three forms of land is bound up with the organization of production in Huasicancha. Here, although the household plays a central role, it is important not to make it the exclusive focus, for this tempts us to impose our own distinctions between the arena of domestic relations and the arena of social relations (Roseberry 1986). The emergence of the household as a distinctive unit as we know it has many implications for understanding the character of social relations among peasants and hence the role of "community." But in the Huasicancha to which we refer here, the distinction between domestic relations and the reciprocal relationships of the community is one of degree only (Harris 1981, 1982; Collins 1986). Nevertheless, the autonomy of the household is an important ideal among Huasicanchinos, and it is necessary to look at the unit in greater detail.

The household usually contains the man and the woman and their unmarried offspring. Often it also contains the widowed parent of one of the couple. In other cases the youngest son remains in the household of his parents after marriage, gradually taking over the role of household head as his father gets older. In order to emphasize the livelihood function of the household, I refer to it as a *domestic enterprise,* that is to say, an enterprise employing predominantly the nonwage labor of members.

Both husband and wife bring land and livestock to the household at its formation, and women continue to regard their livestock and its offspring as their own. The husband, however, is regarded as the legitimate representative of the household in the community. Only widowed and single women household heads are regarded as comuneros. But the household head is not the sole owner of household property, and conflicts are likely to arise where heads attempt to dispose of household goods without consulting the working members of the enterprise.

Members of the household pursue an ideal of autonomy for their enterprise, attempting to provide for the needs of members by using the resources and personnel available within. First the head must seek labor from within the household for cultivating the household's land and caring for its livestock. When seasonally or continually the amount of labor available within the household is insufficient for the amount of land that the household possesses, labor is sought from other households in the village. Such a situation forces the domestic enterprise into relationships with others in the village through the use of institutions for mobilizing labor. Second, when the amount of land is insufficient to provide for consumption, such needs have to be met by offspring offering out labor. As the total amount of land available to Huasicanchinos diminished in the wake of hacienda expansion, so the opportunity of finding such work within the community diminished. Many had to seek employment beyond their own community.

Extrahousehold linkages of this kind are not just a function of the amount of land and labor held by a household but also the kind of land held and the kind of labor available. Household composition is not the same as household size. If we think of the domestic enterprise as being made up of "labor units" and "consumption units" (see Chayanov 1966:60 and ff.), then there will be some who produce more than they consume, especially the mature youths, and some who do the opposite, especially the old, the sick, and the very young. The effect of a household pursuing an ideal of domestic autonomy will be, therefore, to make the family life cycle an important influence on extrahousehold linkages. Greater amounts of certain kinds of labor will be needed at one time, lesser amounts at another. Crop land and pasture, however, require different amounts of labor of different kinds at various times of the year. Shepherding, for example, does not require much labor, but it requires that labor continuously over extended periods of time. Arable plots, on the other hand, require intensive labor but only at certain periods of the year. The kind of land used by a domestic enterprise, therefore, will also affect its links to other households.

The institutions through which extrahousehold labor is mobilized in Huasicancha fall into two categories: relations between the domestic enterprise and the community as a whole, and relationships between one domestic enterprise and another. The operation of the farm is dependent upon the community as a whole. Not only does the production process of the domestic enterprise require the material advantages offered by the community such as its pasture, sheep-dips, and roads, but its reproduction through time requires an entire language of social and legal performance expressed through community institutions: forms of inheritance, marriage, administrative functions, and so on. In Huasicancha in the 1960s and 1970s the community as a whole rather than individuals or households held title to the land.

The demands of social performance within the community include serving on committees, taking official positions (*cargos*) in the fiestas, and numerous far less obvious daily performances. These, together with the provision of labor on the community's arable land, are in fact a cost paid by the household for its continued functioning, a kind of rent through social performance (cf., Guillet 1980:156). The representative of the household holds usufruct rights to land by virtue of being a comunero. Though he or she is a comunero partly by virtue of certain ascriptive givens (such as being born in Huasicancha), it is primarily the performance of the household within the community that ensures the rights of membership. Of course, once social reproduction embraces larger circuits the character of this "rent" changes. As members of households became dependent on links beyond the community for the survival of their domestic enterprise, so social performance vis a vis the community was modified. But so long as elements of social reproduction depended at least partially on community institutions, households were compelled to continue paying some form of rent through social performance within the community.[1]

The most overt community obligation in the 1960s was participation in the faenas. Faenas could be called for any public works, as well as for work on the community arable land. Though by the 1960s Huasicancha had little pasture, and comuneros regarded their household arable land as more or less their own, villagers asserted that in the past the amount of household labor service was tied directly to household size and household use of the communal pastures. Households making use of larger amounts of land, both arable and pasture, were expected to provide more labor. By the 1960s however, the household—rather than its members—had attained sufficient identity as a discrete unit that, regardless of size, each provided one worker per day for the faena, and larger households simply provided two or three laborers for the first day's work in order to forego their obligations on subsequent days. Failure to perform in the faena invokes sanctions, and continual failure to work leads villagers to talk of the household as especially irresponsible community members. In the early morning members of the campo de vara are stationed on the hills around the village, and they call out the names of people seen trying to leave the village. Those not turning up at the faena have to pay a fine or do some other chore for the community.

Work on the faena is accompanied by the music of a band. During pauses in work the community provides workers with *coca* (dried leaves from coca shrubs) to chew and *aguardiente* (cane alcohol) to drink. During these breaks a certain formality is observed, with workers sitting in a line while the band walks up and down playing in front of them with some of the participants dancing. Coca, aguardiente, and *chicha* (corn beer) are passed along the line. By late afternoon participants, affected by the work and the entertainment, begin to forget about formalities, and the whole group dances and sings its way back to the village.

In addition to communal labor, the operation of the farm requires direct links between households for which there are appropriate institutions. Uyay is the reciprocal exchange of equivalent amounts of labor between two or more households. "We help you plough your field today; you help us shear our sheep next Thursday." In fact, exchange labor is rarely measured in such a calculated way as this; nevertheless, the principle of equivalence makes it difficult for uyay to be used as a means for readjusting permanently the labor of the household. It might give a household extra labor today but only at the price of an equal deficiency tomorrow.[2]

Minka offers more flexibility in this respect. Here labor is supplied to a household in return for goods that may be simply consumed during the day of work or taken away at the end of the day. The degree to which the goods given in minka are seen as real equivalents of labor varies considerably. Nevertheless, essentially the loan of labor is repaid in the form of produce, which means that one household can use the labor of four neighbors and pay them in goods, without having to lose four days domestic labor of their own. Thus, while uyay does not have the effect of modifying the composition of the household over the long run, minka can do precisely this.

Other institutions also affect labor supply and productivity. The word *huaccha* originally meant an orphan,[3] but *huaccha* or *huacchilla* refers also to an institution. In the days when Huasicancha was almost entirely a pastoral community, a person, with or without living parents, who reached maturity without inheriting any livestock, being without patrimony, was essentially an orphan. To this day within the community, the institution through which such a person gives his or her labor to a household with animals (but deficient in labor to care for them) in order to receive in payment a certain number of newborn animals for his or her services is called *huacchilla*. In this way the *huacchero* was able—in theory at least—to accumulate some animals. In the case of *michipa,* the shepherd takes in the animals of another household among his own flock. In return, the other household either provides the shepherd with a certain amount of produce from its arable land or provides laborers to work on the arable land of the shepherd. In other words, pastoral is exchanged for arable labor.

Trueque (barter) has become the subject of an extensive literature on the Andean economy (see espeically Alberti and Mayer 1974; Murra 1980; Golte 1980; and Lehmann 1982). In the case of Huasicancha, barter originally took place between the comuneros and households in the higher communities of Huancavelica to the south, those in the intermontane Mantaro Valley, and those in the high jungle to the east of the Mantaro Valley (see map 1). This allowed Huasicanchinos to exchange goods grown at different levels of the Andean ecology, giving them access to salt and fleeces from Huancavelica, cereals from the Mantaro Valley, and coca and corn from the high jungle. By 1960, trueque with households in the Mantaro Valley had ceased entirely. But most households continued to journey once a year to the jungle, where close relationshps had been built up between one household and another. A similar, though less vigorous barter continued with Acobambilla in Huancavelica. Although exchange equivalents between goods is somewhat influenced by their prevailing market price, villagers argue that relative values are less volatile than market prices and hence more reliable.

Before turning back to look at the genealogies of these institutions in the past, there is another important dimension to labor supply and demand. Many of the institutions for mobilizing labor within Huasicancha were also used, though in modified form, by the neighboring Hacienda Tucle for gaining access to the village pool of labor.

Hacienda Use of Community Institutions

On the hacienda, crops had to be harvested, sheep dipped, roads repaired, and stables built and maintained; for each task, workers were needed. Just across the hill in the nearby "indigenous community" (comunidad indigena) there existed a ready-made institution for such work: the faena. It was simply a matter of redirecting its labor away from the community and toward the hacienda.[4]

The hacienda used the institution of the faena, at least partly, by ideological sleight-of-hand: the hacienda became an ersatz member of the community; the hacendada, her husband, and the administrator set themselves up as ersatz community patriarchs—from *patron* to *padrino* (from boss to godfather). At the community faenas the community provided music, drink, coca, and food. Hacienda Tucle did likewise, at least initially. In addition, cigarettes were provided, and, instead of the community dish of soup, a couple of sheep were roasted. Furthermore, acting in the spirit of "community," the hacendada occasionally offered the villagers the services of the hacienda truck, and the administrator gave the village authorities advice on farming and dealings with the government.

Of course this kind of disguising of labor-extraction through the use of an idiom of reciprocity was fraught with tensions. As time went by, Tucle began to find that the music and especially the drink were counterproductive and dropped them. By the 1950s the community was actually being offered cash to provide the hacienda with a faena. Even so, this ideological performance on the part of the hacienda was by far the cheapest way of securing labor and would have remained so, just so long as the appearance of reciprocity could be maintained. The effect was not to dissolve the traditional institution of the faena (for a time the faena even took on an appearance of renewed vigor), but to transform it. So the form of the institution known as "the faena" was not just a function of the reproduction requirements of domestic enterprises that, together, formed the community, but it was also a function of the reproduction requirements of the neighboring hacienda.

Other institutions among Huasicanchino households were also made use of by the hacienda. Members of households were most frequently used as shepherds for the hacienda sheep and cattle. These shepherds were employed by the hacienda by transforming existing extrahousehold economic relations within the village, i.e., huaccha and michipa.[5] As the hacienda began to expand onto the community pasture, the situation changed: where before there had been a few poor Huasicanchinos who had access to community pasture but had no sheep, now there were increasing numbers of Huasicanchinos with sheep but no pasture. Before, a person who cared for the sheep of another was paid by being given some of those sheep for himself or herself, but now a household cared for the hacienda animals in return for being allowed to "enter" the pasture now controlled by the hacienda with a certain number of animals of their own. In effect then, these shepherds rented pasture from the hacienda for a designated number of their own animals and paid in the form of labor as shepherds for the hacienda. The animals they brought onto the hacienda land with them were referred to as the huacchas. So, though the relationship was exactly reversed, the institution maintained its original name (and resonance): huaccha or huacchilla.

Because the task of shepherding for the hacienda demanded the fulltime labor of the entire household (except a few days at harvest time), if these households had their own small arable plots in the village, they could not cultivate them. And if, in addition, these were people who became shepherds because they had so little of this arable land anyway, then they now needed to acquire subsistence crops somehow. In either case, the solution was michipa. Hacienda shepherds (illegally) took in the animals of other villagers among their own huacchas, and these were, of course, referred to by the old term michipas. In return, the shepherd received produce from the other villager, either from that villager's plot or through the labor that villager did on the plot of the absent shepherd. Once again the community-hacienda institution was grafted onto, and became a transformation of, the community institution.

But Hacienda Tucle was not by any means the first noncommunity organization to make use of Huasicancha's institutions. Indeed, the interrelationship between Huasicancha and Hacienda Tucle can only be understood by reference to a long history in which communities such as Huasicancha were inserted into a larger economy and polity; however, the task can achieve very limited historical accuracy. There are by no means the historical resources in contemporary Huasicancha to allow us to reconstruct the specific history of the community from the days of the Inca domination to the War of the Pacific in 1879. Instead, it is necessary to rely on the extant ethnohistorical literature on the Peruvian Andes to reconstruct what Wachtel has called "a retrospectively rationalized image" (1977:65).[6]

La Nación Huanca

> *[In the Inca period] tribute played a double role: it linked the community to a much greater unit, but at the same time it isolated it in its local setting and consolidated its traditional structures.*
>
> —Wachtel (1977:73)

The Huasicanchinos, like most people living in and around the Mantaro Valley, regard themselves as the descendants of the nation of Huanca peoples subjugated by the Incas. Far from being conquered by the Spanish, the Huancas were their allies in the fight with the Incas. The Huasicanchinos argue that this fact provided the historical basis for resistance to hacienda penetration of the area, for Spanish claims to land were never as clearcut as in the areas of imperial Quechua where crown grants were made as part of the booty of war.

The Inca empire of Tahuantinsuyu in 1532, far from being well integrated, was composed of a number of ethnic groups or nations whose degree of subordination depended upon their remoteness from the centers of Inca power. They differed considerably in size and in degree of complexity (Moore 1958; Murra 1958; Espinosa 1972) but were governed by a political regime whose economy was based upon the social organization of these subordinated nations. Despite differences in the degree of Inca control, it seems doubtful that the empire ever radically altered the agricultural structure of any but those groups closest to Cuzco: "In 1500 the State could not afford to interfere with the peasant's ability to feed himself and his kinsfolk when in need; he continued to do so in the Andes by growing without irrigation the locally domesticated tuber crops within a system of traditional lineage and ethnic tenures" (Murra 1958:341). To explore the interplay between the Incas and these subordinated groups we must first turn to a description of the *ayllus* that made up a nation or ethnic group.

The ethnic group was a unit of varying size, wider than the simple lineage but having an ideology of kinship, though not necessarily a traceable set of linkages. It was composed of a number of ayllus (Rowe 1946). *La Nacion Huanca*, for example, which was united by belief in a common ancestor, Huasihuillca, was divided into three maximal ayllus. These were Jatun Sausa, Lurin Huanca, and Anan Huanca, each being roughly equivalent to the present-day provinces of Jauja, Concepcion, and Huancayo that make up the Department of Junin. The present site of Huasicancha would have been on the extreme southern, highland periphery of this nation (Espinosa 1972).

Each maximal ayllu was made up of smaller ones, there being sixty of these in all (Espinosa 1972:35). The ayllu is described by Rowe (1946:255) as "a kin group with theoretical endogamy, with descent in the male line, [which] owned a definite territory." In practice, however, Spalding's more general description of the ayllu is more apt: "The traditional ayllu can be defined as any group whose members regard themselves as 'brothers' owing one another aid and support, in contrast to others outside the boundaries of the group" (1973:583). The ayllu provided members with plots for their households in return for labor on the ayllu common land. This household land consisted of both pasture and arable land. A couple were considered "married" from the time they organized a work team of their neighbors and kin and built a house. Once married, the couple were regarded as mature members of the ayllu. As members, they were expected to contribute to all community work, and in return the household was provided with arable land in proportion to its size. Arable land was reallotted each year to keep up with demographic changes both at the level of the ayllu and at the level of each individual household within it (Wachtel 1977:66).

It is important to emphasize the role of the household rather than the individual. Tasks were allotted to households, not to individuals (Murra 1958), and autonomy was as much a goal for the households as it was for the ayllu as a whole. Work might be extended beyond the household but not a single good was released to individuals. "Nobody, not my *curaca* (head man), nor later the Inca, has rights over my fields or my llamas" (Wachtel 1973:67). For the purposes of distribution among the households, the ayllu land was divided into sectors on the basis of a) where it stood in the system of crop rotation, and b) where it was located in the mountains. In view of the extreme variations in altitude within short distances in the Andes, this latter dimension was largely a function of "verticality": from high pasture, to intermediate tuber-growing lands, to lowland maize. Wachtel writes: "By virtue of the autarchic ideal which ruled the economic life of the Andean societies, each domestic unit could lay claim to a parcel in each of the various sectors (even though this ideal was not always realised)" (1973:63). These sectors were referred to as *mañay* meaning literally "to request" or "to beg." The household requested land from neighbors and kin as a group, represented by its head or heads, the curacas. Neighbors and kin, in turn, requested that the household adults shows themselves to be socially responsible community members. This social responsibility or obligation was expressed through their reciprocal offering of labor in exchange for land. The offering of extra-household labor was seen as a social obligation be it the offering of labor to the community as a whole, or the offering of labor to individual neighbors and kin. Neither a household's request for land nor, conversely, requests to them for labor could be refused.

The reciprocal character of this exchange of household land for labor given to the community meant, of course, that larger households with more labor units could "rent" more land than those with fewer. The *tupu* (the allotting of land according to household size), within the principles of balanced reciprocity, reflected the labor potential of the household but not its consumption needs. Such reciprocity did not in itself serve a "welfare" function (cf., Louis Baudin 1928). In this kind of community the household head who could mobilize a large number of people through generalized reciprocity was in an advantageous position vis-à-vis the community as a whole. Thus a person with a large household could create both a greater debt from neighbors with respect to reciprocal exchanges of labor and also a greater debt from the community with respect to the allotment of land. Where generalized reciprocity begins in the household and moves out to proximate kin, a large household strategically positioned within a larger kin grouping would have offered favorable conditions for making a man "rich." A Spanish chronicler referring to contributions of labor to the communal work force notes: "He who has most assistants and finishes his share of the *suyu* [labour on community land] most quickly was considered a rich man he who had nobody to assist him and hence worked longer, a poor man" (Wachtel 1973:64).

Such a man was well placed to become the curaca or head man of the local ayllu. No doubt, with the advent of the Inca domination, curacas acquired special privileges. But the conflicting reports of their special privileges and their ownership of tracts of land far beyond the needs of their immediate household probably arose not simply from the specific ideas of property held by the Spanish chroniclers who provided us with this evidence, but also from the way curacas manipulated this system of reciprocity. Chroniclers suggested, for example, that curacas held large tracts of private land and large flocks of llamas and that they claimed the services of community labor on their property. Supposedly ayllu members first worked the community land and then the land of the senior curacas, on down to the curaca of their most immediate locality. Curacas also used the labor of *yanas* (owned servants).

The evidence implies that curacas had privileges quite distinct from other ayllu members. Yet, chroniclers were always impressed when curacas were seen at work in the fields with other ayllu members and were required to beg (*rogar; mañay*) for labor services (Murra 1958; Wachtel 1977:65, Spalding 1973:585, Godelier 1977:64).

Distinctive privileges and the ability to secure private land were probably restricted to high ranking curacas, local ayllu heads having very little of either. But important is the way in which a curaca combined an ideology of reciprocity with kinship links. The curaca was essentially the head of the ayllu-family and as such commanded resources that allowed him access to a wide network of reciprocal rights from kin. Thus when Cobo wrote that "No one nobleman or commoner owned more land than was necessary to support his family" (1956 [1653]:XCII, 121) this need not have meant that the curaca was thereby limited in his control of large amounts of land since, in this context, the word "family" could cover a whole ayllu. This confusion, however, between the curaca's possession of land as household head and his possession as representative of the ayllu is significant in understanding the subsequent developments in territorial control in the Andes.

Similarly, curacas, unlike other ayllu members, owned yanas—people taken into the household for life who worked as servants in house and field. The origin of this institution of *yanaconage* is not clear (cf., Murra 1964:93), but any institution that allowed one household to expand its own internal labor pool by drawing in new members would give such a household a dominant position vis-à-vis other households in a system of balanced reciprocity of labor. Yanas would therefore have provided the means by which curacas could overcome the dictates of the demographic cycles and thus solidify their position within the ayllu.

Despite the advantages that the curaca might have derived from the system of reciprocity, the existence of community land and the obligation to give labor to cultivate land had the effect of maintaining the ayllu as a community of people with shared identity. This land was broken down into three categories:

1. communal land administered by the curacas;
2. land farmed to support the worship of the local deities;
3. land allotted to households.

In view of what has been said about the role of kinship in relations of production within the ayllu it is possible to see what would happen to those unable to provide extra-household labor to exchange in return for other labor or goods. The opposite of the "rich" household able to call upon large numbers of kin for labor would be the person unable to call upon any kin. Such a person is typically an orphan, a huaccha, referring also to a poorer person in a relationship. These parentless children, together with childless parents and physically handicapped people, drew upon the resources produced on the communal land administered by the curaca.

Community land worked with labor extracted from each household thus resolved the problem of the debt that would have emerged between deficient households and those well endowed with labor. Resources provided by the community land substituted an overall debt to the community as a whole for what would otherwise have been an ever-increasing debt to any one household (see figure 1). Where curacas used control of this land for the specific advantage of their own households, of course, the communal solution to interpersonal debt was undercut.

An analogous situation existed for livestock husbandry. The person who inherited no livestock gave him or herself as a huacchero to a household seeking labor. In this way such a person could gain access to a number of the newborn animals of the flock each year. This was usually expressed by the adoption of the "orphan" into the household of the flock owner. In principle at least, huaccheros could, once having accumulated stock of their own, strike out and set up house for themselves. In the case of livestock husbandry, pasture might often be at some distance removed from the seat of the ayllu itself. And just as we have seen that an ideal of autonomy was pursued by households (each household attempting to control some land at differing altitudes in the Andean ecology), the same was true for the ayllu as a whole. The seat of the ayllu located at about 3,000 meters above sea level strove to control as many microclimates as possible above and below this level. Moreover, since ecological zones at the extremes of the Andean vertical ecology did not have to be geographically coterminus with the intermediate zones, they could form "archipelagos" whose "islands" achieved unity through reference to the ayllu lineage (Murra 1967:381–406).

The long distances involved meant that colonies of shepherd households arose who maintained their ties to the ayllu and continued to have rights in ayllu land in the other zones. When a household head died or was widowed, the household returned to the seat of the ayllu to be replaced by another (Wachtel 1972:72). Despite these arrangements, the sheer distances involved must have given to the pastoral colonies a certain distinctiveness that would have been increased because many of these distant shepherds shared in common their experience of being huaccheros for better-off households resident at the intermediate Andean level.

At least by the time the Spanish chroniclers were writing, curacas even of a fairly low level maintained their own yanas, which the Spanish translated as "slaves" (Murra 1964; Wachtel 1977; Lumbreras 1980). It is likely that yanas too were found in these colonies. In principle huaccheros were still members of the ayllu, and over a generation, families could dissolve the huacchilla relationship. By the time of the chroniclers in the 17th century it seems

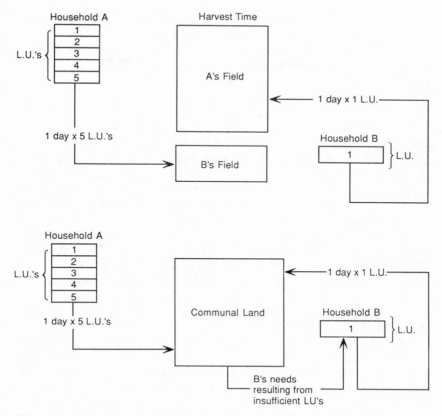

Figure 1.   *Direct interhousehold reciprocity and communal reciprocity.*

that this was not so for yanas, at least one of whose offspring appears to have remained the property of the wealthier household. It seems likely, however, that for huacchero and yana shepherds the social distinctions between them would have become less than the distinction that divided them, by distance, from the seat of the ayllu. The point is that even prior to domination by the Incas and the introduction of *mitmaq* colonies of "outsiders" within the various subordinated nations, there already existed, within the ayllus themselves, a group of pastoralists whose interests and daily concerns may have given them an identity distinct from the rest of the ayllu members, who spent the greater part of the year at the lower geographical levels. This at any rate is the interpretation of contemporary Huasicanchinos, who stress that their independence from lower level ayllu seats goes back to the earliest times. Contrasting themselves with the similar pastoral community of Yanacancha, they point to the distinction in their names: the one a cancha or collection of yanas, the other a collection of huasis or houses. They argue that this suggests that there was a more permanent settlement in their own area, and they point as well to Yanacancha's uninterrupted accessibility, lying as it does, directly up the slopes from the old ayllu seat of Chupaca.[7]

. . . and "El Imperio Inca"

The Inca state apparatus was superimposed on these institutions. Ayllus and the larger nations of which they were part maintained their integrity and identity, but existing institutions had now to serve the needs of the dominant empire. The Huancas were one such group. They were predominantly agriculturalists, and their control over the higher zones varied between one ayllu and another. According to Espinosa, the Huanca had his own yanas who worked land near the capital, and they were held personally by him. He frequently made "gifts" to the *jatuncuracas* or senior curacas, who themselves had yanas and used them for the shepherding of their own llamas (cf., Murra 1980; Samaniego 1974). It is not clear what the extent of the physical might of the Huanca was, but it never appears to have been much more than symbolic and involved virtually no extraction from the ayllu or defense against larger groups. "Battles for the protection of lands were far more frequent between ayllus than ethnic groups" (Espinosa 1972:41).

Once the Huanca ethnic group was absorbed into Tahuantinsuyu in the middle of the fifteenth century, the seat of the Huanca was abandoned and the three *mitades* were set up as Inca *huamani* or "provinces" with jatuncuracas at their heads (Espinosa 1969) and Cuzco as their center of authority. Besides the seats of the three major ayllus, now provinces within Tahuantinsuyu, there appeared two other quite different kinds of settlement groupings. The first of these were the famous Inca *tambos,* placed strategically along the Cuzco-Quito road (Morris 1967). There were four of these in the region: Julca, Jatunsausa, Maravilca, and Huancayo. These were both resting places for the officers of the Inca court and army and also storehouses for the grain and other goods produced by the *corvee* labor of the ayllus. The second of the two introduced settlements were the mitmaqs: certain Huancas were forcibly removed from the area and replaced by mitmaqs from other areas (Espinosa 1972:45).

The most striking feature of this system is the apparent continuity in the community institutions before and after the advent of the Incas. Surplus labor, rather than goods, continued to be the form of extraction from households. Communal work teams continued to take their customary form. Even the use of yanas predates the Incas, though the yanas' role was vastly less important. And while the implantation among conquered peoples of mitmaq colonies far removed from their home base may have been an innovation, there already existed, as we have seen, relatively independent ayllu archipelagos at some remove from the seat of the ayllu.

It is, however, equally clear that this continuity was only on the surface disguising an underlying reality, and this process of disguise was not incidental to the Inca system but essential to it. The Inca state depended upon the productivity of the conquered communities by introducing into the equation of reciprocity a new element: the godlike unity of the Inca. The dominant position of kinship within the ayllu, as the owner of the means of production in its unity and the provider of labor power through its parts, was replaced by the apparent unity of the Inca godhead. The community institutions persisted but were made to serve modified functions. Hence the land of the ayllu was now divided into: Inca state land; Inca deity land; ayllu land; local deity land; and household land. The Inca lands probably did not constitute a very large part of the ayllu.

There is some difference of opinion about who now claimed ownership over land. Moore (1958) and Wachtel (1973, 1977) argue that all land now belonged to the Inca, and Wachtel suggests that this fact underlay the principle by which tribute was extracted through the continued ideal of reciprocity:

> The ayllu . . . enjoyed rights of use of territory possessed in theory by the Emperor. In exchange for this favour, the members of the ayllu owed him tribute. The Inca's "gift" might well be considered fictitious of course, since before its conquest the territory already belonged to the communities. But the fiction was necessary to give to the tribute its character of reciprocal obligation. (1977:66)

Lumbreras, however, writes that, "The ayllu, the family clan, was the possessor and owner of the land. . . . The state was not the direct owner of land but through its access to the labour force of the ayllu, it expropriated the riches generated by the latter. . . . The Inca state was based on its ownership of the labour force" (1970:35). Hence ownership of the populace was the principle justifying surplus extraction.

Either way, the important point is that the ayllu members were called upon to acknowledge the legitimacy of repaying their debt to society through payments in direct labor, such that a Spanish chronicler wrote, "All they gave their kings were personal services. . . . No other obligation but work . . . [to the point where today] they resent it more when they have to give a peck of potatoes than when they work for fifteen days with the community at some task" (Murra 1958). If, as I have suggested above, the communal work team represented the payment of a kind of rent by households for their membership in the ayllu, then it now became a payment acknowledging membership in a far broader social world.

This change meant a transformation in the meaning of the "social responsibility" of each household head. Where before it had been based on the idea of reciprocal obligations between neighbors and kin expressed in the form of labor, now the responsibility that superceded all others was not to the ayllu but to the state. This was still expressed in the form of labor, specifically in terms of the labor obligations on that land that had been ayllu common land but was now Inca land. Thus, as Murra (1958) points out, marriage and the setting up of a house was transformed from a rite of passage into the community, giving the adult a positive status with both rights as well as duties, into an onerous obligation to provide corvee labor to the Inca state. Subsequent institutions used for extracting surplus labor from Andean peasants cannot be properly understood without recognition of this particular heritage of "owing labor" to those with power through manipulating the meaning of social membership.

Tribute could only be extracted through the idiom of the exchange of equivalents by a process of mystification, a form nicely described in another context by Marc Bloch (1974:228) as "reciprocity in unequal obligations." Items offered in return for tribute had to be given a special "value," which was expressed through the increasing importance of a division between utility goods and luxury goods, part of the former being absorbed by the state, while the latter were redistributed in return. Utility goods, especially food, were not redistributed by the Incas from one ayllu to another but consumed in support of state activities (Morris 1967:174). Luxury goods, on the other hand, such as cloth, coca, and maize (for the production of beer) were strategically distributed as "gifts" from the Inca, especially to the jatuncuracas at the head of the nations and the curacas in the local ayllu. "And the reason they went to Cuzco was so that they could [be seen to] come *from* Cuzco" (Morris: 173). The "value" that made it possible for luxury goods to achieve equivalence with utility goods derived from the belief that they had been touched by the godhead, the earthly representative of the potent Sun. Even though the Incas used existing ayllu institutions, the process of surplus extraction could not fail to modify social relations within the ayllu. However small a proportion of land was put aside for the Incas and Inca deities, it had to be subtracted from the ayllu lands, as did the labor given over to the state. The richest and the poorest in the ayllus were most directly affected.

Despite the ideal of equality—expressed in the curaca's need to beg ayllu members to provide him with labor, for example—there had always been room for the assertion of power by particular families. But after the Inca conquest the basis of this power changed. Some of the ayllu land that had previously been administered by the curacas now became the land of the Inca and the possibility of the curaca using his control of the land to maintain his position through what Sahlins (1968) has called "the politics of generosity" was thus reduced. But the Inca was dependent upon the curacas for the local organization of production. Morris suggests that luxury gifts from the Inca served to provide the curacas with symbolic strength and that possibly a small amount of subsistence goods was similarly made available to compensate the curacas and allow them to maintain their positions, "at a level similar to what they were before the Inca take-over channeled a major part of the area's surplus production into the central coffers" (Morris 1967:176). Inca support of the curacas thus rigidified the position of such households vis-à-vis the community and made them surrogate state representatives.

The reduction of ayllu common land also affected the ability of the community to provide for the welfare needs of the poorer ayllu members. But the growing demands of the state for its own labor force led to an increase in the number of yanas drawn from precisely this group within the ayllu. As huacchas had been used for both shepherding community flocks and working within the households of wealthier families, so yanas served both the state directly and the households of the "authorities." With the curacas themselves taking on some of the roles of state representatives, so the new relationships became but slight transformations of the previous ones.

The reduction of common land would also have reduced the incentive for pastoral colonies to maintain links to the seat of the ayllu and thus increased the tendency for them to become a class of their own. The mitmaq colonies through which the Inca rulers introduced "outsiders" into the ethnic nations, far removed from their kin, may therefore also have been but a variation on an existing pattern. It might also be proposed that the growth of a population loosened from the ties of an ecologically autonomous ayllu was an inevitable outcome of the growth of Inca state power and the loss of complete autonomy on the part of the ayllus.

By the time of the Spanish Conquest between 1531 and 1533, the Inca state had inserted itself into the ayllu economy while by no means entirely destroying the autonomy of the subjected groups. The practice of paying tribute in one form or another and to a variety of groups ranging from local curacas to Inca state officials had been established. While the more powerful ayllus and their curacas continued to be located at the intermediate ecological zones—and for the Huancas this meant the Mantaro Valley—the pastoral groups in the higher zones were developing independent interests of their own.

The arrival of the Spanish led to a massive mobilization of the Huanca population against the Incas and a number of battles were fought in the area between the Huancas and the Inca army quite independently of the Spanish. Over the hundred years following the conquest the powerful ex-curacas of the Mantaro made a series of requests to the Spanish crown for recognition of their role in the defeat of the Incas, and the Jatuncuraca of Ananhuanca, Apo Alaya, and his son Cristobal, were among these claimants. Their descendants managed to gain control of much of the highlands to the west and south of the valley in the subsequent period and made successive attempts to establish their influence over the area of present-day Huasicancha.

The Emergence of
the Highland Hacienda System

The economy of the area around the Mantaro Valley experienced a severe collapse through the first hundred years of the Spanish Colony. The population of Ananhuanca fell from about 9,000 households in 1520 to 2,500 in the census of Toledo in 1572 (Espinosa 1972:174). Spanish interest in agriculture was concentrated on the coast until the earthquake of 1687 put the final seal on already impoverished soils. But the central focus of interest in the area was the mercury mines of Huancavelica. While the highland areas to the north of Huasicancha (Laive, Cacchi, Yanacancha) and closer to the Mantaro Valley continued to fall under the influence of the intermediate-level settlements, especially Chupaca and the Apoalaya family (see map 1), the pastoralists of the area around Huasicancha broke their ties to the Apoalayas in 1714 and thereafter were drawn into the orbit of the Huancavelica economy to the south.

Although a few wealthier lowland families ran large flocks on the highland pastures, this took the form of scattered estancias with undefined boundaries and little concentration. Their occasional attempts to lay claim to specific tracts of land (which usually took the form of setting up boundary-marker stones) were met by resistance from smaller flock owners and hence failed to become established. These are the local conditions from which the highland hacienda system emerged.

With the coming of the Spanish a colonial administrative apparatus had been organized to tax the populace, exploit the raw materials in the mines, and prepare the Indian for the civilizing enthusiasm of the missionaries. This was the most visible face of the new colony, and around it laws were made, officials appointed, Indians concentrated into village settlements, and a dual society of Spaniards and *Indios* given recognition. But, after the first century of devastation there grew up beside the official, colonial society an economy of commercial agriculture and trading and with it an indigenous elite that became well established in the Central Andes, with wealthy Indians owning large flocks of livestock, using communal labor for their arable land, and selling commodities to the more accessible villages. Ex-curacas, now referred to as local *caciques,* used their positions in the countryside to control as much land, labor, and trade as possible. The early history of the Spanish Colony was one of tension between a colonial system of state-monopolized plunder that first resisted, then gave way to, and eventually supported an economy of commercial agriculture, commodity production, and trade. As trade and scattered forms of small-scale commodity production increased in importance beside the state-run mines, so colonial offices and decentralized tribute extraction, such as the *encomienda,* yielded fewer riches than could be gained from bypassing the state and acquiring wealth through owning haciendas and drawing rent, or monopolizing a region's trade through the *reparto de marcancías*.

The emergence of large ranches, therefore, followed two often overlapping paths, to arrive at the institution now called the hacienda. On the one hand, there was the formal granting of land to a Spaniard or to a highly placed *Criollo,* together with a grant of *mita* (i.e., corvee) labor to be provided by the local Indians (in principle all adult male members of an Indian community owed mita service to the Spanish vice-royalty). It is this practice that has been given the most attention and that has led to an image of distinctive estates with Spanish descendants owning haciendas and Indian serfs working for them (see, for example, Pearse 1976:64–71).

But there was another path to the hacienda: wealthy members of the *Republica de los Indios* on a much more piecemeal basis (sometimes by renting land from their own or neighboring communities, sometimes simply through expansion of their flocks and de facto possession of pasture), gained access to land and used their position in the community to gain access to labor as well, while themselves becoming increasingly distanced from the Indian communities of their origin (Spalding 1975:113). Claims to this land were often made through the elaboration of genealogies showing their "noble" pedigree in descent from the old Jatuncuracas. It was this second path that led to the initial—and crucial—concentration of land in the highland pastures around the Mantaro Valley. Only later did this less direct path overlap with the direct path, more commonly associated with the rise of the hacienda.

As of the royal decree of 27 May 1631, a powerful family could gradually increase its de facto control over an extension of land and then request the *composicion* of what they claimed to be their land. Since the Spanish crown claimed land not being used by Indian communities, all that was required was a payment to the crown for a deed recognizing private ownership of the land. But there was a major drawback. Consistent with the principles of the *corregimiento* in which the crown undertook to protect a separate Republica de los Indios, these titles were invariably conditional on there remaining "sufficient pastures and fields for the Indians of that area" or on "the continued right of the local peoples to graze their animals freely on said land and pass without let or hindrance." This meant that, while Indian caciques might wish to formalize their titles through composición, their Spanish counterparts might find it equally politic, through marriage or mere sleight of hand, to lay claim to lands through genealogical claims showing their Indian parentage. The paths, then, leading to the emergence of haciendas in the region twist and turn considerably.

Meanwhile the real basis for wealth in the early days of the colony lay of course in the mines, and much of the commercial economy of the central Andes revolved around this nexus (Assadourian 1982). The largest center in Peru, by far, was Huancavelica, which lies to the south of present-day

most certainly along the road from Huancavelica down to the coast. By the
end of the century there was a trend throughout the area for scattered canchas
to be brought together and for groups of peasants to be concentrated into
pueblos de indios. We should also recall that it was around this time too that
the Huancavelica mines began their collapse, reducing the market opportunities in that area. Hacienda Tucle was rented to a Spaniard by the name
of Francisco Lira, and the weakened position of the Indians with the collapse
of the mines and of the colonial administration is reflected in his actions: he
took Huasicanchinos to court for trespassing in 1804 and won.

Apart from this case, there are no records of conflicts between the hacienda
and small herders over land for the first half of the nineteenth century, that
is, throughout the collapse of the colony and the early years of the republic.
Although there seems to be little evidence of territorial expansion, this does
appear to be the period when the fundo at Tucle Pampa was established as a
permanent part of the life of Huasicanchinos. Land, in relative abundance,
was not the major source of conflicts, but tension did exist over the hacienda's
use of labor and the community's misuse of hacienda livestock. Community
records show that poorer villagers were working for the hacienda during this
time, usually in return for being fed but no more. They, for their part, frequently attempted to rustle sheep and carry them off for sale at some distant
market.

Although large haciendas nearby, like Laive (famous in present-day Peru
for its cheese) and Antapongo began in the early part of the nineteenth century
to rationalize production and become major suppliers of wool to the growing
textile industry of the Mantaro Valley, Hacienda Tucle remained a farm, producing anything it possibly could for the owner's family consumption; any
excess was sold through the shop they owned in Huancayo. Thus, in the first
three quarters of the nineteenth century, there were few open conflicts with
the haciendas. The picture that emerges is one of relatively independent highland pastoralists with flocks of varying sizes, engaged in some trade and
muleteering on the one side, and a hacienda gradually specializing in livestock
production for the domestic market but still producing a broad range of crops
of less commercial value on the other.

Growing Lines of Distinction

Throughout the seventeenth century then, the economy of the Mantaro
Valley had been slow to get on its feet while, by contrast, the Huancavelica
mines had come on stream. The highland pastoralists on Huancayo's southern
borders with Huancavelica, specifically the Huasicanchinos, were affected by
this. The trend toward increasing independence from the ayllu seats in the

intermediate ecological zones of the Mantaro Valley—which had started prior to the Inca domination and was accelerated after it—was now given further impetus. Pastoralists were affected by the market nexus, therefore, not to the northeast and through the once powerful Mantaro Valley clans, but to the south, directly to the market in the mining centers.

It is important for an understanding of the political events to be discussed in the next chapter that some sense be gained of the specificity of local conditions, especially the relationship between the highland pastoral haciendas of the neighborhood and the local herders.[15] To begin with, while the viciousness and power of the new colonialists cannot be denied (Piel 1970:115), it is important to bear in mind the role of terrain in Huasicancha's history. Roving, highland peasants are notoriously independent figures throughout history, invariably escaping attempts to control them, and the chasms, slopes, and peaks in which Huasicanchinos worked made this especially so.[16] All these factors combined to give the pastoralists of the region a period of respite in the century following the conquest. While potential landlords showed little interest in the region, to the south there lay a market for their hides and meat (and the possibility of experiencing wide geographical mobility).

With the coming of the eighteenth century a composición de tierras did take place for Tucle Pampa and, generally, in the area there was a changeover from scattered estancias managing the sheep of lowland families to concentration into *fundos* that were eventually established as haciendas. The running of these fundos depended on the continuation of institutions that had remained in place since prior to the conquest.

An important component in the development of haciendas and of the mines in the region was the payment of labor service in its various forms, with little or no expectation that laborers should gain access to land in return. While on-farm laborers at the more feudal-like Spanish haciendas were granted small plots in return for labor services, many other large flock owners received labor services from members of the neighboring communities as an extension of institutions like mita and huacchilla (c.f., Piel 1970:113). Villagers thus had two demands on their labor beyond the immediate household: part was in the form of the mita, and part was in the various forms of extrahousehold labor continued from the precolonial period and now paid to wealthy neighbors. Sometimes this labor was organized and mediated by the local authorities; sometimes it took the form of direct service, as in the case of huacchilla. In this area of the highlands land was not scarce, and the granting of plots in return for labor had no attraction to peasants. And, though other hacendados may have protected their tenants from the rigors of the mita this was not, anyway, especially onerous for the farmers who paid a tasa and supplied the mines, as was the case for the Huasicanchinos. Therefore, wealthy households' access to labor had to be secured through existing institutions and thus involved them in links to Indian settlements.

For the settlements themselves, the requirements of livestock rearing and arable subsistence farming also meant the continuation of these institutions. Instead of the coexistence of people, we are witnessing throughout this period the emergence of opposing groups, already imbued with sharp definition and self-conscious identity as two separate camps. The haciendas emerged along an often poorly defined path. Owners of large flocks such as the Marmanillo and Astucuri families from Ayacucho and Chupaca rented or usurped land in the highlands, but their initial strength came precisely from manipulating their membership in the Indian communities. Nor did they face a group of homogeneous "peasants," powerless and ignorant. Although not powerful enough to request composiciónes, individual highland pastoralists controlled large expanses of land through keeping herds in scattered canchas. The extent of these herds was, in the early period, less a function of territorial control than of the ability to mobilize labor. And for this the emerging hacendado and the pastoralists alike required the existing institutions.

The chief difference between the early highland hacendados in areas as remote as Tucle and some of the neighboring pastoralists was economic stability. For most hacendados, the highland fundo was just one of a number of sources of income and, even where it was not, attempts were made to maximize the mix of produce raised. For the pastoralists a precarious stability relied mostly on the maintenance of control over different ecological zones, which became increasingly threatened by the growing commercialization of the intermediate levels. Highlanders, already with an historical inclination toward independence, were now turned still more into specialized pastoralists with only a minimal amount of arable production in sheltered valleys. As a result families' fortunes came and went; individual Huasicanchino families were using extensive pasture in Acobambilla (in Huancavelica) in the early nineteenth century, and then the same families were reduced to small extensions around Huasicancha a generation later, to be replaced by still other families (CA). Meanwhile on Tucle, owners and tenants came and went while the fundo remained intact.

Throughout the eighteenth century conflicts occurred between those whose form of production and establishment of wealth required the permanent staking out of land—these were the emerging hacendados—and those who continued to see production in terms of ecological diversity and whose use of labor was limited by household composition and the extent of kin and neighborhood ties—these were the smaller herders. Conflicts began to emerge that essentially revolved around differences in the concept of territorial control: absolute control—the right to exclude others—and relative control—the extent of control over natural resources (in this case, pasture) being a function merely of flock size, which varied with a household's generational cycles.

Meanwhile daily and seasonal interaction continued between the two, and what emerges from this interaction is a perpetual dialectic between interdependence and independence. The continuation of the local institutions and their simultaneous subversion, familiar in the move from ethnic nation to Inca state, continued into the colonial period but was complicated by two parallel developments. On the one hand, the colonial administration itself was committed to the maintenance of the pueblos as hot houses producing the human labor for the colony. On the other hand, commercial agriculture grew up beyond the rigidities applied by the Spanish crown. Eventually Spanish ex-colonial officials vied with Indian ex-curacas for direct access to Indian labor. Though this partly relied on the colonial grants of mitayo labor to hacendados, for remoter areas a far more effective way of mobilizing labor was through the continuation on the part of wealthy Indian families of traditional labor services.

Karen Spalding has argued (1973) that because Indians were not in need of land, hacendados relied on the colonial apparatus to use political means for obliging Indians to work on the haciendas. These included the mita, which Indians could avoid by escaping to haciendas, as well as the *corregimiento de mercancías,* which forced the Indians to pay tribute in the form of commodities, indebted them, and thus drove them to work on the haciendas. She argues very convincingly that much of the expansion of the highland haciendas after the founding of the republic depended less on the expanding markets and more on the removal of the colonial political machinery so that hacendados now had to create land scarcity for the Indians (by expanding onto their lands) in order to force them to work for the hacienda.

There is no doubt that the process that Spalding refers to did take place in the Tucle/Huasicancha area, but it was delayed until later in the century. For the central highlands in general, the most striking fact about the coming of the Republic was less the collapse of the colonial apparatus, which had been in disarray anyway since the decline of the mines in the 1790s, than the attack now made on the institutions of the Indian communities through an ideological discourse of private property and individual rights. Gradually the old Indian families with pretensions of aristocracy—the Apoalayas and the Marmanillos—had been giving up their positions in the highland fundos to Spanish families, such as Lira and the Comptesa de Vista Florida (Hacienda Laive) and the Comptesa de San Antonio (Hacienda Tucle).

Though now the fundo continued to be run on the old pattern, with the same old forms of labor recruitment and the same mixed agriculture, the new owners were absentee landlords in a very real sense. An old, albeit much transformed, set of institutions had gone. Or, if they had long since gone, then now even the pretense was lacking. The continuity had been broken. The state pulled out from the bottom of the house of cards the legitimacy of the Indian communities at the same time title deeds (however spurious) signaled possession of the haciendas by absentee "foreigners."

The Early Years of the Republic

The interlude in which the Spanish aristocracy controlled the highland haciendas was a short one. It did not survive the Wars of Independence. The Spanish were replaced in large measure by the congeries of criollo families whose possession of landed property quickly grew into extensive family combines (c.f., F. Wilson 1982:204; Wolf and Hansen 1967) of a very different kind from those of the older, well-off Indian families. Immediately after the war, these haciendas fell first into the hands of *patriotas* rewarded for their endeavors in the military cause and, subsequently, into the hands of those who had been active on the economic front in the years of uncertainty that followed. It was the latter who managed to consolidate their position. In the Mantaro region the three most powerful of these were the families of del Valle, Olavegoya, and Valladares.

Thus Hacienda Tucle was first bought from the will of the Comptesa de San Antonio by a patriota family and then sold to the Valladares family (who subsequently sold it to Bernarda Pielago, of whom we shall hear more shortly. Similarly, Hacienda Laive was first rented to the Valladares family by a relative of the Comptesa de Vista Florida who eventually, despairing of making any income after covering administrative costs, sold the property to the Valladares family, whose original fortune had been made in mining to the north, in Cerro de Pasco (Manrique 1978, 1981; Mallon 1983).

We are now at the watershed. For many years things have been changing while apparently remaining the same. For many years, fundo owners and roving pastoralists have lived in hostile symbiosis (c.f., Wolf 1956 [1971]:58). In the years that followed independence Peru was very far from being a nation: it had neither a national identity nor an identifiable national power bloc (Basadre 1968–1970). Now institutions, groupings of people, and ideas became defined by reference to their opposites in the crucible of the struggles that preceded the War of the Pacific in 1876 and continued for the remainder of the century (Bonilla 1978).

At the local level, I have already shown how territoriality and possession became defined through opposition. But nothing is simple: if roving pastoralists had to make themselves aware of possession by deed, so hacendados could not dispense with the notion of claim by occupation. Local pastoralists were quickly aware of the sale and purchase of local haciendas, watching with interest how new owners established possession. The presence of livestock was still the only means through which legal claim could be turned into de facto possession. Thus the Valladareses paid very low prices for both their haciendas in the neighborhood because they were denuded of livestock; and the family's subsequent wealth stemmed from their ability to restock them systematically. Land was comparatively worthless on the open market, because the vendor's claims about the extent of property by reference to various landmarks and surveys were meaningless given the presence of local pastoralists. What gave substance to a vendor's claims was demonstrated ability to control that land vis-à-vis the local peasantry and to mobilize a labor force. Both could only be demonstrated in market terms by reference to the number of livestock the vendor succeeded in grazing in the area.[17]

The evidence suggests that it is far too simple to explain this change in terms of the degree of naked power held by the owner or even some version of ideological hegemony held over ignorant peasants. But there *was* an interplay between power and hegemony: the two were held in varying degrees by all parties. Thus the history of social relationships discussed here suggests that, within the perspective of Andean ideology, the offering (and requesting) of labor to powerful figures who claim to represent a commonly shared polity is by no means illegitimate, be that polity the family however extended, the natural order of the sun and the earth, the community, or even the state.[18] It is hard not to be impressed by the pastoralists in this area who were making life difficult for those who tried to lay claim to large tracts of land, as far back as the early eigthteenth century (resistance that increased substantially later on). But this determination in the defense of land as the principle resource for maintaining a livelihood did not entail a refusal to offer service to those seen to be higher in the social hierarchy.

What changed this balance of affairs by the mid-nineteenth century was the impetus given to agricultural prices by the guano boom after 1860 (Bonilla 1974). On the one hand large capital—like the Valladares's—shifted attention away from the stagnating mining economy and began to view with interest the potential of the highland haciendas, ill-defined territorially and denuded of livestock though they were. On the other hand, the increased commercialization of agriculture and the overall improvement in the Mantaro Valley itself gave strength to a growing class of independent, commercial farmers and merchants who, either through the purchase of haciendas or through the reactivation of traditional political claims to highland pasture (Samaniego 1974, 1978), came to play their role in the lives of the highland pastoralists.

Conclusion

In the beginning of this chapter, I first described the Huasicanchinos as they embarked on their most recent land recuperation campaign in the 1960s.

We also saw something of the institutions that they took for granted as a means for getting on with their daily lives. Then it was necessary to go back to the past to seek out the genealogy of those institutions. What I have done is to uncover the grass-covered path that leads to the more detailed records of Huasicancha's history. I do not by any means claim that this chapter represents the last word in regional ethnohistory for the area. But although I am no ethnohistorian, I am not thereby forced to deny the relevance of this past for an understanding of the present. Rather as I began to learn more about the rebellious people among whom I was living, it became clear that the institutions they took for granted and yet fought to defend, as well as the sense they had of themselves as a certain kind of people (distinct in some way from other people—their sense of identity as the Huanca people of Huasicancha) were a product of the past, not the singular march of some impersonal and predestined evolution, but the winding, bewildered, uncertain path whose impression on the earth was made by the feet of the subjects of a previous history.

But there is something else: one way in which some insight can be gained into the relationship between the image people have of institutions so much a matter-of-fact part of their lives and the actual use they make of those institutions, is a function of the changing conjunctures of history. A process simultaneously of distinction *and* connection is occurring. Institutions and practices take on specific forms as they are juxtaposed with others. Just as some fusion takes place, so also more clearly delineated distinctions arise, as was the case between "ethnic community" and the Inca state, between kin and nonkin, between pastoralists and agriculturalists, between the small households and patriarchs and their larger "family" and curaca-head, and, in the more recent past, between community and hacendado. And in all cases we can neither reject the sense of distinctiveness and independence between the one and the other nor accept at the same time the sense of their interdependence. This process can only be seen historically. It makes no sense beyond the meandering walk of history. (The march of history is a singularly inappropriate metaphor for what we are talking about.) But in many ways its most important implication is in its effect on the relationship between the practice of an institution and the idea held about that institution encapsulated in the word used to refer to it—the concept of "keywords."

3

The Growth of a Culture of Opposition 1850–1947

We can say that, after the fight of Tupac Amaru, it was the Community of Huasicancha which was the second in the Nation, in the Department of Junin, in the Province of Huancayo, to begin the revindication of our lands.
—Huasicanchino ambulant fruitseller, Lima, 1981

The land recuperation campaign of 1963–1972 is the contemporary expression of a culture of opposition that had been developing through history.[1] On the more distant past can now be superimposed the contours of a more recent culture of opposition, for what we encounter now are variations in the ways contention is expressed as a function of the national political and economic contexts that effectively open and close the spaces for resistance. The first national political context was the Peruvian-Chilean War of 1879 to 1884. The Huasicanchinos, mobilized as guerrilla fighters, obtained a vivid political experience of conflict expressed openly and sustained over a number of years. Moreover, in turning to this more recent history we are dealing now with the not-too-distant memory of today's Huasicanchinos. Old and middle-aged people often refer to the accounts their parents gave of these historically significant events—not just for Huasicanchinos—but for the highland pastoralists of the central Andes as well. And the relevance of this past is not confined to storytelling; it is a part of past experience that provides just one of a myriad of sources for addressing contemporary and daily problems.

In coming to this century, the context changes and with it the arena of conflict and daily survival. An increasingly commercialized regional economy effectively put pressure on both the hacienda and the highland pastoralists to operate competitive enterprises, which provided the pressure for changes in the respective relationships between the two: Tucle and Huasicancha. A new set of contradictions came into play, thus providing a somewhat different space for the expression of contention. To go back for a moment to the metaphor of a river flowing over limestone to suggest different stages of resistance, what we now witness is at first the very visible flow of resistance along the surface, as the Huasicanchino guerrillas take on an open expression of class resistance, and then the more sporadic and less easily visible subterranean flow of daily conflict.

In the first stage the centerpiece of the drama is the *montonera* resistance to the Chileans and to Peruvian collaborators with the Chileans in the war of 1879–1884, which subsequently developed into an independent guerrilla campaign directed generally against a much-fractured regional power bloc.[2] The montoneras were crucial in Huasicancha's political development. But then in the early 1890s the hacendados used the dispersion of the montoneras and the consolidation of their holdings as the basis for a drive toward the rationalization of production. Yet in the case of Hacienda Tucle, this process was very much conditioned by the immediately previous experience of open mobilization on the part of the labor force; these attempts to modify existing social relations of production in the area effectively changed the dimensions and shape of contention. The relevant national context was no longer the political one of a foreign and then civil war but the economic one of sporadic but, in the long run, persistent commercialization.

The period we are dealing with here provides the conditions for the most recent recuperation campaigns. Broadly speaking these were threefold. First, the period witnessed a final shattering of what little was left of assumptions regarding the responsibilities of powerfully placed patrons, still referred to in the terms of kinship. In the first stage of open mobilization this change could be seen as guerrillas were first mobilized as the followers of their hacendada's cousin, General Caceres, then saw their leaders executed by him, and finally found themselves taking on the entire regional power bloc. In the second stage a shift occurred from personalized to commodified relations, as the hacienda administration pressed forward toward the rationalization of farm operations.

Third, where the earlier links between the hacienda and the community might be seen in terms of a benign cancer, the effect of increased hacienda use of communal land after the montonera decade, combined with the growing reliance of comuneros on sources of livelihood beyond the village, reduced the monopoly community authorities had over crucial moments in social reproduction. Such crucial practices as the designating of pasture to certain households lay now in the hands of the hacienda administrator. So while many of the instrumental uses of the community remained, some of its more immediately visible manifestations were seen to be disappearing as better-off pastoralists, finding no immediate economic advantage to be gained, lost interest in political office. In the midst of these changes there emerged new forms of interdependence among Huasicanchino enterprises at the precise moment when their heterogeneity increased as the result of their insertion into ever more widely dispersed sectors of the Peruvian economy. Thus, the hundred years I am about to cover represent two major experiences in the Huasicanchinos' past: one that occurred at the level of history writ large, that of open and sustained political confrontation; the other just as important although far less visible, occurring as it does within the gray monotony of daily living: the commodification of increasing areas of their livelihoods.

From Mobilization to Rebellion, 1850–1899

At the beginning of the period, the relation of Huasicancha (and indeed the surrounding highland area generally) to the national political crisis took on a quite personal character, for there were a number of powerful families who played important roles both in Huasicancha's history on the one hand an in national developments on the other.[3] General Caceres, heroic opponent of the Chileans, fought much of his campaign in the Mantaro area. He was a cousin of the owner of Hacienda Tucle and one of his reserve officers was the hacienda administrator. The Valladares family, owners of neighboring Hacienda Laive, however, were collaborators with the Chileans and members of the *civilista* party to which Caceres was opposed. But as the period developed, there was a shift from a conflict reflecting, "at bottom, the irreconcilable interests of individual chieftains and patrons, and their dependent followers" (Bonilla 1978:100), where great names within the Peruvian power-bloc mattered, to one where great names gave way to broader social forces in which guerrillas—originally recruited through personal ties of loyalty between *patrón* and peasant—became a force of their own pitted against both the large hacienda owners and the valley-based capitalist entrepreneurs.

The montonera campaign started as an expression of resistance to foreigners and those who collaborated with them and ended as a class struggle, a struggle that brought to the surface and set the stage for the ineluctible collisions between classes formed on the basis of the newly commercialized regional economy.

The Pre-War Situation

In the middle of the nineteenth century the Mantaro Valley was a fertile agricultural area surrounded by highland grazing lands and with poor communications over the Andes to the more commercialized coast. The conjuncture of classes, besides reflecting the changes that were occurring in the regional economy, was also spatially situated. The area was dominated by three towns on the left bank of the river: Jauja, Concepción, and Huancayo. Jauja and Concepción retained the character of their colonial past and were still the seats of the largest hacendado families, who found markets for their produce on the coast (Manrique 1978). Huancayo, however, became increasingly the economic nexus of the valley, sharing its vigor with the prosperous smaller towns of Sicaya, Chupaca, and Chongos Bajo situated on the western side of the valley, up against the hillsides that reached up to the highland pastures in which Huasicancha was located (see map 1). Huancayo, the department capital, and these smaller towns (*distrito* capitals) were populated by a few smaller hacendados, independent farmers, manufacturers and *comerciantes*.[4] All of these came to benefit increasingly from the growing mining economy, which, in the 1850s, was scattered through the area, but by the end of the century became concentrated to the north, in Cerro de Pasco. They were, then, distinct from the larger landowners in their reliance on the regional economy or, put another way, in their relative lack of reliance on the coastal markets.

Surrounding the valley was the high pampa best suited to llama and sheep grazing but where arable crops were grown in sheltered valleys for subsistence, and both the larger hacendados and the comerciantes of Sicaya, Chupaca, and Chongos Bajo (which, as distrito capitals and old ayllu seats, laid claim to highland pasture) had interests in these highlands. As we have seen in the previous chapter, the relationship between these groups and the highland pastoralists was one of uneasy tension; nevertheless, at midcentury there was still sufficient pasture to provide for a certain degree of coexistence.

The degree of independence of the pastoralists varied according to their links to the haciendas on the one hand and to the lower distrito capitals on the other. Around 1850 the labor requirements of the haciendas were not great enough to involve all pastoralists for very much of the time. The haciendas' labor force was made up to a small extent of permanent staff located on the estates and to a larger extent of people from the surrounding pastoralist communities. But this still left the majority of the community at any one time independent of the hacienda. For some communities however there were ties to the lowland distrito capitals. Though relatively independent economically, the highland community was, administratively, an anexo (annex) required to perform services for the lower town as a whole, as a means of acknowledging the *de jure* claim of the capital town to this highland pasture. Moreover, within these anexos poorer people acted as shepherds for the livestock owned by the comerciantes resident in the lowland towns and hence had direct ties of dependency to them. Hacendados and lowland comerciantes, then, both had claims on highland pasture.

Huasicancha was on the very edge of the Province of Huancayo, however, and this remoteness diminished the Huasicanchinos' subordination to lowland communities while putting Hacienda Tucle in an especially exposed position vis-à-vis highland pastoralists. In this sense then, Huasicancha was similar to other pastoral communities in the area but with a distinctiveness that de-

rived partly from sheer remoteness and partly from an historical tradition of
resisting intrusions by families from the lowland towns. The combination of
Hacienda Tucle's indirect link through its owner and administrator to General
Caceres and his army of resistance and Huasicancha's relative independence
from the claims of the increasingly commercialized valley towns and their
comerciante inhabitants, gave to the Huasicanchinos a distinctive history in
the formation of oppositional consciousness.

And it was the Peruvian-Chilean War from 1879 to 1884 and the years
following it, which provided the quantam leap in the development of a vigorous culture of opposition born out of the role of the Huasicanchinos in guerrilla fighting. The events of the period vividly reveal how the particulars of
local culture can become extended, through the outcome of historical events,
to represent more universal forces; the pastoralists around Huasicancha began
by fighting against the Chileans, then against specific landlord families whom
they adjudged *colaboracionistas,* and finally against landlords as a class.

At the beginning the personalities seemed to stand paramount: Bernarda
Pielago, the self-educated hacendada and businesswoman; Tomas Laimes, the
ex-corporal and rebel general; and Andres Caceres, the Indios' *taita* (uncle)
and eventual betrayer. At the end, these same personalities were lost in the
greater sweep of forces represented by confrontation between commercial,
predatory haciendas and highland pastoralists. As a result Huasicancha's culture of opposition, once juxtaposed against the names and personalities of
powerful families, became increasingly set within the context of more impersonal forces of which personalities became merely the representatives.

In other words, at the outset what was occurring was not just a struggle
between collaborators and patriots, nor between landlords and peasants, nor
highland pastoralists and valley comerciantes, but struggles between particular families of landlords and comerciantes and particular groups of pastoralists, each pursuing their own goals and policies. By the end of the period,
experience of events as they unfolded gave rise to the beginnings of clearly
perceived conflicting forces. The effect then of this political engagement was
to clarify in the consciousness of all participants a sense of the irresistable
force of the commercializing haciendas and the immovable block of the resisting pastoralists—regardless of the personalities and families involved.

This observation is well illustrated by comparing two similar highland
communities whose historical experience led to the emergence of differences
in the nature of their political consciousness, specifically in the extent to
which their local culture is indeed one of opposition to a prevailing hegemony. One community, Yanacancha (see map 1) used pasture claimed also
by both a hacienda (Laive) and lowland comerciantes (from Chupaca). The
owners of the hacienda, the Valladares, were a powerful civilista family who
had supported the civilista claimant to the presidency, Echenique, and were
later opposed to the war, collaborating with the Chileans. The other commu-

nity, Huasicancha, had successfully fought off claims to its pasture by Chupaca families. The primary link between hostility and interdependence for Huasicancha was with Hacienda Tucle. In contrast to Laive, the owner of this hacienda (Bernarda Pielago) had been a staunch supporter of President Castilla against the civilista President Echenique and then later supported General Caceres, who was Castilla's protegé and the hacendada's cousin. Caceres was the personification of opposition to Chile and actually mobilized the highlanders around Huasicancha to fight as nationalist montoneras. These interpersonal alliances and strategies prior to the war and then during it were to provide distinct experiences for Yanacancha and Huasicancha.

One of the three most powerful families in the region was the Valladares clan who lived in Jauja. Their fortune originated from mining, the profits from which were used to buy up haciendas in the area and restock them. This vast dynasty of interlocking family interests was, up to the outbreak of war, the most dynamic force in the region, owning in 1879 at least twenty haciendas covering over 300,000 hectares (Manrique 1981). By the 1870s it was headed by three men, the two brothers, Juan Enrique and Manuel Fernando, and the brother-in-law, Luis Milon Duarte, who was the political leader of the clan. All three were directly involved in the administration of their haciendas which they aggressively restocked immediately following purchase, with often devastating consequences for neighboring small herders. In 1848, for example, they had bought Hacienda Laive entirely denuded of livestock; by 1878, just before the war that was to shatter their fortunes, they had restocked Laive to the extent of 38,000 head of sheep.

In addition to the large families like Valladares, there were a group of smaller hacendados who often combined the ownership of just one or possibly two ranches with commercial activities in Huancayo. Among them was Bernarda Pielago, who owned Hacienda Tucle. Another of this group was Mariano Giraldez, who owned Hacienda Antapongo, which lay between Laive and Tucle and whose land Huasicancha also claimed as their own. Giraldez, the civilista mayor of Huancayo in 1877, was a political ally of the Valladares.

But the Valley also experienced the growth of local textile mills, a wide variety of craft workshops, and, above all, trade. The distrito capitals of Sicaya, Chupaca, and Chongos Bajo, old ayllu centers of the past, were now thriving trade centers with an important class of people who combined small-scale commercial farming with trading ventures. These towns all had claims to the pasture of their anexos in the higher pasturelands, but their interest in these so-called "dependent" communities was to control the commodity trade with them.

Once the Valladares family bought Laive and began restocking it, they were quickly brought into a potential conflict with Laive's neighboring highland community of Yanacancha, an anexo of Chupaca. Pastoralists had been using land in the area relatively freely because, as a result of the previous owner's depleted stock, many estancias were left unused. The Valladares now pressed these pastoralists either to move back off the land or to remain with their animals, paying a rent in labor service as shepherds for the hacienda and accepting thereby the "protection" of the Valladares family (Samaniego 1974).

But this set off an old conflict between Yanacancha and its distrito capital, Chupaca, which had always claimed legal title to the land. The growing commercialization of the Mantaro Valley farms meant that these highland communities no longer bartered with them but grew equivalent root crops in sheltered valleys instead, while specializing in sheep farming for trade. The Chupacans, for their part, were prepared to leave the highlanders to their sheep farming as long as they sold their produce to Chupacan intermediaries in what was becoming a growing commodity market.

Wool prices remained strong from 1866 to 1876, which meant that the intermediaries became increasingly committed to this trade. But an economic collapse in 1876 led merchants to attempt more direct control of production and hence a greater share of the surplus on what they saw to be "their" highland pasture; it also led the pastoralists, themselves faced with falling prices, to seek out the best bargains by breaking the monopsony of the merchants in Chupaca. In August 1877 Chupacans invaded the pasture used by the Yanacancha pastoralists around Hacienda Laive and demanded both a rent and a commitment to sell livestock through them. The Valladares family, following the strategy of civilistas throughout the department (see Piel 1970:122), sought to mobilize the Yanacanchinos against Chupaca. The Chupacan comerciantes were, after all, far more dangerous and powerful claimants to the pasture that the Valladares family coveted, and, in this manner, the family was able to appear as the benevolent protector of the highland pastoralists. The Chupacans did have the support of a national political party, but it was through the influence of Mariano Giraldez, civilista ally of the Valladares who was mayor of Huancayo, that the Chupacans were removed from the pasture by a cavalry contingent (Samaniego 1974).

At this crucial moment then, just prior to the outbreak of war, when highlanders would be offered the opportunity of being armed and mobilized, the pastoralists around Hacienda Laive were being protected from the aggression of petty capitalist entrepreneurs in the valley by the local hacendado with the help of the armed might of the state, in the form of a cavalry contingent. It is important to contrast this situation with that of the Huasicanchinos, whose subsequent political mobilization was to be so different.

To begin with, Huasicanchino pastoralists had established a far stronger independence from the valley communities than had Yancancha. Indeed this independence and physical remoteness meant that Huasicancha was by no means as integrated into commodity relations as Yanacancha. One result was that herd size continued to be constrained by the availability of "family" labor rather than by the more commercial relationships growing up in Yanacancha. Yanacancha's conflict was a direct result of these commercialized relationships: there were no pastoralists in Huasicancha who could herd over 800 sheep as was the case for a dozen or more families in Yanacancha.

By the same token, Hacienda Tucle lacked the commercial development of Hacienda Laive, and through its remoteness was more exposed to the whims of the local pastoralists. Nevertheless the relationship between Bernarda Pielago and the pastoralists of Huasicancha—one of suspicion and interdependence—was the crucial link between the community and national politics. Bernarda Pielago, with her partner Faustino Chavez, bought Hacienda Tucle from the Valladareses in 1846. This she owned with her two shops in Huancayo. As the most relevant "significant other" in the Huasicanchinos' experience at the time, it is worth dwelling for a moment on the kind of person she was.[5] In her will she writes: "Born poor, I lived under the protection of my parents and when they died I was left an orphan with no more support than that of Providence nor more hope than that of my labours" (*Archivo del Juzgado de Tierra, Huancayo*). Despite her poor beginnings, a local historian wrote of her, "Like women of the period, she lacked any formal instruction, which handicap she overcame by her great intuition; she played the piano, played chess, knew numbers and history, managed her haciendas and was rich" (Tello 1971:28). Married twice ("Of the first I have nothing to say"), she brought to her second marriage (to Fernando Fano) 30,000 pesos. He brought no capital whatever and died ten years later, leaving her childless. Indeed Bernarda had a poor opinion of marriage altogether; it gave her "nothing but pain and suffering."

Once having bought Hacienda Tucle, Bernarda gradually gathered a considerable fortune. Her partner soon died, leaving nothing but debts and, in paying these off on behalf of his heirs, she gained full control of the hacienda. The fundo itself remained a miserable building that she rarely visited, but this contrasted with her Huancayo residence, still inhabited by her heir in present-day Huancayo. This "mansion" was described as,

> Very pretty and charming. Passing from the wide entrance to the house, one arrives at a beautiful garden surrounded by wrought iron railings which enclose vast corridors, from which one gains access to salons, bedrooms and other quarters. Within, the rear door is a special entrance where the llama trains are received, carrying produce from the haciendas. (Moreno de Caceres 1974:78)

The intricacies of personal ties and national politics are well illustrated if we pick up the story on 31 October 1854, when Bernarda Pielago, returning to this mansion from Hacienda Tucle on a mule, encountered the exhausted troops of Ramon Castillo and offered the ex-president hospitality in her mansion. Now in rebellion against President Echenique, Castilla was given Bernarda's full support. She put all her wealth at his disposal, turned the town into an arsenal, and organized the town's myriad tool shops and small manufacturers for the production of the materiel of war. Castilla's first term in office had coincided with the beginnings of economic expansion in the Mantaro Valley, and he, therefore, found support from Bernarda Pielago, whose wealth likewise had increased, as well as from many of the comerciantes of Chupaca and Sicaya.

In raising funds for Castilla, Bernarda turned to her cousin, Domingo Caceres, to raise financial support in Ayacucho. In return for these favors Castillo agreed to become the patron of the son of Bernarda's cousin, Andres Avelino, later to become General and then President Caceres. And when Castilla's rebellion led him to a second term as president, Avelino Caceres became committed to the same kind of professional militarism as his patron.

What we have then, in 1854, is the establishment of a firm alliance between the owner of Hacienda Tucle and national political figures with strong nationalistic and militaristic inclinations. Bernarda's support of Castilla eventually was to provide her with the patronage of General Caceres (himself later to become a president of the republic). And, in turn, it was because of Bernarda, the patron of Hacienda Tucle and its neighboring villages that, in the war with Chile, General Caceres was able to mobilize montoneras. But the experience of mobilization itself gave the pastoralists a new perspective on the world. It is a sign of changing political attitudes that at the outset of hostilities these montoneras referred to Bernarda's cousin, General Caceres, as taita; at the end their leader was sending him a message: "Tell Caceres I am as much a general as he is and will be dealt with as equal to equal."

The War and its Aftermath

The war with Chile (1879 to 1884) marked a turning point in the relations between hacienda and highland pastoralists: from this period on Tucle and Huasicancha were set on a path of perpetual conflict. During the war, highland pastoralists, acting initially as guerrillas in the patriotic cause against the Chileans, became aware of their own potential strength. With the war's ending, however, a political climate adverse to the pastoralists provided the hacienda with an opportunity to expand its boundaries as it had never done before. The war thus gave birth to a fatal combination—a self-confident peasantry and an expansionist landlord.

But the war had a far greater effect than this, for it acted to position the highland pastoralists—politically—in a wider set of class relations. Hacendados, valley merchants, and commercial farmers as well as highland pastoralists all saw the war affecting their interests in different ways. The montoneras around Huasicancha, once mobilized, remained so. But the composition of their enemy shifted. At the beginning of hostilities these montoneras were fighting the foreign invaders; at the end they fought alone against a wide range of opponents—landlords, the commercial classes of the valley, and the agents of the state. Such an experience made a profound impression on their culture of opposition, coloring their attitude toward political confrontation for the century that followed. The events of the war then form a vital part of Huasicancha's contemporary politics.

Peru's war with Chile was a disaster in which successive presidents in Lima sued for peace, while a recalcitrant General Caceres waged his own campaign against the enemy in the central Andes (Bonilla 1978). This enemy included both invading Chileans and Peruvians who, in line with the presidents in Lima, were sympathetic to an early peace. Then, for two years after peace had been signed and the Chileans had left, Caceres continued to fight in the region, this time for the presidency, which he eventually gained in 1886.

To fight the Chileans with a meager force of less than 1,500 professional troops, Caceres embarked on what he called *una guerra en pequeña o de guerrillas* ("a small or guerrilla war"). This meant a sacrifice of control over the campaign in favor of fomenting resistance from independent, local militias of "patriots." By far the most enduring of these forces were the so-called montoneras recruited in the high and inaccessible mountains to the southwest of the valley, around the area of Huasicancha. These forces were originally recruited for a confrontation with the Chileans to be fought at Sicaya, in the valley itself.

After a small victory in the south of the valley in February 1882, Caceres retreated south to Ayacucho, leaving the enemy to occupy the valley. The latter quickly alienated the comerciantes through the administration of a head tax and food levies and then alienated the poorer peasants by their ostentatious cruelty toward "Indios." When spontaneous opposition broke out, it was among the highland pastoralists rather than the valley residents, but not near Huasicancha; rather it was on the opposite side of the valley, where Chilean troops were ambushed at Comas. This appears to have been the catalyst for confrontation. Systematic, organized resistance followed, with Caceres's assistance being focused on the towns of Sicaya, Chupaca, and Chongos Bajo, where the local comerciantes enthusiastically began the task of recruiting militia.

Based in Chupaca, a local comerciante, Jose Gabin Esponda, was commissioned to encourage support from the pastoralists in the highlands behind these towns. He was quickly impressed by the enthusiasm with which he was aided by Tomas Laimes, an ex-corporal, native of Huanta in Ayacucho and veteran of the Miraflores campaign (Tello 1971). Laimes mobilized guerrilleros from Colca, Huasicancha, and Chongos Alto. Soon a stream of peasants was pouring into Chongos Bajo and Chupaca to volunteer:

> Chongos Bajo started up and swelled its forces with volunteers from the high-land zone of Chongos Alto, Huasicancha and Colca. In charge of their prepa-ration was Colonel Ceferino Aliaga of Chongos (Bajo). The patriot fighters from these pueblos arrived in Chongos Bajo infected with the courage, fer-vour and 'voz vanguardia' of the subsequently famous bandolero (sic) Tomas Laimes, acting 'cabo' in the battle of Miraflores. (Samaniego 1972:17)

Troops were organized around the elected authorities of each village, and then battalions were arranged as confederations of neighboring villages. In this way, Tomas Laimes came to head the battalion that revolved around Chongos Alto, Huasicancha, and Colca.

The troops that originally faced the Chileans so disastrously at Miraflores two years earlier had been largely an army of amateurs scorned by the profes-sional soldier, Caceres, and it seems that, on a smaller scale, the comerciantes of Sicaya envisaged a similar field battle: facing the enemy head on with their faithful followers. They were quickly and ruthlessly defeated on 19 April 1882. The Chileans then followed up their victory by driving into the high-lands behind Chupaca and Sicaya and sacking Hacienda Laive to provision their troops with meat, an example not lost on the highland montoneras, as events were to show.

Thenceforth, the only effective campaigns were the guerrilla tactics of the montoneras. As a historian of the war describes it:

> There always existed the right conditions for a retreat into the high ground around Chongos Alto, Ninalanya, Colca, San Juan de Jarpa, Potaca, etc.; it is worth noting that there existed a broad mountainous territory where the en-emy's advantages were rendered null in large part, as much because in ravines artillery and cavalry lost much of their efficiency, as because the soldiers were less well adapted than the guerrilleros to operate in territory with these condi-tions. Peasants with immense endurance capabilities, accustomed to implausi-ble marches who, accompanied by their inevitable *bola de coca* (wad of coca leaves), knew no fatigue, were hence dreaded rivals in a war in the mountains. They were able to count, moreover, on a perfect knowledge of the terrain to compensate for the overall disadvantage which resulted from their meagre and primitive arms (mostly pikes, spears, slings and rocks). (Manrique 1981:171–172)

It is important at this stage to remind ourselves of the alliances and con-flicts that provide the context for the formation of the montonera fighters of this period. The Chilean soldiers, by no means familiar with the Andean In-dios, treated them as scarcely human and this at a time when landlords in the valley were apparently hosting Chilean officers in their houses. Nevertheless the initiation of the montonera campaign followed closely the vertical ties of allegiance associated with patronage. Caceres was in a sense the last of the *caudillos,* commanding a personal following of fighters. His aunt was the patron of Hacienda Tucle, and it was around this hacienda that the montoneras were most successfully recruited. When Caceres advanced back into the valley in July of 1882, these guerrilleros swamped Bernarda's Huancayo house. Against Bernarda's advice, the general let them into the reception rooms where they came forward and kissed his hand, calling him "Taita."

The montoneras' opponents formed around these kinds of allegiances. For the pastoralists around Huasicancha and Colca the enemy were not landlords generally at this stage but specific landlords sympathetic to the Chileans—and anyone who followed their leadership.[6] What this meant for the consolidation of all the pastoralists in the highlands as a body united against a class enemy can be seen by reference once more to Yanacancha. Though pastoralists from all parts were recruited for the Battle of Sicaya, it is worth remembering that those who did the recruiting were the comerciantes of the lowland distrito capitals. These were the same comerciantes who had been intent on maintaining their dominance over the highland pastoralists of Yancancha (and its neighboring communities). In this struggle it had been the hacendado himself, Luis Milon Duarte, head of the Valladares clan, who had "protected" the Yanacanchinos. So, after the defeat of Sicaya, and with Duarte energetically recruiting supporters for the Chileans (Manrique 1981:233–234), the montoneras were unlikely to be focused around Yanacancha.

Meanwhile, enthusiasm for the national cause among medium-sized hacendados and comerciantes began to wane after the defeat of Sicaya, and Caceres, on a brief return to the valley late in 1882, issued orders that patriots were to identify traitors and execute them on their own initiative. When the Chileans reoccupied the valley in May 1883, they were met by a far more docile population than on their previous encounter, and this redefined the objectives of the montoneras around Huasicancha, who were now the only organized body of opposition to the Chilean army that confined itself to the valley. Guerrilla attacks therefore involved forays into the valley and its communications routes south to Huancavelica and Ayacucho, followed by retreats to the highland basecamps.

The campaign then involved two interdependent activities: offenses away from the basecamps and subsistence during the long periods of retreat. The war economy of subsistence (of necessity involving plunder) is simply the other side of the coin in which the more spectacular attacks on the enemy occur. Unless this is acknowledged, we are forced to decide whether the montoneras were either attacking the national enemy (as they maintained) or merely plundering the citizenry indiscriminately like bandits (as landlords and comerciantes in Huancayo later argued).

The first attacks on the Chileans began in July 1883 and doused the last embers of any possible mutual understanding between the commercial classes of Huancayo and the montoneras. As a Chilean battalion moved north toward Jauja, the montoneras attacked its rear from the south. They also used the opportunity to exercise their hostility toward those Huancaínos who appeared to be hosting the occupying army. Whatever their behavior at this time, their arrogant appearance in the town, armed with 200 Remington rifles, was enough for the city's burghers, and a call arose, repeated thereafter, to each and every passing commander to disarm the highland peasants.[7] Such a call, involving as it did the disarming of the only effective resistance to the Chileans (Manrique 1981:308) reveals the sentiments now brought to the surface by the fortunes of this supposedly national war. To the propertied classes of Huancayo, nationalist fears of the Chileans were nothing to the class fears aroused by the sight of an armed and self-confident peasantry swamping the streets of the provincial capital. And as such sentiments of class hatred hardened in Huancayo and were reciprocated in the highlands; the montoneras now turned to the large haciendas to provide the resources for their war economy.

In late 1883 a Chilean advance on Ayacucho, followed shortly by retreat back to Huancayo, provided the montoneras with further opportunities of attacking Urriola's 1,500 men as they passed through the deep chasms leading out of the Mantaro Valley. A reporter from the Valparaiso newspaper, *El Mercurio*, referred to *cholos*, perfectly placed in carefully constructed fortifications, from which they fired down on the troops. A part of the battalion that tried to escape attack passed close to Huasicancha but was ambushed at Macchu, not a mile from the present village.

On the return journey the reporter (certainly with exaggeration) referred to 10,000 Indios molesting the troops from their highly-placed redoubts. Hacendados from Huancavelica provided the Chileans with a militia (Favre 1966:6), but the troops returned to Huancayo exhausted after two weeks of fighting. Leaving a small detachment in Huancayo, Urriola now left for Lima where his troops arrived "worn out and in rags" according to the *El Mercurio* correspondent. This marks the end of the montoneras' strictly nationalist campaign. On 29 November of that year Caceres wrote of the montoneras: "The pueblos' resistence to recoup the integrity and honour of the nation in these last days will merit a special place in the illustrious pages of Peruvian history" (Manrique 1981:343). But within three months he was issuing instructions to sow discord among these same montoneras (Favre 1975:64). From February 1884 the survival of the guerrillas as a consolidated and defensible force therefore began to surpass in importance their forays out of the mountains to attack an invading enemy. And this campaign of subsistence took on a momentum of its own that set the guerrillas against any and all newcomers.

In fact President Iglesias's signing of a peace treaty with Chile the previous October signified, for most of the valley residents, that the war was essentially over. (Around Tarma to the north of the valley, Luis Milon Duarte had been appointing local authorities on the basis of their support for the occupying forces.) But the montoneras remained recalcitrant and began to direct their attacks against all who did not actively support them. They had already expropriated the livestock of Tucle's neighboring haciendas (owned by the colaboracionistas, Duarte and Giraldez), and they now turned against all outsiders who threatened their survival. Early in 1884 both Giraldez and Duarte were executed, and terror was used against inhabitants of Chacapampa (Huasicancha's neighboring village) when a number of men had their ears cut off by the guerrilleros. Discipline among the montoneras themselves was also increased against any changes of heart.

When the remaining Chilean forces retired from Huancayo in May, 1884, and Caceres began to move back north toward Huancayo, the montoneras appeared on the outskirts 5,000 strong and threatened to occupy the city.[8] There appears to have been a general panic in Huancayo, but after the event Laimes withdrew back to the highlands before Caceres's arrival. Caceres's own strategy at this time greatly influenced this new stage of the montoneras' campaign. By the spring of 1884 he was prepared to agree to a peace with the Chileans so that he could turn attention to unseating Iglesias as president of the Republic. To do this he had to reestablish a broad base of support in the valley itself. But what he encountered on his return was an economically distraught group of hacendados and comerciantes united in their demand for the dissolution of the peasant forces in the highlands.

Why had this change occurred? It is necessary to look at the guerrilla campaign which required that between 1,500 and 3,000 people be led and kept in fighting condition, for it was this element of guerrilla warfare that most antagonized the dominant classes of the region. At the outset this part of the guerrilla campaign focused on securing *materiel*—food as well as goods that could be sold for arms. It was therefore directed against haciendas and not personnel (hacendados or administrators). But after Caceres's orders of February 1884 to encourage discord among the montoneras, a campaign to maintain an undivided fighting force (among guerrilleros from neighboring and hence often rival communities) meant increased discipline directed against fifth columnists.

Although the highland pastoralists' mixed economy of herding in the mountains and cultivating in the sheltered valleys was not significantly interrupted by the war (in contrast to the agriculture of the valley which had to feed the occupying troops), 1881 and 1882 were years of drought that severely affected subsistence crops. The attractions of using the large haciendas as the basis for a war economy of plunder, moreover, was made apparent when the Chileans themselves drove off animals from Laive early in the war. Eventually the montoneras occupied all the haciendas of the region and began, in line with Caceres's orders, to confiscate the property of colaboracionistas (i.e., the herds of Laive and Antapongo). By the time these resources became exhausted (by the end of 1883 and early 1884) Caceres had ceased to be an ally and his aunt's hacienda—Tucle—previously occupied by the guerrillas, was now plundered for livestock.[9]

There is no doubt that the pastoralists of Huasicancha did accumulate significant numbers of sheep during this period, and the desire to keep their booty lent great ferocity to their subsequent resistance. But it is also likely that livestock were driven westward to the coast and sold for the purchase of arms, which is what the guerrillas of Comas had done early in the war. Between the montoneras' first appearance outside Huancayo in 1882 and Laimes's capture in 1884, their rifles had increased from 200 to 750. After the war, when the hacendados tried to seek reparations from the peasants as well as turn national opinion against them, they were obviously at pains to exaggerate the extent of their own economic collapse due to the guerrilla campaign. Even so, the extent of the highland pastoralists' destruction of the haciendas can be seen, however partially, from the figures in Table 1.[10]

There was another element in the survival campaign of the guerrillas—the maintenance of solidarity in extremely harsh conditions. This is a problem that inevitably increases over time, especially when large numbers of compatriots are living relatively peacefully by collaborating with the enemy. The montonera army was organized around existing village institutions of the Personero and his elected council and the varayoc who meted out sanctions within the village (see chap. 1). Both institutions, however, existed only within the bounds of each community and could not be extended across villages. Moreover the relationships between villages had traditionally been those of rivalry over pasture rather than cooperation against the haciendas. For example, Huasicancha's claims to land in Hacienda Antapongo were matched by similar claims made by the community of Chongos Alto, and their claims to Hacienda Tucle were disputed by the neighboring communities of Chacapampa and Moya.

Laimes and his right-hand man, Briseño, however, were not from these villages and their presence certainly helped to overcome local xenophobia. When, however, Laimes shared the spoils from the expropriated haciendas, he acted to promote unity. But when this resource ran out, he turned to other methods. Although Laimes and his followers were often later accused by local historians (residents of Huancayo and members of the professional classes) of assassination (as he was at his trial) very few specific cases are mentioned, given the length of the war and the number of guerrilleros. Those that are, Laimes freely admitted to. They were the executions of Giraldez, Wheelock (the Guatamalan Consul and probably with Giraldez at the time) and the gobernador of Moya. The first two he called "spies" and the last he justified in terms of his refusal to cooperate.[11] All three assassinations fall within the bounds of Caceres's earlier orders to identiy and execute traitors. But more

Table 1.   Hacienda Inventories before and after the War

Haciendas	Prior to the war	When reoccupied by hacienda administration

LAIVE
Owner: Valladares/
    Duarte
	38,000 Sheep
	    300 Alpacas
	    100 Llamas
		None

INGAHUASI
Owner:
    Valladares
	4,000 Sheep
	    100 Cattle
	Income: 1600 Soles p.a.	

TUCLE Owner: Pielago	42,000 Sheep	3,000 Sheep
ANTAPONGO Owner: Giraldez	Unknown	Unknown

significantly, they all took place after Caceres wished to sow discord among the montoneras. In other words, terror, directed both outward and inward (against the fainthearted), was introduced to maintain solidarity.

So the success of the montoneras' campaign was dependent not only on their formal and legitimate goal of molesting the occupying army and discouraging collaboration, it was dependent too on a war economy to provision not just a meager band of twenty to thirty professional guerrilleros but between 1,500 and 3,000 men. And it was also dependent on some form of war discipline. These requirements are interlinked, and as a national war turned into a civil war with elements of a class war emerging too (as was the case in 1884) so these facets ran over into one another.

For this Laimes was held responsible. For the dominant classes it was not at all inconceivable that the stone-faced Indios who kissed Caceres's hand in 1882 could become savage and vicious fighters soon thereafter. But it was, so it seems, inconceivable that they could actually plan and organize such strategies. And so within three weeks of his arrival back in Huancayo, Caceres set about the task of capturing Laimes and his three aides, Briseño, Vilchez, and Santisteban.

It was a surprisingly easy task. Caceres had some 1,200 thoroughly worn-out regular soldiers, but no campaign was necessary, no siege, not even threats. It is a fascinating reflection on the complexity of their political awareness that these fighters who knew that they had molested the nation's enemies and that they were feared throughout the area, expected in consequence to be respected and treated on equal terms by the professional army. It is difficult otherwise to explain how Caceres so easily pulled Laimes into his web, there to be executed. Indeed on receiving Caceres's orders to present himself and his troops in Huancayo, Laimes replied from his mountain stronghold: "Tell Caceres that I am as much a general as he is and if he wants me to go to Huancayo he must treat me as equal to equal" (Tello 1971:77). And with a naive faith in Caceres's ultimate justice and fairness the montoneras descended into the valley and proceeded to Huancayo presumably with a view to striking a bargain with respect to the land under their control.

Once there, however, Laimes and his lieutenants were quickly separated from their troops, who were quartered in a schoolhouse (previously requisitioned as the Chileans' barracks) and surrounded. On 2 July 1884 a Council of War tried the four men, found them guilty of assassination, robbery, flagellation, and mutilation and executed them by firing squad. Laimes's statement, as recorded in the national newspaper, *El Comercio* (19 July 1884) is worth quoting at length:

> After cross-examination he confessed having sacked the Haciendas Tucle, Laive and Ingahuasi whose produce had been divided up among his men. With reference to the death of the *Gobernador* of Mayo, he was dead as a result of his hostile reception (of the troops); and to the deaths of Señores Wheelock (Consul of Guatemala) and Giraldez which were done by his aide, Briseño, who assassinated them for having been believed to be spies for the Chileans, *en el trayacto de Izcuchaca donde se les conducía presos;* that he had accepted the honorific tribute of an Inca emperor was because he had been drunk (*beodo*), to which other crimes could be ascribed; that it was certain that he had himself assassinated, or had assassinated, all who were accused of being traitors to la Patria; that thus it was that some had been mutilated who were believed to be enemies and guerrilleros who had incurred 'faltas.'

The montoneras, now supposedly rendered powerless without leadership and anyway in no mood to be left around Huancayo, had to be encouraged to retire peacefully. On 29 July a supreme decree was issued: "offering total guarantees to a comunero of Huasicancha in lands known as Analanya, Ananhuanca, Huaculpuquio and Patapata for having been *servidor como guerrillero en la causa de la Nacion*" (A.C.).[12] The montoneras retired back to the hills, but their control of the area did not cease. Manrique, concluding his study of the Chilean-Peruvian War in the Mantaro Valley, writes "The postwar pacification process was extraordinarily complex and merits a separate study on which I am engaged" (1981:366), and the evidence of Huasicancha's position during this period is scant. But two years after Laimes's execution, the municipal proceedings of Huancayo still recorded discussion of the return of the four haciendas, and Bernarda Pielago's will of 1887 refers to the peasants' control of the hacienda and, more importantly, the hacienda's livestock. Manrique estimates (1981:368) that as late as 1888, 45 haciendas from the south of the region up to Cerro de Pasco were still in the hands of guerrillas.

These experiences are a vital element in the Huasicanchinos' culture of opposition. As recently as 1981 villagers were pointing out bluffs and caves in the highlands and saying, "This is where we [sic] ambushed the Chileans" and "Here is where we hid during the guerrilla war." The war is talked about as a period in which villagers showed great tactical skills and cunning but were constantly betrayed by outsiders. During periods of repression when quiescence is forced upon them, oral histories of this period serve as important means for establishing their interpretation against the more widely accepted, prevailing "official version."

Thus, in 1937, when Huasicancha was engaged in its first major confrontation with Hacienda Tucle since the "montonera decade" (that period from 1882 to 1892) a prominent figure in Huancayo, later to become an APRA senator (Alianza Popular Revolucionaria de America [Popular Revolutionary Alliance of America])[13] wrote of the guerrilleros: "Laimes with the pretext of combatting the Chileans only dedicated himself to committing crimes. He and his *compañeros,* far from confronting the enemy, killed defenseless compatriots. He went to his death a palid cholo of small build, with all the signs of a bad man, more dead than alive, weeping and in a cold sweat" (Tello 1971:75). This is far from the memory shared by the Huasicanchinos. Among them, the violence remembered is that perpetrated by Laimes's enemies. According to the popular history of Laimes's end, on his way to a conference with his cofighter Caceres, Laimes, unarmed because he trusted his companion-in-arms, was ambushed and then savagely and brutally executed.[14]

The "montonera decade" was a drama which began with all the intrigue of the heroes in a Greek play and ended with the plebeian chorus taking center stage and refusing to let the curtain fall. It might be possible for a historian to uncover the economic forces and social structure that gave rise to the conjuncture of events around the Mantaro Valley, but I am more concerned here with the results of the political mobilization of Huasicanchinos than the cause. I think in this respect it is important to stress two elements in the unfolding of the campaign. The first is that it isolated the highland pastoralists around Huasicancha and broke their ties to the personal figures of patronage that opened this period. Despite the propensity to dwell on the character of leaders such as Laimes or the political ambitions of Caceres, the evidence suggests that these personalities became less and less decisive in the course of events. The highlands were not pacified, for example, until at least five years after Laimes's death.

And the second element offers something of an explanation of this. At a certain point political mobilization took on a momentum of its own. Too often, in our concern to get at social and economic causes of political movements, we tend to forget that the movements themselves create their own institutions and ideas. For the purposes of understanding contemporary Huasicanchino culture, the important point to remember is that these do not entirely disappear with the end of hostilities. The institutions and ideas through which daily life is expressed in periods of apparent quiescence contain also a perpetual resonance of this oppositional culture, as is suggested by the statement of the Huasicanchino migrant, which opened this chapter.

The Response to Hacienda Expansion 1900–1947

The overt and concerted resistance of the previous two decades set the conditions for the Huasicanchinos' ongoing struggles as they entered the twentieth century. But many of the tendencies were contradictory. The montonera decade established the reputation of the Huasicanchinos as recalcitrant fighters, but the hacienda now laid claim to much larger stretches of land than ever before and hence made the pastoralists in fact weaker. As the century progressed the commercialization of the Mantaro Valley encouraged the expanded hacienda to rationalize production, which in turn reinforced the decline in the role of a patrón as the protector of her or his peasants, a decline that had already occurred in the bitter wake of the guerrilla campaign that had turned Caceres from patrón to enemy. But, ironically, the expansion of hacienda control of pasture effectively made the hacienda administrator the distributor of pasture, thereby preempting the ability of the community authorities to do so and hence undercutting their role in the reproduction of the pastoral households. Finally, though the hacienda's expansion in effect encouraged the Huasicanchinos to migrate away, depopulating the village and temporarily shattering the old ties of interdependency within and between households, the long-term effect of the Huasicanchinos' involvement in the highly volatile marginal economy of Lima and Huancayo was to reformulate those ties and eventually to put pressure once more on the land.

It is now to these more daily aspects of struggle and interdependency, that I turn, focusing first on the hacienda and then on the Huasicanchinos themselves.

The Social Relations of Hacienda Production: Tucle 1900–1920

Under successive governments in the period following the 1880s the land of the peasant communities of the central Andes was swallowed up by expanding haciendas. The rebellion of the montoneras had not been an isolated incident. To the north of the area the Atusparia rebellion had gained a brief success (Stein 1976) and to the south the rebellion in Huanta from 1890 to 1896 had resulted in Ayacucho being taken over entirely by the rebels. But then a reaction set in. An upswing in agricultural prices beginning in 1896 gave impetus to unprecedented offensives on the part of hacendados, aided by a sympathetic central government. This political and economic climate remained favorable to the hacendados until the early 1920s. Wool prices steadily increased from 1914 until 1921, when they collapsed. Meanwhile the persistence of adverse conditions suffered by peasants eventually led to further outbreaks of rebellion from 1918 onward, chiefly in the south of the country, which led to a softening of attitudes with the coming of Leguia's government in the following year. From 1919 to 1923 there was a brief period in which communities were able to reassert their claims to land, but again this was followed by repression.

The owners of Hacienda Tucle responded to the pacification of the guerri-lleros by making sweeping claims to land. At the time of Bernarda Pielago's will in 1886 the hacienda claimed 12,000 hectares of land. In 1906, her heirs registered the hacienda in Huancayo's registry of properties as covering an area of 103,274 hectares, over eight times as much land and an area greater than the combined total of all three major haciendas—Laive, Antapongo, and Tucle—at the time of the Reforma Agraria of 1970!

Huasicancha, as a community, made claims against the hacienda in 1889 and 1902, but they had little effect. However, the new constitution of 1919 provided for the registration of all Indian community lands as well as the set-ting up of a *Dirección de Asuntos Indigenas* under the direction of the founder of Peru's Socialist Party, Castro Pozo. In November of that year Huasicancha registered its claims to land in the Huancayo registry office. It claimed all the land of Hacienda Tucle and Rio de la Virgen, much of the land of Ha-cienda Antapongo, as well as the pastures of the neighboring communities of Palaco and Chongos Alto. Such claims were of little practical significance at the time, of course: nine other communities laid claim to parts of Hacienda Tucle, and Chongos Alto claimed most of Hacienda Antapongo. Although the registration of deeds in 1919 was later to become crucial in proving legal claims to land, its effect at the time was minimal. By 1923 Castro Pozo was driven into exile, and the cause of Indian communities was left in the hands of a variety of nongovernmental pressure groups in the rising tide of 'Indi-genismo' in Lima.

In turning to the relations of production on Hacienda Tucle, I shall refer in turn to the hacienda's control over land and its mobilization of labor. The two are crucially tied together. Tucle's claim to land was not less legiti-mate than that of most other highland haciendas, but Huasicancha's persistent counterclaims and the pastoralists' insistence on their own rights to pasture their animals were an endemic hindrance to the hacienda's attempts to rationalize relations of production along capitalistic lines, that is to say, along lines based upon contractual rights to property on the one hand and contractual transactions based on the payment of a wage for labor on the other.

What then was the basis of Hacienda Tucle's claim to ownership of its lands? In fact there were, eventually, two haciendas involved, Tucle and Rio de la Virgen. Bernarda Pielago's claim to Hacienda Tucle was based on two forms of evidence appropriate to two concepts of possession. Vis-à-vis her fellow landlords she had her deed of sale from the Valladares: vis-à-vis the neighboring peasants there was not a contract but a performance, mediated by a judge of the province of Jauja and witnessed by Don Mariano Tacona, representative of the community of Huasicancha, together with other comuneros from the village:

> All these being gathered here at this place Doña Bernarda de Pielago proceeded to take the judge by the hand and thus took possession by the authority of the nation and in recognition thereof she did throw stones, pull up plants and perform other demonstrative acts of taking real and corporal possession, saying in a loud voice, "Possession, possession, possession." And under the same procedure we went on to Huaichan-puquio and from there to Yutempampa where there is a round corral of stones. . . . Taking all these places in this form, encountering complete quiet and no opposition or contradiction in any way. (Signed by the judge and all witnesses; F.H.T.)[15]

Ownership of Hacienda Tucle was never based on any other evidence. Throughout all the litigation that followed in the hundred or so years after this, the owners of Hacienda Tucle never produced this nor any other evidence of the legitimacy of their claim to the hacienda (Juzgado de Tierra, Huancayo).

Bernarda left the hacienda to the three illegitimate children of her housekeeper. That they shared the name of Bernarda Pielago's onetime partner, the now defunct Faustino Chavez, allows us to speculate that these were his offspring. In any event, Maria Luisa Chavez, who eventually bought out the shares of her two brothers, was the daughter of a woman of Huasicancha where she continued to have cousins throughout the struggles that followed. (There was not much of the "radically distinctive" Spanish landlord left among the owners of Tucle.)

Although Maria Luisa Chavez was not herself especially concerned with the efficient running of the hacienda (in contrast to Bernarda Pielago), which she inherited thoroughly denuded of livestock, she was always intent on consolidating her landholdings. It was she who expanded Tucle's claim eightfold in 1906, and soon thereafter she married Manuel Duarte whose kinship ties to the Valladareses would have allowed their son to consolidate Haciendas Laive and Tucle under one owner. So aware of this were the Huasicanchinos that, when Manuel died leaving one son and Maria Luisa married her tenant (of Hacienda Tucle), villagers believe that she allowed the two subsequent offspring to die so as to ensure the unpartitioned succession of her son by Duarte.

In 1920 then, Maria Luisa Chavez rented 50 percent of Hacienda Tucle to Manuel Pielago, whom she was later to marry, in 1937. Her attempts to restock Tucle had been only partially successful, and the increment in wool prices after 1914 had for her the adverse effect of driving up the price of the stud animals she needed to buy. Pielago, however, was an aggressive member of Huancayo's commercial class whose interests included the growing and milling of flax, a hide processing business, and firms connected with mining supplies (see Roberts 1974b). From his tenancy onward there was a concerted effort to rationalize production on Hacienda Tucle.

To this end, Pielago became interested in the small neighboring hacienda of Rio de la Virgen whose irrigated land made possible the growing of crops that Pielago intended to use for fodder in order to raise dairy cattle. This hacienda had been bought by a certain Juan Bazo Velarde from the Parochial Council of Huancayo in 1926. The title to this land (that Huasicancha claimed in its entirety) was based simply on the council's claim to the land "from time immemorial and at least the past forty years (sic!)," but there were no documents and the council sold Velarde much more land than he was ever able to find (see documents of Juzgado de Tierra, Huancayo). Pielago was able to buy the hacienda because Velarde, on his death, left 54 percent of it to his wife and the rest to his eleven children. Under such circumstances most heirs chose to liquidate their holding and split the cash. Such were the bases upon which the landlords of Haciendas Tucle and Rio de la Virgen "owned" their land.

But how did they meet the need for labor on the hacienda? The annual demands of the enterprise required three types of labor: permanent shepherds; seasonal team labor (chiefly for sowing and harvesting at Rio de la Virgen); and occasional day labor. All three were met, in principle, without cash changing hands.

The most important work required by the hacienda was shepherding, which required the services of a family of two or three adults and a number of children. These were the huacchilleros discussed earlier. After 1900 Hacienda Tucle had acquired virtually all the pasture suitable for sheep grazing, while the Huasicanchinos, for their part, had as a result of the guerrilla campaign of the 1880s acquired a considerable number of sheep (as well as llamas and alpacas). A family undertook to care for the hacienda's animals in return for being allowed to "enter" the hacienda territory with a designated number of their own animals: the huacchas. Substantial numbers of animals were pastured in this way. Of the roughly 250 households in Huasicancha, Tucle employed about thirty at any one time as shepherds. Agreements between the hacienda administration and the shepherds allowed the latter to bring often as many as 200 head of sheep with them. While a few families held these jobs for extensive periods of ten to fifteen years, most were dismissed after a year or two or themselves chose to leave, so the position of huacchillero moved through the community.

The administrator, of course, sought reliable and skilled shepherds, but rarely if ever did Huasicanchinos graze just those animals agreed upon in the contract. Apart from the natural increase in flocks through the years, most shepherds were also grazing the animals of neighbors from the village and, with Tucle still understocked, it is likely that huaccha sheep accounted for at least 50 percent of the animals using hacienda pasture.[16] In the early part of the century the administration was less concerned about the huacchas' use of pasture than the fact that shepherds devoted much of their time and energies to their own animals and polluted the hacienda flocks by interbreeding with their own *chuscos* ("mongrels").[17]

The hacienda's requirement for team labor was met by the community institution of the faena. Correspondence between the hacienda and the community authorities in the first two decades of the twentieth century indicates that faenas were mobilized for the hacienda on the basis of the hacendado being an ersatz member of the community who, like the curaca in days past, had rights to the occasional labor of the community as a whole. Faena work was taken by both parties as an obligation of the community to the patrón, repaid only by the traditional gifts of coca, chicha (maize beer), and a meal on the day plus gifts to the village on feast days.

Day labor was the least important requirement for a livestock hacienda but even so there were always jobs that had to be done on the basis of the *jornal* (i.e., by the day). This demand was met chiefly by the use of *pasaderos*, that is, those villagers who were caught trespassing on the hacienda pasture with their animals. In these circumstances, the animals were driven off to the hacienda's *"coso"* (described by the villagers as "the animal prison"), where they were kept until their owners had performed sufficient day labor to gain their return.

Bearing in mind that the owners of Hacienda Tucle were laying claim to lands that they could not possibly stock with sheep, historians must ask the question: What was the relationship between Tucle's insistent claims on territory (despite evidently shaky foundations) and its mobilization of labor? If the question is asked slightly differently—What was the mechanism that induced peasants to leave work on their farms and in the community to labor for the hacienda?—the answer to both questions seems at first obvious. Haciendas expanded their claims to land (even when they did not use it) in order to create a scarcity of land for Indians and hence induce them to work for the hacendados, that is, the so-called primitive accumulation (Marx 1976: 873–895).

This is a nice argument, although care must be taken not to confuse cause with effect. It is undeniable that the effect of hacienda claims was to make community lands scarce, leading peasants into relationships with the hacienda, but haciendas may nonetheless have expanded for a variety of reasons to give this consequence, intended or unintended. By claiming community land without stocking it, the hacienda was, I shall argue, not creating land scarcity for pastoralists per se but rather undercutting a resource on which the politics of the community depended, in favor of the patron of the hacienda. Regardless of the motive of the hacendados, the effect of hacienda expansion at the beginning of this century was to channel important community institutions through the medium of the hacienda patrón, rather than the community authorities.

Obviously the social relationships between hacendados and neighboring comuneros varied considerably from one place to another,[18] but even in Huasicancha where a long history of confrontation and independence existed, it would be incautious to underestimate an equally long history in which Andean peasants have been expected and, in their turn therefore expected, to offer services to superiors who often went under kin terms or pseudo-kin terms such as taita or *padrino/patrón* (godparent/patron) (see chap. 2). This is not to deny that such an ideology could not have been maintained without at least a minimum of political might and, as ideas lost their intensity, so the political means might have gained theirs. In the aftermath of the montonera decade, for example, Tucle had the political backing of the state (the army, the police, the legislature), but the ideology of hierarchy had taken a severe beating during the guerrilla campaign.

The mechanism inducing peasants to work for the hacienda then, could have been of three kinds. It may have been, to all intents and purposes, a tradition in which villagers accepted as the order of things that they should offer labor to certain superiors: curaca, Inca, patrón. It may have been that an element of physical force was used to set the process in motion and then maintain it. Or it may have been that peasants were driven, out of necessity, to work for the hacienda to gain access thereby to resources insufficiently available on their farms and in the community. While one or other of these ideological, political, or economic mechanisms may at times have been paramount, the important fact is that all three played a role in the social relations of hacienda production.

In this initial period of hacienda expansion, Tucle continued to mobilize labor through the manipulation of traditional community institutions whose functions they thereby transformed. The direct result of this was to deprive the formal community of Huasicancha of its political component and to substitute the hacienda administrator for the village elders (essentially the better-off family heads in Huasicancha). Because Tucle was unable to restock, its claims to territory did not immediately create land scarcity for comuneros of

Huasicancha, nor did it deprive better-off families of extrahousehold labor since the hacienda's demands were not great. Indeed expansion, if anything, increased the availability of impoverished households willing to work for better-off families. What it did do, however, was to reduce the role of the community authorities in the organization of pastoral production:

1. By depriving the community of its lands, control over pasture—specifically allotting highland estancias to shepherds—was taken away from the community authorities, thus depriving them of the basis for their power.
2. Because community lands were so decimated, the role of the faena was proportionately reduced. Insofar as I argued in the previous chapter that this was a form of rent-by-performance in payment for household plots distributed by the authorities in direct proportion to work done at the faena, so reduction of faenas on community land undercut the reciprocal tie between the formal "community" and access to household plots, so that these plots came to be seen as private property whose distribution was removed from the hands of community authorities to those of the family head. Arable landholdings were thus effectively privatized once access to them was no longer a function of the obligation to work on the community lands, which in turn resulted from the decimation of those lands by the hacienda.

The effect of hacienda expansion at the beginning of the century was not to deprive better-off pastoralists of land nor of labor but to reduce the power they derived from holding political office as community authorities. This could no longer be used either as a means of securing the best pasture sites nor of steering community labor in directions best suited to their interests. I shall argue in a moment, after we have looked at the Huasicanchino petty production side of this, that despite this reduction in the political component of community, the social and economic reproduction of only partially commoditized petty production continued to require the essential features of community social relations of production.

Hacienda expansion at the beginning of the century then did not mean a clean sweep, a revolution in the social relations of production in which ideological and political mechanisms were replaced by the iron hand of economic necessity. As a result, the conversion of the hacienda into a capitalistic firm was delayed. Day labor was only available when peasants obliged, by trespassing and then getting caught. Faenas were the occasion for much socializing and rowdiness. And shepherds were, in effect, sheep farmers competing with their employer for pasture. With the arrival on the scene of an aggressive, entrepreneurial tenant in 1920, therefore, attempts were made to rationalize production so that, through the use of cash relationships, labor would become more responsive to the needs of capital. Of major concern is how this process affected petty production in Huasicancha.

The Social Relations of Petty Production: Huasicancha 1900–1947

A description of the social relations of production in Huasicancha must deal with the same two dimensions discussed for the hacienda: the relationship between control over the physical resources needed for production and the organization of the labor process. The nature of petty production changed over this period, and these changes provide the basis for the heterogeneity among Huasicanchinos. The route along which these production relations developed was to give rise to structural incompatibilities between the community and the hacienda, which, in turn, became the source for political unrest.

At the beginning of the century, the people of Huasicancha maintained tenancy relations with the hacienda, and despite their remote location, also worked in a local mine (Cercapuquio), and engaged in widespread trading. These links in turn served to increase the heterogeneity among the different units of production. Changes in the form of petty production, moreover, must be placed within the context of national and regional developments. For the past eighty years this has predominantly been a reflection of the growth of different sectors of the Peruvian economy such as cotton production, mining, smelting, banking, wool production, and manufacturing.

The most immediate and oldest of these relationships has been the one between petty production units and Hacienda Tucle, which, at the beginning of this century, controlled at least 30,000 hectares of land.[19] For a long time changes that occurred in petty production in Huasicancha were closely related to the operations of Tucle. The fortunes of Tucle, in turn, were closely intertwined with changes in the Peruvian economy. At the beginning of the century, Tucle was not participating in the expansion of wool production that occurred among other highland haciendas. It claimed large amounts of the community's pasture, but the real effort to turn those claims into effective control, as also the attempts to rationalize production along cash lines, were delayed until after the First World War, twenty years later. This means that two periods in the history of the Huasicanchinos' petty production between 1900 and 1947 can be distinguished.

> *1900 to 1920.* The hacienda's operations were diversified. Wool production was the mainstay, but arable crops were also produced. A limited amount of labor from Huasicancha was required and claims were made on the community's pasture.

1920 to 1947. The hacienda specialized in livestock production, both sheep and cattle. This led to real expansion onto the available pastures and an attempt to rationalize production. Huasicanchinos began to enter other areas of the labor market so that extrafarm income became increasingly important, and ties to the hacienda were made less important.

1900 to 1920.   The nature of petty production during this period was greatly influenced by the decision of Hacienda Tucle not to become heavily involved in the expanding wool production that took place in Peru after 1890. (Over this period, both the neighboring haciendas, Antapongo and Laive-Ingahuasi, were taken over by a banking consortium which turned them into part of the *Sociedad Ganadera del Centro,* and sold shares to Lima businessmen.)

Huasicanchinos were involved in a variety of different activities in addition to farming. A certain amount of specialization occurred from one household to another, and this had three important implications for social relations. First, complementary ties occurred between households of differing specialization. Second, these at first minor differences in "occupational mix" gave rise to differences in wealth. And third, specialization and wealth differences in turn gave rise to distinct social relationships both within and between households. The forms of specialization were herding, agriculture and trading.

Pastoralism. While none of Huasicancha's flock owners was fully committed to herding activities, the dictates of llama and sheep farming dominated the organization of production. Llama and sheep husbandry at high altitudes has three important characteristics: it is transhuman; its success is greatly dependent upon the skill and conscientiousness of a small number of shepherds; and it demands a heavy input of relatively skilled labor at certain periods of the year. Each of these characteristics has important implications for organization within the production unit, as well as for the nature of its ties to other units.

The year-round labor of household members varied seasonally. During the rainy season (October to April) sheep could be pastured within easy reach of the village, at lower altitudes. Shepherding during this season was therefore undertaken by all members of the household from the age of ten or twelve and older. Llamas, however, were only brought down for short periods during the season, so that shepherding at high altitudes was still necessary. During the dry season (May to September) sheep and llamas alike were moved up to seek out the scarce grasses of the high zone. Access to these pastures was of great importance and highland estancias (the shepherds' dwelling and corral) were usually shared among a number of households. The task of shepherding at these altitudes was a far more arduous and vigilant job than lower down. Flocks were most vulnerable during the dry season, and the strategic location of high altitude estancias was, therefore, an important variable contributing to the success of the farm.

Much of this pasture was held by Hacienda Tucle, so that hacienda shepherds became the nodes of sets of relationships involving ownership of sheep concentrated at one particular estancia. (In other words a hacienda shepherd's huacchas were not necessarily all, or even principally, his own.) Much pasture, however, was held in such remote areas that, claimed by the hacienda or not, it was "no man's land." Though in principle this pasture was not held privately, in practice, as pasture became scarce, estanceros began to guard with some jealousy what they regarded as their grazing area. Fights to establish grazing rights over pasture often involved conflicts between villagers and between communities (as well as against the hacienda), so that it was important to have a concentration of mature men at the estancias.

The organization of the estancia gave rise to a complex set of interhousehold ties, as households' flocks were intermingled on the estancia. Although this meant that for herding, households did operate in complementary clusters, the corporate nature of these clusters was weakened because of the multiplex ties of each household to a number of estancias and the short-lived nature of each of these ties. Since a newly-formed household received animals from parents on both sides, its partnership in a particular estancia had to be negotiated from the start. In fact households did not necessarily concentrate all the animals to which they had some claim in any one estancia flock. Rather they were scattered through a variety of estancias, reflecting both inheritance claims and the various prestations of households over the years. The composition of estancias was far less a function of kinship than of instrumental decisions by livestock owners in the entire operation of their production unit. Apart from the various obligations to others emerging in the spheres of, say, arable farming and intervillage trading, a household's ties into an estancia reflected both the hazards of animal husbandry itself and the changing labor composition of the household over its life cycle.

But the given nature of household composition could be adjusted to the needs of livestock farming through two kinds of reciprocal arrangement. The first of these was the huacchilla. Relationships among Huasicanchinos (as opposed to relationships between them and the hacienda) functioned much as they had in the past: when the household lacked young men for high-altitude shepherding, members of households deficient in livestock were recruited. Such people became shepherds for a household with sheep, being rewarded with a share of the lambs and llama calves. The accumulated animals grazing alongside those of the larger flock owner came to be known as the huaccha animals. The second institution was that of michipa. Here the flock owner took in and cared for the animals of another household. A multitude of exchanges of goods and services were taken care of in this way, such as labor on the flock owner's arable land, transportation services on the part of a muleteer, and so forth.

These two institutions allowed a flexibility in the operations of the herding sector of the production unit. A household with a large number of women, for example, found it convenient to maintain its livestock as michipas in the estancia of another, while performing arable farming tasks in the vicinity of the village, in return. The huacchilla, on the other hand, allowed for the accumulation of sheep beyond the constraints deriving from the composition of the household. This arrangement was used to advantage by some households insofar as livestock owners were in the habit of delaying the handing over of huacchas to the shepherd when, for example, he chose to marry and set up house. Pressures were then brought to bear by the community or the relatives of the huacchillero or his wife, but in many cases this led the better-endowed household to adopt the huacchillero as a son rather than release him with all the sheep to which he could lay claim.

In fact, much of the hacienda shepherd's flock consisted of michipas, that is to say, many of the animals grazing on the hacienda were in fact owned by households having no direct ties to the hacienda but having instead relations of reciprocity with the households employed by the hacienda because the demands made by the administration on its shepherds were such that the job required all the time of all the active members of the household. As a result, hacienda shepherds became increasingly indebted to other households who fulfilled tasks for them in the village, especially on their arable plots. While these arrangements did give rise to some socioeconomic differentiation (see Smith 1979a), they also involved essential links of interdependence between heterogeneous domestic enterprises.

Pasturage for sheep and alpacas was available to Huasicanchinos, therefore, either through seeking out high puna unattractive to the hacienda or through taking huacchas onto hacienda land while acting as employees. If all else failed there was always trespassing. Since the boundaries of Tucle were ceaselessly in dispute, this was anyway an occupational hazard for all herders. But the most consistent pasaderos were the small herders with ten to fifteen sheep—the majority of Huasicanchinos. The hardest time for these farmers was the dry season, when grasses were most scarce, and this was the period when they were most consistently caught by the hacienda's *caporales* (foremen). Offenders had to pay a fine in labor-service, but this was the season when there was little work to be done on the arable plots, so that the household suffered little in loss of labor. So astute were the villagers in gearing their trespassing to the seasonal demands of their farm operations that the hacienda administration had to adjust *its* operations in order to take advantage of the excess of labor which thus arose as a function of the farming rationale of the petty producers.

Although Tucle's real control of pasture was limited, its expansion at the beginning of the century was an overall constraint on comuneros' accumulation of livestock. But, if anything, this gave the edge to the few households with well-located estancias. At the same time those with larger flocks were encouraged to find means for pasturing them that tied them neither to the hacienda nor to the community. In the latter part of this period two brothers (Pedro and Silvestre Hinostrosa: see chap. 4) actually began renting pasture from communities in Huancavelica for an annual cash fee. And the wool boom from 1914 to 1921 (in which international wool prices doubled) gave opportunities for a few others to secure jobs as caporales and *mayordomos* on those haciendas a little removed from Huasicancha that were becoming more commercialized and paying good wages for such jobs.[20]

Nevertheless, there were constraints on the long-term and systematic accumulation of livestock, and these were connected to the personal skills and conscientiousness so valued by highland pastoralists everywhere. As far as year-round shepherding was concerned, the necessary personal commitment was encouraged because inheritance was partible—including adopted workers. But this in turn split up the large herds in each generation. Meanwhile the demand for skilled seasonal labor led to crises for the overexpanded during those seasons of the year, such as shearing and parturition, when such skills were required.

Agriculture. Arable farming was by no means as important to the Huasicanchinos as livestock husbandry. Many of the household needs in this sector had been traditionally obtained through bartering livestock products for goods grown more easily at lower altitudes. However, households became increasingly involved in arable farming over this period, firstly because Hacienda Tucle's expansion onto grazing land reduced Huasicancha's bartering power, and secondly, because farmers in the Mantaro Valley, who had hitherto bartered their crops for livestock products, were increasingly producing commercial crops for the national market. Thus during this period, the majority of households witnessed a reduction of herding in favor of arable farming.

The effect was to reduce the importance of the communal organization of production while giving greater dominance to reciprocal ties negotiated directly between households. In the past, arable land was divided into two areas: "communal fields" farmed by the community as a whole, and fields farmed by each household. These latter took the form of strips of land (faldas) running down the hillsides and controlled by the village's three barrios. This situation changed with the growing need for arable land. The effect of increased demand for this land was to reduce the overall land area devoted to the communal arable fields and of practically ending the barrios' planting decisions and redistribution rights. Plots were not returned to the village authorities when heads of households died but were handed on directly to offspring on a partible basis. A patchwork quilt of small arable plots began to obscure the old logic of the barrios.

As with herding, the fixed nature of household labor in any one year could be overcome through various reciprocal arrangements. Extrahousehold labor was necessary especially at ploughing and harvest times, but, as with herding, its amount and form were a function of the relationship between the composition of the household and the amount of property worked. Harvesting could be undertaken with the aid of uyay, which involved the reciprocal exchange of labor or minka, which further involved the payment of part of the harvest for labor. There was as much heterogeneity in arable farming as there was in raising livestock. Apart from division of labor resulting from differences in crops produced from the microclimates and soil differences of each household's plot, ploughing with oxen involved clusters of households forming around the rotation of one pair of oxen, and in some cases ploughing teams offered their services out to those unequipped for the job, payment being through minka or michipa arrangements.

Trade. Trade beyond the village also involved some specialization among households, basically of two kinds: trueque (bartering) with households in the high jungle and muleteering, with some trading, among the small mines of the area. While the latter had always been the affair of a few specialists, trueque had originally been an activity shared by all households, but no longer. As bartering relationships with households in the Mantaro Valley dried up, trueque continued with households in the high jungle, which was at a lower ecological niche than the Mantaro. But, as arable land became more important, the demands for labor at harvest time increased. Since harvest and jungle trueque occurred at similar times, the effect of increasing arable work was to put great pressure on the household's labor. So, where originally each household was involved in the trueque journey, now a small group of young men were assigned the task on behalf of a number of households.

Trueque's contribution to differentiation derived from this growing, if minimal, degree of specialization. It was not limited to the exchange of equivalents between direct producers whose differing ecological locations led to complementary demands for different use-values: a Huasicanchino herder exchanging fleece for a jungle-dweller's corn, for example. Those who undertook the trueque journey obtained rock salt and dried meat from the higher-altitude community of Acobambilla in Huancavelica. Raw wool, spun yarn, hides and animals on the hoof were provided from various households in Huasicancha itself. All these were exchanged for corn and coca leaf in the high jungle. But part of the return consignment was then used for obtaining commodities in the cash market of the Mantaro Valley on the return journey. These commodities were in turn exchanged with other households (in Acobambilla and Huasicancha), leaving the trader with a profit.

Hacienda Tucle's expansion at the beginning of the century, then, by no means shattered the preexisting social relations of production, driving land-starved peasants into a purely economic relationship to the hacienda. The effects were somewhat more complex. Membership in a community of Huasicanchinos continued to be important for the functioning of petty production through the social relations upon which it relied—that is to say, the bundle of institutions such as huacchilla, michipa, minka, and uyay. But these were now far less mediated or controlled through the community officeholders' abilities to exercise authority. The allotting of estancias and of arable plots was now out of their hands.

The better-off pastoralists were, through the hacienda's decimation of community resources in land, deprived of the political means for securing their positions through office in the community at a time when their economic well-being was increasingly linked to relationships beyond the community—to renting land, shepherding for the hacienda, and earning a salary as caporales. Nevertheless, insofar as many of the relationships on which petty production depended were still a feature of the community, Huasicanchinos continued to have a shared interest in its maintenance.

1920 to 1947.   The overall trend in this period was the growth of the hacienda as a commercially oriented firm and a severe reduction in the operation of the Huasicanchinos as small wool and meat producers. During the latter part of the previous period, both the hacienda and the larger village herders sold some livestock to the commercial market; from 1920 onward the larger-scale firm was progressively to dominate in supplying this market. This process was a direct result of changes that were occurring in the structure of the Peruvian economy.

As the resource base for the Huasicancha's farms was eroded, social relations became increasingly dominated by the dictates of nonfarm, petty commodity production in the urban centers and of wage labor. Insofar as increasing amounts of labor power were shifted from within to beyond Huasicancha, the parameters for the expropriation of surplus labor were expanded to include other sectors of the economy. Here relations of production and distribution were far more thoroughly expressed in terms of commodities than had hitherto occurred within Huasicancha. This increased commoditization of social relationships and the extension of these relationships to a variety of nonagricultural pursuits provided a new set of forces for heterogeneity among Huasicanchino enterprises.

In Huancayo too, the balance of social forces changed. Nationally a commercial bourgeoisie gradually replaced the previously dominant rentier class, giving a new direction to the development of the Peruvian political economy, and this transformation was especially noticeable in Huancayo. Wool, Peru's fifth largest export at that time (Thorp and Bertram 1978), doubled its price on the United States and British markets during the First World War (Mitchell

1962; U.S. Department of Commerce 1960). Such a market attracted a Huancayo businessman, Manuel Pielago, to rent 50 percent of Hacienda Tucle from Maria Luisa.[21] But no sooner had favorable wool prices on the international market attracted a capitalist farmer to Tucle, than the economic scene changed once more. The hacienda never supplied raw wool directly to the international market because the domestic demand for livestock products picked up in the 1920s while international raw wool prices declined.

The effects of all this on Hacienda Tucle were slow. In the early 1920s the American-owned Cerro de Pasco Corporation set up its smelting operations to the northwest of the Mantaro Valley. Much of the city's commercial growth was tied to provision of goods and services for the mines and smelter (Roberts 1974b). Huancayo was also the site of two medium-sized textile mills (Roberts 1974b), and there were mills in Lima too that were supplied by highland haciendas (Thorp and Bertram 1978). The railway now made it possible for highland cattle ranchers to supply dairy produce to Lima, and meat was also being transported down to the national capital from the haciendas of the central Andes (Miller 1974). The combination of Hacienda Tucle's remote location and the sustained resistance of the local peasantry, however, meant that it still lagged behind its neighbors. During the 1920s the hacienda increased its emphasis on wool production, but it was not until near the end of this period that its cattle stock was significantly improved.

The effects of Peru's changing economic structure on Huasicancha were threefold: in the transformation that occurred in the village's relations to Hacienda Tucle; in the growing influence of the Huancayo nexus on the economy of the Huasicanchinos; and in the demands that occurred in the labor market first on the part of coastal cotton plantations, and second in the construction industry.

Where the Mantaro Valley had hitherto been just one of the economic areas in which Huasicanchinos were involved, it now became increasingly influential. The operations of the smelter as far to the north of the valley as Huasicancha was to the south, the penetration of the railway again from the north and ending midway down the valley, and the termination of the central highway to Huancayo by the same route in 1939, were all to change the center of gravity for the village. Even so, the effects of the opening of the smelter were by no means as direct or as thorough (in terms of labor recruitment or the opening up of demand for farm produce) as they were for the communities situated to the immediate north of Huancayo (cf., Laite 1981). Rather it was the cotton plantations of the coastal region to the west of Huasicancha which now came to modify social relations within the village.

During the 1920s and 1930s, under the entrepreneurial influence of Manuel Pielago, Tucle began actually to use the pasture it had hitherto only claimed. It increased its own stock of animals, and it increased its demand for skilled and conscientious shepherds. This had profound effects on the Huasicanchinos: by reducing the local resource base it also reduced the strength of the interhousehold ties described above; it drove a few herders ever higher into the mountains; and it made trespassing onto the hacienda land a way of life. In retrospect it can be seen as a watershed for petty commodity production in which the linkages between units were reduced to be reformulated once more during the 1960s.

Pielago employed a Scottish administrator and commissioned an agronomist to do a thorough report on the hacienda. It was found that hacienda stock were greatly at a disadvantage as a result of the practice of paying shepherds in the form of the huacchilla. The administrator pressed for the upgrading of the sheep to Corriedale purebreds, and the agronomist pressed for the introduction of wages in lieu of huacchas. If shepherds became entirely dependent on a wage their first commitment would be to the hacienda, whereas huaccheros were in fact small-scale farmers whose first commitment was to the maintenance of their own herds (F.H.T. and A.R.A.). Time and again shepherds, obeying the seasonal demands of their own animals, simply deserted the hacienda sheep in their care and went off in search of other estancias. Agreements with Antapongo and Laive not to employ such shepherds were hard to enforce, and anyway those that did not so leave were frequently found to have increased their huaccha herds inordinately. Moreover the hacienda was not only providing the shepherds with pasture but with sheep as well: the agronomist's report found that 73 percent of newborn lambs were reported to have been lost in birth or carried off by "foxes" (the foxes, of course, being the Huasicanchinos). However, if hacienda sheep could be upgraded then they would produce more wool from a given amount of pasture than the shepherds' chuscos, so that the wages paid to shepherds could be worth more than the value of their sheep but less than the value of the upgraded purebreds that replaced them, thus benefitting both parties. Similar arguments were made for the use of team labor that could either be paid per head or in a lump sum. As for trespassers, they would now be required to pay a fine in cash and thus release the hacienda from the inflexibility inherent in the present system.

These proposals were a direct threat to the social relations of petty commodity production among Huasicanchinos. I have already shown that through michipa, it was not the hacienda shepherds alone who benefitted from the practice of huacchilla, now to be replaced by wages. The huacchilla was not merely important for the direct cash equivalent of the livestock involved but because it fitted into a particular slot in the operation of a small enterprise run with extremely scarce, unstable, and varied resources. For the large flock owners too, their mountain estancias were further depleted by the renewed vigor of the hacienda administration. This drove them still further toward renting land from other communities and even from a number of small haciendas in Huancavelica. Others who had taken up jobs as caporales on other haciendas, while maintaining their houses and small plots in Huasicancha, moved their households away from the village and began to send their sons to Huancayo for schooling or apprenticeships that would prepare them for nonagricultural pursuits. These, however, were the better-off households.

The poorest households were the hardest hit and the most isolated from the old interhousehold economic relationships. Their abilities to pasture sheep—for themselves or on behalf of others in return for reciprocal services—were forestalled because they could not find the cash for pasadero fines. Some were able to take advantage of the labor shortages in better-off households who sent their children to school in Huancayo. Now these households needed huacchilleros. Others were maintained by specializing in skills that had hitherto been undertaken by all households as part of the peasant farm, such as pottery, weaving, and making harnesses, so that the division of labor between households became more emphatic.

Between these two groups, the remaining households became involved in the seasonal migration of selected members. With the exception of the poorest, virtually all households sent members to work on the coastal cotton plantations at some time during the period 1920 to 1939. The demand for labor was greatest from March to June (thus absenting men from the village during the beginning of the harvest), but in fact many people tried to find other casual labor for longer periods. During the second presidency of Leguia (1920–1930) the government devoted more of the national budget than ever before to construction work, so that the most usual job was labor on construction projects, some on the coast, some in the Mantaro Valley. Virtually all those who eventually worked under the *contratos viales* (the road construction program of Leguia and, later, Benavides) after 1936 were recruited while on the coast.

Although remittances were insufficient during this period, by the end of the period the scene was set for increasing the role of extrafarm income through migration, firstly to Huancayo and later to Lima. From the 1930s, households that had sent members to Huancayo began to move their residence to the town. What commitments they still had in Huasicancha were now maintained through members of the immediate household returning during important periods of the year and through huacchilla arrangements in the case of livestock farming. Then, in 1938, the bottom fell out of the cotton market, while those who had been working on road-building gangs were released. A number of these people journeyed up the coast to Lima. Few of them remained permanently in the city, but by the end of this period there was a small colony of Huasicanchinos established in an inner-city slum.

In the previous period there was considerable heterogeneity in the form of the petty production unit. Most were involved in a variety of different occupations, but the various permutations of these occupations within each unit led to significant differences between one and another. These internal properties of the units of production had an effect on the relations between them. With the exception of those involved directly in providing labor for the hacienda, the bulk of productive relations were concentrated within the community itself. A household possessing a certain ratio of personnel to types of available resources at a particular period in its development cycle sought out others to complement its own productive operations.

During the second period, however, changes in the configuration of the regional economy—especially Huancayo's increased economic expansion as a result primarily of the Cerro de Pasco's operations—led to the involvement of dynamic commercial interests in the running of Hacienda Tucle, leading to its increased use of pasture. Reductions in livestock production by small farmers followed, and thus changed the internal configuration of each unit. These changes varied from one unit to another, depending on the particular commitments and resources of each during the early years of this period. In a few cases larger herders reduced their livestock commitment, bought property—like a small corner shop—in Huancayo and finally moved their entire household there. If they kept a few sheep, they were cared for by poorer households within the village, while members of the wealthier household returned during crucial periods to keep up minimal arable production.

But for the majority, the transformation took the form of maintaining the units' multioccupational character while fragmenting it as a nucleated household. Internally, the increase in nonfarm occupations did not have the effect of reducing the importance of producing subsistence items on the farm. On the contrary, great emphasis was now placed on the ability of the unit to produce subsistence items, which in turn modified the role of women. Such was especially the case for livestock farming. Women increasingly took over the running of the estancias for long periods during the year. This was then reflected in inheritance patterns; many newly-formed households received the larger share of their livestock through the wife, and the location of their estancias thus tended to be determined by reference to the wife and her mother.

With respect to relations external to the production unit, the new occupational combinations meant that the unit, as an integrated functioning entity, had far fewer sets of ties with other such units. Production relations were no longer confined to the community of Huasicanchinos: households, straddling uncomfortably across wide geographical regions for long periods of the year, had few resources to commit to the continued reproduction of such relations. So the configuration of a household economy came to depend increasingly on nonfarm occupations. The diverse directions of their subsequent development were now dependent upon such factors as: (a) the character of the particular sector of the national economy to which members were tied, be it agriculture, mining, or urban commerce; (b) the nature of those ties, for example, whether they involved the sale of labor or the sale of products; and (c) the degree to which they were committed to that sector, in terms of capital invested in nonfarm operations on the one hand, and the amount of farm resources to fall back on, on the other.

By the end of the period a system of closely interrelated petty production units whose reproduction had been a function of the unmediated social relations of the community was being threatened by a process of commodification. In fact the same development of the Peruvian economy which, by stimulating the hacienda to rationalize production, was pushing these people off their land, was simultaneously creating the interstices in the cash economy that they were to occupy. But whether drawn into the cash economy as commodity producers, whether drawn in as wage laborers, whether left behind with the drudgery of subsistence, or whether a combination of all of these, each Huasicanchino household had reasons for resisting this process or at the least trying to control its direction. Against the steadily mounting pressures to erode Huasicancha as a community, following the montonera period, this common ground within heterogeneity coalesced once more around the (much modified) institutions of (a now geographically dispersed) community.

And, insofar as the imperatives of capitalist development that were enveloping the highland pastoralists in a variety of ways were most immediately visible in the form of the neighboring commercializing hacienda, Huasicanchinos concentrated their resistance in that direction. In effect this meant what it had always meant, in one way or another: a question of control over resources. But the parameters were different, for this now represented an attempt to replace the pasture hitherto made available through being hacienda huaccheros and pasaderos, with pasture gained by invading the hacienda. The hacienda was therefore faced with Hobson's choice: the "legitimate" encroachment on their pasture by huacchilleros contracted by the hacienda or the less controllable "invasion" of pasture by land-hungry herders (cf., Barona 1963; Martinez-Alier 1973, 1977).

Throughout the 1930s and 1940s this stalemate continued, simultaneously preventing the hacienda from developing into a streamlined capitalist enterprise, and also restricting the development of Huasicanchino petty commodity production. And it is from here that we shall take things up in the next chapter. But what occurred between 1947 and 1948 encapsulates the contradictory processes that have been described. A concerted campaign to recapture land on the part of the Huasicanchinos met with a disappointing settlement in 1948, resulting in increasing out-migration throughout the repressive Odria years that followed. Ironically though, the configuration of the Huasicanchino economy that resulted did not, over the long run, reduce the number of their livestock. Although increasing engagement in nonagricultural occupations temporarily reduced the number of livestock from the 1920–1947 figures, village households as a whole began to hold ever greater numbers of sheep from 1950 to 1972, thus providing the basis for the major mobilization that ended in the later years. To understand why this was so and why, albeit in much modified form, the institutions of community remained the means of its expression, I turn now to the participants in that mobilization, in order to get to know them better.

4

Making a Living

You think we are like cunning old spiders weaving a wide web, but you are wrong. We are like the flies caught in the web. And you know what happens to the fly. Each twist and turn to be free just strangles it a little more.
— Tomas Pomayay, Huasicanchino migrant in Lima, 1973

Past experience—of political conflict, of unfolding social relations of production—combine with the conditions people face in the present to influence the way in which they engage in political activity. And so we turn from past experience to, if not the present, then at least the recent past. The purpose of this chapter is not so much to provide an economic anthropology of the Huasicanchinos as to be able to understand their political activities within the context of their present conditions: to know the kinds of things that matter to the Huasicanchinos in their pursuit of a living; to understand the way in which their domestic enterprises work to keep them alive; in short, to gain some sense of what their concerns are, their interests, their ambitions, and their worries. Not surprisingly, we discover from looking at the great variety of such enterprises that there is variety too in the concerns of the Huasicanchinos. It is best to begin by looking to the past, and for the Huasicanchinos that past lies in how migration became institutionalized.

The Institutionalization of Migration

Early Days

Long a characteristic of Huasicanchino domestic enterprises, variety was vastly increased once migration broadened the base of the economy. It was this early variety though that determined the differing participation of Huasicanchinos in the migratory diaspora that occurred following the disappointing settlement with Hacienda Tucle in 1948. A number of Huasican-chinos became part-time farmers or left their agricultural operations in the hands of others, until by the end of the 1970s half the people registered as comuneros of Huasicancha maintained residences outside the village.

By institutionalization of migration is meant essentially two things: first that it became a planned course of action for a household in which uncertainty was minimized through the use of existing contacts with out-migrants; and second that at a certain point, the existence of out-migrants earning some part of their living in other sectors of the economy began to generate its own dynamic. Of course the process by which migration became institutionalized was a gradual one, and the ability to organize and plan migration was confined to a few families whose numbers increased through the years. There were always migrants whose experience was unanticipated and still more whose best laid plans were disappointed. Generally speaking, however, it was those families originally well endowed with livestock who had the best chance of successful migration, and hence it is they who became the first permanent out-migrants, or "ex-residents," as they are known among Huasicanchinos.

To say that migration creates its own dynamic does not mean, in this case, that migration leads to more migration. Although this was originally the case and to some extent still is, it is far more important to see that as migration became an institutionalized way of life, so it acted to select out some for ex-residence while confining others to the village. The way in which some ex-residents and some returned migrants have continued, and often expanded, their agricultural activities has resulted on the one hand in a number of vil-lagers being retained in the countryside to provide labor, and on the other hand in others being pushed out of the village to complement their own farm incomes, as local resources become concentrated in the hands of others.

Although "ex-residence" became an established part of Huasicancha life only after 1948, migration itself was by no means a new phenomenon.[1] In the past some of the better-off pastoralists found themselves on grazing lands far distant from Huasicancha, while others acquired jobs as caporales on ha-ciendas further off than Tucle. Meanwhile many of the less well-off engaged in seasonal migration to the cotton plantations on the coast to the west of the village. These kinds of migration allowed for continued contact with the vil-lage, however, so that most older Huasicanchinos regard work on the con-tratos viales as the most radical experience, because it drew them away from the village for years at a time. These contratos were forced labor services for the government in the campaign to extend Peru's transport infrastructure, and they took peasants away from the villages for periods often in excess of two years. Many of the first migrants to Lima had experience first of work on the cotton plantations and then on the contratos viales.

Finally there is the role of the rapidly expanding economy of the local provincial capital of Huancayo. The sons of a number of the better-off pas-

toralists, especially those working as caporales, became interested in edu-
cating one or possibly two of their sons there. In the 1930s this education
concentrated much more on apprenticeships as mechanics, electricians, and
so on, than on formal education, and it was therefore through hacienda connections with the town that fathers were able to find "masters" to whom their
sons could be apprenticed.

Statistical data rarely capture the character of migration (Roberts 1973;
Connell, Dasgupta, et al 1974) and because ex-residents virtually always keep
up houses in Huasicancha (referred to in the village as *las casas con can-
dados*, "the padlocked houses") as well as their status as comuneros, the task
is made the more hazardous. Nevertheless life histories taken from 187 Huasicanchinos living in the village or Lima in 1972–1973 give some guidance.
There were 1,567 people in Huasicancha in 1936, making up 320 households
in which there were 45 more adult women than men. By the 1962 census the
population had declined by 22 percent but migrants' practice of maintaining
residences in the village as well as my own data suggest a figure nearer 40
percent. The life history data shows a solid cluster of migration from 1937
to 1942 mostly connected to the contratos viales program and the opening of
the Cercapuquio mine (see below) and then another significant increase from
1948 that was maintained throughout the 1950s.

All this forms an essential background to the growth of institutionalized
migration after 1948, and the experience of Salvador de la Cruz captures the
character of this process well.[2] Salvador, now a long-established resident of
Lima, was an illegitimate child who found work in Huancayo at the age of
twelve as an assistant to a man who sold herbal emollients at a stall in the
market. When his employer decided to move to Lima in 1934, Salvador went
with him. He stayed there for six months before returning to Huancayo. In
1938 Salvador, then sixteen years old, was recruited to work under the contratos viales program. He had a two year contract building a service road from
Huancayo to the Ica reservoir system on the western side of the Andes. When
this contract was up he found lodgings with an older Huasicanchino, Elias
Tacunan, in Lima.

Tacunan's experience of migration was quite different from Salvador's.
Tacunan came from a very different background in the village. His father was
an employee on Hacienda Antapongo and Elias, the eldest son, was sent to
Huancayo where he received three years of high school education before
being apprenticed as an electrician. Joining APRA in 1931, he was forced to
flee to Chile five years later. Then Salvador managed to find him in Lima in
1941, and it was his hospitality that allowed Salvador to remain in Lima. But
in 1945 Tacunan got work in La Oroya, the central smelting town of the
American-owned Cerro de Pasco Corportion, where he set about forming the
Federación Regional de Trabajadores del Centro. Tacunan's departure left
Salvador to search out new quarters.

He found that a number of villagers had secured work as *peones* on the hacienda of a family who grew cotton on land around Lima. These peones squatted on the land of their employer. By 1948 these few migrants had concentrated their dwellings on a small plot of land that lay on the edge of Lima's two most opulent suburbs, San Isidro and Miraflores. The strategic location of this land encouraged them to begin selling fruit from door to door, and Salvador took up this occupation too. The establishment of this "Petit Thouars" *coralon* (as it is known among Huasicanchinos) coincided with the disappointing end of the community's campaign to recover land from Hacienda Tucle and became the first focal point for migration to Lima.

It was in fact this settlement which provided the catalyst for the growing ex-resident migration which occurred after 1948. The 1930s and 1940s had been a period of struggle against the hacienda, offering hopes for the continuation of a viable local economy. Once Huasicancha's recognition by the government as a *comunidad* indigena had been achieved in 1936, a legal basis was established for the recuperation of land. But the open confrontation with the hacienda and army in 1947 culminated in a disappointing settlement. Meanwhile the economies of Huancayo, Lima, and the mining towns were expanding so that villagers began to turn attention to already-existing ex-resident households as the channels for what became increasingly institutionalized migration.

By 1972 half the comuneros of Huasicancha were distributed in Huancayo, Lima, and the mining centers of the central Andes and the high jungle area of Chanchamayo (roughly, 15, 25, 5 and 5 percent respectively). In assessing the effect this migration had on the Huasicanchino economy, two facets are of special importance: the nature of the receiving areas to which migrants went, and the different kinds of households in Huasicancha that fed this migration.

The Receiving Areas
from 1948 to 1960

Huancayo's economic expansion took the form of the multiplication of myriad small enterprises: mining supply houses, transport, workshops (*talleres*) and then shops, marketstalls, and street traders (by 1972, 80 percent of employed males in Huancayo were in enterprises with fewer than twelve employees [Roberts 1974*b*:69]). Nowhere could the line between the so-called "formal sector" and "informal sector" of an economy be more imprecise. The Huasicanchinos entered the pile very much at the bottom. By the early 1950s there were a few who had established themselves with a shop or workshop, and a few others were traders or skilled independent workers (electricians, mechanics, carpenters, etc.).[3] These people became the center of a Huasicanchino colony in Huancayo, but by far the majority of migrants had more un-stable and unremunerative work.

In Lima too the Huasicanchinos were engaged in mostly unstable jobs. Then Lima's informal economy expanded rapidly from the late 1950s on-wards resulting in the establishment of a few stable enterprises about a decade later than in Huancayo; through the 1960s. Unlike in Huancayo, in Lima they concentrated in just one profession: fruit selling, with a seasonal specializa-tion in strawberry selling. But the two colonies had one thing in common: apart from a few highschool graduates and apprentices, Huasicanchinos were never involved in wage labor either in Huancayo or Lima. And even at the mining and smelting centers of La Oroya and Moracocha most migrants were only briefly wage laborers. Married women operated marketstalls, and men were involved in various petty trading ventures. Work in the mines was a source of pride, but many men had worked only briefly for a wage (while their wives worked in the market) and then moved into the informal economy.

But of more direct influence on Huasicancha was the nearby mine of Cer-capuquio, just a three-hour walk from the village. This was a small but im-mensely rich mine, extracting lead and then later zinc and cadmium. The mine came on stream in 1937 and achieved the height of its production in the late 1940s and through the 1950s, exhausting itself after 1962. Roughly 300 men were employed. Most of them came from Huasicancha's neighboring village of Chongos Alto and from a village near Jauja at the north end of the Mantaro Valley. Nevertheless during the 1950s and early 1960s, eighteen Huasican-chinos had full-time work at the mine for periods from two to ten years. Many others found work at the mine for shorter periods, from one to eight or nine months in a year.

The Sending Community
from 1948 to 1960

In turning to Huasicancha as the source of migrants, it is important to re-member that all households were not alike. Even though village households represented "mixes" of commitment to various sources of income, there were households that were predominantly pastoralist, and the most economically secure of the Huasicanchinos were among them. Besides these were others who devoted a larger part of their time to arable farming and still others who were involved in petty trading and a variety of skilled jobs, such as har-nessmaker, carpenter, tinker, or smith. Some of those with little commitment to pastoralism gained a reasonable if unstable income. But by 1948 *all* house-holds were on the edge of poverty in Huasicancha because pastoralism was the basis of the economy, and it had been severely eroded.

Those who had nonetheless managed to maintain a viable household through sheep and llama herding in the difficult years of the 1930s and 1940s were also those who had, through those herds, maintained extrahousehold ties. And these households were most immediately affected by the cessation of the campaign against Hacienda Tucle brought on by the settlement of 1948 and the repression of the Odria years that followed it (see chap. 6). At the same time, these people had the easily convertible resources of sheep as well as the personal linkages that went along with pastoralism to enable them to embark on migration with a greater possibility of success.

For the others the threat of reduced pastures was not so immediately apparent, though as this basis of the village's economy declined so too did their own livelihoods. But the resources they had were not of the kind that could be easily converted into cash for a child's education or for setting up a small independent operation in Huancayo. And the continuity of extrahousehold linkages had been severely damaged through the previous period. For these people migration in the 1950s was accompanied by fewer successes, with many returning to the village and then trying again to migrate in subsequent years. As a result it took longer for migration to become institutionalized for them. It was not that they did not migrate during the 1950s but rather that the experience was a much more hazardous one and hence less capable of taking on a systematic form (see Roberts 1973). Nevertheless, by the 1960s nonagricultural sources of income were becoming increasingly important to the Huasicanchino economy, and as a few of these people achieved some stability outside the village, so they became nodes around which migration could become institutionalized. Moreover, while this occurred, households sought to reduce the instability of their uncertain urban incomes by investing in sheep.

Thus, with the coming of the 1960s, the fact of Huasicancha's integration into the nonagricultural economy through migration became an increasingly important variable influencing the differing forms of petty production enterprise. But the historical paths along which households travelled to reach that point were different. Some had used sheep to diversify into nonagricultural pursuits (through migration), while others, once having migrated and established some form of nonagricultural pursuit, diversified by investing in sheep. For both groups, by the 1960s pastoralism was an important component of the economy, but the experience of the two groups, which brought them to this convergence, was distinct.

Thus enterprises we find today with ostensibly similar structural characteristics might have emerged from quite different past experiences. Some of this difference can be captured in the following way. The word Huasicancha means house (*huasi*) and corral (*cancha*). Since those people with greater commitment to livestock have to spend much of their time among the corrals of their mountain estancias, while those with greater commitment to arable farming, trading and so on, spend more time among the houses of the village itself, I will use the two terms to refer to the migrants who emerged from these two bases. Those who based their migration on their original pastoralism I shall call the *canchas* and those whose base for migration was more varied, the *huasis*.

The Canchas.   All Huasicanchinos took great pride in their past history of opposition and gained much of their cultural identity therefrom. But the canchas had been especially deeply involved in the almost daily war of pastoralism, not just in resisting the hacienda, but in resisting too, encroachments from neighboring herders of all kinds, not just trespassing on hacienda land but rustling as well. It was these people's fathers and uncles who were the famous fighters of the past, and a few of them had also seen the inside of a jail for *bandolerismo* as well. Their politics (and in most cases the politics of their ex-resident sons and daughters) were those of rural radicalism, and their ideology was appropriately idiosyncratic.

So, with the coming of repression in 1948 and with some of their best-known leaders in jail, they were the most immediately affected. They now sought avenues that would direct them or their sons away from the village, at least temporarily. For a number of the sons, this meant being sent to high school in Huancayo. But the end result was varied. A few completed three or four years, but most did not. They sought out training for skilled jobs or went into street trading. Others went directly into various kinds of independent activities in Huancayo. For the most part a certain investment could be made in these initial steps through the sale of livestock, and often there were personal contacts too that were of use in getting started. In August 1945, they founded the "Club Cultural Deportivo de Huasicancha."

In Lima, it was the canchas too who initially monopolized the coralon of Petit Thouars, where Salvador had found his base in Lima. Here migrants were quickly thrown into the hazards of life as independent street traders, gaining their apprenticeship by migrating seasonally to Lima for the strawberry-selling season from November to February. But uncertainty and risk were reduced through the intensive use of contacts within the coralon, so that the chances of sticking it out in Lima were rendered far better by this dense network.

Canchas were generally prepared to dispense with some sheep in order to set up in other operations away from Huasicancha and were thus not especially attracted to wage labor in the mines. Nevertheless for a few, the proximity of the Cercapuquio mines, which allowed them an added source of income without absenting them for too long from the village, meant that a few canchas did seek and find work there. Thus, through the 1950s a process of diversification transformed the traditionally pastoralist households, pushing them out into petty production and petty trading in Huancayo and Lima.

The Huasis.   But, as migration took hold, another group emerged. They were not just drawn partly from the poorer families of Huasicancha, they came too from the few traders, skilled craftsmen, and shopowners as well as farms more strongly committed to arable farming than livestock. They had fewer resources to invest in migration and fewer contacts, but for many of them a fairly hazardous geographical mobility was already part of their experience. Initially they were not as directly hit by the 1948 settlement with Tucle. As a result it took longer for these—the *huasis*—to institutionalize migration. There was far more early failure during the 1950s, with disappointed migrants returning to the village for a year or more. They became a tough breed of mobile and streetwise people, many of whom joined APRA in the 1950s and became engaged in the growing political movements of opposition in the central region of Peru from then onward. In 1959 they founded the "Club Social Deportivo de Huasicancha," as an alternative to the older club.

These migrants were to be found in the same occupations as the canchas in Huancayo, though in different proportions and at a later date. Many of them became involved in trading in Huancayo, and a few acquired low-level semi-clerical jobs, such as postman, school porter, and so on. It was from these people that the mining migrants emerged. And, in Lima one or two got a foothold in Petit Thouars and then were able to set up another coralon in Surquillo, which then provided an alternate bridgehead for Lima migration. So, just as the canchas had dominated Petit Thouars as a migrant base, so now the huasis set up Surquillo as their base.

The important point is that there were *some* who managed to get established: as traders in Huancayo, streetsellers in Lima, or miners in Moracocha or Cercapuquio. And, as this occurred, so these ex-residents provided the basis from which migration could become institutionalized for the huasis, as it did from the beginning of the 1960s.

One wave of migration, then, took place very shortly after 1948 and became institutionalized in the 1950s. This was mostly fed by families who had been strongly committed to pastoralism—the canchas. But, as migration took hold, another group emerged whose migration in the 1950s was more uncertain but who, by the early 1960s, had themselves established their own institutions for migration—the huasis. They formed different ex-resident clubs and lived in different parts of Lima, but they relied nonetheless on similar enterprises for their livelihood. It would be wrong to overemphasize the distinction between these two groups. I am referring to a style of migration and to some extent even a style of life and of clothing. Obviously the two categories overlap and what rivalry there was between them at this stage was exorcised in the football matches between their clubs.[4]

The Variety of Enterprises Today: the Locations

It is now possible to outline the forms of the Huasicanchinos' livelihood during the 1960s and early 1970s. In this period capital was attracted away from largescale livestock operations toward industrial and commercial concentration to a large extent on Lima but also to a lesser extent on Huancayo. Economically the vacuum thus created provided a possibility for small-scale enterprises whose barrier to entry—the haciendas' continued claim to territorial control of pasture—could only be removed through political means. For Huasicancha, the effect of Hacienda Tucle's extension of land use in the area following the 1948 settlement had been to provoke out-migration and prevent significant capital concentration in smallscale livestock operations. Instead a wide variety of smallscale enterprises emerged in the migratory diaspora. But the instability of their various sources of livelihood always served to keep alive the agricultural alternative, resulting in perpetual pressure on the hacienda that took an overt political expression in the mid-1960s.

Huancayo

By the 1970s the significant core of permanent residents in Huancayo were either running small household enterprises or had one chief source of livelihood deriving from reasonably reliable wage jobs, either in lower levels of government offices or in one of the myriad small enterprises that abounded in Huancayo, especially in shops and *talleres* (workshops). These latter were people whose parents had committed resources to getting their children high-school and/or apprenticeship education in the previous two decades.

Among the small household enterprises variation was chiefly a function of the form of capital and the nature of interpersonal relations. Obviously the crucial determinant for setting up small household operations was a minimal amount of seed capital, and the way in which this capital was obtained influenced the subsequent pattern of development of the enterprise. Hence there is a distinction between enterprises set up by canchas and by huasis.

For the early cancha migrants capital was raised by selling off livestock, and today a number of these households maintain stable and independent enterprises in Huancayo. Where the sale of livestock did not result in enough cash for initiating the enterprise or initial setbacks called for more capital, canchas too were often well placed in a social network to call for credit from friends and relatives. Where this occurred, however, it significantly affected the subsequent pattern of development of the enterprise; credit was often advanced without interest, but its use effectively made the creditor a partner in the enterprise. Intricate credit relationships thus developed that had the effect of spreading risk through enterprises engaged in different sectors of the economy.

For others seed capital could derive from previous migrant activity, such as mining, petty trading, and the practice of some skill or other. This was most often the case for the huasi migrants who set up operations in Huancayo in the late 1960s. Often the amount of capital was very small, and the number of personal contacts who could be relied on at the onset of adverse conditions was similarly restricted; a number of these migrants responded to these conditions by going into high-risk ventures (both economically and legally). The failure rate was, therefore, of course, greater, but occasionally the successes appeared to Huasicanchinos impressive, and such people acquired the sobriquet "vivo" ("smart" or "sharp"). Their smartness was to be admired; possibly their cunning could be used by others to advantage, but the watchword in such dealings was caution.

Lima

By the beginning of the 1970s Lima took in at least 50 percent of Huasicancha's ex-residents. They were concentrated in two inner city coralones, canchas in Petit Thouars and huasis in Surquillo, and three barriadas or shantytowns on the edge of the city. Huasicanchinos developed a specific trade in Lima to which all were at one time or another attached and which still occupies in one way or another the vast majority of ex-residents. They sell fruit on the streets of Lima, from stalls, from mobile tricycles, or from baskets. In fact, all Huasicanchinos regard themselves as essentially strawberry sellers. Many people who sell a variety of fruit will still say "I sell strawberries." Initially, former residents were agricultural peones working in cotton plantations near Lima, who took to selling strawberries on the streets from November to February. Gradually, as more migrants arrived, something had to be done to get by in the remaining part of the year, and so they went into retail fruit selling. Strawberry selling continued to occupy a central place in their lives, however, and many villagers arrive in Lima and stay with friends and relatives during this period. Some of them take baskets and sell fruit on the streets. Others are employed out on the farms around Lima, picking strawberries. Most do both.

All ex-residents have established themselves through entering the fruit trade as retail sellers. Beginning as ambulant sellers with one or two baskets of fruit provided by a more established ex-resident, a man usually attempts to move up to the use of a tricycle, which allows him to carry more goods and cover more ground. There are also a number of ex-residents who run established stalls, either at street corners or in the large market places. Residents of the inner-city coralones are well placed for ambulant selling. But those who have moved out to the barriadas have traded off this advantage for the various benefits of the barriadas, and they, therefore, store their tricycles and fruit at the coralones of these other Huasicanchinos.

Many of those who have moved to the barriadas have moved down the chain of the fruit trade and thus moved away from their total reliance on retail selling. Fruit is brought to Lima down the central highway from the highlands and jungle and sold at the central market. Strawberries are grown on farms around Lima where irrigation water is available. In both cases retailers have to face a transportation problem in which time plays a very important part because fruit spoils, but strawberries, especially, spoil rapidly and have to be picked around 6 A.M., sorted, and then sold on the streets. Overnight storage is virtually impossible, so that the entire batch must be sold each day, and the early-morning pilgrimage repeated the following morning. When overnight spoilage does occur, fruit has to be taken to one or another of Lima's conserve factories for sale. In all cases, buying fruit at the central market, strawberry-picking in the suburbs, and sale to conserve factories later, transportation of fruit is required and is provided by a number of ex-residents who have invested in pick-up trucks or somewhat larger light trucks.

A few ex-residents managed to rent some land in the early 1970s with plans for growing strawberries on it. But they soon scrapped this plan. Instead, a number of ex-residents equipped with trucks have become involved in the contract strawberry-picking business. They advance cash to the farmer at the beginning of the year. This secures a certain acreage of his production for their exclusive use, and, for his part, allows him some cash for production expenses. The contractor then faces the task of maximizing the income from strawberries, which means managing the picking process carefully so that plants are not damaged in the hurry to get their fruit. The farmer must also regulate the planting so that not all fruit ripens at once, creating a glut on the market. To do this contractors rely on Huasicanchino labor, and at the height of the season villagers arrive in Lima for the picking and selling of fruit.

Contractors and transporters face a slack season after the strawberry crop is exhausted. At these times, those with larger trucks park them each morning at well-known spots and wait for one-time jobs that might be local or might take them on trips distant from Lima. Many, however, get through the remainder of the year by maintaining their retail operations, which has the effect of placing great emphasis on the household as a pool of domestic labor. If retail operations are focused on the tricycle, then one or two sons are roped in during the strawberry season when the father is too busy. But in many cases an essential source of continual income is provided by the women whose husbands have secured a truck. The wives of such men, aided by their daughters, set themselves up with a permanent stall, which becomes the major income for the rest of the year.

In Lima, the most severely impoverished are those entirely committed to the retail end of the business. In sheer numbers (though not in their influence over the Huasicanchino economy) these people constitute the bulk of the Lima residents: some 50 percent of the households. They are almost entirely concentrated in one or another of the inner-city slums. Invariably both husband and wife work, the latter taking the children with her and selling from a basket, the former using a tricycle if the family's resources extend to such an investment. In some cases the wife's involvement in selling is concentrated on that period of the year when strawberry selling is at its height. In other cases, an older relative or unmarried female cousin might be brought down from Huasicancha to care for the children, allowing the family to move out to the more salubrious barriadas.[5]

At the opposite end of the economic spectrum are to be found enterprises whose initial basis in retail selling had led to the investment of capital into one operation that now provides the major source of a family's livelihood. Three ex-residents, for example, have substantial shops in the older barriadas and have given up retail fruit selling entirely. Two others rely entirely on in-city trucking and no longer transport fruit at all. A further three own small minibuses and are members of one of Lima's many colectivo cooperatives, transporting barriada-dwellers to the city. In each case money was generated in retail fruitselling, but today the household has concentrated its source of income in one venture in the city.

The remaining migrants are involved in multioccupational enterprises (Long 1979). The economic unit is extended to include, besides the fruit trade, perhaps also some pig breeding, the repairing of ambulant tricycles, the retail selling of cosmetics, some dressmaking, and a few casual jobs. Of course all adult and not-so-adult people are involved in the enterprise. In 1973 I found households with as many as fifteen regularly undertaken occupations carried out by just four or five members. But then, in many cases, the enterprise itself—let's say a tricycle repair shop—is run with two partners from Huasicancha, who head two other households from which they draw labor for the *taller* and which households themselves have perhaps as many again operations attached to them, all making their demands for capital and labor as well. It can thus be seen that the line between one domestic enterprise and another is often very hard to draw, as is the line between wage labor and domestic labor.

In fact, not only do the lines between enterprises and between domestic and wage labor become obscured, but so too does the line between owner and worker. In a number of cases, *taller* owners, faced with a choice of buying a new piece of equipment or going out of business, have raised credit from their own wage laborers (who themselves have a number of other sources of income besides their wage) on the basis that the creditor becomes a partner until the debt is repaid. Besides working alongside their employees then, the initial owners of enterprises are often only so in name, being in fact partners with their own workers. A number of informants pointed out that it was in anticipation of just such an occurrence that they favored employing relatives and close friends from Huasicancha.

Thus, in Lima are found a large number of very poor ex-residents whose economic ties are quite limited and who rely on just one, very unstable source of income: retail fruit selling. There are besides them, perhaps fifteen or twenty better-off ex-residents who have concentrated investment in one source of income to the exclusion of others. And for the remainder, income derives from a variety of operations.

Once again, as in Huancayo, differing past experiences of their members cut across the structured variety in enterprises. In the case of Lima the distinction between canchas and huasis is reflected in the migrants' places of residence. Early migrants around 1948 set up the Petit Thouars coralon, and they were mostly the younger sons of pastoralist families in Huasicancha. They, in turn, were the first to partake in a barriada land invasion and set up house in what is now an old and established barriada on the road to Lima's airport. Then, in the early sixties a second group from Petit Thouars began to seek barriada homes and eventually established another colony in La Campina to the south of the city. These people continue to have close ties with Petit Thouars where they keep their equipment and where they pass on and acquire information of social and economic importance. The heritage of these people then is broadly what I have described as cancha.

Another group set up a coralon referred to as Surquillo and which is in fact within the area of Surquillo market in Lima. This occurred only in the early 1960s, and it was followed by a major land invasion in which Huasicanchinos played an active role in 1968. As a result many migrants now live in the relatively new barriadas of Villa Maria del Triunfo, especially in the area known as Mariano Melgar. The heritage of these people is roughly speaking that of the less pastoralist-oriented huasis.

Huasicancha

Most of the ex-residents in Huancayo and Lima maintain ties to households in Huasicancha. The complexity of these ties varies in relation to the particular form of the units of production in question. The poorer villagers who are casual migrants to Huancayo are enabled by the proximity of town and village to return for important periods in the agricultural cycle, thus obviating the need for partners in the village to do tasks for them. For the poorer Lima migrants this is not possible, however, and although they attempt to strike reciprocal bargains with villagers, hazards in their volatile trade usually prevent them from cementing ties over any length of time.

The more prosperous migrants in both towns began, through the 1960s, to reestablish ties to various enterprises in the village. In the case of arable farming, the arrangements rarely involve sharecropping. Rather village households enter into agreements with ex-resident households such that no direct payments are involved. In principle, the village household receives the full fruits of the arable land they work regardless of whether they own it or not. Their "generosity" in sending food supplies to their ex-resident partners is not at all a function of the amount of the ex-resident's land used and scarcely susceptible to any very arithmetic calculation at all, reflecting as it does the need of both parties to maintain the proper links of friendship, possibly a past call on the ex-resident's household for cash in the previous year, or the need of the ex-resident's Lima-based enterprise for labor during the strawberry season.

Pastoral farming began increasingly to reflect the way in which ex-residents sought to offset the hazards of their city-based enterprise by investing in sheep. In some cases the care of these sheep is based on a scheme similar to that just described, but because pastoralism is not a seasonal occupation allowing for occasional migration to the cities, it is more often the case that the village household receives some of the new-born lambs each year in line with the old custom of huacchilla. In a number of cases, however, lack of pasture means that flocks cannot be increased and periodic sales are made. Pastoralists continued to care for the capital (in the form of sheep) of their ex-resident partners, but in so doing they acquire the status of partner either in the ex-resident's overall bundle of enterprises or, more often, in just one of those enterprises. Thus one Lima resident who had bought land for strawberry growing in 1973 had three pastoralist village households as partners in the venture, all of whom cared for some of his livestock.

In return for services performed in the village, ex-residents lodge the villager's children in the city during their high school training or apprenticeship, notify their village partners of temporary casual jobs becoming available in town and then lodge those who come to do the job. In some cases they simply advance cash to a needy partner for some emergency; in others they arrange a villager's *tramites* with a government agency or attend to any possible legal affairs that might come up. In effect, the complexity of interhousehold relationships that had existed prior to Hacienda Tucle's expansion and then had been reduced through the 1950s now reemerged though radically transformed.

I refer to these clusters as "confederations of households." Virtually all Lima-based multioccupational enterprises and many of the better-off Huancayo-based units are involved in these complex sets of ties. The degree to which they complement the operations of each enterprise is such that the rationality—the developmental path—of any one unit becomes closely associated with the others to which it is associated. Investments of time and money are crucially influenced by the imperatives not just of any one enterprise but of the confederation as a whole. For example, a Lima-based household with close ties to another in Huancayo and two others in Huasicancha mobilized capital for investment in a small *taller* (workshop) by tapping the salary of the Huancayo household head and the livestock being shepherded by the village households. Later on, the same household postponed a subsequent decision to buy a piece of machinery in favor of investing capital in an operation initiated by the Huancayo partner.

It must be remembered that the complexity of these ties between Lima, Huancayo, and Huasicancha is just the tip of the iceberg; beneath the surface each participating enterprise is itself multioccupational as the above discussion of Lima-based migrants has shown. Thus, in the example just cited, the Lima enterprise eventually resolved the need for equipment by raising money from its existing workers who then became partners in the *taller* or, more specifically, in the ownership of one piece of the *taller*. Since this *taller* was already owned by both the Lima household and one of the Huasicancha households who shepherded their livestock, in effect, the two new worker-partners in the *taller* were also becoming partners with the village pastoralist.

Confederations of households are subject to constant flux and reformulation. While interhousehold alliances prior to institutionalized migration had been subject to schisms resulting from changes in the composition of each household, schisms now were primarily a reflection of developments occurring in the various sectors of the national economy to which each household was connected (cf., Deere and De Janvry 1981). Schisms could also be influenced by inflation, which could subside in a particular sector, and attack another, or by the collapse in demand for luxury fruit in a third. Such risks were reduced by the household confederations.

But, as we have seen, besides Huancayo and Lima, Huasicanchinos also migrated to the nearby mine of Cercapuquio. Since the work center was no more than a morning's hike from the village, the work at the mine involved a quite different kind of migration from that described so far. Migrants to Cercapuquio were in a good position to maintain their village-based enterprises. This was the only form of migration for wages in which ex-residents did not remove their immediate families from the village. Migrants used their wages primarily to buy sheep, and, when the mine began to lay people off in the mid-sixties, pastoralism became the household's major source of income.

Because their households were not removed from the village, these residents could use domestic labor to accumulate livestock. Wives especially took on an important role in the management of the enterprise. This meant that there was no necessity to acquire extrahousehold obligations in order to accumulate sheep in the village. As flocks became too large to be managed by domestic labor, in the late sixties, these enterprises began to employ workers on a contractual basis, referring to them by the old hacienda term, *peon*. They reinvested surplus back into their own enterprises, rather than spreading it through a number of confederated operations, and by 1972 four out of the six wealthiest farmers in Huasicancha were men who had spent from six to ten years in Cercapuquio and hence had few obligations to other Huasicancha households.

Ironically the scarcity of pasture after the expansion of Hacienda Tucle, which drove Huasicanchinos to migrate, did not in the long run reduce the pressure on pasture but increased it. The requirements of both the few simple commodity farmers on the one hand and the confederations of households on the other, led to a steady rise in the number of livestock and hence to a rise in the pressure for a resolution of the endemic conflict with Hacienda Tucle. Inasmuch as the relationships necessary to pastoralism were mainly expressed through the noncommodified sphere, so these institutions—anchored to the notion of "community"—were recomposed.

But the growing importance of nonfarm sources of income meant that it was no longer just those families predominantly tied to pastoralism (whom I have called the canchas) that spearheaded the movement for land recuperation. Therefore in order to get some sense of the differing pressures felt in a variety of enterprises it is necessary to look more closely at the rationality of their operations through the examination of case studies.

5

Ghostly Figures
Outside the Domain
of Political Economy

*Political economy . . . does not recognize . . . the
working man so far as he is outside the [wage] relationship. Thieves, tricksters, beggars, the unem-
ployed, the starving, wretched and criminal working
man, are figures which do not exist for political economy, but only for other eyes; for doctors, judges,
gravediggers, beadles etc. They are ghostly figures
outside the domain of political economy.*
—Marx, *Economic and Philosophical Manuscripts*

The structure of Huasicancha as a community was changing quite strikingly during the period of confrontation with the hacienda. Enterprises were
inserted into the larger socioeconomic formation in a multiplicity of ways,
so that as economic conjunctures affected one sector and not another, they
influenced directly enterprises linked into that sector and only indirectly others
not so linked. But the response of enterprises cannot simply be understood
by reference to their different structural features at that moment. Differences in the interpersonal resources available for dealing with economic
conjunctures play a role in determining the development of the various Huasicanchino enterprises, and these resources are not instantly available in exchange for cash but rather derive from an experiential history, the variety
of which has been captured by use of the terms huasi and cancha. In this
way, data relating to contemporary structure is combined with that of past
experience.

This noncommodified component for the reproduction of enterprises faced
by uncertain economic conditions goes some way to explaining why Hacienda
Tucle found itself opposed, not by a united body of hacienda peones or scattered groupings of individual peasants but by a body of people whose collec-

tivity resided in the notion of "the community of Huasicanchinos." Were all Huasicanchino enterprises individual atoms—simple commodity producers bereft of the interpersonal ties of the community—any given development in one sector of the Peruvian economy, let us say a fall in the price of fruit in Lima, would lead to ever greater heterogeneity among enterprises along the lines of their differing relationship to each economic sector, but because the interpersonal ties of the community have played a major role in help- ing the Huasicanchinos resist the hazards of being small fish in a big sea, these noncommodified ties have remained a significant variable in the de- velopmental path of each enterprise, offsetting the process of polarization. As a result economic conditions directly influencing one enterprise can have a domino effect on a multitude of other enterprises with the result that inser- tion into a larger economy, in the case of the Huasicanchinos, has not so much shattered the sense of community as given it a heightened degree of plasticity. This plasticity, moreover, has been a constant feature throughout Huasican- chino history.

But plasticity over time is not the only dimension; plasticity must be seen too from the specific vantage point from which one or another member of an enterprise perceives "the community." Thus, for the canchas who in the past tended to have a far more extensive set of interpersonal ties and the huasis whose ties had less historical depth, the character of this community compo- nent is likely to be different. Hence, it is by examining the case studies that we can acquire the bases from which to understand the different purposes and meanings that key Huasicanchino institutions had for participants.

These case studies represent the variety of Huasicanchino enterprises. It is not so much that they can be understood as being involved or not in commodification—to some extent they all are—nor is it simply a matter of the degree to which commodification has taken hold in each case. Rather, it is a question of examining the effect of commodity penetration into different areas of the operation in such a way that the potential developmental trajectory of enterprises varies. Faced with specific crises the ability to remold the shape of the enterprise is of course conditioned by the labor process within the household. But it is also conditioned by the differing kinds of social relation- ships to which members of the enterprise are committed for its continued operation. It is therefore important to examine in some detail social relations both within and beyond the household seen as an enterprise.

It is important as well to remember the goal of this method. I am not con- cerned simply with the economic development of certain kinds of small-scale enterprises *tout court*. Rather the trajectory of one enterprise and its diver- gence from that of another had quite specific political implications: these trajectories were a major factor giving shape to the culture of opposition that finally took expression in the land recuperation campaign of the 1960s and

1970s. The presentation of statistical data on the percentage of enterprises using wage labor, the amount of machinery they owned, etc., cannot provide the kind of information needed to get at this dynamic component. And so we turn to five case studies.[1]

From these case studies the extent of heterogeneity is apparent. We can begin, very schematically, with the well-known polarities of peasant villages: in Huasicancha there are eighteen enterprises (of a total of 402 households) in which commoditized relations of production enter most facets of the operation. In these enterprises the labor of impoverished households is exploited in various approximations of the wage form, and surplus is reinvested more or less systematically back into the enterprise. Though such households continue to maintain some interpersonal ties for economic purposes, these remain few though often significant. While small in number, these households have had a strong directional influence on the Huasicanchino political economy, and I use our final case study of Urbano and Paulina to exemplify such households.

At the other extreme are families whose holdings of livestock and arable land are so insubstantial that they can rely only on their meager subsistence crops and a perpetually unstable demand for their labor, either in the village or through migration. One group of such households is in a sense a macabre image of the former category: deprived of resources and faced with perpetual instability, they lack the continuity of social relationships built up through the reciprocal institutions of the community and rely instead on casual jobs as peones, the instability of which they try to mitigate by asserting admiration, respect, and so on for the one or two persons who have employed them occasionally but with some consistency. Eighteen households or 6 percent of the village comprise such a group. But these do not exhaust the labor pool available to farmers in need of workers. Besides other impoverished households who seek out livelihoods through haphazard migration, there are a large group of minifundia farms where farm income must be supplemented by other activities. For all these, the most significant form of income is the sale of labor power as a commodity.

In neither the case of the independent commercial farmers nor the peones, though, are we dealing with the majority of households in both Huasicancha and Lima that constitute the core that gives to Huasicanchino social structure its principal character. These are enterprises in which the characteristics of commoditized social relationships are found alongside relationships that rely for their continuity on the maintenance of some form of affect such as we associate with the community or the family. What we find here, however, is not just a hodgepodge of different mixes in which the impersonality of the marketplace vies with the continual need to maintain the position of the household vis-à-vis more personal ties. We find, instead, articulated within each of these enterprises a pattern of forces whose shifting relative weight provokes a variety of developmental responses on the part of the enterprise, giving it a form with varying degrees of plasticity. It is the texture of this process that is described by case studies. While the threads of connection are sufficiently complex to make distinctions hard to see, there is indeed a distinction between small-scale enterprises whose reliance on interpersonal resources has been extensive and continuous and others in which the confrontation with the marketplace—for goods, services, and labor—has taken place from a less secure background of interpersonal support.

Clusters of households that possess continuously-used networks of inter-household linkages I refer to in their most institutionalized form as "confederations of households." They characteristically span the urban and rural locations of the Huasicanchinos—Huasicancha, Huancayo, Lima, and in some cases the mining centers. A feature of such households, especially the urban ones, is the multifarious sources of income on which they rely. Of the 187 households on which I have detailed information, 99 or 53 percent are linked into confederations of households. It is to the establishing and maintenance of these confederations that we turn in the first three of the case studies.

I said that these kinds of households give the principal character to Huasi-canchino social structure, and yet 53 percent is a narrow majority. Nevertheless, there are households who are in the process of attempting to build up such sets of ties. And there are others who are attempting to extricate themselves from what must seem at times like molasses. And both have varying degrees of financial success. The existence of these confederated households has an effect on the character of Huasicanchino social relations that extends beyond a synchronic moment in time captured in a fieldwork survey.

The case studies deal too with members of enterprises whose network of interpersonal ties has emerged from a more recent past (they constitute roughly 30 percent of Huasicanchinos). Such is the case for Eulogio and Eufresenia, whom we meet in the fourth study. The contemporary structure of enterprises, seen as individual production units, is superficially similar to those just mentioned. Here too there is a mix of market relations and personal ties, but the form differs from the confederated households according to past experiences.

Amid this heterogeneity, however, each of these enterprises is dynamic, in the sense that it must be understood in terms of an ongoing trajectory of development. For any one enterprise to ensure the relationships essential for its reproduction, certain requirements have to be met, and these requirements are clearly not the same for each of the case studies. The implications over time of engaging in certain kinds of relationships may, other things being equal, commit the unit of production to a certain logic of reproduction. This is the centrifugal tendency. But the erratic nature of that part of production that relies primarily on commodity relationships—both rural and urban— means that these varied enterprises have in common their use of the noncommodified social relations for access to both resources (land and livestock) and personnel, and these social relations are expressed through institutions having a community referrent. This is the centripetal tendency.

Of the five case studies, the first is used to set the scene historically; it allows us to place the remaining studies into an historical past peopled by personalities we have already met. In a way it gives us the genealogy of a set of domestic enterprises as I found them in 1972–1973, during fieldwork. It also provides important background information for the subsequent two case studies. Of these two, the former is located in Lima, the latter in Huasicancha. In both we are seeing the way in which confederations of households seem to work in the process of reproduction.

The fourth case is immediately striking for its difference from the previous three. This case represents those Huasicanchinos whose reliance on a variety of nonmonetary extrahousehold linkages and strong ties with Huasicancha are based on social relations with a shallow basis in the past. We begin by meeting Eulogio and Eufresenia in Lima, but we find that their enterprise lacks long-standing personal networks. We will quickly gain the sense that there is a qualitative difference in the kind of enterprise of which this fourth case is an example. It is tempting to suggest that the difference is one of increased commoditization and market incorporation. And Eulogio, Eufresenia, and I all share somehow in the view that they *are* in some way less "traditional" than the previous examples. But in chapter 6 I shall have cause to question this superficial appearance.

Finally, I will turn to a case taken from the few independent commercial farmers in Huasicancha, and here too I shall be cautious about rushing to ascribe this case (and the others it represents) to the category "simple commodity production," despite the combined use of domestic and wage labor, increasing production for the market, and other possibly persuasive evidence. Indeed the question of trying to come to grips with the entire labor process as encapsulated in these case studies will be taken up in the next chapter.

Perhaps the greatest danger of all lies in semantics: in referring to the households of the Huasicanchinos as "enterprises" I have underemphasized the degree of their poverty. By seeking to distinguish between them I have obscured this one thing they have in common. It is hard to convey this in any absolute sense. Were the traveler or census-taker to make the journey to this remote mountain community he or she would be most immediately struck by the uniformity that poverty imposes on its victims. Were the same traveler or census-taker to seek out the Huasicanchinos in Lima, perhaps there too he there too he or she would be impressed by their likeness to the ghostly figures whose absence from political economy Marx noted.

Victor and Juana Hinostrosa's Domestic Enterprise

Victor Hinostrosa, 63 years old.
Juana Cano de Hinostrosa, 60 years old.

Amid the variety we find today among the Huasicanchinos each enterprise still emerges from a past set of social relationships. And this "genealogy of the household"—the path it has followed to arrive at its present—affects its character as an enterprise today. But the storehouse of past relationships from which an enterprise draws more closely resembles a genealogy for the canchas than it does for the huasis, because cancha enterprises came into existence on a base of the family's past involvement in pastoralism. This, then, is where we pick up our case studies: not quite in the present but instead in the context of their past (see fig. 2). From the perspective of Victor and Juana, we can gaze back for a moment toward their antecedents. But by starting from their doorstep we can set out too, along a number of different paths into the present to reach households with economically active adults operating today. So to understand the operation of these latter households (nos. 12 through 29 in fig. 2) we begin with a somewhat older couple, because they occupy a central position and thus allow us to branch off and look at others.

By 1972 the household of Victor and Juana had gradually been reduced from its former dynamic position. Their eldest daughter (no. 15, fig. 2) was married and running a multioccupational household with her husband in Lima. The same was true for their eldest son Salvador (no. 16). (Both these enterprises were similar to the case of Mauro and Guillermina described in detail below.) Donato (no. 17), the second son, lived in Huancayo and had a government job as a forestry engineer, having received a diploma from the provincial university. The youngest daughter (no. 18) had just set up house in Huasicancha, and she and her husband helped the old couple run their farm. But the child of whom they were proudest was Donato, who had studied forestry at the local university in Huancayo and then won a scholarship for two further years' study in Belgium. For Victor, Donato's was the crowning achievement at the end of a long life of struggle.

For five months of each of the past nine years Victor journeyed to Lima where he sold strawberries on the streets. Initially he stayed with his brother's son, Mauro (no. 14) whose animals he cared for at that time in Huasicancha.

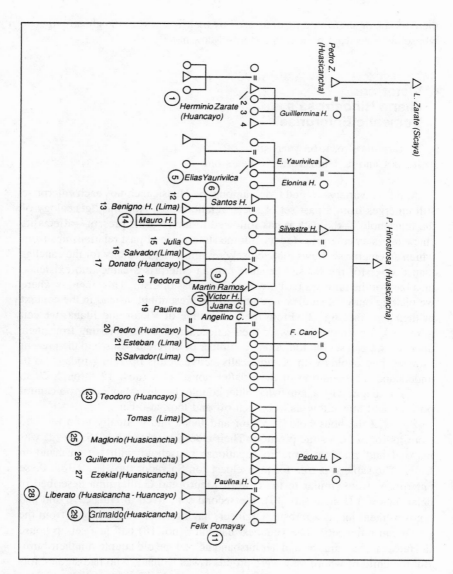

Figure 2. Victor Hinostrosa's relevant kin.

But gradually he shifted so that by now—1972—he stays with his son Salvador (no. 16). I have stood on a street corner and watched Victor from a distance, selling fruit at the doors of wealthy people's houses in Miraflores. He appears to be a shy and somewhat confused Indio, possibly a little stupid in matters of bargaining over fruit prices but no doubt to be trusted for all that. The appearance is misleading. In Huasicancha, more at ease, he is so articulate that young people sit for hours listening to him talk. Nevertheless, in the village his life is now wrapped in the tight constraining blanket of poverty. It was not always so. His father, Silvestre, together with Silvestre's brother, Pedro, had been relatively well-off pastoralists, owning flocks in excess of 1,500 animals each. When Hacienda Tucle began to become jealous of the land it claimed, they moved off to more distant areas where they rented land from communities to the south in Huancavelica and to the north in Yaulis and near Sicaya. Eventually they even rented land from haciendas in Huancavelica, and their sister, Guillermina, married a big pastoralist from Sicaya (Pedro Z., in fig. 2).

Victor was one of just four children and so stood to inherit much of the flock, always assuming that there would not be any pasture left to graze it with the haciendas expanding, apparently forever, onto all available grazing land. (Pedro, Victor's uncle, however, had a vast family of eleven children who could not expect much inheritance once the flock had been depleted to meet the costs of their upbringing). At eight, Victor began to receive somewhat haphazard private tuition from the roving teachers who passed through the highlands, giving lessons in return for food and lodging. Then in 1922 he went to Huancayo where he received three years of primary education. It was the only formal education Victor ever had.

He spent the five years from 13 to 18 in Huancayo, returning frequently to Huasicancha, and during this time he became friends with two other, similar migrants, Elias Tacunan and Martin Ramos (who later married Victor's sister). The three of them set off for Lima in 1932, and Victor found work selling pastries in the market. He stayed for two years and then returned to Huasicancha where, in 1934, he married Juana Cano and built a house. He started out his household at an initial cash investment of $125.00 (U.S.), which came chiefly from the sale of sheep.

Victor, his cousin Elias Yaurivilca, another cousin who lived in Huancayo, Herminio Zarate (no. 1, son of Pedro, the Sicaya pastoralist and Victor's aunt Guillermina) and Martin Ramos (no. 9, now Victor's brother-in-law) began to get very involved in Huasicancha's campaign to regain its pastures around this time, and the political climate was such that by 1938 Victor fled to Lima for two years, where he lived with Elias Tacunan and once more took to selling pastries. He was back in Huasicancha throughout the 1940s however and has become remembered as one of the significant figures in Huasicancha's land invasion of 1947–1948, and indeed he was imprisoned in Lima's infamous island prison, El Fronton (G. Smith 1975).

Victor was one of the few pastoralists to remain in Huasicancha during the 1950s. He actually sold some livestock and bought arable land during that time. But meanwhile his peers were pursuing a different strategy. Elias Tacunan was a qualified electrician working in La Oroya. Herminio Zarate (no. 1 in fig. 2), who had spent eight years as a junior clerk in government offices in Huancayo, began to work as an itinerant accountant doing the books of local craftsmen in the town, "because the maestros didn't know commerce" (*porque los maestros no sabían el commercio*). Herminio's father put a lot of pressure on him and his brother to go into livestock rearing, but they both resisted, Herminio eventually setting up his own watch repair shop and silversmith, and his brother setting up a bakery in Huancayo.

Martin Ramos (no. 9) too was rarely to be seen in Huasicancha. When one tries to inquire just what he *was* doing, people smile and say, "¿Martin? *¿Quién sabe?* He lived off the *hombres grandes* wherever he could find them." In fact during the 1950s Martin Ramos was the mayordomo of a hacienda in Huancavelica and then went into small-scale mining. Another close associate of Victor's, who had been alcalde in 1948, was his wife's brother, Angelino Cano. He too left the village and remained away in Huancayo and Lima throughout the 1950s and 1960s, eventually going into fruit selling in Lima.

If we look for a moment at the offspring of these people, we get some idea of the extent to which Huasicanchinos became involved in nonfarm activities in the lean years of the 1930s and 1940s.

Herminio Zarate (no. 1) himself left Huasicancha very young (14 years old) so that it is not surprising that none of his children have spent any time there. Herminio himself has now reduced his livestock holding in the village to a few token animals and his children told me, "You know more about the village than we do."

Elias Yaurivilca's (no. 5) children have a shop and a garage in Huancayo. They are very involved in Huasicanchino affairs in Huancayo and continue to have livestock in Huasicancha. Their father is famous in the village and in Huancayo as the longtime secretary of the local arm of APRA.

Santos Hinostrosa (no. 6), Victor's brother, had three children, all of whom live in Lima and all of whom have interests in Huasicancha (I discuss one of these enterprises, that of Mauro, no. 14, in detail below).

Martin Ramos (no. 9) had five children. The three eldest and the youngest daughter are all married and live in Lima. The penultimate child, a son, remains in Huasicancha.

Victor Hinostrosa's (no. 10) children all live outside the village, though they maintain their interests there.

Angelino Cano had three sons. The eldest, Pedro (no. 20) got through high school during his military service and then went on to the local university. He now works for the ministry of education, but his wife brings in at least half their income by running a market stall. The next eldest (no. 21) operates a light truck as a *flotero* in Lima, picking up onetime jobs as he can. In the strawberry season he contracts to pick and transport strawberries for retail sale. His wife works at home; they have five children. The third son lived in Lima too but was killed in 1972 when, trying to get home late at night and very tired, he fell from an overpass on to the downtown Lima thruway.

Felix Pomayay (no. 11) is also mentioned on the diagram, though more distantly related to Victor, through his marriage to Victor's uncle's daughter. But our discussion of the case of Grimaldo and Angelina below will bring us into contact with many of Felix's children.

The picture that emerges from the above list is that at least for this slice of the Huasicancha totality, migration has had a significant effect. The majority of children are no longer resident in Huasicancha, though few of these are entirely without some interest—usually in the form of livestock ownership—in the village economy. So now let us look in more detail at the enterprises of the contemporary generation. Just as Victor and Juana were the node from which we moved out to other households, so this time first the household of Mauro and Guillermina Hinostrosa (no. 14 in fig. 2) and then that of Grimaldo and Angelina Pomayay (no. 29) can now be similarly treated. The former household is located in Lima, the latter in Huasicancha.

Mauro and Guillermina Hinostrosa's Domestic Enterprise (no. 14 in fig. 2)

Mauro, father (fa), 38 years old.
Guillermina, mother (mo), 34 years old.
Son (so$_1$) 14
Daughter (da$_1$) 13
Daughter (da$_2$) 11
Son (so$_2$) 8
Son (so$_3$) 3

Mauro and Guillermina's household enterprise is typical of those migrants to Lima who arrived in the late 1940s and early 1950s establishing themselves first at the coralon in Petit Thouars and then eventually moving to the barriadas (shantytowns) that were to emerge as so distinctive a feature of the Lima landscape from the 1950s on (Matos Mar 1961; Mangin 1970; Collier 1971; Turner 1972*a*, 1972*b*). Of the roughly 1,000 adult Huasicanchinos living in Lima, some 40 percent gained their living in enterprises similar to Mauro and Guillermina's.

Mauro and Guillermina live with their five children (all under 15 years old) in a barriada called La Campiña, a half hour bus ride from the commercial area of Lima. The household as a unit is engaged in at least fourteen different kinds of livelihood, and each of these involve household members to varying degrees with extrahousehold people. They have had their house of part concrete slabs, part straw-matted walls for the past eleven years in the barriada, and before that Mauro had been living in the Petit Thouars coralon since 1958.

For all household members skill in systematic, long range planning is less useful than skill in rapid responses and adaptibility to opportunities as they arise. Indeed, in turning to Mauro and Guillermina's household, it is well to remember the haphazard nature of opportunities: it is not easy to convey time and energy expended in tasks nor the unpredictable nature of daily meetings with other Huasicanchinos at which information is exchanged, credit and labor arrangements made, and so on, nor even the very small amounts of cash and material which each small operation involves. To get some sense of this, I will describe a day's fieldwork in 1972 (see table 2).

I first met Mauro at Petit Thouars in October of that year before the strawberry season had begun. It was three in the afternoon, and he was reorganizing the fruit on his tricycle prior to handing it over to his eldest son, who had just arrived from school to take over the selling. "I do the regular customers, going from door to door," Mauro said. "Then Felix, he is young and can move the tricycle fast; he unloads as much of what is left as he can, by touring the streets for casual sales." He then invited me to join him in his 1950 Ford pickup for a trip to his piggery. After about an hour's journey out of Lima we turned off the main road and followed a track over a hill in the desert to encounter a sight perhaps beyond the inventive powers of the greatest satirist. Stretching beneath us in neat rectangular plots was a vast shantytown made up of what appeared to be miniature shacks. Many had small gardens laid out before them with a few flowers and possibly a vegetable or two. A few even sported the Peruvian flag. It was a barriada of pigs. In reply to my astonished inquiries, Mauro laughed and said, "It is forbidden for people to stay here overnight. Only the guard lives here," and he pointed to the guard house as we passed. The bloated carcass of a dead pig lay beside it on the road. We had loaded the truck with spoiled fruit from the coralon, and after feeding it to the pigs—seventeen full grown and a litter of eight—we fetched water from a large tank at the end of the road. Mauro told me that he is one of seven partners in the piggery and that they take turns in coming out here each

Table 2.   Economic Activities

Activity	Months per year	Hrs. per day or days per wk.	Participants
Tricycle fruit selling	12	6 hrs. for 5½ days	fa, so$_1$
Fruit transportation	7	2 hrs. for 6 days	fa
Strawberry picking contract	5	3 hrs. for 6 days	fa
Strawberry transportation	5	1 hr. for 6 days	fa
Strawberry spoilage selling	5	1½ hrs. for 5 days	fa
Strawberry picking	5	3 hrs. for 5 days	mo, da$_1$, da$_2$
Strawberry retail selling	5	6 hrs. for 5 days	mo, da$_1$
Agriculture	12	When possible. At least 1 day	fa, mo, so$_1$.
Piggery	12	3 hrs. for 1 day	fa
Washing	12	cachuelo[a]	mo
Child-minding	12	cachuelo	da$_1$, da$_2$.
Saxophone playing	7	Average: 1 evening per 2 wks.	fa
Car-washing	7	cachuelo	so$_1$, so$_2$.

Notes: The table is meant to be used only as a convenient point of reference. Time and participation information are only rough guides.

[a]"Cachuelo" is the term used for occasional or "casual" work. Underlining indicates the participant contributing the major amount of work.

day. His partners were all Huasicanchinos, and they hoped to expand to about forty pigs.

We returned home via Petit Thouars. It was now after six o'clock. Felix had returned with the tricycle but had disappeared again. Nobody knew where or if he was coming back. Most other tricyclists had finished and either gone home to their barriadas or sat outside their shacks at the coralon. A couple of tricyclists passed by on their way back to the Surquillo coralon, and there was some discussion about a social event. The two men began to apologize to Mauro because he was not included in the band which was to play that night. Mauro replied that he was not at all put out. He had enough work as it was, and he was going to give up saxophone playing anyhow. Discussion turned to fruit selling: the unstable prices, the relative value of domestic versus Chilean apples, a particular wholesaler who had cheated them in the morning, the risks of tampering with their own weighscales on the tricycles, and the uncertainty of the enforcement of new laws concerning ambulant selling.

We then drove back to Mauro's barriada, about three quarters of an hour's drive away. On arrival I met Guillermina, and we began to talk about her day. It had consisted of shopping, then picking up two children from a neighbor for the day, then preparing food, then receiving a visitor who brought a pile of washing for her to do, then putting aside food preparation to attend to the washing, then persuading her second daughter, who had returned from school at the lunch break, not to go back to school but mind the children while she did the washing, then back to the food preparation, then returning the two children to their home, then cooking the meal, and now talking to a polite but somewhat inconvenient gringo visitor. At this, she laughed and left me with Mauro as she went to the kitchen to finish preparing supper.

Mauro started working in Lima when he was eighteen, twenty years ago (the "present" now being 1973). He was a bachelor, and he lived with his aunt at Petit Thouars. He started out by selling fruit from a basket, walking the streets. He did this on behalf of another, older migrant who gave him an allowance, but for the first year he did not partake in the profits and losses of his sales. He then began selling on his own account. By 1958 he had bought a tricycle with credit from his uncle, Victor, at no interest. He had married Guillermina in Huasicancha the previous year, but she did not move permanently to Lima until 1961, when they moved to the barriada. At that point the livestock that Guillermina had been shepherding were moved into Victor's flock.

Mauro and Guillermina are engaged in the running of a multioccupational enterprise. During much of the day Mauro is engaged in selling strawberries from a tricycle, but he stores his tricycle at Petit Thouars, together with other barriada dwellers, as well as the people who live in the coralon themselves. In return for this he transports fruit each day from the central wholesale market to the coralon. The fruit is bought in bulk by partners who then divide it up before setting out on their day's selling. Those not involved either in Mauro's buying partnership (there are five of them) or in storing his equipment, pay him a fixed amount per day for transportation.

From roughly 9:30 to 3:00 p.m. Mauro is involved in retail selling. But he also devotes time to a number of other ventures, one of which is the piggery already described and which takes up one afternoon each week. Another is his ownership of a small plot of irrigated land on the edge of Lima. This is owned by Mauro and three Lima partners who work the land with him and two Huasicancha partners who were asked for credit when the land was bought. One of the Lima partners is Mauro's brother (no. 13, fig. 2), and one of the Huasicancha partners is his uncle, Victor. Their ambition is to grow strawberries and other cash crops on the land, but at present all the land is devoted to growing foodstuffs for the immediate families. This plot of land requires considerable attention that Mauro and Guillermina can ill afford to give. For two years, Victor's unmarried daughter (no. 18) was brought from the village and lived at the plot, working the land, but she had recently married, and now Mauro and Guillermina have to try to get there as often as possible.

For five months of the year, Mauro is involved in various aspects of straw-berry selling as are most other ex-residents. The work involves Guillermina too and often the children. Mauro advances cash to the owner of the straw-berry fields in order to acquire rights to buy his strawberries. He then makes agreements with various Huasicanchino retail sellers to come out with him between 5 and 6 a.m. and pick strawberries. Mauro divides up the unsorted fruit among the pickers and sells it to them. He then pays the grower on the basis of what has been picked. He claims that his profit covers no more than the costs of transport and other "costs." The pickers are then brought back to the inner city where a hectic job of washing the strawberries and sorting them into categories according to size takes place. They then, by about 9:30, set off for their various locations in the city where the strawberries are sold from baskets.

The strawberry pickers consist of two groups. On the one hand, Mauro brings down people from Huasicancha for this job. Victor comes down each year, as do two other men with whom Mauro has a variety of other economic ties (one of them is Grimaldo of our next case study). Whether or not these people sell entirely for their own account or pay a small amount to Mauro per week, depends on the degree to which they are performing tasks for him in Huasicancha. It also depends on the continuity of their past connections with him. Thus, in 1972 Victor stayed with Mauro, ate at his table, and used his equipment (baskets, scales etc.), but sold for his own account. But at that time he was deeply involved in Mauro's affairs, caring for his sheep, and having advanced capital for at least two of his Lima ventures. But, by 1981 Victor was still doing the same thing, and still selling on his own account, though by then he no longer performed any reciprocal favors for Mauro.

The other group of pickers and sellers are people already living in Lima. For these people the relationship with Mauro is based strictly on cash terms and, moreover, on daily cash terms; fruit is paid for before Mauro pays the grower. These people arrive for the picking either by turning up at Mauro's point of departure in the morning or by getting word to him the previous day so that he can pick them up. The number and personnel of the team, then, varies each day, and this is primarily because retail selling is so hazardous that people do not know from one day to the next if they will be able to gen-erate enough cash to buy the next day's fruit. Even so, Mauro only takes people he knows well and whom he can trust not to damage the plants or pick fruit before it has properly ripened, or avoid picking fruit that may appear overripe and thus subject to quick spoilage. Since pickers are likely to be tempted to do these things, depending on the going price for fruit, it is impor-tant for Mauro to be able to control the quality of picking through personal influence. Hence, Mauro favors pickers from the Petit Thouars coralon where he has much influence. Some loss from spoilage can be marginally offset by taking the fruit to the conserve factories in the evenings where a price, usually below the original purchase price, is paid. Mauro uses his truck for this job. He collects the fruit, sells it, and then delivers the money the next day, taking off a fixed price for transportation.

Finally, Guillermina usually tries to sell strawberries on her own account during the season, though she often finds it hard to put together the time. Mauro encourages her in this because they always need the money but also because Guillermina is able to provide him with reliable information on trends in retail selling: prices are very volatile from day to day, and Mauro must know them in order to negotiate the price he pays to the grower.

The Hinostrosa domestic enterprise is, then, a composite of multifarious activities. And just as this variety of occupations should reflect for us, not wealth, but poverty, so we should be careful too not to overemphasize the systematic nature of the operations. If there is anything of regularity it is a propensity to act quickly in response to opportunities and the absence of any huge bounty deriving from them. Despite the continual manipulation of trading capital and the number of activities that are undertaken, the insubstantial and spasmodic nature of the income thus generated mitigates against its being systematically accumulated. Moreover calculating the "profits" from the various livelihood activities is further limited because the Hinostrosas do not make a distinction between domestic outlay and entrepreneurial outlay.

Household consumption, capital, outlay and expenses for social events are all lumped together as the overall costs of reproducing the viability of the enterprise. And this is to be expected. Take the example of the household's need for rice. To get it cheap Mauro buys in bulk at the wholesale price, and then Guillermina sells off the balance. She does this partly through the network she has available within the context of the confederation of households, partly through a looser network she has with other women in the barriada, and partly by herself selling small quantities in the barriada market on subsequent days. In all three cases, however, the price is scarcely above the original cost. Even if she sells at cost, "taking a position" in rice has still allowed them to acquire domestic needs below retail prices, and the entrepreneurial function and household consumption have been united.[2]

This is not to say that savings are never accumulated, but in this respect it is important to note precisely what was involved on those occasions when Mauro and Guillermina needed to produce cash for investment into fixed equipment such as the plot of land, the piggery, or the old pick-up truck. On all such occasions money was raised, without interest payments, through interpersonal ties, and in most cases this was done through the sale of livestock.[3] Advancing credit in this way is an essential component of keeping a wide network of interpersonal channels open, and a persistent inability (or unwillingness) to find such credit when called upon can have the effect of isolating an enterprise. As a result household members will liquidate one branch of the household's operation to provide capital requested by a confederate household elsewhere. In this way Mauro and Guillermina sold their entire holding of pigs and terminated their partnership in the piggery in 1974 to provide capital for a confederate in Huancayo.

The use of credit to maintain relationships and the use of relationships to acquire credit are two sides of the same coin. But what are the kinds of relationships in which Mauro engaged to acquire labor? Broadly speaking they were of three kinds: labor mobilized by the use of a domestic relationship, labor mobilized by the use of a relationship to a broader field of reciprocity, and labor mobilized by the use of (a relationship to) money. The implications of these differences are the subject of the next chapter; here I may simply note that the first two require the parties involved to stand in a particular relationship to one another prior to the transaction: they must be categorized as domestic and community members respectively (G. Smith 1986). As for the third, the relationship is indifferent as to person. In Mauro's case this only occurred with *some* of the people who picked strawberries and, even here, the parties were not entirely "indifferent as to persons," but came in great measure from the Petit Thouars coralon.

Besides the various occupations of the Hinostrosa's enterprise in Lima, they are also tied into a confederation of households in Huancayo and Huasicancha, of whom I have so far mentioned only Victor's by name. In fact, however, the confederation of which Mauro and Guillermina were a part is going through a process of reformulation. Victor, who provided one of the chief partners in the pastoral side of things, is getting old. Moreover many of his Lima connections are being concentrated in the enterprise of his son, Salvador (no. 22, fig. 2), who has gradually become established there. Indeed in 1973 and 1974 Victor no longer stayed with Mauro on his trips to Lima. As a result Mauro is becoming increasingly involved in another confederation that itself is undergoing reformulation. This link has been made because one of its members is Victor's next-door neighbor in the village, Grimaldo Pomayay (no. 29 in fig. 2), who has increasingly through this proximity been of assistance to Victor. In anticipation of this new alliance, to oil the wheels of good will as it were, Victor agreed to become Grimaldo and Angelina's padrino at their wedding in 1972. So we can turn now to Grimaldo and Angelina's enterprise, focusing this time especially on their links into the confederation of households of which they are part.

Grimaldo and Angelina Pomayay's Domestic Enterprise (no. 29 in Fig. 2)

Grimaldo, 24 years old.
Angelina, 23 years old.
Son, 3.
Daughter, 1.

Although Grimaldo and Angelina only became formally married in 1972, they have been living in *convivencia* for four years.[4] During this time they have lived in the house of Grimaldo's parents, and, with the coming marriage, Grimaldo built a house attached to the yard of the old house. The Pomayays are not especially well off by village standards. Although Grimaldo's mother comes from a well-known pastoralist family, there were eleven offspring who had to divide up the patrimony, and Grimaldo's father is not remembered for having been especially successful at the height of his career. Grimaldo has five years of primary schooling that he received in the village, and, like 90 percent of his peers, he can read and write.

After his schooling he spent four years in Lima at the house of his brother, where he contributed his labor to his brother's enterprise and also sold strawberries on his own account during the season. He returned to the village to take up residence with Angelina, and four years later they own outright a few sheep and insufficient land to meet their consumption needs, which include, besides themselves, their two small children and a third that is on the way. The demands on Grimaldo's time are seasonal, but he spent 60 percent of his time in 1972 working on arable land. With only 0.8 hectares of land of his own, it is obvious that this time is not confined to his own chacra. In fact it is directly a function of the household's links to others.

As for Angelina, she brought no land with her. She is the illegitimate child of a widow who has one surviving legitimate son. Her mother's flock of sheep numbers between three and four hundred head, but four years after her partnership with Grimaldo, Angelina remains uncertain about her share of this flock. Although her half brother has recently begun to spend more time at the estancia (to solidify his claim), Angelina spent all her working life prior to marriage shepherding the flock. Her mother recognizes Angelina as her daughter, so that she should be able to claim between one and two hundred head of sheep.[5] Angelina, however, divides her time between her mother's estancia and that of Grimaldo's brother Maglorio (no. 25 in fig. 2). Both estancias contain sheep that belong neither to Angelina's mother nor to Maglorio, and Angelina's work at these estancias reflects the fact that these other animals belong to enterprises to which the couple have economic ties.

It is clear that for both of them, their allotment of labor does not reflect so much their own property but the linkages they have to other enterprises whose particular characteristics thus influence the development of Grimaldo and Angelina's enterprise. It may be a simplification to suggest that the Pomayays are arable and pastoral farmers to the extent that their closest economic partners are not so, but it does help to stress the point that their linkages to nonfarm sources of income are greatly dependent upon extrahousehold ties that in turn are maintained by their contributions of labor in agriculture.

Since Angelina is an illegitimate child who spent most of her life on the lonely estancia of her mother, the couple initiated their economic ties through the use of Grimaldo's connections. Gradually however the initial advantages of making extrahousehold ties along the lines of past close relationships, i.e., in this case Grimaldo's siblings, have come into contradiction with the requirements both of Grimaldo and Angelina's enterprise and those of the other confederates. Grimaldo and Angelina therefore decided to use the occasion of their marriage to establish close ties with Victor Hinostrosa by asking him to be the padrino of the marriage. This serves as the beginning of a new confederation that is likely to extend toward Angelina's half brother in one direction, to the gradual exclusion of Grimaldo's existing ties to his brother Maglorio, and toward Mauro Hinostrosa, in Lima, to the exclusion of Grimaldo's brother there, Tomas (no. 24). To see how this development has occurred, we must look at the enterprises involved.

Grimaldo's eldest brother, Teodoro (no. 23), lives in Huancayo. He has four children, all of whom are at school. His wife does some dressmaking at home, but by far the greatest part of their income is derived from Teodoro's job as a shop assistant in a hardware store. His six brothers consider him fortunate in having a regular and reasonably secure income, and Teodoro gives the impression of being the most affluent of the brothers, with a large adobe house in a suburb of Huancayo. He was the only one earning regular cash wages, and there is a sense in which his livelihood was a mirror image of Grimaldo's. While he did indeed spread his resources through the confederation, holding sheep at Maglorio's estancia, investing in two of Tomas's operations, and having Grimaldo cultivate his chacra, he was becoming increasingly unenthusiastic about this. His wage provided him with what he saw to be a solid base substituting for the security deriving from a wide network, and he was anxious to use his savings for trading ventures in Huancayo. At the annual reunion of the confederation at Maglorio's estancia in August of 1972, he announced that the distribution of his livestock and other capital all over the place was inconsistent with good accounting practices, and he thought this would be the last year that he would have the time for visits such as these. Earlier in the year, though, Grimaldo had gone to Huancayo, prompted by Teodoro, where he had spent the days selling some "damaged" hardware around the markets of Huancayo. He had split the profits with his brother and used the proceeds toward the costs of his wedding party.

Tomas (no. 24 in fig. 2), the next eldest brother, is 38 and lives in Lima where he and his wife run a multioccupational enterprise that in 1972 included, besides selling fruit from a tricycle, a small marketstall in the barriada run by Tomas's wife, and two plots of land, one within the barriada but with access to some water on which he and a partner grow ornamental plants for sale in Miraflores and San Isidro, the wealthy suburbs of Lima, and one plot of land an hour and a half down the Pan-American highway, which he owns with five partners (two of whom are Teodoro and Maglorio) and on which he grows subsistence crops and some cash crops including strawberries and flowers.

Tomas and his wife, Feliciana, have six children, none of whom are yet old enough to help them run their domestic enterprise, and the pressure on the two of them is immense. In 1972 Tomas's greatest hopes were in the distant plot of land on the Pan-American highway that had been expropriated under the new agrarian reform. But a condition of purchase had been that all land be put into use, and Tomas was scarcely cultivating a fifth of it. He was constantly pressing his confederates for labor, but increasingly the demands of their own enterprises made these requests futile and embarrassing to all concerned. Indeed as each brother approached a period during which he had nonproductive young children, he was no longer able or interested in working with Tomas.

Tomas's first recourse was to his spiritual sister, a single parent, the cousin of his wife (who was not from Huasicancha). He suggested that she and her nine-year-old son join his household but not in sociable Lima, rather out there on the lonely plot of land down the Pan-American highway. And there she lived, caring for the plot of land but unable to extend the area under cultivation.

Perpetually afraid of losing the land, Tomas and Feliciana decided to invest in a mule and approached Teodoro for funds. Teodoro, however, declared himself to be overextended, a declaration that Grimaldo found hard to believe, since this request followed immediately after the little windfall he had shared with Teodoro. Then tragedy was added to misfortune when Tomas's spiritual sister became ill alone in the remote shack with her small son, and she died. This left the land unattended and Tomas with one more mouth to feed. By 1973, it was clear that Tomas was no longer able to maintain his links in the confederation and that he had exhausted the obligations that derived from his past interpersonal relations.[6]

Eventually, in fear of it being expropriated, the land on the Pan-American highway was sold by Tomas and Feliciana at a loss.[7] Then the cost of water at the barriada plot led to the folding of the ornamental plant venture. Feliciana now increased her market operations, but the children were always a problem, and in the end Tomas gave up his tricycle and spent the time at home. There he bought condiments in bulk and spent the days repacking them into smaller containers, which he sold to retail sellers.

Returning once more to Grimaldo, he has the use of the Huasicancha chacra of both Teodoro and Tomas. This is not a sharecropping arrangement, however, in which owner and tenant share the proceeds. The food produced on this land is Grimaldo and Angelina's, and what he takes to either of his two brothers when he visits them, he considers gifts subject to his own generosity. In reality the arable land around Huasicancha is too high to offer very good returns for the work that must go into it, and virtually all of it is consumed in Huasicancha. Few ex-residents show much interest in the produce from their chacra and, although this is partly a strategic attitude in the politics of reciprocity, it also reflects the low value they place on their chacra. Grimaldo therefore derived few resources for maintaining extrahousehold ties through his arable farming. In effect he was allowed to be the beneficiary of the chacra so that his labor would be available during the rest of the year to be used by other confederates.

While this situation means that Grimaldo and Angelina are best shielded from swings in the market economy, it consigns them to perpetual inability to develop their enterprises and, as their children multiply and Grimaldo becomes less mobile, he is less prepared to provide labor to others. Hitherto Maglorio, the third eldest of the brothers, had done most of the shepherding of confederates' animals, but Grimaldo and Angelina were now beginning to offer that service too, through access to Angelina's mother's estancia, to which Grimaldo was devoting increasing amounts of time. Tomas, in Lima, of course was at this time in no position to invest in sheep, but Grimaldo had already given a few lambs to Mauro, his potentially new confederate, an act that was intended to encourage him to keep sheep at Grimaldo and Angelina's estancia.

So a shift was taking place in the confederation of households that embraced Teodoro, Tomas, Maglorio, and Grimaldo. This was given further impetus when Teodoro lost his job as a shop assistant and was threatened with imprisonment for theft. By this time he had already made his own attempts to reduce his extrahousehold commitments within the confederation, and this unfortunate development had the effect of cutting off his advance into petty commodity relations without hope of retreat into the reciprocal links of the confederation (see the next chapter for further discussion of this phenomenon). He immediately sold virtually all his livestock held by Maglorio and set himself up as a *carnicero,* an intermediary, buying sheep in the highland villages and selling them in the Mantaro Valley markets. In this role he told me that he hoped to perform an essential service in the links necessary to the confederation and one that had hitherto always been performed by outsiders.

But his relatives were not of the same opinion and told him emphatically that there was no room for a livestock intermediary within the bounds of the confederation. Livestock is, in effect, the commodity face of the village households, just as fruit is the commodity face of the Lima households. They become commodities the moment the carnicero digs his fingers through their fleeces to feel the meat on the ribcages. The activity of the carnicero was therefore seen to be incompatible with the social relations among members of a confederation. So the confederation that had seen Grimaldo and Angelina's household established as an enterprise began to disintegrate and this now led them toward a new set of relationships more suitable to the requirements of their enterprise.

Both multioccupational enterprises and confederations of households are means for reducing the risks inherent in concentration on any one operation on the margins of the economy. Existing institutions based on various forms of reciprocal exchange are amenable to such a strategy and essentially incompatible with its converse: the concentration of resources into one operation within the domestic enterprise. A prerequisite for reciprocal relationships is continuity in interpersonal ties (a feature not required for relationships mediated through commodities), and this means that where the integrity of past relationships had not been broken, potential channels are available to the enterprise.

This is certainly what occurred in the cases so far presented, all of whose participants would fit firmly into the category of pastoralists referred to earlier as canchas. For other migrants, however, while the institutions remained available in principle, in fact the continuity of personal relationships had been reduced, limiting the use to which those institutions could be put. Nevertheless the unstable conditions of the informal economy that they faced remained the same for these people as for those discussed in the case studies so far. So we must now examine another set of cases to see what occurred there. The essence of the distinction between these two kinds of Huasicanchinos—those who used past ties for mobilizing resources versus those who lacked such ties—makes the kind of genealogical diagram presented in figure 2 an unsuitable means for getting at the character of these latter kinds of enterprises. For the people I am about to discuss, other means had to be employed for mobilizing resources.

Eulogio and Eufresenia Ramos's Domestic Enterprise

Eulogio, 33 years old.
Eufresenia, 34 years old.
Son, 11.
Daughter, 9.
Daughter, 5.
Son, 1.

In the previous case studies the continuity of the past made an impact on the relationships internal to the household itself. Family members' past connections, beyond the immediate household, had a powerful effect on the way the domestic enterprise itself operated, indeed so much so that the boundaries of the domestic sphere itself become obscured. The rationality of one domestic unit cannot be understood when isolated from the web of other, confederated units. The difference between those cases and this one of Eulogio and Eufresenia is perhaps nicely summed up by the genealogical chart: while a genealogy of these linkages provides such a useful organizing principle for looking at the former cases, it would not work so well for the case of Eulogio and Eufresenia. And where it would be impossible to draw up a meaningful balance sheet of profits and losses for any single domestic enterprise in our previous examples, such a balance sheet becomes a key organizing principle for the case we are about to embark upon and, with some limitations (as we shall see), does make sense for the Ramoses.

For the kind of Huasicanchinos to whom I have referred as the huasis, and of whom this case study provides an example, migration to Lima was institutionalized somewhat later—in the mid-sixties, rather than the early fifties. And, in the absence of extensive sets of relationships embedded in the past, it began as a makeshift and individual experience. Migration initially lacked well-placed stepping stones so that makeshift arrangements made by individuals acting alone replaced the plans of a number of households, endowed with extensive ties acting in conjunction. Then such a past experience subsequently affects the rationality of the enterprises as they operate today in Lima; while the long-run intentions of these migrants may be directed toward the initiation of a confederation of households in response to the hazards of single-occupation livelihoods in Lima's volatile economy, the real limitations of their interpersonal resources restrict the possibilities of their succeeding in doing so.

Nevertheless, it is still through a network of Huasicanchino relationships that they (and domestic enterprises like theirs) obtain cheap food, find aid in times of family crisis, seek out a squat in one of the newer barriadas (or get involved in the invasion of land to form a new barriada), and seek out partners for their small ventures. But in the absence of long-established direct relationships between households both in the city and in the village, these people have to seek out another arena in which contacts with Huasicanchinos are made. To do so they are inclined to make more public symbolic statements of their "Huasicanchino-ness" than would people in the previous cases.

This takes on specific expression through two institutions: Huasicanchino football clubs and a Huasicanchino *Sindicato de Vendedores Ambulantes de Frutas* [Union of Ambulant Fruit Sellers]. The former, ostensibly formed for the preservation of village traditions among the young, provide an arena in which migrants with less well-established direct interhousehold links can interact to seek out information, possible partnerships, and so on. The latter, ostensibly formed as a union of those sharing a specific occupation and working in a certain series of locations on the Lima streets, is in fact entirely composed of Huasicanchinos and provides an arena for similar interaction. But while the former is expressed through reference to symbols of the rural community and its central occupation as farmers, the latter is expressed by reference to the occupation of fruitseller through the urban institution of the sindicato. But to arrive at these broader arenas of their interpersonal relationships, we must begin with the experiences of Eulogio and Eufresenia themselves.

They now live, together with their four children (of which the oldest is eleven), in a recently-formed shantytown of shacks made of reed matting some hour-and-a-half by bus from the commercial center of Lima. Eulogio and Eufresenia took part in a land invasion in order to squat on this land in the barriada of Mariano Melgar. This move was essential once they had decided, five years ago, to bring Eufresenia and the children down from Huasicancha permanently. Prior to that Eulogio had been living in the second of the Huasicanchino's two inner-city coralones, Surquillo (see chap. 4). This coralon has not attained the strong association with Huasicancha and Huasicanchinos found at Petit Thouars, the older coralon, partly because it came into existence ten years later and hence is less well established and partly because the Huasicanchinos do not monopolize the entire coralon.

Eulogio's migration history (see table 3) serves as an excellent example of the kind of uncertainty involved in migration prior to its becoming an institutionalized procedure. By the time he first arrived in Lima in 1958 at eighteen, he was a well-seasoned migrant. The initial impetus for migration had come when a relatively poor farm enterprise in Huasicancha began to collapse as a result of a domestic crisis. When he was eight his mother died. He and his brother remained with his father, but his two sisters were given over in adoption to another family. Eulogio's father supplemented farm income by traveling around making and repairing harnesses. His long absences made it hard to keep the boys at home, and in 1954 he remarried and soon began to have more children. At this point Eulogio left. He was fourteen.

That year he was in Huancayo selling newspapers, working in a bakery, and getting occasional work around the market. He had trouble finding any permanent place to sleep and simply moved from one place to another each night. His sister meanwhile was working as a domestic in Tarma, a town on the road to the jungle, and he went there twice for periods of a few months, but no long-term jobs arose. So he then moved to La Oroya, the large smelting town. There he found a job in a shop, and he started to go back to school at night. But he says that he kept falling asleep and in the end gave it up. After six months he moved to Moracocha, a nearby mining center, where he found work as an assistant to a Huasicanchino who worked in a bakery there. This lasted for three months. Then he returned to Huancayo in search of work.

Huancayo had nothing to offer him, and Eulogio decided to invest what little money he had in getting to Lima, where he made his way to Surquillo.

Table 3.   Eulogio's Life-History Outline

Year	Age	Event
1940		Born, Huasicancha
1948	8	Mother dies
1954	14	Father remarries
		Moves to Huancayo
[Over next four years. . . .]		Sells newspapers, Huancayo
		Works in bakery, Huancayo
		Visits sister, Tarma
		Works in shop, La Oroya (6 months)
		Returns to school
		Works in bakery, Moracocha (3 months)
		Returns to Huancayo, finds no work. . . .
1958	18	Sells strawberries, Lima ("Surquillo" Coralon)
1962	22	Marries Eufresenia
		They return to Huasicancha
		Eulogio stays 1 month
		Returns to Lima, leaving Eufresenia in village
		Return trips to Huasicancha at least once a year
1968	28	Returns to Huasicancha "permanently"
		Takes up junior political position
1969	29	Returns to Lima with family
		Participates in land invasion in Lima
1970	30	Builds house in "Mariano Melgar" shanty town

He had a number of friends there but none was able to help him much. It was however the strawberry season, and he started selling from baskets. He carried on this trade for four years. During this time he met Eufresenia who was working as a domestic servant. She too was from Huasicancha.

Surquillo was not in their view a good place to start a family, and so, in 1962, they returned to Huasicancha. They both remember the return after such a long absence as an alienating experience. Eulogio was not welcome at his father's house, and he had few friends in the village. He stayed only a month. Leaving Eufresenia with her family, he returned to Lima where he bought a tricycle.

At this point it is worth reflecting on the situation of Eulogio and Eufresenia. They were both in their early twenties and about to start a family. Neither of them had an extensive or reliable network of personal ties around which to build up a domestic enterprise as we have seen in the previous two cases. Eulogio was working in Lima independently as an ambulante, Eufresenia was living with her parents, working on their chacra and helping tend their few sheep, in return for bed and board. The year was 1963, and a number of Huasicanchinos whom Eulogio did not know especially well were turning attention once more to a land recuperation campaign against Hacienda Tucle. Eulogio made frequent returns to Huasicancha over the next five years. Eufresenia had two more children, and they began to accumulate a small flock of sheep. A number of migrants with backgrounds similar to those of Eulogio and Eufresenia became supporters of the national political party APRA; they were following a similar pattern and began to take on increasing influence in the direction of the land recuperation campaigns.

By early 1968 the land recuperation campaign was showing positive gains, giving people a sense of optimism, and Eulogio joined a group of Huasicanchinos with a similar background who were also supporters of the national party, APRA, and they ran for municipal office under the leadership of a man named German Ojeda. They were elected, and Eulogio built up a friendship with German. As a result of these events he returned to Huasicancha to take up residence there. He was anticipating that his newly acquired political position would give him access to a wider range of personal contacts within the village itself through which he could embark on some kind of coordinated enterprise. This plan was not successful, and Eulogio and Eufresenia's financial situation did not improve with his return to Huasicancha; within a year they both left the village and returned to Lima. For new conditions had arisen which were now to effect the trajectory of their enterprise in a different way.

Visiting Lima ostensibly for the baptism of a friend's child, Eulogio found that, with the coup d'état of October 1968, Surquillo was alive with discussion of a possible land invasion to the south of the built-up area of Lima. Plans were being made with systematic intensity, and Eulogio returned to Huasicancha, discussed the situation with Eufresenia, and they, with their four children, returned to Surquillo.

The planning of the land invasion now became a major preoccupation of their domestic enterprise. Eulogio became a member of one of the planning committees for the area of the Surquillo market, which took much time. Certain bars were known to be the places where people met to exchange information, and a number of people were known as experts who made a full-time career of checking the land registries and the records of deaths and testaments to locate land that was in legal dispute and thus suitable for squatting. The invasion itself (which included vast numbers of people of whom the Huasicanchinos were merely a part) involved the coordination of numerous trucks, minibuses, pick-ups, and buses for transporting families all of whom had to be equipped with enough material to start the semblance of a house as well as staves for marking out the plot.[8]

For Eulogio and Eufresenia, Eufresenia's role was essential in the invasion, as was the children's. Eulogio stayed on the site for the first two weeks, but thereafter he had to get back downtown to continue selling fruit. Shacks left empty during the day were inevitably invaded by others, so that the shack could not be left, not even for minutes, for what thread of ownership there was lay in permanent occupancy.

Once established at Mariano Melgar both Eulogio and Eufresenia ran tricycles. Now far removed from the downtown area, they were faced with the problem of finding a place to store them overnight, and through his activities at football club meetings on Sundays Eulogio found seven other Huasicanchino ambulantes with whom to rent a small space in an enclosed parking lot. This partnership dissolved within a year as did two others set up in subsequent years for this purpose.

Although they had two tricycles, whether Eufresenia went out selling or not depended on the conditions of the market and other demands of the domestic enterprise. The larger, more impressive tricycle was used by Eulogio in the morning to serve a regular clientele at the suburban houses in the morning. It would then be parked on a street corner in the afternoon for Eufresenia to operate for the rest of the day, while Eulogio took to the smaller tricycle, selling fruit at a slightly lower price than slower moving ambulant tricycles. At other periods of the year Eufresenia stayed at the barriada and did some corner selling from a blanket on which was laid out a small selection of fruit.

Eulogio and Eufresenia's contemporary operations, though in many ways resembling the petty commodity operations of Mauro and Guillermina in our second case study, are in fact of a different character. Still they provide us with an opportunity to use conceptual tools of a more strictly economic kind to understand the rationality of their enterprise. By the end of 1973, Eulogio had abandoned his tricycle and bought a second-hand pickup truck. As Mauro had done some years before him, Eulogio made a contract to buy strawberries from a grower. Unlike Mauro, however, he used *jornaleros* (day laborers), none of whom came from Huasicancha, to pick the berries. He then transported them to the gathering spots from which tricyclists set out on their retail selling rounds. This took up the four to five months of the strawberry season, and during this time Eufresenia ran a fruitstall, now permanently established on a corner in a Lima suburb. Eulogio usually relieved her around noon so that she could return to the barriada. For the remainder of the year, Eulogio used the pickup to transport fruit from the central wholesale market to the various tricyclists' gathering points and then opened the stall around nine a.m.

This is by no means a stable position, however. A crisis is looming. Each day, after using his truck for transporting fruit to gathering points, Eulogio once more engages in selling by tricycle, leaving the stall to be operated full time by Eufresenia year round. There are no resources to replace the truck, and Eulogio recognizes that its replacement costs are growing much faster than any chance he has of accumulating money. Eufresenia is complaining of the increasing cost of the food bill, and the two youngest children are showing signs of malnutrition. Faced with the hazards of this situation Eulogio and Eufresenia are relying on the systematic accumulation of the sheep they have been buying in Huasicancha over the past few years. These they both see as the "bottom line" of their capital resources.[9]

By combining data gathered directly from Eulogio and Eufresenia with budget material gathered from 37 other similar informants it is possible to get some idea of the economic circumstances they face.[10]

A tricycle with as many as fifteen varieties of fruit carries between 3,000 to 4,000 soles of fruit on it (say, $70.00 to $100.00).[11] Of this the tricyclist expects to sell between 1,000 and 2,000 soles worth per day at between 15 and 20 percent over cost price, to produce between 150 and 400 soles per day ($3.50 and $9.30). Working six days a week, this brings in a gross total of between $87.50 and $229.00 per month, against which must be deducted the basic daily costs of transportation (for Eulogio from the wholesale market, and for Eufresensia, from the barriadas), tricycle storage overnight, lunch, licensing fees, fines, and bribes. The total comes to $40.50 per month, leaving a net profit of between $47.50 and $188.50. Obviously there are good days and bad days and better and worse locations and so on. But the lower of the two figures represents by no means a disastrous day. It still assumes a considerable turnover of stock at a reasonable markup.

Eulogio and Eufresenia had a family of six people, and a very rough calculation of domestic outlay can be made, though this takes account of no exceptional costs, such as a trip to Huasicancha or the costs of taking on a *cargo* (official position) in a fiesta, or of becoming the godparent of a child— all of which must be considered essential for the reproduction of the enterprise over the long run. In other words, what is included here is the absolute base line of domestic expenses. The amount devoted to "social obligations" (see table 4) does not refer to the personal consumption of the adult male getting drunk on the weekends; it refers to costs incurred by both adults through participation in club events and the life crisis events of others, such as attending baptisms, marriages, etc. Eulogio and Eufresenia's outlay per month is presented in table 4. As can be seen in good months, or in good locations, or possibly with better trading skill, *some* accumulation is possible. But if income is only "reasonable," then a household of Eulogio and Eufresenia's size would run at a deficit of at least $27.00 per month.

In the early years Eufresenia added further income by selling small amounts of vegetables each day in the barriada market. Later on she started selling from a tricycle too, as did Eulogio. But for the moment, I will assume that she is working at her former occupation, which is more representative of other informants in the newer barriadas. This will give us some idea of the degree to which such activities contribute to the viability of the domestic enterprise. I give two sets of figures in table 6. The first assumes that the wife works in small-scale vegetable retailing for four days a week for twelve months of the year. The second assumes that she works for five days a week

Table 4.   Monthly Household Expenses (1973)

Expenses	Soles	U.S. Dollars
Food (including on the job lunch)[a]	2190	51.00
Clothing	100	2.50
Medicine	350	8.00
Educational Expenses	100	2.50
Housing expenses	430	10.00
Social obligations	650	15.00
	3820	89.00

[a]The calculation for food was made at 12 soles per head per day irrespective of age. This was arrived at from my calculations and correlations with a nutritionist, Hilary Creed, who was working in the barriada. Food costs were less elastic than change in diet, i.e.: people changed their consumption patterns rather than spend more for the same food.

Table 5.   Monthly Income from Tricycle (1973)

	Reasonable	Good
Tricycle Income	$47.00	$188.50
Less Household Outlay	$74.00–89.00[a]	$ 74.00–89.00
Potential Accumulation	$00.00	$100.00

[a]The $74.00 figure assumes no expenditure on social obligations.

Table 6.   Monthly Sidewalk Vegetable or Strawberry Selling

	Monthly Income (averaged out over twelve months)
Vegetable selling 4 days a week in barriadas, for twelve months.	$20.00–$63.30
Strawberry selling 5 days a week downtown, for five months.	$10.00–$31.67

for only a certain amount of the year—in this case, five months. Informants felt that it was reasonable to assume that a woman selling strawberries for five months of the year, if she were energetic and lucky, would earn about the same figure as the woman selling a few vegetables for twelve months (hence the Huasicanchinos' attraction to strawberry selling).

If tricycle sales are only reasonable then, a successful sidewalk trader, working five months of the year, could make up the deficit (allowing for no outlay for social obligations). If the man's tricycle sales are "reasonable" and his wife sells strawberries with some success for five months of the year, they will be able to meet social obligations but fail to accumulate. In the case of Eulogio and Eufresenia, her vegetable sales in a good month covered nearly all the immediate household expenses (not including social obligations), leaving Eulogio to use income from tricycle sales both for accumulation and for social obligations. This division, of course, is a significant one, and it reflects the relationship between them: all Eufresenia's labor power is used for direct household requirements, regardless of whether they are the domestic labor of caring for the children, washing clothes or cooking meals, or the income-producing labor of sidewalk selling. While some part of Eulogio's tricycle income *is* used for family expenses and while much of that income and much of his activity *is* directly concerned with the viability of the household as a domestic enterprise, the priority for that income is toward entrepreneurial ventures, and the focus of that social activity is outward and away from the household itself. It is important, therefore, that we turn attention now to the means by which this domestic enterprise extends its social relationships through personal ties beyond the household.

Eulogio and Eufresenia need partnerships for running the various aspects of their enterprise. They need a partnership with somebody in Huasicancha who will care for the sheep they are trying to accumulate and for the chacra they want to maintain in use. They also need a set of partners to share in renting a location for the storage of the tricycles. Once Eulogio decided to buy a pickup truck, he needed to find credit to help pay for it, and the way open to him was to make somebody else a partner in the ownership of the truck until the debt could be paid off.

While Eulogio himself was disparaging of the extent to which the confederations of households put constraints on the initiative of members, he was nevertheless aware of the advantages pertaining to their operation, and he was continually trying to construct a network of partners along similar lines. But the preconditions were not in place either for him or Eufresenia. Their enterprise today is the product of a history of their (and their parents') specific insertion into the social relations of Huasicancha's past. Both Eulogio and Eufresenia's parents had a very narrow range of interpersonal connections; this in turn affected their ability to make use of migration as a livelihood strategy, giving to Eulogio's career a discontinuity which, in itself, worked against establishing enduring interpersonal links. So Eufresenia and Eulogio have to find an arena in which first to seek out such linkages and then to provide a context that will give them stability and endurance. This is done by making use of Huasicanchino institutions in Lima, but because these institutions are of more recent origin and more tenuously linked to the community of Huasicancha than those reciprocal practices that have emerged (with relative continuity) both within the village and also among the confederations of households, so the ritual activities attached to these institutions are more self-conscious and vivid. This becomes clear when we compare the relationship of the fiesta of Santiago to the confederated arrangements among households on the one hand, and the relationship of a marriage ceremony to the institutions that serve to actualize linkages for migrants like Eulogio and Eufresenia in Lima, on the other.

A major social event for households involved in confederations is the return to Huasicancha in August for the Santiago festival that takes place at the estancias where their sheep are kept. In these events as many of the households as possible, be they from La Oroya, Huancayo, Lima, or Huasicancha, journey up into the pasture lands to the various estancias in which their sheep are kept. The ceremony of Santiago ostensibly involves the ensuring of the fertility of the flock for the coming year, but it is essentially a period during which the reallotment of animals to various *pastores* [shepherds] takes place, and the claim of the estancia to its specific location is reasserted by the presence of a large number of people around its hearth, which in effect is a statement of its legitimate existence on that particular stretch of pasture. Santiago then expresses the precise relationships of the households engaged in livestock rearing on any one estancia. Because confederated households may have sheep located in a variety of estancias, these arrangements are quite extensive. As a result it is not surprising that many confederated households spend as much as four or five weeks celebrating Santiago in the puno of Huasicancha.

Eulogio, by contrast, if he happens to be in Huasicancha for the fiestas patrias in July, may attend a small, almost token Santiago just above the perimeters of the village, and Eufrensenia never attends. They do, of course, have a village household caring for their sheep, but this arrangement is unlike those of the confederations. Eulogio pays the old woman who cares for their sheep with what he calls a *propina* ("tip"). This is done on a regular basis, only allowing her some of the newborn lambs when they are unable to lay hold of the necessary amount of cash for the propina. As for their chacra there is so little of it that Eulogio's sister and her family are unable to live off it plus their own small plots, so that her husband supplements the household's income by weaving ponchos, *mantas* [shawls] and *costales* [woolen sacks].[12] Eulogio receives no produce from this land and keeps it cultivated partly for the sake of his sister and partly so the land cannot be claimed by some other villager as unused land.

Far more important for Eulogio than Santiago are the events that revolve around the football clubs and the ambulant sellers' syndicate of which he is the president. Apart from football, many clubs have virtually no existence at all in the minds of members, until some issue or other brings them together. Such issues may be matters affecting just one family or those affecting the

Huasicanchinos as a whole. As such issues occur, different clubs have adjusted their form of response to them. Thus through the 1960s all clubs became active in raising funds for the land recuperation campaign back in Huasicancha. Then, more recently, the newer clubs have provided an organizational focus for land invasions near Lima. These are often the clubs too that organize the ceremonies surrounding the weddings of members or sponsor the Lima enactment of a seasonal fiesta normally performed in Huasicancha.

Indeed the extent to which football clubs respond to the present needs of members is nicely illustrated by an extreme case where eight members of one club formed a partnership for growing and selling ornamental plants. This activity prevailed while football became so secondary that the other club members left to join another club. These partners quickly explain that they were hoping to imbue their business partnership with all the characteristics of solidarity and village patriotism that they had seen occurring when the clubs had been used in the Huasicancha recuperation campaign. In this particular case then, the idiom of the football club was being made to serve— effectively or not—the continuity function found among the confederations of households.

Clearly then, the social life of the clubs is a stronger symbol of Huasicancha identity for those migrants whose center of activity has been Surquillo and whose institutionalized migration has occurred more recently. This fact is expressed in the impatience among most members of confederations of households (like Mauro and Guillermina's, in the second case study) with the social affairs attached to football clubs. They say that not only do these take time away from the running of their multioccupational enterprises, but they are tasteless and offensive.

One such event was a wedding I attended with a tricyclist I had worked with. The ceremony was organized in identical fashion to such an event in Huasicancha: the couple sat at a table beneath a canopy while we sat around the walls of the inner patio of the house in the barriada of Mariano Melgar. But in front of the table, unlike anything I had seen in Huasicancha, stood a new knitting machine. After the meal a person designated "the Secretary" of the event, reflecting the office held in the football club, took out an exercise book, seated himself at the side of the table, and began inscribing the names of the padrinos of the wedding. Both placed a one hundred sole note in a plate on the table. Now each guest came up to the table and put a sum of money in the plate, the amount being recorded by the secretary, who turned out to be Eulogio. The amounts were recorded in two ways—in the exercise book and, somewhat humorously, aloud as follows:

"The great hacendado Don Esteban Hinojosa has given 35,000 soles" [the actual figure being 35 soles].
"This character tells me he has sold two good ewes for this gift."

"Aha, and here we have Señor Tomas Rojas who has given ten soles *more* than his brother."

Eulogio's behavior, which in fact caused much laughter as well as occasional embarrassment, set the tone for the evening, though it would have been regarded as aggressively tasteless in the village. But the wedding was not taking place in Huasicancha; it was taking place in Lima, and its purpose, just as would have been the case in the village, was to allow the couple to set up a domestic enterprise of their own. The couple had been living together for some time in Surquillo, and a number of guests insisted to me that the money was being used toward the purchase of the knitting machine. Lest I should miss the significance of this, one informant said: "For some it's the roof that keeps them together. Like in the village. In the village it's the roof that keeps them together. Here it's the knitting machine." And she went off laughing.

Because domestic enterprises like Eulogio and Eufresenia's are somewhat different in character from those of the previous case studies, the way in which they are presented is different too. In looking at the texture of their past, we find it characterized above all by discontinuity. I have then examined the contemporary conditions of their domestic enterprise, and if I have addressed the question of its viability as a unit more specifically than for the previous cases that is because these are the first-order conditions of its viability, creating the preconditions for extrahousehold linkages. Finally I have clarified how these extrahousehold linkages are different from those of the more established household confederations.[13]

Nevertheless both must invest in the maintenance of the arena within which these linkages are made available to them. Hence these external relations in turn feed back to affect relations internal to the enterprise itself. The clubs contain a broad and shifting category of people in comparison to the specific partners of a confederation. As a result, the boundary between the domestic enterprise and its outside links is far clearer. In the earlier case of Mauro, his commitment to the members of his household is a kind of intensification of his broader commitments to a wider set of partners that in essence make up a confederation. Moreover those interpersonal resources are as much a function of Mauro's activities as they are of his wife, Guillermina's. By contrast, for households like Eulogio and Eufresenia's, extrahousehold linkages have become increasingly initiated and maintained through institutions in which only men participate.

Because the extra-enterprise links essential to reproduction are found in the arena of club and union events that take place beyond the household and are dominated by men, gender divisions within the household are thereby modified. Although the domestic unit still remains a source of labor, unlike in the previous cases, the reproduction of the enterprise is not a function of interpersonal linkages deriving from the past social network of both husband and wife, and hence penetrating to the heart of the relationship between them. The domestic sphere is no longer simply an intensification of a broader network of social relations, but a sphere distinct from them in which the wife's role is largely confined to direct labor, while institutionalized extrahousehold relations necessary for the economic reproduction of the enterprise become confined to the husband.[14]

But, where discontinuity in the past has restricted the maintenance of long-established networks, these institutions provide far more than an arena in which interpersonal resources can be tapped in an immediate economic sense. They also perform a more extended but equally essential function in the reproduction of domestic enterprises, for they provide an opportunity for members to express openly their identity with others. This identity provides at least some continuity that is a necessary basis for partnerships. And it is through these partnerships that individual enterprises gain vital access to informal sources of credit and labor.

It is important to grasp the mutual reinforcement of these two functions. If clubs were only for playing football they would get a very low profile. It is when critical moments arise that one or more clubs become intense arenas of activity. The land recuperation campaign in Huasicancha provided a continual series of such moments for the clubs of both Lima and Huancayo, as we shall see. Then, once in place, these arenas of activity are available to serve quite different purposes. Thus, as the oppositional solidarity of the land recuperation campaign declined, links that had been thus maintained, as well as the cultural and political sentiments they expressed, were redirected to address the issue of territoriality and livelihood not in the mountains but in the city, with the forming of the tricyclists' syndicate.

Urbano and
Paulina Llacua's
Domestic Enterprise

Urbano, 42 years old.
Paulina, 41 years old.
Son, 23.
Daughter, 15.
Daughter, 13.
Son, 12.

The case studies so far represent the core of the Huasicanchino economy. We turn now to the smallest group of domestic enterprises among the Huasicanchinos: the relatively independent small enterprises. In the village itself

I refer to these as the independent farmers, and in the past two or three years, as the land recuperation campaign looked increasingly promising, their numbers have increased to 18 of the 402 households in the village. This increase is partly because of the larger amounts of pasture becoming available that have placed more villagers among this group and partly because some villagers, driven away after 1948, have now returned. It is from among these eighteen that I have picked a case study for discussion. Be they in Huasicancha today or in Lima a year or so ago—at the height of the land-claim campaign—these few enterprises have a political and economic significance out of all proportion to their small numbers.

Such independent farmers, as the term implies, have few linkages of reciprocity with other households, either within Huasicancha or among migrants beyond the village. The trajectory of these enterprises has involved a relatively systematic accumulation of livestock and other forms of capital, the labor for which has either been provided by the immediate household or has been found from among the more impoverished households of Huasicancha. It is by no means always the case that such labor is mobilized through commoditized relationships, however; in many cases traditional institutions have been used to mobilize labor, but in such a way as to maintain the independence of these households from extensive obligations.

Indeed among these independent farmers Huasicanchino "patriotism" runs very high indeed. They voice constant concern with the maintenance of Huasicancha as a community and bemoan the erosion of community institutions, and they have done so from the beginning of the land recuperation campaign as far back as 1963. Why farmers whose daily operations seem to other Huasicanchinos to be relatively free of the mesh of community obligations, are nonetheless deeply involved in the community's institutions and have played an important role in the regaining of the land is the question I hope to answer by reference to the case of Urbano and Paulina (see table 7).

In 1963 Urbano was thirty-two years old. Paulina was thirty-one. They had four children, the oldest of whom, at thirteen, was in high school in Huancayo; the other three children were all too young to contribute to household tasks. But also included in the household were two of Urbano's widowed aunts. In addition to a small shop in Huasicancha run chiefly by Paulina, the family had 170 head of sheep, 30 llamas and alpacas, and 2 cattle. But they possessed a relatively small amount of arable land: two hectares. Most of their sheep and cattle were kept on land that Urbano rented from the distant Huancavelica community of Acobambilla, but the llamas and alpacas were kept specifically because they could be situated on pasture that was too high to be of interest to the hacienda with its high grade sheep.

In 1973 the widows are no longer a part of Urbano's household. Although the oldest son is now at the Universidad del Centro in Huancayo, he is talking of leaving, his degree incomplete, and going to work in the *selba* (high

Table 7.   Summary of Urbano's Career

Year	Age	Event	Location
1931		Born	Huasicancha
1938	7	School	Huasicancha
1943	12	School	Huancayo
1946	15	Leaves school	Huasicancha
1948	17	Apprenticeship at mine	Cercapuquio
1950	19	Marries Paulina	Huasicancha
1954	23	Father dies	Huasicancha
1955	24	Sister, America, marries	Huasicancha/La Oroya
1956	25	Mother dies	Huasicancha
1958	27	Quits Cercapuquio. Opens shop	Huasicancha
1962	31	Father-in-law loses job as shepherd	Hacienda Tucle
1964	32	First year of land recuperation campaign	
1965	33	Buys house	Huancayo
1966	34	America's husband killed	La Oroya
1972	41	As *Personero* Urbano concludes campaign	
1973	42	Buys high-jungle land	Satipo

jungle). The second child, a daughter, has already left her secondary education in Huancayo and is working for the domestic enterprise in Huasicancha, while the remaining two children work as shepherds on the estancia and also aid in the cultivation of the arable land. Much of this latter work, however, is now undertaken by peones: people from Huasicancha who work for Urbano for a wage. For agricultural work, Urbano pays 50 soles (just over $1.00) per day without meals and bonuses such as cigarettes and coca, and a little less with meals and bonuses. He himself tells me that this is at least 25 soles less than the minimum rate he would pay were he to employ peones on the open market.

In 1972, when I began fieldwork, Urbano and Paulina held over 300 head of high grade sheep, 15 cattle, and 15 llamas and alpacas.[15] Improved access to the lower land of the hacienda and the increasing success of the recuperation campaign had led the family to reduce its llama and alpaca holdings and upgrade its sheep flocks, while increasing the number of both sheep and cattle. This was done not just by breeding, but by actively buying high grade animals. But by the following year, he had sold off a sizeable number of his livestock and entered into what he called a "partnership" with another villager to start a farm in the high jungle near Satipo. This land is made up of mature and young coffee plants, as well as some land used for growing *yuca* (an indigenous tuber) and coca (coca shrub, grown for local consumption of the leaf). Despite Urbano's reference to "partnership" (*un socio*), all the cash for the purchase of the land was put up by him, and the "partner" is to provide the labor and management of the jungle operations, while Urbano's oldest son learns the ropes.

The entire purchase of the high jungle land had been financed through the sale of livestock. Two hundred head of sheep were sold as well as seven cattle. Although this still left Urbano with a sizeable herd, it means that he and Paulina have now diversified their enterprise, though not away from agriculture and into commerce but rather into that sector of agriculture that the government is supporting with big propaganda campaigns.

In 1972 it was Urbano who, as personero of the community, negotiated the final land claim settlement. A year later he no longer holds any political office, but is secretary of the community's livestock cooperative. He is a respected figure in the community, though he rarely speaks up at village meetings and is not a popular figure among his own immediate kin.

The running of Urbano and Paulina's enterprise does involve them in extrahousehold economic ties, and both the past and future condition of their enterprise is dependent upon Urbano's social and political position within Huasicancha as a community. But the nature of these various extrahousehold linkages both economic and sociopolitical is somewhat different from the examples we have so far seen. Indeed from quite early on Urbano has had few economic linkages with his immediate siblings, and Paulina is an only child. Increasingly he prefers to enter into arrangements with people who can make no reference to family ties. As one of the better-off and respected members of the community, he is approached to provide loans to others, usually for family emergencies but, unlike the better-off confederated households, he never takes on a partnership in other enterprises as part of the loan arrangement but rather is known to ask for collateral in the form of livestock or land. Such an arrangement however would be humiliating for the debtor, and so neither Urbano nor those to whom he might have loaned money like to talk about this.

To understand the position Urbano and Paulina now find themselves in, it is necessary to juxtapose the personal life history of Urbano against the prevailing historical conditions facing Huasicancha that led up to the migrations after 1948. At that point Urbano's father and mother were still alive (see table 8) and holders of a reasonable amount of land and livestock. Urbano was the eldest of seven children. His parents had ten hectares of arable land and sufficient livestock to warrant renting some land in Acobambilla on the far side of Hacienda Tucle. After completing three years of secondary school in Huancayo in 1946—something that placed him among the better educated of the villagers—he returned to Huasicancha with a view to settling into livestock farming. Plans were afoot to press the hacienda and the government

Table 8. *The Life Cycle of the Household of Urbano's Parents*

Year	Andreo	Juana	Urbano	America	Artico	Victor	Nicolasa	Cartujos	Davida
1931	?	?							
1932			Born	Born					
1933			1	1	Born				
1934			2	2	1				
1935			3	3	2				
1936			4	4	3				
1937			5	5	4	Born			
1938			6	6	5	1			
1939			School	7	6				
1940			8	8	7	2			
1941			9	Estancia	8	3			
1942			10	10	9	4			
1943			11	11	School	5			
1944			12	12	11	6	Born		
1945			13	13	12	7	1		
1946			14	14	Estancia	School	2		
1947			15	15	etc.	9	3	Born	
1948			16	16	15	10	4	1	Born
1949			Mines	17	16	11	5	2	1
1950			18	18	Hyo	12	6	3	2
1951			19	19	18	13	7	4	3
1952			Marries	20	19	14	8	5	4
1953			Blds	21	Marries	15	9	6	5
1954	Dies		House	22	21	16	10	7	6
1955			Returns to Hcha	Marries	22	17	11	School	7

Year								
1956	8	9	12	18	23	24	25	
1957	9	10	13	19	24	25	26	Dies
1958	10	11	14	20	25	26	27 Rents shop	
1959	11	12	15	Marries	26	27		
1960	12	In next village	16	22	27	To Mines	29	
1961	13	Hcha	17	23	28	30	30	
1962	14	16	18	To jungle	29	31	31	
1963	15	17	19	Hcha	30	32	32	
1964	16	Jungle	20	27	31	Husband dies	33	
1965	17	19	21	28	32	35 Hcha	Buys house in Hyo also, land from sister	
1966	18	Hcha	22	Lima	33	36		
1967	19	21	23	30	34	37		
1968	Dom servant	Marries	24	Mines	35			
1969			25		36			
1970	Hyo	23	26	32	37	38	39	
1971	Hcha	24	27	33	38	39	40	
1972		25	28	House	39	40	41	

for acknowledgment of Huasicancha's claim to pasture then being used by Hacienda Tucle, and there was a militant mood in the community that Urbano very much shared.

But two years later a disappointing settlement was made out of court with Tucle. At this point Urbano's eldest sister and next eldest brother were working on the family's estancia and had no experience beyond the village. Urbano found work in the hydroelectric plant of the local Cercapuquio mine. In the period that followed the migratory exodus of 1948 many of the well-established intra- and interhousehold linkages were cut or severely weakened until the process of migrating to the various centers could be properly institutionalized. This period, which lasted until the mid-1950s, appears to have affected all households (see G. Smith 1979a) and this was certainly the case for Urbano, whose linkages with his siblings seem to have been especially weakened over the two years that followed his taking the job at the mine.

After two years he was advancing in his apprenticeship so as to make sufficient money to save. The year was now 1950, and livestock farming was looking especially bleak for Huasicanchinos: Artico, Urbano's next oldest brother (see table 8), who had been working on the estancia, decided to leave and try his luck in Huancayo. Since the next brother after Artico was then only twelve years old, this left America, the oldest daughter, to do the bulk of the shepherding.

Urbano chose this moment to go in search of a wife, building a house for Paulina, an only child whose family had a small estancia on Hacienda Tucle, where they worked as huachillero pastores (shepherds working with huacchilla contracts [see chaps. 2 and 3]). This gave him access to some pasture, but there was no possibility of expanding livestock holdings, and Urbano continued to work at Cercapuquio. Then, in 1954, 1955, and 1956 family crises reduced still further the resources of domestic labor available to him. First his father died, then America married, and finally his mother died (see table 8). Two years later, Urbano gave up his Cercapuquio job and returned to the village where he and Paulina set up a shop in a house they rented from a migrant.

In the early 1960s Paulina's father lost his position as a huacchillero on Hacienda Tucle partly because he had been upgrading and increasing his own (huaccha) flock of sheep by illicitly interbreeding with hacienda fine grade animals, partly because Paulina's mother died. With Urbano insisting on Paulina running the shop, there was insufficient family labor for the old pastor to fulfill his duties,[16] and finally losing his job was the result of Hacienda Tucle's attempts to reduce huaccha sheep in favor of wage payments to the shepherds.

This created a crisis for Urbano and Paulina who had been upgrading their flock and now found themselves with a lot of livestock but no labor and little pasture. The first problem was solved initially by bringing Urbano's youngest sister, Davida, into the household to act as shepherd and, later, replacing her by first one and then a second widowed aunt. As to the second problem—that of land—it became increasingly clear that it could be resolved only by political means (to which I turn in chap. 7).

There is no doubt that Urbano was especially fortunate in being the eldest son of a reasonably well-off family who were thus able to support his early education, which, in turn, gave him the opportunity in 1948 to take advantage of the rapid developments at the Cercapuquio mine. This job then made it possible for him to marry a woman who brought with her a sizeable flock of sheep and—initially at least—secure access to pasture. Even so this pattern could easily have locked the couple into a set of confederated households, as we have seen was the case for Grimaldo and Angelina. Indeed Artico, the next eldest brother to Urbano, feels that the couple's success has always been at the expense of other family members, and he himself evolved a confederation of households that included Victor and Cartujos (see table 8) as well as Victor's father-in-law.

Urbano and Paulina, however, never became involved in such arrangements. Up until 1964, he was getting an increasing percentage of his income from the shop. From that time forward he became one of the younger advocates of an attack on Hacienda Tucle's use of the pasture Huasicancha claimed as its own, and he performed an important role as one of the intermediaries between the villagers and the Huancayo residents. But despite his views with respect to Huasicancha's claims, he was not prepared to put all his eggs in one basket ("I had learned my lesson from what happened in 1948, when everybody waited optimistically and what happened? Not much"). He and Paulina began investing outside the village in the only way possible in the absence of a well-organized confederation through which it might otherwise be done: he bought a house in the Chilca area of Huancayo at a cost of $700 (U.S.).

By referring to table 8, it is possible to see that at this time Urbano was the only one of his siblings with any significant amount of convertible capital. Artico had some sheep and a little arable land, but was essentially running a small-holding subsistence farm. Victor had just returned from Satipo, in the high jungle, in ill health, and Cartujos was only eighteen. Both Nicolasa and Davida, the unmarried sisters, were part of Artico's and Victor's households, changing around from one month to the next as requirements dictated, in the usual pattern found for confederations of households.

So, when America, the eldest sister, was suddenly widowed when her husband was killed in a mining accident, it was not unreasonable for her to turn to Urbano for help. He, however, was caught fully extended, having just bought the house in Huancayo. He showed some reluctance to help. At this point too he was paying out money, as were all Huasicanchinos, for the campaign against the hacienda. He did however sell some livestock and provide

America with the necessary cash. But he did something which was a relatively new practice for these kinds of dealings between one member of the Huasican-chino community and another (though not for dealings with outsiders). It was a move that led Artico and Victor to refuse to talk to him in the street. He asked his sister for collateral. It was to be the produce from all of the arable land America received in inheritance from her parents for a period of years.[17]

If we come back full circle now, to Urbano and Paulina's enterprise as we left it in 1973, the shop has long since disappeared from Huasicancha, and the house, once ostentatiously boasting a corrugated roof and private water supply, is not notable beside newer ones in the village. But Urbano antici-pated the eventual saturation of Huasicancha's newly gained pasture. Through a process of vigorous (over-) grazing, he has generated considerable capital, but this has put him, and other independent farmers like him, in conflict with the main body of Huasicancha's middle peasantry—both migrant and non-migrant, involved or not in confederations—over pasture.

The hacienda is no longer there to provide the focus for potential expansion nor to be the catalyst for the wartime patriotism of community from which certain benefits derived. This has had an effect on both the capital and labor components of Urbano and Paulina's enterprise. In the first place, they have shifted from a concentration on livestock, to use of livestock as a means to diversify into coffee production in the jungle.[18] In the second place, they first rationalized their labor requirements by substituting peones for the fixed com-mitment to supporting Urbano's two widowed aunts. Despite the flexibility of using commodified labor, however, Urbano is coming to rely increas-ingly on the domestic labor of his children; both his adult children are giving up formal education in favor of a fulltime commitment to the enterprise, a pattern shared by other independent farm enterprises. In the next chapter I shall address in some detail the question of the oscillation between the use of commodified and noncommodified labor by independent farmers and other petty commodity producers. Here, however, I think it is worth stressing two important factors that affect the position of these kind of farmers within the community.

The first has to do with the reduction in the power of community sentiment to act as a means for segregating the labor force in order to provide cheap labor. Peones, some of whom are beginning to benefit from the community's acquisition of pasture in order to reduce their need to sell their labor power, have now increased their wage demands; also loyalty to co-members of the community seems less important now. The result is that Urbano has trans-formed the segregation of the labor market based on personal proximity from the level of the community to the level of the domestic unit—specifically to his adult children. Second, the need for high quality labor in a situation where close supervision is made difficult by the spread of the enterprise, places em-phasis on the committed labor of the household, both in the tending of sheep and, in the future, in the tending of coffee plants. This latter has been resolved in the immediate period by the use of a partner and in the future by his anticipated replacement by Urbano's son.

But it would be quite mistaken to anticipate the alienation of independent farmers such as Urbano from the community and its institutions. With specifically notable exceptions who provide useful scapegoats, independent farmers remain central to Huasicancha's community affairs. Indeed Urbano's elusiveness in the village belies his importance and that of others like him. As their children become more involved in both the labor and management of the different branches of the enterprise, Urbano and Paulina's daily tasks are increasingly bound up with village politics. Urbano has taken on the role of running the village cooperative farm that produces high-grade sheep and cattle. But he finds it useful not to draw too much attention to himself or to his own entrepreneurial activities; he is secretary, rather than president of the cooperative, and he declines to express opinions publicly at meetings.

The Llacua's reduced public involvement in political office in the community has revealed something of a contradiction to which I have alluded earlier. Because the successful running of their enterprise means greater use of finite amounts of community pasture, their farming practices are in conflict with community development. But insofar as they have demonstrated skills both in husbandry and in dealing with state officials, it is expected that those skills should be made available to the community as a whole. The present resolution to this problem has placed Paulina in a role hitherto unique in Huasicancha. On Urbano's refusal to run for the presidency of the community, Paulina was voted into the office.

It is clear that enterprises such as that of Urbano and Paulina's are geared around a rationality of systematic accumulation in a way that the other cases are not, with the result that these relatively independent enterprises are more openly exposed to the hazards of an uncertain national economy. There is a very real possibility that Urbano and Paulina's enterprise will fail in a very dramatic way, having reduced many of the risk-reducing linkages available to them. But then there will be others like theirs which will not. For this reason the daily affairs of enterprises of this kind are so difficult to divorce from the politics of Huasicancha, the subject of chapter 7. In the following chapter I will suggest that it has been attempts to preempt this threat that accounts for these people's attachment to the community, but a community whose meaning is at variance with the views of other Huasicanchinos.

There are three points to bear in mind, then, when turning to the interests that underlie the political involvement of enterprises such as these. First, the idioms of "the viable enterprise," "rational business practice," and so forth, are never foreign to the discourse of these independent farmers, but this is by no means incompatible with many of their views of community institutions, whose maintenance provides for the essential infrastructure of their enterprises, such as sheep dips, the maintenance of roads, and the systematic organization of access to pasture, specifically with reference to their claim to that pasture as a legal corporation (the comunidad campesina) recognized as such by the state. Second, the use of unpaid domestic labor is an essential element in the viability of these concerns but lies in conflict with the ambitions of household members who wish to turn the wealth of the domestic enterprise into educational diplomas for upward mobility. When this occurs, the cheapest substitute for such labor is provided by using community sentiment (and community institutions) as a means for segregating the labor force in such a way that wages can be kept well below the prevailing average for the region. Finally, systematic expansion of livestock within one domestic enterprise does not extend the benefits of good husbandry among a widespread set of other comuneros but concentrates its benefits within one enterprise, while inevitably involving the need for greater amounts of pasture within the strictly delimited confines of what is available to the community as a whole. The only means of resolving this conflict is by finding a political solution to the problem of pasture shortage—the land recuperation campaign.

It would of course be nice to present the reader with a far richer variety of case studies from which to gain some insight into the lives of the Huasicanchinos who were involved in the land recuperation campaigns of the 1960s and 1970s. No one case can be perfectly typical. Here I have tried to present the complexity of variation between enterprises. In the next chapter I will try to draw out the essential elements underlying this complexity.

6

Commodification and Culture

> *[With money]* the individual carris his social power, as well as his bond with society *in his pocket. . . [T]his is indeed a condition very different from that in which the individual member of a family (or . . . community) directly and naturally reproduces himself, or in which his productive activity and his share in production are bound* to a specific form of labour *and of product, which determine his relation to others* in just that specific way. . . . *The less social power the medium of exchange possesses . . .* the greater must be the power of the community which binds the individuals together.
> —Marx, *The Grundisse* [emphasis mine].

Throughout this book I have sought to emphasize the close connection between the contemporary practices we find among a group of people and the past experiences from which they emerge. And so the discussion of their contemporary lives in the previous two chapters was preceded by discussion of their grandparents' engagement in local insurgency at the end of the last century and the unfolding of their conflict-filled interdependency with the hacienda. And earlier we found that even the social relations of the peasant community itself and its relationship to the hacienda had to be seen within the context of a still longer process of transformations in the practice and meaning of key institutions.[1]

And in the last two chapters, when we turned from Huasicancha's history as a whole to looking at individual Huasicanchinos, we found once more that the structural features of their enterprises had to be understood within the context of the different "data banks" of experience they had to draw upon. Moreover this is not just a question of past experiences as recorded in memory but past experiences that have provided crucial material and personnel resources. A past background of access to certain material resources (e.g., livestock) facilitated the maintenance of personal ties, which, in turn, were translated into retaining some continuity through adverse times. Lack of resources at crucial historical moments, however, was translated into radical breaks at moments of adversity in people's past, resulting in genealogical discontinuities and hence a smaller personnel resource base. Such factors have, in turn, strongly affected the character of enterprises otherwise superficially quite similar from the point of view of their structure at any one moment in time.

Despite this heterogeneity in the requirements of people's enterprises and hence in their daily livelihood concerns, the Huasicanchinos continue to rely on institutions of community, and their political activity is crucially mediated by the role of those institutions. It is impossible to understand the character of the political mobilization to be discussed in the next chapter without first addressing this question. My task now is to examine this variation not in isolation and by means of classifications but for the specific purpose of understanding the politics of mobilization expressed through the various land invasions of recent times. For example, after the repression of the 1950s, a heterogeneous and differentiated peasantry were brought together for mobilization around the idiom of common identity as a community (of Huasicanchinos). So this chapter must address the question of what threads existed *prior* to the mobilization of the 1960s and 1970s that served so to pull people together. Put another way, I shall argue later that during this intensive period of mobilization, Huasicanchinos of varied past backgrounds and present livelihoods found themselves engaging in vigorous discussions of what they were up to. This chapter provides the field within which this discourse and negotiation took place.

Acknowledging the crucial differences in Huasicanchino enterprises then is not merely a question of classification but of recognizing that certain features of forms of production, combined with the larger economic environment, tend toward certain lines of development for the enterprise.[2] It would seem that, among the cases presented here, there are enterprises exhibiting many of the features of simple commodity production that would suggest a line of development—albeit modified by the specificity of local economic conditions—outlined by writers who have addressed the issue of simple commodity production. It would seem too, however, that there are enterprises whose social relations of production in no way conform to those features. Broadly speaking, these people more closely resemble the conventional view of the peasantry.

Under simple commodity production all moments of production but one are expressed through commodities (Friedmann 1980; Kahn 1980; J. Chevalier 1983a). Inputs are bought on the market, produce is sold on the market, interest on credit is paid at the market rate, and rents reflect the differential value of land. The commodification of social relations between households and the domestication of labor within them, serves to individualize simple commodity production units from one another, eroding social relations of community where they previously existed and preventing their emergence where they did not. The viability of this form of production derives from the fact that one moment of production remains uncommodified: either through the use of domestic (i.e., noncommodified, intrahousehold) labor (Friedmann 1978), or the use of labor that is paid no more than the component necessary for its immediate subsistence needs (Kahn 1980), simple commodity producers remain competitive within the overall commodity economy. Access to domestic labor allows simple commodity producers to stay in business though it obviates their expansion, hence making their reproduction simple as opposed to expanded. It is to be noted then that a crucial characteristic of simple commodity production is its reliance on a category of labor that is made available through noneconomic means.

For better or worse these kinds of structural features have received far less attention in the case of "peasantry." Nevertheless we can say that they too are usually supposed to rely predominantly on domestic labor (Friedmann 1980; Ennew, Tribe, and Hirst 1977; Wolf 1966; Franklin 1969; Shanin 1973, 1979). And their distinction from "natural economy" or "tribespeople" is conventionally seen to rest on their linkage, however partial, to the commodity market. This is another way of saying that some part of peasant reproduction takes on a commodity form. But, unlike simple commodity production, peasants engage in production through the use of many institutions that allow them access to resources and to labor *unmediated by the commodity form*. As we have seen, for example, in the case of Mauro and Guillermina in Lima, or that of Grimaldo and Angelina in Huasicancha, where goods and services cannot be found from within the household they are sought through a variety of reciprocal arrangements with neighbors and kin. Access to land, be it controlled by an outside landlord, by some other villagers, or by representatives of the community as a whole, requires a "cost," but that cost is not calculated by reference to the commodity market in land. And more generally, the infrastructures necessary for the running of any individual enterprise are provided primarily either by a landlord of this traditional type or by the community, and only in very small part by the state. It is argued therefore that for these reasons, despite the peasants' production of commodities, the logic of development of the peasant farm cannot be predicated on the same principles as those set out for simple commodity production (Friedmann 1980).

Nevertheless, I shall argue that the line between simple commodity production and peasant production, as laid out here, is not as clear-cut as is often supposed. And this has great significance for the politics of rural, small-scale producers. So a detailed understanding of their forms of production is a necessary precondition for understanding these people's politics (and hence the literature on simple commodity production is of value), I shall argue that these writers have tended to divorce the structural forms of production of enterprises—issues relating to the immediate reproduction of livelihood—from the political and ideological factors that also condition the reproduction of these enterprises. As a result their studies have failed to see some of the major factors that condition the developmental trajectories of these forms of production.

Moreover the particular characteristics, even of a hypothetical, pure form of simple commodity production make untenable the use of Marx's categories for his analysis of capitalism; and they become still more untenable once we turn to the more empirically widespread associated forms of small-scale production using domestic labor. I shall argue in this chapter that the formal subsumption of labor, which primarily prevails amid all this variety of small-scale enterprises—makes it impossible to ascribe certain logical properties to the development of these forms of production akin to those Marx developed for real subsumption under capitalism. I shall return to a more detailed explanation of formal subsumption later in the chapter. Here it is simply important to note that the use made, under this form of production, of noneconomic incentives, makes it the more dangerous to disaggregate social relations of production in a very strict sense from the entire process of social reproduction, because such reproduction requires investment on the part of members in political and cultural resources for the maintenance (or expansion) of those conditions.

It is at this point that the rigor with which authors have sought to distinguish between simple commodity production and peasantry appears to be misguided. Simple commodity producers, we are told, depend on a pool of labor access which is dependent upon some form other than the commodity relationship. Peasants on the other hand, it appears, organize production through noncommodity relationships but nevertheless produce (some) commodities. Hence both forms of production have in common that they are made possible alongside large-scale capitalism (i.e., full-blown and continuous production of relative surplus value [real subsumption]) by the fact that one or more elements are not priced on the open market. In the case of simple commodity production this requires a category, "domestic labour"; in the case of the peasantry this also requires a category, one which extends the noncommodified field to embrace a wider arena, i.e., the "community."

If a distinction can be made between these two forms of production, therefore, it must rest on the relative amounts of investment put into the maintenance of these categories. This is what the term "cultural production" means. But if this is the case, then it no longer becomes possible to separate the "categories of political economy" (Friedmann 1978) from political struggle and cultural production. If the viability of all enterprises, across their variation, is linked to the use made of "unpaid" labor and other forms of noncommodified relationships, then the struggle for the protection of the conditions that allow those relationships to be maintained—a political struggle—

becomes as much a part of social reproduction as does the more daily struggle of livelihood. And people can be expected to mobilize around such issues. Among the Huasicanchinos people engaged in political struggle for the maintenance of a quite disparate collection of enterprises, and they did so chiefly by mobilizing institutions that were used in the daily round to mediate noncommodified social relations, the package of which was referred to as "the community."

In short, *if* there is such a thing as the appropriate form of struggle for a particular class, then fighting for the maintenance—possibly even the expansion—of these kinds of relationships might be the appropriate form of struggle for people whose livelihoods depend on these forms of production units. In this sense the culture of the community is not distinct from class consciousness but an expression of it. Inasmuch as the sphere of affectual, particularistic ties used by each domestic enterprise varied and was a matter of negotiation through time (both within and between households) so the idea of "the community" and of "being Huasicanchino" had great plasticity. As we shall see in the coming chapters, once the political struggles acquired greater intensity, so the purposes various institutions were properly supposed to serve and the meanings attached to the words describing those institutions became subject to perpetual reformulation. But because the institutions and their words were essential, just as they were being struggled for, so this process of reformulation generated a very committed involvement on the part of the participants who were struggling and wished to assert that what they were struggling for had the meaning and served the purpose they ascribed to it. This process—of heterogeneity and discussion—rather than the more familiar process associated with political mobilization—homogeneity and unity—best characterizes the form Huasicancha's political activity took.

The detailed data emerging from the case studies of the previous chapter suggest that the Huasicanchinos rely on quite a broad range in forms of production units to make their livelihood. Among them there are those whose developmental trajectories suggest many forms: commodified, cumulative reproduction; commodified, simple reproduction; noncommodified simple reproduction; as well as commodified and noncommodified enterprises that fail to reproduce themselves. Moreover many enterprises show evidence of what Guy Bois (1984) has called "discontinuous accumulation." And even these structural classifications do not take account of the great variety in precisely which relationships in each enterprise have been affected by commodification. Nevertheless I want now to use a self-consciously hypothetical frame of reference to uncover the specific implications of these various trajectories, diverse though they may be. But to do so, I must begin by emphasizing those elements of commodification and the formal subsumption of labor that have useful implications for our understanding of the Huasicanchinos.

The Implications
of Commodification
and Formal Subsumption

Rather than entering into a lengthy discussion of the characteristics of commodities (Marx 1976:125–177), I want simply to stress the important characteristics of the process in which some of the social relations of a group become expressed by reference to commodities. Two features need emphasis: (1) the commodity as the representative of direct relationships between people, and (2) the exchangeability of commodities.

Commodity fetishism occurs when a material item is used to stand for the social relationship between producers. Instead of the actual relationship having to be referred to (or performed) each time, reference can be made to the commodity. In the course of time it is no longer the relationships that appear to have value but the commodity that represents them. While Marx confined himself to the discussion of commodity fetishism in reference to the labor process narrowly defined, he was also aware that commodification had similar effects to the touch of Midas. Once not just labor power but other forms of social performance can be replaced by a material item that is said to serve in place of the actual social performance, then the scene is set for forms of development of particular enterprises that would not otherwise be the case. To begin with, where direct labor or social performance cannot be so represented, then it has to be carried out when required. It cannot be stored up and accumulated over time.

The second characteristic of the commodity is that it achieves its exchange value through general circulation.[3] It is important to bear this in mind, because items can be exchanged in a very localized context at relative prices that do not reflect the prevailing equivalents in the larger market environment. Items can also be exchanged at prices that vary according to the status relationship between the parties concerned. In neither case are these commodities in the strict sense. Just as labor must be entirely "freed" for it to become proper wage labor under capitalism, so material goods must be similarly "freed" from let or encumbrance for them to become commodities. To the degree that other factors, such as regional loyalties or proximity of family ties, can be used to influence the price of labor or goods, we must be cautious about referring to them as commodities, and we must seek out what those factors are and how they are socially reproduced.

Amid this variety of Huasicanchino producers it would appear that none is entirely committed to commodified social relations, nor are the noncommodified relations of any of them limited only to the domestic sphere as is supposedly the case for "pure" simple commodity production. Rather, partial commodification is a feature, in varying degrees and forms, of all enterprises.

The persistent use of a particular, commodified social relationship is invariably constrained by impediments imposed by other social relationships. Such a situation contrasts with Marx's example of the use of wage labor in conditions of simple reproduction. There he shows that even where no accumulation takes place, once a person pays labor to work his means of production, the mere repetition of the process imposes new characteristics on the enterprise: "And although this reproduction is a mere repetition of the process of production, on the same scale as before, this mere repetition, or continuity, *imposes on the process certain new characteristics,* or rather, causes the disappearance of some apparent characteristics possessed by the process in isolation" (Marx 1976:712; emphasis is mine). It is not just that a new social relationship has occurred but that the imperatives of the new relationship have a demanding logic if it is to be repeated. In this case, for example, Marx explains that "Entirely leaving aside all accumulation, the mere continuity of the production process, in other words simple reproduction, sooner or later, and necessarily, converts all capital into accumulated capital, or capitalized surplus-value" (1976:715). But in the case of the Huasicanchinos the process that might result from a wage relationship of this kind is less likely to be systematic and unimpeded than discontinuous and at best cyclical.

Structuralist analysis has performed a great service in lifting the study of social relations out of a static frame of reference and demonstrating the dynamic properties of certain kinds of relationships along lines similar to the above example from Marx (see Friedmann 1980; Kahn 1980), but in the conditions that exist in the vast majority of examples of small-scale, domestic production, detailed study (as opposed to macrolevel surveys), suggests that we should be aware *at the same time* of the implications of commodification (which social anthropologists have not been) *and* of the force and dynamism of the whole variety of more particularistic relationships (which political economists have not been).

Simple commodity production never thoroughly shatters preexisting relations of production. Its historical existence therefore is always a function of its relations to large-scale capital on the one hand, and the use it makes of preexisting relations of production on the other. This makes it extremely hard for commodity relations to become so perpetually repeated that they are thoroughly embedded in the social fabric. Rubin notes:

> Only at a determined level of development, after frequent repetition, do the production relations among people leave some kind of sediment in the form of certain characteristics which are fixed to the products of labour. If the given type of production relations have not yet spread widely enough in the society, they cannot yet give things an adequate social form. When the ruling type of production was crafts production, where the goal was the 'maintenance' of the craftsman, the craftsman still considered himself a 'master craftsman' and he

considered his income the source of his 'maintenance' even when he expanded
his enterprise and had, in essence already become a capitalist who lived from
the wage labour of his workers. (1926:23–24)

Nevertheless it would be equally inaccurate to depict the enterprises we
have been discussing devoid of *any* of the characteristics of capitalist social
relations, such as owners of private means of production and employers of
paid labor. Thus, what Marx has described above, "is the general form of
every capitalist process of production; at the same time, however, it can be
found as a *particular* form alongside the *specifically capitalist mode of production* in its developed form, because although the latter entails the former,
the converse does not necessarily obtain" (1976:1019). There are *elements* of
capitalism but not the *specifically capitalist mode of production*. This, the *formal* subsumption of labor (as opposed to the real), seems an accurate account
of even the most apparently capitalistic of Huasicanchino enterprises, but this
immanent relationship continuously fails to become a source for the accumulated extraction of relative surplus value because in Marx's words there is a
perpetual starvation in "the volume of the means of production invested" and
hence "the number of workers under the command of a single employer"
(1976:1022).

In order to survive in an environment of capitalist enterprises that are so
equipped with means of production (i.e., with a higher organic composition
of capital) Marx asserts that "The work may become more intensive, its duration may be extended, it may become more continuous or orderly under the
eye of the interested capitalist, but in themselves these changes do not affect
the character of the actual labour process, the actual mode of working. This
stands in striking contrast to the development of a specifically capitalist mode
of production" (1976:1021). Under these circumstances the operators of small
enterprises are almost in the inverse position to the pure capitalist: they have
a low commitment to capital and a high commitment to labor; they may even
fetishize far less the technical value of machines and fetishize instead the
value of personality, of the individual, and often the localized skill/knowledge
of individuals. There is room for considerable speculation here. My concern,
however, is only to stress the relatively greater importance of existing institutions and practices—the local culture—for the elements of formal subsumption to be put into practice (encouraging longer working hours, intensity of
work, etc.), than would be the case for "the specifically capitalist mode of
production" where increasing investment in means of production is the major
path toward greater productivity of labor.

The effect of all this is to suggest that we should be cautious about assuming that enterprises showing quite significant commodification necessarily exist amid increasingly atomistic social relations beyond the "domestic sphere"
and a decreasing interest in "the community." Rather these key institutions

should be treated like "keywords" (Williams 1976), and we should watch for the changing resonances in their meaning and perceived purpose that result from interaction between the very different forms of enterprise we find in Huasicancha.[4]

Limitations to
the Commodification
of Production Relations

I can begin constructing my hypothetical frame of reference by positing a cluster of production units similar to that found in the village of Huasicancha: most labor is mobilized through noncommodified forms, as are the entire package of factors of production. There is relatively little sale of land, and credit for the few cash items needed is found from within a community of friends, neighbors, and kin. Though some portion of agricultural produce reaches the market, much is consumed locally. Though the reproductive cycle depends to varying degrees on this market, it depends too on the package of noncommodified relations into which the unit of production is inserted. The "community" is both an effect and a precondition for the reproduction of these units of production, just as the "family" is an effect and a precondition for the domestic unit (Harris 1981, 1982). Indeed the line between the domestic and the social, here not delineated by the line between commodified and noncommodified relations, is a source of great cultural and ideological manipulation.

A number of students of the domestic sphere under advanced capitalism have suggested that the unpaid domestic labor, largely of women, in effect subsidizes the reproduction costs of the "breadwinner." Mingione (1983) has extended this view, seeing the household as a livelihood-seeking enterprise in which cash income, domestic work, and self-provisioning (extended domestic work) are combined in various permutations. Increased self-provisioning, for example, may reduce reproduction costs and hence make cash available for other purposes. Such costs can further be reduced by drawing on resources provided by membership in some association, be it a confederation of interlinked households, a sindicato or migrant club, or the community. The community is a source of unpaid labor through myriad varieties of labor exchange institutions: it offers potential marriage partners; in communal work teams, it dips sheep and cleans irrigation channels; politically too, the community has recognition and provides both access to land and what little solidarity poor and otherwise atomized petty producers can hope to secure in defense of the institutions and resources necessary for their survival.

What makes these kinds of relationships especially different from commodity relations (which are indifferent to person) is that they are particularistic. That is to say, for reciprocal agreements to be possible it is necessary for the parties so engaged to stand in a particular position to each other. Insofar as such relations rely on the categorization of persons, distinguishing who is and who is not subject to sanction and hence can offer some assurance that they will be there tomorrow when today's debit must be balanced, then they require a *bounded* field of participants.

There is a cost for such a community, one which Huasicanchinos know and talk about and which members of certain enterprises can weigh quite precisely, as we shall see later. If a person wants the community to provide a roof on the school he or she must be prepared to sacrifice a few hours of labor from his or her own farm to work on the communal work team. And this is only the most obvious social cost: *any* performance that serves to establish and locate the production unit within a network of access to all those components necessary for its reproduction is a cost payable to the community. As such it is not unreasonable to assume that, where it is possible to make such a calculation, participants regard the return to be at least equivalent or greater than their outlay. In effect we are talking of a community "tax" that is paid through social performance.[5]

In this sense, "unpaid" labor is not entirely unpaid. It does involve a cost to the enterprise, but this is paid in terms of an ideology of direct exchange unmediated by the wage form. Much has been written in anthropology about how such exchanges take place in terms that reflect the specific status of the parties vis-à-vis one another (Sahlins 1968). Thus those who wish to maintain that status vis-à-vis an extensive group of kin, all of whom they wish to make appear "close kin," have to make certain "investments" to maintain a position that puts them in an advantageous situation for the exchange of labor. The devotion of time and resources toward this end goes back to the days of the curacas, when the heads of the larger and more powerful families benefited because there was no clear distinction between the "family" (the ayllu) and the community (see chap. 2). While the distinction between an extended family and the "community"—now a legal entity, *La Communidad de Huasicancha*—is sufficient to make this practice virtually obsolete among the Huasicanchinos, more prosperous people do attempt to position themselves to tip the balance of reciprocity in their favor, thus deriving sources of labor from "close" kin.

The manipulation of this practice is a continual source of discussion. The confederations of enterprises are clearly a means for institutionalizing forms of proximity to serve the specific ends of each enterprise in a situation where kinship is no longer the most suitable medium, and their constantly shifting reformulations reflect this manipulation.[6] The particularistic nature of the community as a whole, however, is relevant to the reproduction of the more independent farmers such as Urbano and Paulina (in chap. 5) because community sentiment serves to restrict the mobility of labor. Besides being interested in community officeholding to influence the course of the land invasions, these people were also most vociferous when holding office in emphasizing that the young men should not leave the community and that working within the community was a good in itself. The community therefore is relevant to the reproduction of these enterprises precisely in its characteristic of segregating the social world, specifically the labor market.[7]

But for these aspects of "community" to retain their affective component, the community "tax," as well as the majority of direct interhousehold labor exchanges, must be expressed in terms of direct labor or (in the broader definition of "tax" I have used above) *actual* social performance. Once such tax can be provided not by direct labor but by the material objects that represent that labor and can be given a universal (nonparticularistic) value—commodities—then the opportunity cost vis-à-vis the equivalent labor lost in direct labor given over to the domestic enterprise becomes transparent. This need not be a problem as long as the productivity of all domestic enterprises is much the same, or close to the community average. But once the productivity of labor *within* a production unit is consistently higher than the community average, then the amount of productive labor such a household has to forego at home in order to participate in the community tax is greater than the (immediate) returns they derive from communal labor as members of the community. So the cost to the enterprise of giving up some work time in the enterprise to work on a community project is greater than the value of what the community can offer the enterprise in return.

This disparity can be partially resolved by using political office to ensure that what one derives from the community more than repays what one puts out, and, to some extent, this accounts for the interest of better-off heads of families, such as Urbano, in local-level politics. Once, however, labor power or social performance does not have to be expressed as actual labor or actual social performance but rather can be frozen into small cubes of ice, called commodities, then the one household with higher labor productivity can resolve its relationship to the community as a whole. Because the labor power to be foregone in the capitalized household is more productive than that of its neighbor, it can pay a "wage" to this neighbor to turn up for communal work in place of any member of the better-off household. Such a "wage" is attractive to both households involved because of their differing productivity as production units: the "wage" is less than the value produced within the first household but greater than the value produced in the second.

While this kind of analysis is most easily seen in the case of communal work, it can be applied with greater or lesser effect to all forms of interhousehold exchange and indeed to the commodification of social performance itself. In lieu of actually attending a wedding a household will send an especially generous material gift. In lieu of actually attending a village meeting, the household willingly pays the fine. And so on. Thus released from interruptions in the labor process on the farm, a cycle is made possible that allows for differential accumulation. The hoary hand of commodification touches first one then another and then another direct social relationship, freezing it and replacing it by its commodity equivalent. The effect of this is that the labor process becomes differentiated within itself: labor within the more capitalized production unit takes on distinctive characteristics from extrahousehold labor.

The line between the domestic and the nondomestic, once a very tenuous thing, is now being drawn in ever sharper and clearer lines. As with the numbered dots making up an invisible figure in a child's play book, so the parameters of the domestic sphere come to be drawn. This is made possible by the commodity form that in turn is called into being by the differential access to capital of at least one unit of production.[8] Such a situation of extrahousehold relations is the one usually described for simple commodity production.

And yet for the Huasicanchinos the anticipated generalization of commodity relations has not taken place because there is a cyclical process built in to the simple commodity producing enterprise just described, regardless of the various conjunctures and crises in the dominant capitalist economy (cf., Kahn 1980). In effect, simple commodity production operates within the two extremes of the expansion and contraction of the sphere of noncommodified labor. In its pure form this sphere is confined to "domestic" labor, the labor available within the immediate household. But because simple commodity production retains much of its competitiveness because it does not have to calculate for profit, the shrinking of its unpaid labor pool, as it withdraws from community social relations, also reduces the amount of labor it can formally subsume and hence drives it back into the community in search of a wider field of unpaid labor. This acts as an incentive to restore its position within the institutions of the community, in order to have access to the cheap labor pool those institutions provide.[9]

Such institutions can be viewed through the interconnected facets of idiom, identity, and use, and it is by tracing changes in these three facets that we can see the process of transformation taking place. Thus we can see that the idiom of certain reciprocal exchanges of labor within the confederations of households may remain the same and may even encourage people to maintain their close identity with the co-participants in that institution, while the use made of this institution by various production units may be changing.

Inasmuch as many of these kinds of noncommodified social relations are necessary for the reproduction of production units despite their variety, so the political struggle expressed in terms of "community" cannot be separated from the daily conditions of these people's existence. For petty commodity producers the prevailing conditions are uncertainty and competition. Community "culture" becomes an oppositional expression essential for survival within the cut-throat competition of dominant capitalist relations for both simple commodity producers and "peasants." The use made of this community culture may differ, however, and thus provide the basis for transformations in the idiom, identity, and use of the community as an institution.

What has been said here applies, in different measure, to a wide range of enterprises among the Huasicanchinos—by no means just the more independent farmers in the village. It may seem that I have devoted undue attention to the rural end of the Huasicanchino economy, but it must be remembered that, in the last analysis, it is the political mobilization expressed by the land recuperation campaign that concerns me. The involvement of the ex-resident (i.e., largely urban) Huasicanchinos in that campaign influences the mechanisms I have described here. The chief characteristic of petty commodity activity on the margins of the urban economy is instability. It is the persistent topic of conversation with interested outsiders just as it is an acknowledged but unspoken chorus in daily discourse among themselves. Within the context of this instability the institutions of the past are put to use to serve contemporary needs.

Conclusion

I have tried to explain why the institutions of the community of Huasicancha retained their dynamism and viability over a period of time—roughly 1948 to the mid-1960s—when people's domestic enterprises became increasingly dispersed and heterogeneous, and the campaign for the land was greatly in abeyance. Once the campaign was reactivated many existing institutions were put to work to serve the political ends of the campaign and that in turn modified those institutions. I have already cautioned against making too radical a separation between political activity and daily livelihood activity. But my purpose here has been to address this question: once the political mobilization reemerged, why was it expressed in the idiom of the community? How did such an expression actually serve to gather together nearly all Huasicanchinos despite the heterogeneity and differentiation that by then characterized them?

There undoubtedly was a period just after the 1947 settlement when numerous interpersonal ties among Huasicanchinos were shattered, and community institutions served very few purposes (see G. Smith 1979a), but as domestic enterprises became more involved in petty commodity production and sale through the 1950s, so endemic institutions reemerged.[10] But they re-emerged now in new economic and political conditions, and as a result, the uses now made of community institutions effectively modified their purpose and meaning for each participant. Nevertheless the words themselves remained the same and retained resonances of the past, so that at one level—their "proper" usage—they remained a common, if never fully explored source of agreement.[11] The heightened political activity of the land invasions then simultaneously gave rise to intensive discourse over the meaning of "key" components of social life and required the outward presentation of a unity that could only be expressed by reference to the old, "proper" usage or "tradition." Thus a struggle to further the class ends of these people takes on the appearance of a fight "for the preservation of tradition" (Hobsbawm 1959). But tradition is no more being preserved than it is being invented from scratch (cf. Hobsbawm and Ranger 1983); rather political engagement provides the arena within which it is continually reinvented.

Thus those enterprises closely approximating simple commodity production in Huasicancha were rarely eager to dispense entirely with the institutions of the community, but this effectively modified the use and hence meaning of those institutions over time. As a result, as will be amply illustrated in the next chapter, persistent internal crises, resolutions, and redirections of the campaign resulted from attempts to specify—and potentially rigidify—the meaning of crucial terms, usually in response to initiatives taken by outsiders. Whenever, for example, the distinction between the fight for the "community" of Huasicancha as a set of particularistic ties and the "Community of Huasicancha" as a state-recognized, legal unit with a specific locale potentially embracing the disputed land was clearly articulated, it led to a local crisis and the reformulation of leadership. Both components were essential for the survival of the various enterprises but in each case for different reasons. Here I have tried to explain this phenomenon by reference to the divergent requirements of social reproduction felt in a variety of enterprises. Where I have discussed experience I have done so by reference to different life histories. I have avoided reference to people's *lived* experience of political engagement itself. Once we become familiar with this phenomenon in the next chapter, the discussion I have presented here will be shown to be necessary but not sufficient. Political struggle itself is not only a necessary part of Huasicanchino survival, but the dynamics inherent in the political mobilization of people having quite heterogeneous livelihood interests (as we have seen here) are at least as important in our understanding of Huasicanchino identity as are the more directly economic elements discussed hitherto. Now that I have said something about these people, while attending to the complex and locally specific details of the social relations of production that so clearly affect their livelihoods and hence their interest in politics, we can turn to the recuperation campaign.

7

The Land Recuperation
Campaign, 1930
to the Present

A movement which only claims to "recuperate" communal lands illegally alienated may be as revolutionary in practice as it is legalist in theory. Nor is the line between legalist and revolutionary an easy one to draw.

—Hobsbawm "Peasant Land Occupations"

Chapter 1 began by drawing attention to the Huasicanchinos' long, drawn-out campaign to recuperate lands they claimed to be theirs, a campaign that culminated in the final "reivindicación" (as they call it) from 1964 to the time of fieldwork in 1972–1973. What little fame the Huasicanchinos might claim for themselves they would claim through this. And now, as we turn to that time and the moments that immediately preceded it, we do so with some awareness of the people involved. We have become familiar with the changing configuration of Huasicanchino social relations and the role of political conflict in their past experience in chapters 2 and 3. And, turning to the contemporary period in chapters 4 and 5, we have seen in some detail that, within the parameters of a common use of the domestic enterprise, there is great heterogeneity among Huasicanchinos' livelihoods. This heterogeneity is indispensable for understanding the form the recuperation campaigns took and then the way in which those campaigns entered the experience of the Huasicanchinos.

Over the past 100 years the highland peasant has been a thing of supreme irrelevance to the proper conducting of state business. Such conditions give rise to rural unrest that then enters the national consciousness as an isolated "incident." These apparently isolated incidents that are reported in the national press or elicit a response from the government are, from the local point of view, one contiguous, political experience in which the *form* of struggle is dictated by actions most appropriate for taking advantage of conditions as they prevail at the level of the region or the state. So we must tackle Huasi-cancha's mobilization along two fronts simultaneously: the crises at the center that provide the opportunity for local initiatives, and the parts played by different groups among the Huasicanchinos as a function of the way in which *they* interpreted prevailing conditions.[1]

In effect this means that after a certain period of engagement, the political campaign itself takes on its own autonomous momentum. We have seen this for the montonera period of the 1880s, when the initial mobilization gave rise to what might almost be termed a mobilized "way of life," working to provision the resistance and resisting to protect the conditions for carrying out such work. And, with the broader resources and intimacy of the more proximate past, we are able to see more intricate dimensions of this process. The picture that emerges is one in which the perpetual debate that emanated out of the heterogeneity described in chapter 5 (over strategy, over goals, over the roles of various parties and so on) gives a heightened color to the power of debate, of language, such that this experience itself had its own significance, its own call for undivided attention—in short, commitment.

Two points follow. First, much can be lost from trying to separate participation in particular events, such as confrontations with the army, arrests, and imprisonments, from the recounting of those events as experience. As events of intense conflict accumulate and are recounted, they become linked together. Because intense events do not remain safely in the past but continue to occur in the present, so the accounts and the events become integrated, the one into the other, so that the experience of the account and the account of the experience are both combined to make up the totality of political experience, giving it an intensity and an autonomy that carry it forward. We have to understand this political experience not as one that occurred despite the Huasicanchinos' heterogeneous livelihood concerns, but because of them.

Second, this rather exciting narrative of political struggle must be reintegrated into the parallel experience of each participant in trying to keep bread on the table. This seems to me to be the opposite side of the coin. On the one hand, then, the politics of Huasicancha were by no means simply a reflection of their social relations of production; on the other, in among the confrontations, the discussions, the decisions to make one more daring move here or there, there was a bottom-line issue of hunger, of getting into the chacra to sow the barley, of keeping an eye on the sheep, or—for the migrants—of keeping the urban enterprise going on its daily rounds.

One final point in the way of a caveat, before I turn to the campaigns themselves, inasmuch as I can take any position besides my own, I want to provide details of the campaigns from the point of view of the Huasicanchinos. Through the success or failure of the campaigns, the fact that a decision was made to go in this direction rather than that and the actual form the confrontations and legal disputes took, were all themselves a direct reflection of the kind of opposition the Huasicanchinos faced, yet I have chosen not to discuss at any great length why that opposition chose to act in one way or the other. This is partly because I don't know. But then the Huasicanchinos didn't know either.

Initiatives Early in the Century

The great surfacing of resistance that had occurred at the end of the last century had done so, of course, in the context of a crisis of the center: the War of the Pacific and the civil war that followed it. The next such crisis came with the accession to power of Augusto Bernardo Leguia to the presidency in 1919 when attention shifted once more to the "peasant question." Huasicancha's response to the confused role and intentions of the state vis-à-vis the peasantry, resulting from the contradictory currents of state policy in the following five years, provides a theme that runs through the ensuing years, one in which chaotic and cynical struggles among political parties attempting to capture the leadership of Peru's elusive power bloc repeated themselves again in the early 1930s, again in the late 1940s, and again in the early 1960s.

The constitutional assembly that Leguia convened in 1919 tackled its task in an atmosphere of unrest in the countryside and renewed delight with the charms of *indigenismo* in the salons of Lima society (Chevalier 1970; Klaiber 1977: 71–91). It was then, amid the widespread belief that the new constitution would reestablish the legal integrity of the Indian communities and the inalienable nature of their title to land, that Huasicancha now registered its old documents in the Property Registration office in Huancayo on 20 November 1919 (RPH).

In 1920 the constitution duly surfaced recognizing comunidades indigenas and prescribing the setting up of a *Sección de Asuntos Indígenas* (Office of Indigenous Affairs) through which such registration should be channeled. Hildegardo Castro Pozo, an energetic and articulate *indigenista* and subsequently one of the founders of the Socialist Party, was to head the new bureau. But the contradictions soon emerged. It was five years before the bureau began to process claims, by which time Castro Pozo had been driven into exile. Moreover the climate of optimism created by decrees was belied by the absence of any real reform, and uprisings took place in the south that were ostentatiously and bloodily put down by the army.

"The peasant question" was to disappear from national discourse once more. But this momentary spotlight did have its effect on the Huasicancha campaign. For the institutional role of the community now superseded individual herders in the struggle over land titles. Henceforth no claim to land could bypass the community authorities and, conversely, no community authority could expect support in office without asserting his unerring opposition to the hacienda's claims. This, in effect, reintroduced the institutions of the community into the question of access to land. For it will be recalled from the latter part of chapter 3 that the expansion of Hacienda Tucle at the end of the last century had precisely undercut the community and its authorities insofar as access to pasture was either mediated through the hacienda administrator (who gave out pasture in return for labor-service, leaving the community authorities minimal amounts of land to distribute to comuneros) or acquired through payment of rents to remote highland communities in Huancavelica.

Once again, in 1933, a constitution was drawn up. Once again provision was made for peasant communities to acquire legal recognition as comunidades indigenas. Once again Huasicancha responded to this situation at the national level and, by 27 October 1936, had achieved recognition through the Sección de Asuntos Indígenas. There was a nice circularity to the situation, however, a kind of Catch 22. Legal recognition was a precondition for repossessing lost lands, but de facto occupancy was a precondition for establishing legal recognition in the first place.

This was not especially shocking to the Huasicanchinos. Recognition had the effect of affirming the inalienable nature of community lands and was therefore a sine qua non for claims against Haciendas Tucle, Rio de la Virgen, and Antapongo on the grounds that they had expanded by alienating communal land. But for the Sección de Asuntos Indígenas, documentation was by no means sufficient evidence. Besides the vagueness of the terms of reference in the documents—reference to ancient-named landmarks and ambivalent notions of what constituted "possession"—it was obvious that the enforcement of all such claims would involve a major redistribution of property that was far from the intention of government.[2] An essential part of the recognition process therefore involved official inspections of the area to report on the actual disposition of claimants to land. De facto possession was thus an essential precondition for recognition that a community did indeed have a claim to specific territory.[3] This meant that a campaign of actual repossession had to accompany the legal campaign for recognition in the Lima Offices of the Sección de Asuntos Indígenas. Thus while the 1919 registration of property as communal gave renewed impetus to community institutions and prepared the way for legal battles, so the 1936 pursuit of legal recognition introduced the strategy of simultaneous legal and extralegal adversarial tactics and initiated the use of a head tax to cover expenses (Hobsbawm 1974).

For the sake of clarity Huasicancha's recuperation of land can be referred to by means of the three areas of territory that they acquired at each stage (see map 3):

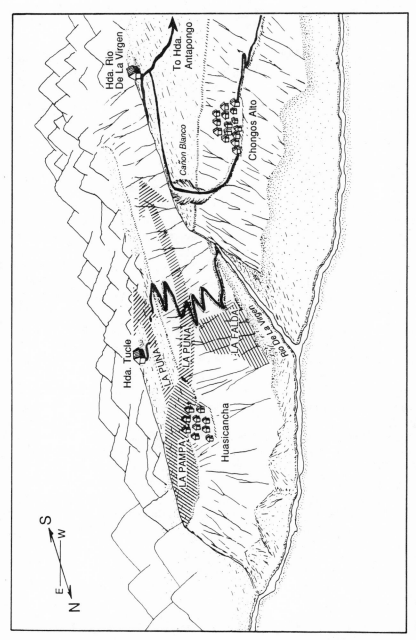

Map 3. Stages in the land recuperation campaign.

1. "La Falda," a small area of hillside land (falda) suitable chiefly for arable plots in the 1930s;
2. "La Pampa," a stretch of flat pastureland, in the 1940s;
3. "La Puna," the remaining area of disputed land, and by far the largest amount, including high mountain pastures, in the 1960s and early 1970s.

La Falda Invasion

The National Context

It is not possible to address the 1930s stage of the campaign by remaining within the confines of Huasicancha alone. Instead we must draw together a number of threads to construct a quite complicated net of national, regional, and local social, economic, and political factors. This is hardly surprising since we have seen in chapter 4 that a number of Huasicanchinos were, by this stage, involved in work on the contratos viales, seasonal migration to coastal plantations, and migration to Huancayo that involved a combination of formal educational and work experiences. The Mantaro Valley was increasingly becoming a region of small-scale commercial operations (Long and Roberts 1978) and in August 1937 the *Minas Cercapuquio S.A.* was established.[4] Reference to chapter 3 will remind us that it was precisely during this period that Manuel Pielago, operator of Hacienda Tucle, was rationalizing operations, expanding his flocks, reducing areas of pasture available to villagers, and attempting to tighten control over his own employees, the shepherds.

Though like all periods of crisis in Peruvian national politics, the issue is controversial; it is important for us to attain some distinct characterization of political conditions at the national level. Huasicanchinos were themselves attempting to reach some such conclusions about the national political situation, and discussions to this end were now part of daily village discourse. From 1930 to 1933 "the centre did not hold." Julio Cotler (1979: 229) describes the situation as follows:

> All the while the popular masses were organized rapidly particularly around APRA and its chief Haya de la Torre. It was from here that the confrontation between the propertied class, now politically disintegrated, and the popular masses, in the process of consolidation, defined the situation as prerevolutionary. Nevertheless, three years later, in 1933, this period closed with the trend being thrown into reverse. The propertied bloc united around Benavides . . . and the military, defeating the popular movement which had tried to destroy the oligarchic state.

There was indeed a period of civil war that most immediately affected the coastal towns but nevertheless had the effect of opening political debate after a long period in which it seemed irrelevant. A massacre in Trujillo in July 1932 set the course for mutual hostility between APRA and the military for subsequent decades. Leguia's successor, Sanchez Cerro, was assassinated in 1933, as a result of which APRA went underground once more. Meanwhile, in the central sierras, in November 1934 uprisings occurred in Ayacucho and Huancavelica while unrest was sufficient in Huancayo itself that the Third Infantry Batallion was dispatched from Lima (Tello 1971: 123).

To understand the role of rural insurgency, indeed of any rural political expression at this time, it is important to recognize the precise character of this period, which revolves around the specific nature of Sanchez Cerro's *caudillaje* and the stage of development of the Peruvian Left. Sanchez Cerro, who often described himself as *El negro* and whose Indianess was sufficiently shocking to the Lima bourgeoisie for one contemporary to liken him to an orangutan (Werlich 1978: 187), was not part of Peru's military establishment and could not count on its unquestioned support. His presidency therefore cannot be seen as one that posed an alternative between an authoritarian military figure and a popular, democratically run political party of the left, headed by Haya de la Torre. And among the Huasicanchinos, while a few significant figures, chiefly migrants (among them Elias Tacunan, see below) became active in APRA, others became outspoken *"cerristas"* (i.e., supporters of Sanchez Cerro).

Much of the discussion in Huasicancha must be seen in the context of the chaos within the Peruvian left. Mariategui, who had resisted Soviet control over the Peruvian Socialist Party, died in the same year as Leguia's term ended, and the PSP split along national versus Moscow lines. APRA was in the process of being reorganized along emphatically authoritarian lines by the Huancayo school teacher who remained a staunch advocate of this "vertical organization" throughout his political career: Ramiro Prialé (Werlich 1978: 204; see also Klarén 1973). Indeed APRA during this period is best understood less as a party of the left than as the petty bourgeois nationalist party that Mariategui called it in 1928.

The prevailing national political conditions within which Huasicanchinos operated then are characterized by a situation in which struggles over control of the state persistently neglected "the peasant question." Crises at the center arose that were not immediately resolved, and in this atmosphere peasant initiatives secured minor footholds. As the century progressed, a new element was added to the pattern: peasant initiatives in the highlands, combined with the failure of one side or another to resolve the crises at the center, acted to force the relevance of the peasantry into the programs of national political parties. The continued absence of any decisive victory of such parties, however, left the peasant question—and the relation of the parties of the left to it—unresolved, and, hence, the failure of those parties to succeed in providing any leadership or control of the movements.

The Local Situation

Such at least was the case for the Huasicanchinos. We must remind our-selves of their composition at this stage. On the one hand, the period of un-easy tension with Tucle was giving way to open conflict. Many pastoralists continued to tackle the problem of their access to pasture by either taking jobs within the haciendas that gave them grazing rights or seeking out remote pas-tures, which either remained freely available for high altitude llama grazing or were rented from communities in Huancavelica. On the other hand, we have seen at the beginning of chapter 4 that many domestic enterprises were undergoing a process of fragmentation as individuals sought income sources beyond the community, while the interhousehold institutions for dealing with the situation had not been adequately established.

We can now turn to the roles of three Huasicanchinos during this period. By the time of the Peruvian crisis of 1930 to 1933, a number of the sons of Huasicancha's better-off pastoralists had achieved some degree of formal edu-cation in Huancayo and were working there or in Lima. Elias Tacunan was one. The son of a caporal working on neighboring Hacienda Antapongo, he had trained as an electrician and joined APRA in Lima in 1931. He was active in the village during the national elections, but by 1936 had fled to Chile as a result of the persecution of APRA activists. But by then he had transmitted his interest in APRA, if in a somewhat confused manner, to a number of the Huasicanchino pastoralists, one of whom, Sabino Jacinto, was alcalde of the newly formed municipality.[5] Jacinto was, for the hacienda and villagers alike, a symbol of the kind of independent-minded pastoralist who was a perpetual scourge to authorities. It was he who provided the frontline tactics of the cam-paign for La Falda.

Involved throughout the period prior to 1930 in various incidents of vio-lence, rustling, and banditry, Jacinto had been born in a mountain estancia sometime around 1885. With the return of hacendado control of the area in the 1890s he went to Huancayo at the age of seven and was earning his own living there soon after. This was followed by eight years as a shepherd on Hacienda Laive and Hacienda Ingahuasi and then as a butter maker there. Around 1910 he was involved in a battle over land that broke out between Huasicancha and the neighboring community of Chacapampa. Although there were a number of deaths, neither side was prepared to refer the matter to out-side authorities and, to this day, nobody is prepared to discuss the casualties.[6] Jacinto was accused of violence and imprisoned, which was only the first of many sojourns in prison. He then found work as a shepherd on Hacienda Tucle where he worked from fifteen to seventeen years.[7] But as tensions rose between the neighboring communities of Chongos Alto and Colca over attempts to set up municipalities independent of Colca, Jacinto became involved again, and in 1927 there was a fight in which one person died and a number were injured.

This then was the pastoralist alcalde who held office as Huasicancha pursued its recognition as a Comunidad Indígena. He, and pastoralists like him, were to spearhead the de facto recuperation of lands. But first the legal proceedings had to be set in motion. And for this part a number of the young Huancayo migrants were to play their roles. One of these was Martín Ramos, and his role in this campaign forms an important part of local history. To grasp the importance of this account it is worth remembering that the 1930s was a transitional period for the Huasicanchinos both in terms of the reformulation of their domestic enterprises and in the reformulation of their political experience. Oral accounts of Martín's participation in events at this stage represent attempts to resolve many of the contradictions and uncertainties that resulted from these objective conditions.

Unlike the villagers in Ciro Alegría's *El mundo es ancho y ajeno* (Broad and Alien is the World), the people of Huasicancha were never assured of the responsibility or loyalty of one leader over another.[8] Nor were they certain of the kind of wiles required for the successful pursuit of the campaign. And these are factors that are contained in the account that follows. What is being discussed at the opening of this account—told on numerous occasions by the old people of the village—is who should handle the legal side of community recognition and what kind of skills such a person would require, for they would undoubtedly be opposed by the hacienda owner.[9]

> Martín arrived back in the village. He had been away for a long time. He found the villagers drinking aguardiente provided for them by the hacendado. He lectured to them on the need to do something in the courts about legal recognition. But they told him to go away. He was just a young man who should respect his elders.
>
> But when they sobered up, they thought well of Martín's advice and sought him out. They told him to go to Huancayo and represent Huasicancha to the government officials. So Martín said,
>
> "I will need money. A lot of money."
>
> So the authorities went away and that same night they went to each house and they collected a *cota* (head tax, quota) from each household head. Then Martín set out for Huancayo that same night, by foot.
>
> When Martín arrived in court (sic) Duarte saw him and was furious because he knew that Martín was very cunning.[10]
>
> "Why is this man here," he said. "He cannot be a Huasicancha delegate. He was born in Colca. Therefore he cannot be a legitimate comunero." Martín was very disheartened and he left the court.
>
> He returned to the village and told the authorities. It was very late at night.

"This is not a problem," they said. And the alcalde made up a new birth certificate for Martín saying that he was born in Huasicancha. Martín returned to Huancayo.

Duarte was furious to see him back. But Martín produced his birth certificate and showed it to him.

"Look!" said Duarte. "He is not yet twenty-one. He cannot be a comunero." So Martín was downcast once more. He returned to the village. But, once there, the authorities simply laughed. The alcalde was brought in once again and the date duly changed. Martín returned that same night to Huancayo. But this time Duarte complained that he was not married and therefore not a household head and could not be a proper delegate.

Again Martín traveled back to the village, certain this time that nothing could be done. But the authorities once more found a solution. It was very late, but they went from house to house and all the young women of the village were brought and lined up. Martín went down the line and picked one. He was married that night, but before they could even consummate the union, he had to leave his wife in a cold bed and go back to Huancayo.

Later the villagers built Martín a house by communal labor. Today he travels all over the mountains and no longer lives in Huasicancha.

So goes the constantly-repeated account of Martín's successful application for Huasicancha's recognition, played out against the persistent opposition of the hacendado. In fact his activities were directed toward the Sección de Asuntos Indígenas in Lima and were carried on chiefly through the mail. The first thing Huasicancha had to do was to establish that it could claim recognition as a native community. Later their claims to lands as being inalienably those of the community would be verified through ocular inspections of de facto possession. So Ramos initiated proceedings in Lima on 8 April 1936. The statements that were drawn up were composed by him and two colleagues with similar backgrounds. The request, apart from laying claim to the majority of Tucle's land, all the land of Hacienda Rio de la Virgen, part of Hacienda Antapongo, and some of the land presently used by Chongos Alto, also stated that:

1. the present tenant, Manuel Pielago, goes so far as to claim that the owner, Maria Luisa Chavez, possesses the entire strip between the pampa and the river;
2. he has been "disrupting our tranquility" [a direct quote from earlier documents], abusing his influence in Huancayo and even sending some of us to jail without the least motive;
3. we cannot survive economically without this land;
4. recognition will give us more power to repossess our rightful land.

It is important to note that the request makes little reference to the titles that Huasicancha possessed, relying rather on the claim of "economic necessity."

It is important to note that the request makes little reference to the titles that Huasicancha possessed, relying rather on the claim of "economic necessity." Secondly, there is no attempt to disguise the motive behind the request for recognition—to repossess the land.

Huasicancha was then told to present any documents that the community might possess, and Ramos requested that the Huancayo Property Registration office send the notarized documents registered in 1919. The letter he later wrote to the Sección complaining of the bureaucratic inefficiency in the registry is revealing. Ramos's suspicion of the motives of the petty bureaucrats is nothing new, but his confrontational attitude toward them and his propensity to write critically of political authorities generally (not just as they affect Huasicancha) is a measure of the radicalization of Huasicanchinos that had occurred through the heightened discourse of the early 1930s:

> The notables and members of the Community of Huasicancha inform me that it is two weeks since the *primera autoridad* of Huancayo received the request for the respective statement concerning the titles of the Community. But despite telegrams sent by you, said authority remains determined to withhold the statement, thus hindering our recognition in this way . . .
>
> It appears that political authorities in the provinces systematically dedicate themselves to withholding reports for month after month without justifiable cause and against the completion of the legal proceedings which are required in these cases which, in fact, should be speeded up because, as indigenas we require protection and the permanent solution of our claims. (O.A.J.)[11]

Huasicancha received recognition on 27 October and the center of interest moved back to the village.

There Jacinto had to busy himself and other villagers preparing the scene for the ocular inspection of de facto possession. An initial claim was made in Huancayo that reflected Huasicancha's own belief that they had acted as the focal point of the montonera campaign of the 1880s, for the Huasicanchino claim was for the return of virtually all the land that had been occupied by the montoneras prior to the reestablishment of hacendado control in the mid-1890s (see chap. 3). Claims were laid to pastures in all the local haciendas: Tucle, Rio de la Virgen, Antapongo, Laive, and Ingahuasi, as well as to lands claimed by some other local villages. A correspondent from Laive wrote that the campaign, "has been thought up, they tell me, by one Sabini or Sabino Román who used to work on Ingahuasi and who has recently been made alcalde" (Hobsbawm 1974: 137ff).[12] Though he referred to the claims as "baseless and absurd," it is interesting to note that in claiming such a sudden expansion in territory, Huasicanchinos were only following the example of Hacienda Tucle at the turn of the century.

Even so, apart from the opposition this generated from other communities (Chácapampa, with whom Huasicancha had fought earlier, wrote to the

Sección de Asuntos Indígenas suggesting that the municipal center should be moved from Huasicancha to their village, in view of Huasicancha's aggression), it is obvious that the Huasicanchinos could not occupy anything like this area. In order to establish de facto possession a different piece of *real politique* came into play. The area of land chosen lay between Haciendas Tucle and Rio de la Virgen. If it belonged to either of the two haciendas rather than to Huasicancha, it was obviously Rio de la Virgen's, but that hacienda was in a chaotic state owing to family squabbles, and so Pielago and Mackenzie were using the land themselves. This land, known as the falda of Pachacayo, was occupied after the harvest of 1937.

Precisely who occupied this land? Nominally those who occupied the land were "those who owed friendship to Sabino." Insofar as Sabino was alcalde of the village, this in effect meant all the villagers of Huasicancha. Nevertheless, a specific quality of village leadership inherited from the past that I emphasized in chapter 2 was that the line between community leadership and headship of a family branch was often unclear, and village leaders frequently used this lack of clarity to the advantage of their most immediate kin. There is evidence that Huasicanchinos were already worried about this aspect of Jacinto's leadership from the moment the land occupation took place (Letter Juez de Paz, Huasicancha to Hacienda Tucle 5 July 1937. A.R.A.). And as the events proceeded, discussions ensued in the village over the character of the elder members of a family on the one hand and the offices of community authorities on the other. "One day he [Jacinto] tells me he commands here; the next day he tells me, 'Uncle? Do not call me uncle. I am no uncle of yours" (minutes of community meeting, 1937, day and month not recorded, A.C.). Engagement in this discussion was made the more pressing because most of the land occupied was arable, and while all communal pasture was held communally, most arable land was held de facto by individual households.

In any event Mackenzie made a deal with the Huasicancha authorities for a very small portion of the land on condition that the villagers fence it. They agreed to the deal, but neither fenced it nor budged from the falda. The administration of the hacienda were considerably alarmed, therefore, when in August of that year they heard that the Sección de Asuntos Indígenas were sending officials to conduct an ocular inspection of the boundaries.[13] Determined to have at least some documentary evidence to fall back on, Maria Luisa Chavez now registered Bernarda Pielago's "taking of possession" document with a notary.

During the ocular inspection Jacinto became increasingly unhappy with the behavior of the man sent from Lima, eventually concluding that he had been bribed by the hacienda. An argument ensued, and Jacinto was arrested. He was taken to Huancayo where he was accused of being a communist agitator disturbing the otherwise peaceful communities of the area. He was shipped thence to Lima, and two men from the nearby community of Moya were found to give evidence against him. According to Jacinto's account of events, he was beaten with a rubber hose and kept in a darkened cell, and at one time was offered a bribe to sign a statement that he refers to as *un canto* (a song).[14] He claims that he was planted with political leaflets and that the statement he made was altered. Finally he was moved to the prison island of El Fronton from which, he says, "He sido loco saliendo de la carcel" ("I was mad on leaving the prison"). Importantly, while obviously Jacinto's account has its own perspective, like Laimes before him, he never denies being a troublemaker, nor that he was a supporter of APRA during this time. At one point in the interview he said, "No estaba por la izquierda, sino por nuestros derechos" ("I was not for the Left, but for our rights"). Eventually, in 1940, the Sección did recognize Huasicancha's claim to a small piece of land on the falda. Meanwhile Hacienda Tucle settled a piece of land on the community that was claimed entirely by Jacinto and his immediate relatives. Once in possession of this land, moreover, Jacinto began to work for the hacienda.

There were then lessons to be learned from this settlement. Not only was undue support given to Jacinto's leadership, but the precise nature of the land being struggled over and Jacinto's role in that struggle, though debated, was never settled prior to the hacienda's concessions. And not only was the amount of land thus gained disappointing, but the settlement neither effectively challenged Maria Luisa Chavez's claim to the pastures used by the hacienda nor established the community nature of the land-claim (and hence the rights of all comuneros). And finally the identification of the hacendada and hacendado with the national government was made manifest when, in 1939, Manuel Pielago became a senator for Huancayo.

La Pampa Invasion

June 1972, Victor Hinostrosa describes the events as follows:

> In 1947. In the year 1947 once more: again. But this time all of the village went in [to the hacienda land] with all the animals, the whole village went in. We made an invasion with all the animals. Everything! All there was, we drove them on!
>
> Those of us who were living in Huancayo—who had some work there—it was they who had the idea. I will tell you how it happened. Wait. Three of us were in charge here in the village. We were the leaders. They were the ones who had the idea but we were the ones who executed the plan. At first only we three knew, you understand. Then later, the village. Nobody. Nobody else knew. There was a guardia post here in those days, so it was all secret.
>
> I was the gobernador.
>
> Those from Huancayo arrived late at night. It was Christmas Eve [1946]. We met secretly in the school building. I remember. It was raining very hard. The rain was sounding on the roof as we talked. Then I ordered the small boys, the little ones, to go from house to house, in the night with the rain. Rain. Rain.

It was to be for the following day. Silence. Nobody said a word. With all the animals in the night we went. Not a chicken, nor a guinea pig [was left in the village]. Everything! At six in the morning we were on the land, the *chosas* [huts] smoking, the women cooking.

That morning, the police commander got up: "What's happened? Nobody! Where? Aha!" Silence! We were up on the pampa of the hacienda with our animals. We stayed there for three months.

When those of Chongos Alto had heard of our plan, they had said: "You are foolish. What can foxes do against the army. You are cunning but the army have guns.[15] We call them clipped hens, you understand. We are the foxes. But then they saw that we had entered [the hacienda land], then they went on the land of Hacienda Antapongo. They had no plan. No leaders. They had no cunning [*astucia*] like the foxes! The army came. A battalion from the 43rd *Cuartel*. After we had been on the land for four days they came.

Before they arrived, they went through Chongos Alto. They were stupid. They threw stones at the soldiers. They jeered at them. There was a massacre in Cañon Blanco. Nine were killed. Many were wounded. Later I, Martín, and Antonio, we passed through on the way to Huancayo. There were wounded here. They were there. Many people.

We were waiting on the hill near Huaculpuquio. We were very afraid because we could hear the shooting. At two in the afternoon there arrived an officer called Mora, with the hacienda administrator, employees of the hacienda and troops. Mora took out his revolver. The people, they stayed back. Behind us. We were the leaders. Only we spoke to the officer. We spoke very forcefully. He said that he had been told that we had invaded the land. "How can that be, señor?" we said. "This is our land. Look here at our huts. How can we invade our land? You see [the straw on] the roofs of the huts, how old it is. It is a mistake."

At that moment there began a big thunder storm. Lightning! Big thunder. Hail! A very big storm. The army commander was afraid. The troops were in line abreast with their guns ready like this. They were afraid too. The officer decided to go back to the farm buildings. He went on his horse. The soldiers, they went on their feet, hah! They didn't come back. They went back to Huancayo.

We stayed on the pampa. The leaders we went to Huancayo. We got a lawyer. The hacendado tried to frighten us. He came with his truck and shot our animals. Five animals. My mule was shot here [points to his thigh]. But it got better. Only a flesh wound.

We wanted a judge, you understand. But we were accused of being Apristas again. Me, Elias, Martín. And now Antonio. Again my father too. Because they said we were agitators.

That land. That land up to Huaculpuquio. We got that land then. In the quality of a sale. Not in court. But by sale. The payment took the form of a long ditch which we had to build between that land and the hacienda. That was the price. Then they continued the persecution from Huancayo. I became the Justice of the Peace in the village. Still they accused me. This was 1948. Always they were after me. I had to hide. But they caught me here. Here in my house! Just like that. Two sergeants came. They took me to Huancayo. Two weeks in Huancayo. This was 1948 or 1949.

What did he say the Prefect of Huancayo? He said, "Send an officer to the Prefect of Lima. That this person is a very dangerous Aprista. Against the government. He must be eliminated. Because of him there have been massacres in Cañon Blanco. He was the leader there."

In the village though, we had the land. We were using the pasture.[16]

The events that preceded and followed the Pampa Invasion of 1946 described here by Victor Hinostrosa were far more dramatic and confrontational than those of La Falda. Moreover, while they were similar to previous confrontations in that they took place in the context of a crisis at the national level, they differed in two important ways. First, as we have seen in chapter 5, by the 1940s Huasicanchino enterprises were becoming much more heterogeneous than before, and second, a broader spectrum of comuneros were becoming involved in the direction of the campaign, replacing the few significant figures of the 1930s.

The National Context and the Changing Local Resource Base

As for the crisis at the center, despite the superficial alliance between President Bustamente's party and APRA between 1945 and 1948, Haya de la Torre's engagement in legitimate politics was accompanied by APRA's hitherto most energetic drive toward extralegitimate political engagement. Bustamente entered office firm in the belief that Peru was approaching an APRA-inspired revolution (Werlich 1978:234), and throughout the period APRA's organization drove toward that end. APRA itself was nevertheless fundamentally split not just between those who courted a more conservative constituency and applauded Haya's newly-found friendship with the U.S., on the one hand, and the party's radical left, on the other, but also between Haya's highly authoritarian kitchen clique and the middle and lower level party organizers.

In the region this split within APRA was significant. It was represented in the persons of Ramón Prialé, APRA senator for Huancayo who was unwilling to condemn the local hacendados; and Elias Tacunan, a Huasicanchino *hijo del pueblo* and middle level party organizer. As this dichotomy became apparent it gave rise to a wide variety of views of APRA that were superimposed on an increasingly heterogeneous variety of Huasicanchino domestic enterprises. The heightened political discourse among the Huasicanchinos which thereby resulted had a significant effect on the form of the 1947–1948 campaign. Meanwhile, at the local level, it must be remembered that by 1947, all households in Huasicancha were on the edge of poverty because the basis of the economy—pastoralism—was being eroded by Hacienda Tucle's persistent attempts to establish exclusive control over the pasture of the area.

As we have seen in chapter 4 the result of this attempt was to increase the heterogeneity of Huasicanchino domestic enterprises, while simultaneously putting a great strain on the linkages between them. With livestock and arable resources subject to attrition at a time when the Huancayo and Lima economies were expanding, Huasicanchinos began to enter other sectors of the economy so that extrafarm income shifted from symbiotic links of one kind or another with the hacienda to income sources in Huancayo and (in a very few cases) Lima. This process took different forms for different enterprises. A number of pastoralist enterprises began to establish their children in Huancayo and, to a lesser extent, Lima. The effect was for households to shift their emphasis on a local resource base without actually terminating their involvement in farming. Other households with a smaller pastoralist base relied on providing artisan and other services to those neighbors in the local, highland economy that had hitherto drawn on their own households for such things: pottery, weaving, trading, etc. The overall effect of this was to weaken the interhousehold links of these people, isolating them from reciprocal linkages and thus eroding the bottom-line security base in times of crisis. These were the households from which sprang those people I have called "huasis." They were both less immediately involved in migration and partook less in the direction of the 1940s campaign than did the "canchas."

The push for La Pampa, then, reflected a response on the part of Huasicanchino households either fragmented by migration or rendered insecure by a diminished personnel resource base to reassert their integrity by reformulating their intrahousehold and interhousehold links ("confederations of households") that predated the period. It turned out to be a qualified failure. Not only did it result in a very small acquisition of land but the land was acquired through a deed of sale by the hacienda, not through the exercise of claims made by the comunidad indigena through the courts. Far from underscoring the illegitimacy of the hacienda's claim, therefore, the sale actually implied hacienda ownership. The effect of this disappointment was to institutionalize extrafarm incomes—especially, but not specifically through migration—in the subsequent period.

The Local Situation

From 1945 to the invasion of land by Huasicancha as a body in late 1946 tensions mounted both specifically between hacienda and pastoralists in the region around Tucle-Huasicancha and, more generally, as Huasicanchino migrants became engaged in the political atmosphere of confrontation in the region and nation. Ironically it was APRA that provided the incentive both for the hacienda and for the Huasicanchinos to increase their pressures on one another. And so before discussing the events of the invasion itself and the debates that revolved around them and thus gave continual momentum to the Huasicanchino campaign, we must turn first to the development of these conflicting forces prior to the 1947 invasion, first at the hacienda, and then among the migrants in Huancayo.

Ramón Prialé, the APRA senator for Huancayo, and his allies on the Huancayo municipal council endorsed Haya's slogan of 1945: "We do not want to take away the wealth of those who have it," and he stressed support for those landlords who were prepared to transform their properties into capitalist operations. Under such optimistic conditions, Manuel Pielago was trying to rationalize his operations on the hacienda. Hacienda Tucle and Hacienda Rio de la Virgen were brought together and run as a single unit and attempts were made to establish greater control over territory. Because fencing was financially impossible and of proven impracticality against Huasicanchinos, this meant more vigilant patrolling. This in turn required the employment of those most familiar with rustling and trespassing techniques, i.e., ex-rustlers and trespassers.[17]

An agronomist was hired to do a report on the running of the hacienda and found 17 percent of the hacienda's livestock were being lost per annum. It was feared that much of the problem lay with paying shepherds through the institution of huacchilla. But attempts to move into a wage relationship with employees and to replace the arrangement for *pasaderos* ("trespassers")—in which animals caught were returned to their owners in return for labor—by a cash fine, had the effect of reawakening animosity over the legitimacy of Tucle's land claims.

Both huacchilla and pasadero were fraught with tensions in the past. But in both cases they did allow for some use of hacienda land by Huasicanchinos. And in both cases this was regarded as legitimate practice. The move toward cash relationships quickly revealed the differing interpretation of the meanings of these institutions on the part of the two parties involved. In the case of the huacchilla, while Huasicancha and the hacienda administration agreed that the custom was an old and well-established one, the Huasicanchinos also included within the huaccha animals they pastured on hacienda land michipa animals too. These latter were animals hacienda shepherds grazed on behalf of villagers who cared for their arable plots in the village in return, and neither hacienda shepherds nor their village partners could afford to do without that institution. The hacienda, however, specifically did not recognize the presence of michipa animals in the contracts they drew up with shepherds. Because they made no such recognition, they misjudged a) the degree to which hacienda shepherds were in fact tied into their home communities, and b) the extent to which the move to a wage relationship would be a threat to the community as a whole as opposed to just the immediately-affected shepherds.

In the case of the pasadero, the differing meanings held by the two parties were in some ways even more revealing of the link between the commodification of the labor relationship and a contractual claim to territory that was, by definition, exclusive of joint use by both parties. Correspondence between community authorities and the hacienda administration at this time reveals that what most infuriated Huasicanchinos was the newly developed habit of the administrator or his foreman to lecture to the pasaderos on their infringement of the law by "trespassing." It is clear from the correspondence that the practice of spending occasional days on hacienda land and, if caught doing so, being expected to do some work for the hacendado in return, was by no means considered by the Huasicanchinos to be an acknowledgment of the hacendado's claim to the land as an exclusive one.

Labor difficulties then, mounted from 1945 onward, and Hacienda Tucle attempted to deal with this by making joint agreements with the neighboring haciendas to prevent employees blacklisted on one hacienda from taking up employment on another. When hacienda employees began to attend meetings of the newly-formed employees union at Haciendas Laive and Antapongo, the Tucle administration did not object. It was hoped that the unions would replace the now fully legalized communidades indigenas as the representatives of the shepherds and thus drive a wedge between employees and local comuneros.

On 24 July 1946 Laive sent a letter to Tucle saying that they had fired seven employees, including Sabino's son Julio Jacinto, because they were considered "subversive elements." These people then returned to their home community of Huasicancha, where they found a lively discussion in progress revolving around complaints about Hacienda Tucle. This inevitably close relationship between the hacienda employees and the nearby village from which they came cannot be overemphasized. Although Tucle attempted to reduce its commitment to Huasicanchino labor, the strength of the offensive in 1947 (and later, in the 1960s too) lay as much in the fact that hacienda shepherds were persuaded, willingly or otherwise, not to cooperate with their employer, as in the actual occupation of the land itself. During 1947 Haciendas Tucle, Laive, and Antapongo were forced to fire *"por elementos indeseables"* over fifty employees (ARA). As a result, animals went unguarded at times when they were most vulnerable to "foxes," and there was a danger that the harvest would rot in the field for lack of a work force to reap it.

But pastoralists—both hacienda shepherds and roving flock owners—were now sharing their influence in the community with an entirely different and ever-growing group: the migrants who had become established in Huancayo and, in a few cases, in Lima and La Oroya. To these migrants it was not the senator from Huancayo who represented the true spirit of APRA but Elias Tacunan, who had been sent by the party to La Oroya to help found the *Federación Regional de Trabajadores Mineros del Centro (F.R.T.M.C.)* (Handelman, 1975:140). Tacunan and other Huasicanchinos were associating with migrants from villages in the Mantaro Valley itself that were far more commercialized than Huasicancha. Such migrants saw a different kind of capitalist development in APRA's program than did Prialé. They were reinvesting back into their communities and wanted every barrier to that activity removed.[18] For Huasicanchinos that barrier was Hacienda Tucle.

Even so the significance of migrants in Huasicancha during this period should not be overemphasized. The diaspora came after, rather than before the invasion of La Pampa. A number of the children of pastoralists (people I have referred to as "canchas") were by now living in Huancayo and a very few in Lima. Migration had just begun as well to Cercapuquio, the nearby mine, but the numbers were small and the people involved were not immediately involved in the direction of events. For households with less livestock and often therefore somewhat poorer in material resources (people I have referred to as "huasis"), seasonal migration continued to the cotton plantations on the coast, and sporadic work was found in Huancayo, when possible. While the majority of migrants in Huancayo were of this rather unstable kind, it was the few more established Huasicanchinos, trading or working in such skilled jobs as carpenters, electricians, and mechanics, whose participation in the campaign contributed to its particular form.

On 20 August 1945 the *Centro Cultural, Huasicancha* was formed in Huancayo. It soon became the locale for discussions about the future of the community. These discussions were made more relevant because at no time were the migrants prevented from holding office within the community itself, by virtue of nonresidence. Reference to the membership roster and minutes give some idea of the kinds of discussions that were taking place at the time.[19] Included in the Huancayo club were Martín Ramos, who had played an important part in the legal and financial arrangements in the previous campaign; Elias Tacunan, some ten or fifteen years older than Martín, but active by 1947 in La Oroya; Elias Yaurivilca, later to found the local branch of FENCAP (the APRA peasant league) and to act as APRA's provincial secretary; Antonio Y., the illegitimate son of a Huasicancha woman, who practiced in Huancayo as a pharmacist's assistant; Herminio Z., married to the only child of a flock owner from Yanacancha, who also had a small shop in Huancayo. (Herminio was the brother of Victor Hinostrosa, the narrator of the above text and a village leader of the invasions; see fig. 2). A number of members of the club were from similar, essentially pastoralist, backgrounds in Huasicancha but were in fact resident not in Huancayo but in Lima. There were

five or six migrants there who kept pressure on the Lima-based Sección de
Asuntos Indígenas, and who paid a head tax to cover expenses and also had
among their number the then personero of the Community of Huasicancha.

Essentially it was discussion among these migrants and the villagers that
gave the campaign its specific character. There were plenty of people who
migrated sporadically to Huancayo, a few who had found work in the local
mine at Cercapuquio, and of course the seasonal plantation migrants. As
events took shape they undoubtedly began to form opinions about the way
things should go, but the real migration had not yet occurred. The campaign
for La Pampa took place around a heightened discourse between those who
shared a common background in pastoralism but whose contemporary sources
of livelihood had now begun to vary, giving them different concerns for the
reproduction of their particular domestic enterprises.

Migrants not only affected intravillage discourse but also played what little
role there was to play in intervillage discourse. The administrations of the
haciendas, as we have seen, feared that there would be concerted action on
the part of the communities that surrounded them, and they conveyed this
impression to the authorities in Huancayo. The evidence that such an alliance
ever came anywhere near fruition, or that it was even considered in the village
itself, is nil. Huancayo migrants from these villages did talk about the simi-
larity of their problems and entertained the possibility of at least some form
of alliance, at some rather vague time in the future. None of them was in
sufficient control of things in his own village, however, to be able to solidify
such ideas. It was therefore only after an invasion had been initiated by one
village (Huasicancha) that there was any possibility of a more general confrontation and then only as a result of a chain reaction rather than a well-
planned series of invasions or a longer term strategy. Exchanges of ideas and
strategies between villages took place not directly between one set of village
authorities and another but between migrants who were often members of the
same political groups in Huancayo and between the hacienda workers who
themselves were members of the surrounding communities.

In any event, both Huancayo migrants and hacienda shepherds were represented at the first secret meeting, held in early December 1946. The strategy
of occupying the long flat pampa between the fundo itself and the community
(see map 2) was agreed upon in principle although the ultimate goal was never
clarified and was later found to be quite different for different groups. The
tactics of the land-occupation were left to the village leaders. Apart from the
formal officeholders, these included a number of others who were voted into
their positions by all household heads and were referred to as *delegados* (delegates). Of greatest importance for the direction of these tactics was a core
of village residents, whose migration experience never included more than
trips to Huancayo, work in Cercapuquio, and past experience on the contratos
viales. These men were, generally speaking, the larger flock owners who re-

lied for pasture on the high altitude land on the other side of the hacienda, near the Huancavelica village of Acobambilla. Victor's father, for example, Silvestre Hinostrosa (who was also Martín's father-in-law), and his brother (see fig. 2) had rented land there but had found that labor conditions on Tucle were forcing the villagers there to use the pasture themselves.

From 15 December onward, robberies of sheep from the hacienda increased, and shepherds began leaving their estancias on the hacienda. The administration complained to the local civil guard posts in Chongos Alto and Huasicancha, but tension was already high, and the officers were reluctant to leave their posts and still more reluctant to confront village authorities (ARA; FHT). On 23 December another secret meeting was held and the events described by Don Victor occurred shortly thereafter.

Seeing Huasicancha occupy hacienda land, a number of other communities did likewise. But none of them was able to deal with the opposition of the hacienda staff, the army, the civil guard, or the political and legal authorities from Huancayo—or a combination of them all—and they retreated. Huasicanchinos today ascribe this difference to their own past experience in mobilizing against the regional power bloc. A meeting was held on the pampa on the first day and on almost all days during the subsequent month. Small huts were built using fire-scarred stones and old thatching straw to give them the appearance of having been there "since time immemorial." A small school was set up for the children; much time was spent teaching the children the false names of prominent landmarks and how to refer to their parents so as not to give their names away. Lookouts were posted in such a way that they could report the approach of any vehicle three hours before it could arrive on the pampa. Finally relatives of hacienda employees were encouraged to visit their estancias to persuade them to drive their animals and those of the hacienda into the peasant camp.

Hobsbawm (1974) suggests that soon after this the invasions subsided, but this is far from the case. On 26 February the Huancayo migrant representatives began moves toward what they saw to be their goal in the campaign: to use confrontation on the pampa as a bargaining card to obtain an agreement from the Sección de Asuntos Indígenas acknowledging Huasicancha's claim to at least some land (how much was never very clear). A temporary agreement was reached to acknowledge a piece of no-man's land between the hacienda building (the fundo) and the invaders' camp. But that was the closest thing to an agreement. On 17 February Tucle, fearing things were getting out of hand, sent a letter to all nearby communities warning them that invaders would be treated harshly. The community authorities replied in the humble and deferential tones usual at such times. But at least two of these communities had invaded Tucle by the end of that year.

Together with squatting, the community also withdrew all its traditional labor services to the hacienda. When the hacienda then tried to use the remaining shepherds—from Chongos Alto and other nearby villages—to bring in the harvest, there were strong objections from their community authorities, insisting that such labor could only be derived from a communal faena organized through the acknowledged community authorities (Letters of Chongos Alto and Moya to Hacienda Tucle, June, 1947 ARA). Moreover the squatting on La Pampa was just the tip of the iceberg. At night the pampa provided a bridgehead for incursions by parties of pastoralists deep into hacienda land. Something of what these incursions were like is captured by this report from a junior officer to his lieutenant, explaining his actions following the orders he had received:

> Following the orders you gave me today to send a 2nd sergeant and six men to the place named 'Analanya', where the mayordomo of this hacienda, Don Alejandro Tembladera, had seen the comuneros of Huasicancha invading the pastures of the hacienda with sheep, cattle and horses.
>
> I found myself in the place above named at around 1330 hours with the mayordomo, Tembladera, and the caporales of the hacienda, who showed us the place where there were approximately 2000 animals.
>
> To undertake my commission I ordered that the soldiers JD, JB and VF accompany the foreman and his caporales to make certain that we were necessary, remaining myself with the rest of the personnel (according to my orders) in the place known as 'Cabildo-Pata' with the aim of preventing the enormous quantity of Indian men and women—more than a hundred in number—from advancing. The soldiers dismounted to stop the transit of the animals, something which was impossible. I and the other three were insufficient to be able to control the invasion in the upper zone.
>
> Taking advantage of our small numbers and seeing that we were dismounted in the pampa of 'Analanya' they threw stones at the employees of the hacienda and at us, shouting that it was by order of . . . the Judge of Huancayo, that they had permission to stay there in that place because that was their legitimate property and for that reason they were decided to die before they would allow their animals to be taken away to the hacienda.
>
> They offered in this way a tenacious resistance and set upon us, surprising us in such a way that, as a result, the soldier VF was thrown to the ground from his horse breaking his gun near the bolt. Under these conditions of the fury of the attackers, I ordered that shots be fired in the air, thinking that this would drive them off but it was useless; to the contrary, they attacked more, such that I had no alternative but to go along with your orders and fire again, wounding a bull which died from the injury. Only in this way could I get them to retreat and leave us to take the animals—in the small numbers that were by then left to us—180 sheep, 24 cattle and 7 horses. (ARA, 13 August 1947)

Asked by Asuntos Indígenas officials to explain this behavior, in view of the temporary agreement reached, the Huancayo residents were embarrassed and sent representatives to the village to point out that squatting on La Pampa was enough to make a symbolic point while legal channels were followed to bring pressure on the hacienda, but that further incursions, undercutting as they did the agreement they had made with the Sección, only acted to reduce any residual goodwill felt toward the villagers in Huancayo (AC).

Whether these representatives then returned to Huancayo bemoaning to the officials their poor reception in the village is unclear. But soon thereafter, on 15 March, the commander of the civil guard and members of the hacienda administration arranged to meet with the village authorities to find out just what *they* were after, as opposed to their Huancayo representatives. Finding that no agreement was to be reached the civil guard used an old tactic, one the villagers of sixty years earlier had fallen victim to. They promptly arrested people identified by the hacienda as "leaders."[20]

Characteristically this in turn led to the reenactment of an old and proven response. The villagers withdrew from offensive positions, respecting the established no-man's land. The civil guard, interpreting this action to signify the success of their tactic of arresting the leaders, withdrew all but a handful of troops. The Huasicanchino villagers then advanced as before. Thus deprived of what they considered adequate protection, the hacienda fell to taking action of its own. Squatters were attacked, their huts burned, their animals taken and their corrals destroyed. They also tried to introduce a strong dose of fear into their relationship with the shepherds, who themselves addressed a petition to the representative of the Sección in Huancayo complaining of their harsh treatment at the hands of the administration. Then, on 30 April ten employees resigned their jobs. The hacienda correspondence suggests that the administration believed that they were persuaded to leave through threats from their relatives of fines from the community authorities, ostensibly for their absence from community faenas (FHT).

While tension continued high for both the community and the Huasicanchinos who had been shepherds on the hacienda and had now resigned, in Huancayo the migrants were employing Oscar Bernuy, a sympathetic lawyer, with a view to approaching Pielago for a settlement. For those who were directing events in the village—those who came from pastoralist families in the past and were themselves trying to maintain domestic enterprises based on local resources—the squatting on La Pampa as well as the incursions it allowed were virtually an end in themselves: if they could be carried out long enough they would become a way of life that was essentially an ancient *status quo ante*. But for the migrants directing affairs in Huancayo—who also came from pastoralist families in the past, and hence drew on a similar resource bank of experience as the village leaders, but were now themselves trying to establish domestic enterprises based on a delicate balance between the urban petty commodity economy and the rural, peasant economy—the invasion of La Pampa was only a means to an end. Living in Huancayo as they did they would never be able to have the whip hand on pasture in the area through the old symbiotic relationship between Hacienda Tucle and Huasicancha. For them the end was a legal contract which established exclusive rights to specific plots of pasture. And the invasion was merely a form of political leverage to get it.

The lawyer's position made it possible for both views to be held concurrently. He felt that the hacendado had been sufficiently inconvenienced, if not intimidated, to come to an agreement on terms favorable to the Huasicanchinos. He suggested that what the hacienda most feared was some kind of acknowledgment on the part of the Sección that Huasicancha had a legitimate claim to some vaguely defined piece of land. Instead what he suggested was that an out of court "sale" by the hacienda to Huasicancha of the Pampa land then being squatted on would certainly give the Huasicanchinos undisputed control of that land. But strictly speaking such a sale would be illegal and hence not recognized under the terms of the 1933 constitution, should the community later manage to fight a further case against the hacienda—one which he certainly planned on encouraging them to do (Bernuy, Interview, Huancayo, September 1972). The hacienda was approached and agreed to a sale, payment for which would take the form of the digging of a dividing ditch, a *sanja,* between the two properties to be undertaken by community faenas.

The proposal was taken to a community meeting in Huasicancha. For the reasons already mentioned, the pastoralist families with most influence at this time were opposed to any such arrangement, especially one which, because of the *sanja,* would make night incursions dangerous for the animals. But there were others in the village, as well as the more sporadic migrants to Huancayo, who had far less of a direct or pressing commitment to livestock and hence need for pasture. The old pastoralist households argued that the situation could do nothing but get worse for the hacienda because the Huasicanchinos' livelihood was not as directly dependent upon getting goods to market at very specific times as was the hacienda's economy. But many other villagers were straining under the weight of persistent tensions, movement to neighboring villages had been badly disrupted, and relations with them were often so poor as to make sales of craft skills and trade very difficult (AC).

Much of the discussion was interlarded with patriotic speeches on the importance of preserving Huasicancha's heritage both cultural (way of life) and material (claims to pasture) so that nobody could be heard publicly to voice the opinion that the struggle should be terminated. Instead much could be heard of complaints that had the effect of implying criticism of one group or another and, near the end of the meetings, hints were made, at least among some of the village residents, that if a few delegates chose to make an agreement with the hacienda, well we might always see what happened after that—a hint that past agreements had not always been abided by (AC).

After these meetings a "sale" was arranged with Augusto Duarte, son of the owner, Maria Luisa Chavez, on 28 May 1948. Work was begun on the ditch but remained intermittent and was far from complete by the end of that year, suggesting that the villagers had by no means accepted the agreement in good faith. Their assessment of the predicament facing Hacienda Tucle and indeed of the local environment generally was sophisticated. But what may well have encouraged the migrant representatives to settle for a quick sale was their assessment of the changing regional and national climate, for the instability at the center that had always been used to such good purpose by Huasicancha gave way, after February, to the ousting of all APRA members of municipal councils and calls from the military to ban APRA once more.

By October APRA's coup d'état having failed, the party was once more repressed and APRA supporters, so-defined rather indiscriminately, imprisoned. In a sweep that surprised even the cautious villagers, the army picked up most of the village's authorities, now out in the open following the settlement. They were shipped to Lima where they were imprisoned in El Fronton as "political subversives" (See G. Smith, 1975). General Odria took over the presidency, and in July of 1949 civil liberties were suspended. Taking advantage of the situation, Manuel Pielago, husband of Tucle's owner, had authorities appointed in the community who were favorably disposed to the hacienda and, on 22 August, had a second bill of sale signed by these new authorities.

The invasion of La Pampa was over, and a long period of repression was to set in. For the Huasicanchinos much of the optimism that had driven the campaign forward was now replaced by dismay at the future of a life in the village, and as we have seen, a wave of migration followed throughout the 1950s.

Evidently a broader section of the Huasicanchino population were now involved in the direction of the campaign compared with the previous campaign for La Falda. Then it was possible to restrict attention to two or three key figures—Elias Tacunan, Sabino Jacinto, Martín Ramos—all of whom emerge from a background closely tied to pastoralism, what I have called "the cancha" families. However the past background of the members of a domestic enterprise is no longer sufficient to explain the interests of households in the campaign. Now it is necessary to add to this past genealogy, the present pattern of the varying livelihood pursuits of different domestic enterprises.

Because the people who first got established in Huancayo were those whose past family background had been in pastoralism, it was they among the migrants who influenced matters. They were nonetheless from the old pastoralist households and in fact were often related to the authorities resident in the village itself who were themselves "canchas." So in effect, while canchas continued to take a lead in the recuperation campaign, their voice was no longer one. Their sense of identity that derived from a common background—one in which, as pastoralists, the struggle over control of pasture had always been of central concern—was now crosscut by contemporary concerns having to do with the future reproduction of enterprises that were based on different sets of resources.

A dialogue sprang up, provoked by the campaign and put into ever clearer focus as it developed, between the heads of enterprises in which the balance of agricultural and nonagricultural income differed. The dialogue was, to a great extent, restricted at least in its immediate significance to pastoralists or to the progeny of pastoralists. But by the end of the campaign other voices were becoming more insistent. And with the coming of the campaign for La Puna in the 1960s these voices were to contribute a major part to the form the struggle took. But the point is that this dialogue foreshadowed a new Huasicancha. While most of the words remained the same, the Huasicanchinos using them became more varied, so that different inflections of meaning were put on those words. Much of the impetus of the 1947–1948 campaign evolved from that internal discourse among an albeit restricted group of Huasicanchinos. With the coming of the campaign for La Puna, a still greater variety of Huasicanchinos had a role to play, and the discourse became still more heated and again gave great momentum to the struggle itself.

La Puna Invasion

> With great urgency I write to put you in knowledge of the following: The personnel of this hacienda, having already been considerably threatened have now become aware of a veritable invasion by the community of Huasicancha. These are in the following places: Analanya, a large flock of sheep, cattle and horses. In Picpish they are building huts and there is an alarming quantity of livestock of the community. In the zone of Anchi a large quantity consuming the best hacienda pasture—this confirms that by night they passed through the areas of Huachamachay, Arauca Pachca [etc.] with many animals. This movement of the comuneros of Huasicancha was still continuing at 1 PM and at Cabildo Pata there is a community authority (Ascensio A) who is giving orders to all who leave the village telling them where to go and with what flocks, all of them carrying staves and other moveables in the direction of the puna of the hacienda.

> The matter must be dealt with urgently in order to avoid confrontations with the hacienda staff and the mixing of their animals with ours. Pedro P has already lost 10 of his animals and we shall certainly lose more.

> I am sending this with the truck driver to make clear to you the gravity of the situation which faces us here at Tucle.

> —Letter from Administrator to Manuel Duarte,
> Huancayo, 24th April 1964 (ARA)

COMUNEROS BREAK PACT: INVASION AT TUCLE

Approximately a thousand peasants of the community of Huasicancha yesterday morning invaded the lands of the Tucle Livestock Co. in an area covering over 10 kilometres.

Carrying flags, sticks, and banners with the phrase "Land or Death" on them, the peasants installed themselves—challengers—some 3 kilometres from the hacienda buildings.

The residence is guarded by 40 employees.

Included with these acts of invasion the comuneros trespassed 5000 head of sheep and 1500 cattle and have taken over the area, putting up their own shepherd's huts.

Manuel Duarte, the chief administrator of the hacienda, said he thought the invaders were being organized by foreign elements with communist inclinations.

The Tucle Livestock Co. is one of the most important of the region. It covers an area of 45,000 hectares and owns 20,000 Corriedale sheep and 2000 Brown Swiss cattle.

—Huancayo newspaper, 25 April 1964

The period of Odria's presidency saw relative quiescence around the hacienda and Huasicancha. True the telephone wires were cut on average once a year; true too that pasaderos continued their activities. But wool prices remained high during the first three years, and Pielago hired one of the inheritors of Hacienda Rio de la Virgen, an agronomist whom he had bought out, to take over the administration of both haciendas. The latter succeeded in systematically improving the hacienda's flocks and established better control over pasture by signing an agreement of friendship with Huasicancha in 1951 and employing Sabino Jacinto as a watchdog over hacienda pastures. Persistent attempts to move shepherding contracts from huacchilla arrangements to wages met with only partial success and remained—with similar attempts to institute pasadero fines in lieu of labor service—the most continual source of tension between hacienda and community.[21]

As the decade progressed, however, the hacienda family's early optimism gave way to frustration, gradually increasing to desperation by 1958. After 1951 international wool prices began an erratic but general decline. In 1954 Pielago died and Maria Luisa Chavez, searching in vain for a buyer, withheld wages from her employees for long stretches of time. Then in 1956 the repressive years of Odria came to an end. It is a little remarkable how quickly the Huasicanchinos returned to the offensive. In 1948 they had been so successful in besieging the local civil guard post that in October of that year, it was decided to withdraw the post. Only the accession to power of a repressive military regime reversed the decision. In the year following that regime's departure (i.e., 1957) the Huasicanchinos began a two-year campaign to have

the civil guard post removed from the village. Basic amenities dried up—
fodder for horses became so scarce that the officers were reduced to patrolling
on foot—and attempts to supply the post from the hacienda were unsuccessful
(FHT, ARA). After one attempt by a senior officer to reinstitute the post, it
was withdrawn in 1959.[22]

Meanwhile community authorities insisted that faenas were only available
to the hacienda for specifically agricultural work and the road to the fundo
of Hacienda Tucle fell into such disrepair that, by 1958, Maria Luisa Chavez
bought out her husband's other heirs and moved the administration to the
more accessible fundo of Hacienda Rio de la Virgen (ARA). Two years of
hoof-and-mouth disease struck the herds as the sixties dawned, and this made
the administration try still harder to keep peasant animals separated from the
hacienda flocks by reducing huacchilla and trespassing. But this, in turn, only
increased tension with the villagers, especially as a drought in 1962 forced
them to seek pasture over a still wider area and hence increased trespassing.
Pressures from the village were increased further when the local mine, Cercapuquio, began to close down operations and lay people off, while a minor
recession took hold in the Huancayo economy.

We are already familiar with the configuration of the Huasicanchino economy during this period from the details of chapters 4 and 5. It will be recalled that throughout the 1950s a number of families hitherto reasonably
endowed with livestock holdings had now begun to institutionalize a process
of migration that began with Huancayo and then extended to Lima. For these
households there had been a considerable strain on previous interhousehold
linkages, but interconnections nevertheless remained. For others, less able to
liquidate their resource base, migration was characterized by considerable uncertainty and had the effect of stretching the household enterprise (as members
worked in different locations), while also isolating households from very
extensive personal networks. There were still other households—mostly of
very young or very old couples—who suffered from extremely impoverished
conditions.

The Re-Awakening of the Campaign

With the end of the repressive years of the Odria government, open political debate returned, and in the Mantaro Valley an increasingly commercialized small, independent farming population began to seek political leverage
through a multitude of *federaciónes campesinas* (peasant leagues). Essentially
populist in character, most of these federations were given support and guidance by local lawyers, schoolteachers, and small merchants.

Among the Huasicanchino migrants who were now well established in
Lima, there were a small number of people who had left the Petit Thouars
coralon and had set up in the more spacious surroundings of a shantytown

near the airport. At the same time, those who did not have some special skill, such as electrician or mechanic, were shifting into investment in small shops or marketstalls. Confined to no more than eight to ten migrants in Lima, this process was far more widespread in Huancayo, where it included as well as offspring of the old cancha families, a few successful huasi families as well. Two such people were Elias Tacunan and Elias Yaurivilca, both Apristas just out of hiding.

People such as these saw the institution of the federación campesina as a channel through which the land recuperation campaign might be steered. They saw the land recuperation campaign, moreover, as just one of a number of issues that Huasicanchinos should address to improve their lives. To this end in 1958 Tacunan, long since a stranger in the village, ran for the position of personero in Huasicancha, together with similar figures drawn from the migrant Huasicanchinos in Lima and Huancayo, all supporters of APRA.

Sympathy with APRA brought migrants into contact with party members in Huancayo who sought a political voice for small entrepreneurs and independent farmers in the Mantaro Valley. It also brought those who were now involved in village office holding into contact with neighboring highland communities. Through APRA colleagues in these villages Tacunan organized a meeting at the small settlement of Vista Alegre, at the gates of Hacienda Laive, and formed the first of his federaciónes campesinas, the *Movimiento Comunal del Centro,* based on five municipal districts: Huasicancha, Chongos Alto, Chicche, Colca, and Yanacancha. Although the recovery of "communal" lands was a major source of enthusiasm for the Movimiento among the highland villagers, Tacunan intended to spread the federation to include the more commercial farmers of the Valley, whose privatization of their own communities' land would make such demands embarrassing. He therefore stressed the more vague platforms of better conditions in the villages and improved educational facilities.

From 1958 to the national elections of 1962 and again in 1963, those in office, both in the village and in the migrant clubs, channeled much of Huasicancha's campaign for the restitution of land through the federaciónes campesinas. Then, in 1959 Tacunan split with APRA and, with the support of a number of political figures from the more commercial Valley towns, founded the *Universidad Nacional del Centro,* and followed this by forming a "peasant" federation aimed at a broader constituency than the highland communities: FEDECOJ (*Federación Departmental de las Comunidades de Junin*). This, in turn, split the Huancayo migrant population, some of whom felt committed to APRA, others of whom found little relevant to their concerns in the founding of a local university. Under the influence of Elias Yaurivilca, who in 1958 had been active in setting up the local branch of the APRA federación campesina (FENCAP: *Federación Nacional de Campesinos del Peru*), in 1959 a group formed a new club, the *Centro Social de Huancayo,*

which became the focal point for many of those Huasicanchinos just beginning to institutionalize their migration from Huasicancha—the people I have
called the "huasis." There were thus now two clubs in Huancayo: the *Centro
Cultural,* dominated by canchas, and the *Centro Social,* made up predominantly of huasis.

So the federations did provide a forum for discussions among Huasicanchinos—both those in Huancayo and those in the village— about the two different federations. The fact that the community's personero, Elias Tacunan,
was actively involved regionally in the national election campaigns (which
began in mid-1961), moreover, drew Huasicanchinos directly into those debates too. And in every instance, the anchor around which discussion floated
was the issue of the restitution of land claims (AC).

But village records, two old diaries, and informants' accounts give the impression that most Huasicanchinos in the village itself, and indeed the bulk
of the poorer migrants too, looked upon the activities of the federations with
a certain bemusement, as though it were a conversation taking place on the
other side of a partition, in an adjoining, crowded, and ill-lit room. The Huasicanchinos' attitudes even to the original Movimiento Comunal were by no
means unequivocal or unanimous. Many of those still in the village who had
been involved in the 1936 and 1947 campaigns were lukewarm toward an
alliance with other neighboring communities whose record of success in confronting the haciendas was, in their view, not great (AC and Interviews). And
then, with the founding of a larger, more inclusive federation the sense of
being marginalized grew still stronger. For the commercial farmers of the
Valley the federations may have represented a genuine attempt to acquire a
voice for an increasingly large and powerful petty bourgeoisie. But such was
never the case for those highland communities whose future development was
conditional on a redistribution of property that required a radical social read-
justment, not merely a changing of a few taxes and subsidies.

There was then plenty of debate in the air among Huasicanchino migrants,
among villagers, and between migrants and villagers when, from 1960 onward, spontaneous land occupations and other rural insurgencies throughout
Peru began to be reported in the papers with increasing frequency. Around
the haciendas Tucle, Antapongo and Laive there were signs that renewed confrontation between the communities and the haciendas would not be contained
by the promises of political parties or participation in peasant federations. And
this renewed local activity was a sign that different forces were becoming influential in controlling the direction of the recuperation campaign.

The Realignment of
Forces, Within and Without

The dominance of the community's offices by migrants was an especially
visible expression of a process in which Huasicanchino social relations had

become increasingly dominated by the dictates of nonfarm economic activities beyond the highlands. Changes in the fortunes of the various sectors in which enterprises were inserted had combined with the dominance of the hacienda in controlling pasture to undercut the preeminence of the community as an institution. The instrumental use made of community officeholding by migrants like Tacunan served less to integrate the highland pastoralists into national and regional political institutions than to draw attention to the distinctiveness of their interests (compare the evidence presented here to Tullis 1971; Bourque 1971; Handelman 1975). Meanwhile the hacienda was bypassing the community institutions by dealing directly with pasaderos, increasingly settling disputes between villagers by reference to the police of the hacienda administration, and recruiting faenas for hacienda work on an ad hoc wage basis rather than formally through the community authorities.[23]

What we witness now, therefore, is an attempt by various factions of the peasantry in Huasicancha itself to reassert the *community's* control of the key areas for the social reproduction of enterprises. First the police post was removed in 1959, putting increased responsibility on the village's gobernador to handle local disputes, then in the early 1960s, largely as a result of this, the hacienda agreed to return to the old practice in which villagers signed a promissory note with the community authorities in order to have their pasadero animals released by the hacienda.[24] The specific form the campaign took—which involved a massive invasion of the hacienda after 1964—must be understood in terms of the community authorities attempting to maintain leadership over otherwise individually initiated trespassing by Huasicanchinos acting in small groups.

We get some sense of the situation prevailing just prior to 1964, if we recall what the possibilities were for sheep pasturage (apart from employment on the hacienda). They included: 1) using llamas to graze on pasture too high for hacienda sheep—this remained the monopoly of the larger village flock owners from the old pastoralist families; 2) trespassing on the more remote areas of hacienda land, and since these bordered on the high pasture, it too was often undertaken by the larger flock owners; 3) brazen trespassing on the best and most easily accessible hacienda pasture, usually by the smaller flock owners. In all cases the activities were undertaken by groups of Huasicanchinos banding together.

Through 1962 and 1963 the threat of foot and mouth disease made hacienda staff especially diligent in preventing the unbathed animals of the villagers from straying onto hacienda land. Meanwhile among those caring for the smaller flocks pressure to trespass grew: drought made pasture scarcer, encouraging greater movement of flocks; villagers hitherto working at the local mine were returning with cash that they invested in sheep; and the number of animals owned by migrants and held in village flocks on the basis of reciprocal arrangements between households was now steadily increasing.

As a result the number of conflicts occurring between hacienda staff and villagers increased (See ARA, AC, and FHT for 1962).

The inability or reluctance of the Civil Guard to act as a third party between the hacienda caporales and the villagers displaced conflict directly onto hacienda and village figures. The caporales in the hacienda were increased in number from 1963 onward even though they were almost impossible to come by (ARA, 1963); while in the village, the gobernador and his tenientes came to see their mandate as the defense of villagers attacked by hacienda personnel, rather than the policing of conflicts internal to the community.

By comparing the pasadero records of Hacienda Tucle (ARA, FHT), the community records for the period (AC), and the questionnaires administered during fieldwork, it becomes clear that the bulk of these violent confrontations took place between hacienda staff and groups with small flocks, some of whom were returned migrants acting largely on their own account but most of whom were villagers who, during the 1950s, had managed to evolve sets of reciprocal links with migrants—the confederations of households.

Initially there was a possibility that this would lead to a rift because the community authorities were the better-off Huasicanchinos, most of them migrants.[25] In the community meetings throughout 1962, these people were urging discretion on the local front while the national political scene clarified itself (AC). And increasingly the community personero, Elias Tacunan, fudged his position on land redistribution the better to keep his hand free for bargaining with national political figures on behalf of his federación campesina. A rift was avoided, however, because interhousehold linkages acted as a centripetal force to crosscut quantitative differences in wealth and qualitative differences in the sources of household incomes. Moreover, as the large flock owners saw many villagers taking matters into their own hands, they began to share a common interest with the bulk of migrants who needed the community institutions as a means to keep formal control over the direction of events in Huasicancha, where they were now investing some of their resources.

Pressure for the removal of Tacunan came initially then from those villagers caring for the smaller flocks, because the areas that were left to them to pasture were most easily accessible to hacienda staff. Many of these people had confederated household ties with Huancayo and Lima migrants, whose animals constituted part of the flocks being pastured "illegally" on hacienda land. Minutes of community meetings held during 1963 reveal that one of the prevailing views was that unless something was done about this tension migrants could not be expected to maintain their interest in the village; two speakers went so far as to use the expression "invest in the community." In other words, both from a community and a household point of view, villagers were worried that migrants would cease to build up obligations in the village, which in turn would prevent villagers from taking up favors outside the village. As temporary migration and off-farm incomes began to play an increasing role in household reproduction, even for the village households, so these ties were essential to ever larger numbers of Huasicanchinos.

On 11 April 1963 Tacunan was removed from office as personero and was accused of stealing money from community funds. Now, while some of the migrants were worried that events would go so far in Huasicancha that they themselves would lose their influence, others, who at this time had less livestock in Huasicancha, saw overt support for the incoming village leadership as a means to increase their leverage in the village. Thus members of the Centro Social in Huancayo, more closely associated with APRA since Tacunan (in the other migrant club) had broken with the party, gave unanimous support to the new authorities despite the villagers' refusal to have anything to do with party politics.

The replacement of Tacunan and his colleagues appears then to have been the first of what became a series of attempts to kick the more "incorporated" Huasicanchinos upstairs, as it were. These incorporated migrants had established their domestic enterprises during the lean years in Huasicancha—from the 1936 campaign through the repressive years of the Odria regime in the early 1950s. While their attachment to Huasicancha was emotionally very strong, therefore, the reproduction of their enterprises was tied to commitments in their place of migration rather than in the village. In Lima this included those migrants who were first to leave the inner city slum of the Petit Thouars coralon to become established in a suburb near the airport, where they had invested in their houses and shops or marketstalls. In Huancayo this included migrants who, as a result of high school or apprenticeship migration in the 1930s, had found skilled or semi-skilled work.

There were three elements that carried out this "coup." The first and strongest were the migrants and villagers who were tied into household confederations with each other. By the mid-1960s huasis as well as the longer-established cancha migrants had begun to get involved in household confederations so that confederations were sufficiently widespread through Lima and Huancayo to include members of both the migrant clubs. Secondly there were those few better-off, relatively independent flock owners who had either remained in the village after 1948 or who had returned from migration and were beginning to invest in sheep. Finally there were a group of poorer migrants in Huancayo and Lima who had no strong interhousehold links to Huasicancha to speak of because of the restricted networks available to the families from whom they had emerged. More than any others they had been pushed from Huasicancha because of land shortage rather than pulled toward Lima. They, together with their relatives in the village, tended to move in the direction of whichever immediate tie to a member of one of the other groups offered the best advantage.

Thus we find Tacunan naming as the troublemakers who had unseated him those leaders of the 1947 campaign who had not left the village, such as Victor Hinostrosa (chap. 5) as well as many of their "allies" (in his words) who now lived in Lima and Huancayo; secondly, people who had returned to the village and were, in Tacunan's view, selfishly increasing their own flocks (see, for example, Urbano and Paulina, chap. 5); and finally those APRA supporters whose motivations he put down to revenge because of his leaving the party (see, for example, Eulogio and Eufresenia, chap. 5) (AC. Flier distributed to the migrant clubs).

The authorities who replaced Tacunan were small flock owners who received the support of the older pastoralist families. Reliant as they were on funds raised from the migrants, the new authorities were unable to take a particular direction in the campaign without migrant support. So they decided to petition the president of the republic and get the migrants directly involved in the process (de la Cruz Diary, Huasicancha).

Belaunde had come to the presidential palace with promises of a sweeping land reform for those peasants who would move back off the land they had invaded and agree to be adjudicated by the Sección de Asuntos Indígenas. Recognizing that the most pressing cases would be dealt with first, many peasant groups petitioned the president directly. Themselves pursuing this course of action, on 3 September 1963 the newly-elected Huasicanchino authorities sent their personero, Demetrio de la Cruz Lazo, to sound out the various migrant groups.

In Huancayo, de la Cruz received the unanimous support of the Centro Social. He received support too from the Centro Cultural, but here it was suggested in addition that a legal complaint be lodged against Hacienda Tucle, and the members of that club agreed to make the necessary legal contacts. In Lima, de la Cruz felt that the migrants fell into two categories: those whom he spoke to in scattered meetings throughout Surquillo (i.e., the more recent, usually huasi, migrants) who were willing to back the new authorities in whatever course of action they chose, and those whom he addressed at a formally called extraordinary meeting of the Club Cultural Deportivo at Petit Thouars.[26] This was a club originally formed as a branch of the Centro Cultural in Huancayo and centered on the Petit Thouars shacks. But by 1963 it included the older migrants now living in the well-established suburb near the airport, a number of other migrants who, having recently participated in land invasions, were setting up in shantytowns south of Lima and were tied into Huasicanchino household confederations (see Mauro and Guillermina, chap. 4) and the residents of the Petit Thouars slum itself.

Dominated by the more established Lima migrants who had supported Tacunan, this meeting produced both opposition to de la Cruz and qualified support. Apart from the importance of financial support from this source, de la Cruz also needed their approval because they were his connection to Tacunan, and Tacunan had supported Belaunde's candidacy for president and hence could rely on his patronage. There appears to have been general opposition to the idea of petitioning the president personally, a number of migrants arguing that they should wait until the land reform bill had been passed. The mood of the meeting changed, however, once it was agreed that not de la Cruz, but selected members of the Lima migrant community, petition the president.[27]

A petition was then approved which began,

As special delegates of the community of Huasicancha we beg you to put in order the recuperation of our lands which have been stolen from us by the Hacienda Tucle and which are of vital importance to our survival, being good pastures which are indispensable for the upkeep of our livestock and therefore of special economic and social importance . . .

The petition went on to assert that:

1. the land was taken violently and led to costly legal battles over the past hundred years that destroyed the economy of the village and led to little recuperation of land;
2. reclamation would be vital to the survival of the community since the high altitudes made arable farming very risky and increasing amounts of arable land had to be devoted to livestock pasture;
3. increasingly comuneros were being forced to migrate to the cities and mines where they contracted fatal illnesses;
4. the litigants should be indemnified for the extensive riches which the landowner had managed to accrue from lands that were not his own: he had been able to diversify into other business in Huancayo as a result of the peonage of the Huasicanchinos;
5. finally it outlined the titles in possession of the community which, it claimed, dated back to 1607 (AC; diary of Demetrio de la Cruz Lazo).

Duly dressed in ponchos and felt hats rounded up from more recent migrants, the Huasicanchinos did obtain an interview with the president in which the petition was delivered. And on 30 November an agreement was signed with Hacienda Tucle stating that there would be no more trespassing until the government adjudicators had made some decision. Community authorities now reminded villagers at every meeting that aggression would lose them the support of President Belaunde. Whatever their feelings had been when they had ousted Tacunan in April, de la Cruz's visit to the migrants convinced the Huasicanchino authorities that they should commit themselves to legitimate channels for the recuperation of land. In this they followed a practice common to virtually all similar rural insurgencies of the period: they exercised the patience of Job in pursuing all and every formal and legitimate channel before resorting to extralegal action (Huizer 1972, 1973). But things were to change in January of 1964 when, after an inspection by the civil judge of Huancayo, the stance of the community as a whole vis-à-vis the hacienda changed.

To assess who was involved in the campaign and how, I must pause for a moment to record who participated in this inspection of Huasicancha's landmarks. To begin with, the hacienda sent no representatives, which led the authorities of the community to conclude that the judge had already been bribed. The community, on the other hand, provided the following entourage: the personero, the alcalde, and the gobernador, three other members of the *junta directiva* of the community, and three other members who had been elected to deal specifically with legal aspects of the campaign. There were two representatives from the migrants in Huancayo and two more from Lima. Also present were a cook and three assistants, plus a "waiter" (*mozo*) and two men to look after the horses. Two more went as experts on where the landmarks were and two more to carry the beer. The whole task took two days, and on the second the judge was entertained by the migrants at the nearby Cercapuquio mine, whence he returned to Huancayo (AC).

This event seems to have tested the patience of many villagers who now dispensed with the cautions of the authorities and began to invade land in groups, causing the hacienda administrator to believe that a fullscale invasion was occurring (ARA). Similar invasions continued throughout February, prompting the community authorities to call a meeting in March that placed them in charge of a land occupation to *reivindicar nuestros pastos legitimos*. Three authorities who felt unable to support a policy of confrontation were permitted to resign and were replaced by others. On 16 March de la Cruz went to Huancayo where he appeared before a judge with the community's lawyer to denounce the violent acts of the hacendado. In the subsequent six weeks invasion tactics were discussed, areas of the puna allotted to particular groups for invasion, and attempts made to persuade hacienda employees to leave their posts. Then on April 24 the invasion was carried out, eliciting the responses of the hacienda and the local press as appear at the beginning of this section.

The army was called in, creating a climate of fear in Huasicancha, for by this time the so-called "land invasions" were occurring throughout the central highlands, and confrontations of varying degrees of violence were reported in the press almost daily. But in the event, possibly because of widespread commitments elsewhere, only a small detachment arrived and then, to the administrator's disgust, refused to leave the fundo buildings. Even so the people in the village felt that the time for compromises had passed, and when a ministerial inspector was sent once more to survey the landmarks on 7 May, de la Cruz had a violent argument with him and left. On his way back from this inspection, he and another community authority were captured by the civil guard. Three other elected authorities were captured and all were accused of being communist agitators and imprisoned without trial (JT; de la Cruz diary).

While there seems little doubt that the government hoped to dissipate the momentum of the campaign in this way, the effect of the arrests was to throw the Huasicanchinos into yet another period of intense discussion. Soon after the arrests Belaunde announced that no land being occupied by squatters would be considered for land reform, and throughout Peru many peasants withdrew from land. From the point of view of those migrants in Huancayo and Lima who were in touch with national and regional developments this seemed to be a promising development favoring a conciliatory stance. However, the extent of rural mobilization in the central Andes was far greater than anybody had witnessed in this century, and the preoccupation of the army in numerous separate areas had given the Huasicanchino land invaders more success than they had anticipated. They saw that Hacienda Tucle, despite the employment of more caporales, was unable to contain their activities. So the pressing question of finding a new set of leaders provided the opportunity for further debate along these lines.[28]

Political Perspectives Arising from the Heterogeneity of Enterprises

In prison in Huancayo, Demetrio de la Cruz recorded in his diary the name and club membership of each migrant who donated money to the fund of the imprisoned men. He noted the unanimous support of the Centro Social in Huancayo, the majority of whose members were APRA supporters and were people only beginning to get themselves established in Huancayo, only a few of whom had much of a personal network to rely on. From the Centro Cultural, de la Cruz records support from its rank-and-file membership, most of whom were people now reestablishing confederated household linkages, but he complains bitterly of the lack of support from the club's executives, the old, established migrants who associated themselves with the more commercially-minded entrepreneurs from the valley towns and who still supported Tacunan's peasant federation.

The case studies of chapter 5 represent quite well the variety of participants in Huasicancha's land recuperation campaign at this time. The families in the village who still felt a strong association with the old pastoralist authorities of previous invasions, represented by Victor and Juana Hinostrosa, had a very strong influence over the opinions of many of the poorer Huasicanchinos from whom they received what the younger Aprista migrants regarded as somewhat old-fashioned respect. Of especially significant influence on the character of the campaign at this time, moreover, were the domestic enterprises engaged in household confederations.

But by this period another group of Huasicanchinos was beginning to institutionalize its migration from the village. They were a group of people who, lacking a significant base in livestock, had been deprived too of the kind of personal networks that had allowed others to institutionalize migration earlier. Nevertheless over the years these people had become established in Huancayo, where they joined the Centro Social, and in Lima, where they gathered around the inner-city slum area near the Surquillo market. The case study of Eulogio and Eufresenia Ramos exemplified these people.

And then a very small group of "independent farmers" in Huasicancha are exemplified by the case of Urbano Llacua, who had returned from work in the Cercapuquio mine in 1958, and his wife Paulina. In this, the last of the case studies, I suggested that enterprises closely approximating simple commodity producers began to take form in Huasicancha. Nevertheless as early as 1964 Huasicancha still controlled insufficient secure pasture for such enterprises to become well established. They were not yet therefore at the forefront of Huasicancha politics.

Finally there were an initially influential group of well-established migrants (not covered by the case studies) both in Huancayo and in a suburb of Lima near the airport (referred to by Huasicanchinos as "the Callao residents") who, in the unfolding of the land recuperation campaign, were gradually excluded from the Huasicanchino social economy. In retrospect their delegation to the presidential palace was their swan song. Always personified in their subsequent accounts to me by the figure of Elias Tacunan, these few well-established migrants were justified in their complaints to me in 1972–1973 that they had born a disproportionate share of the financial costs of the campaign at this stage. The fact that livestock were being used as part of the campaign (to "eat up the hacienda" in the words of informants) meant that Huasicanchinos were reluctant to sell animals to raise cash for legal fees, and it was therefore the more established migrants with access to cash and credit who took most responsibility for paying legal fees. But refusal to pay the *coto* (head tax) was assumed to mean renunciation of comunero status and hence any claim to pasture or to a voice in the community. This meant that so long as there was a significant body of Huasicanchinos determined to continue the campaign, any backsliders wishing to gain from the eventual outcome had to keep up their participation. As a result, heated discussion took place to influence the course of events, but threats to withdraw support were never especially effective. Moreover the village residents were aware that they had the whip hand, inasmuch as a steadily increasing number of migrants from one year to the next were investing in sheep. In the last analysis, as de la Cruz put it a few years later, "We had their sheep."

I have suggested earlier that, far from the Huasicanchinos' solidarity and effectiveness deriving from their singleness of purpose, it was precisely this heat of discussion over different perceptions of purpose, combined with the real commitment people had to the outcome (in terms of the future of their livelihood) which gave momentum to the campaign. Under these conditions it is not just any debate that creates momentum but rather the combination of the degree of participation with the degree of investment in the outcome which does it. Now the need to find officials to replace those in prison provided a forum for such a debate. A number of migrants and even a few of the older village pastoralists were anxious to persuade the villagers to accept a negotiated settlement with the Ministerial Commission of Enquiry. In this matter their interest was similar to others, the hazards of whose enterprises on the margins of Peru's unstable urban economy meant that the major attraction of investing in livestock was not vicarious dreams of sudden wealth but a more pressing need for solid security. For them too the pasture would only be a useful way of accumulating savings if it was secure.

However, there were people who articulated their position in terms very much like those suggested by Hobsbawm. They were "inclined to reject as morally invalid and 'unnatural' laws which, however constitutionally correct, [took] away common lands" (1974: 124). We are of course unable to probe into people's consciousness at that time. We can therefore only note the use of this viewpoint in debate. But, as such, it was no less instrumental than that of the Huasicanchinos who wanted to use the invasions as a means to achieve the end of a good bargaining position for a negotiated settlement. There were those among the Huasicanchinos who were not seriously hindered in the running of their enterprises by a long drawn out war of attrition. Notably they included those households who found group trespassing at least an improvement over individual trespassing. They were not preoccupied by difficulties deriving from unsystematic husbandry such as irregular sales or care during the lambing season (they observed no special season for lambing), because it was not a view of farming that prevailed in their enterprises. And these villagers were supported by the migrant households with whom they had confederated arrangements. This attitude toward time was shared as well by villagers and migrants with few or no livestock whose only possibility of such investment lay in the future. Most articulate among them were the young APRA supporters who were members of the Centro Social in Huancayo or residents of the Surquillo area of Lima.

The Momentum of
Discourse and Increased Participation

Among and between these groups debate set in. Village records of the time, together with informants' accounts, suggest that, from the forum of the Sunday meetings in village or migrant club to urban workplace and village streetcorner, to the confines of the household "patio," discussion was animated. As one informant put it (now resident in Huancayo), "At meetings did we talk about what to do? Of course we did. But we had already discussed it the day before. And the day before that. We talked of nothing else. What else mattered? After all, we are talking of a moment when it seemed as though everybody ruled in Huasicancha. Hah! And those with office did not rule [*Y ellos con cargos no mandaban*]. And so it was" (fieldnotes, Huancayo, February 1973). "Everybody ruled" and, "those with office did not rule." The conditions facing officeholders while Demetrio de la Cruz and others languished in prison, together with a meeting called by the Interministerial commission, both serve to clarify the situation this informant is referring to.

With de la Cruz and his colleagues in prison a new set of authorities were decided upon from among the old established migrants resident in Lima and two of their village relatives. Their ability to assert their own interests however was proscribed by a generally held view that they were now only superficially leaders for the purposes of dealing with outsiders and that others really "ruled in the community." This form of realpolitik was sufficiently acknowledged among Huasicanchinos to have a name: *La cumbre oscura* ("the summit hidden [by clouds]"). And when the Interministerial Commission asked that a community meeting be called in the village itself, these new officials asked Tacunan to attend. The debate it now engendered, as Huasicanchinos with ministerial backing tried to browbeat recalcitrant hardliners, is captured by these outraged words noted down by a village resident after the event and inserted into the community records:

> It was set up at the request of Manuel Duarte who had bribed (*habia comprado*) the two delegates of the Ministries who came to Huasicancha . . . The community received them with a band and then a general assembly was summoned by the guests, in which the two officials took over entirely. The official delegates of the community were not permitted to speak. Señor Elias Tacunan who represented FEDECOJ as the general secretary, was however permitted to use his words which he did entirely in favour of the *gamonal* (i.e., the hacendado) and for expropriation by the agrarian reform and not by the demand which is being made by the community. From this date Tacunan has lost all prestige as a representative of the community. (AC)

It is to be noted that "the official delegates of the community" were not the newly appointed authorities but the old leaders who had been brought up from the prison in Huancayo especially for the occasion. Tacunan, moreover, is carefully referred to as the representative of the peasant federation and not of his fellow comuneros.

The next day the Huancayo newspaper carried the headline, "PROBLEM TUCLE-HUASICANCHA STILL AT PAGE ONE." But the hacienda administration had been impressed by the evident differences of opinion among the Huasicanchinos, and a few days later another headline appeared in the paper, "TUCLE: WE ACCEPT AGRARIAN REFORM." Underneath this title it was recorded that the hacienda administration was aware that the villagers of Huasicancha only wanted the land in order to rent it out to those who were not residents of the village (the migrants?), and therefore it would accept a limited amount of expropriation on condition that the beneficiaries were to be found among all neighboring communities save Huasicancha.

Within a few days the hacienda appeared to achieve what it had been seeking. On 4 November, the newspaper carried a large public announcement: "TO PUBLIC OPINION: Act of Agreement Between the Community of Huasicancha and the Tucle Livestock Company." The commission had arranged an agreement between the hacendado and the representatives of Huasicancha, Santos C., Ramon M., Francisco Y., Hermino Z., and Cleto Y. After much deliberation, it said, an agreement had been reached between both parties.

1. The community agreed to the Commission's request to retire from the disputed area, "for the best interests of the Government, to satisfy the justice of Indian reclamations and to better their case";
2. The hacienda conceded an area denoted by the following landmarks . . . ;
3. Where there were no natural boundaries the comuneros agreed to build a ditch, wall or fence, materials to be provided by the hacienda;
4. Both parties to desist from further litigation;
5. Both parties to desist from any acts which threaten the peace for any motive whatsoever in the face of punishment by the power of the state;
6. Pasaderos of either party (*sic*) to be punished according to the law and *costumbres ganaderos que sobre ellos existan en la region* ("farming customs which with respect to them [*pasaderos*] exist in the region").

The abject defeat this settlement represents is sufficiently evident to require little comment. What it would mean to the villagers can be imagined by reference only to the last clause. As far as the Huasicanchinos were concerned there had never existed a "law" with respect to pasadero, and the local customs were in dispute between the hacienda and the community. Nevertheless an immediate result of the settlement was that the imprisoned authorities were released. By January, following a pattern established with the downfall of Tacunan in the community, the new authorities who had signed this agreement were removed and replaced by their predecessors. The settlement was then rejected on the grounds that it had been signed by people who had never had the proper credentials from the community.

Throughout 1965 the "readings" of prevailing conditions by the urban centers and by those in the remote area around Tucle and Huasicancha were strikingly at variance. Belaunde had declared that the Departments of Junin and Pasco would be the targets of land reform in that year but that land reform would be pursued vigorously only in 1966 (Petras and Laporte 1971: 94) and then only in favor of people who moved off land they had invaded. In the rural areas of the department, however, government presence was not represented by these generous intentions but rather by the suspension of individual guarantees and the presence of U.S.-trained "rangers" in pursuit of the guerrilla fighters calling themselves the "Tupac Amaru" cell (Bejar 1970).

The mounting tension was felt on Tucle Pampa. It increased the sense that there was now a dangerous state of siege on while evidently the army was present only in small numbers and then only at the hacienda buildings themselves, concentrating on preventing the destruction of the physical plant. The effect of the guerrilla campaign was to draw army attention away to the opposite side of the Mantaro and into the high jungle where the guerrillas were concentrating their attacks.

The increased guerrilla activity, however, meant that government sympathy with those especially stubborn peasants who, suspicious of promises, refused to withdraw from land, was now replaced by a campaign of fear. This substitution of a climate of fear for the previous government policy of negotiating, effectively drew more sharply the line between "within," where discourse proceeded apace, and "without," where it had ceased altogether. The sense of confrontation was now very high, when two apparently unrelated occurrences gave raise to overt resistance. First the army contingent at the fundo was withdrawn, then the Huancayo court delivered a judgment in favor of Tucle in the civil case with Huasicancha. The judge announced that he doubted the validity of Huasicancha's 1607 document and, referring to the state of emergency in which all land invasions were to cease, he proposed that the Huasicanchinos' de facto squatting rendered them ineligible to make appeals over land in any event. In the wake of these two superficially unrelated events, an apparently mysterious fire occurred at the hacienda. The growing middle-class hysteria vis-à-vis the peasantry is reflected in the local newspaper headline: "RED TERROR CONTINUES: HACIENDA BUILDING BURNT DOWN."

With the return of de la Cruz and his colleagues many of those from the Centro Social in Huancayo who had so ostentatiously helped them while in prison began to feel that they had more control of things in Huasicancha. With Tacunan's supporters offstage, a number of APRA supporters both in the village and in Huancayo became increasingly vocal at village meetings, promising that through FENCAP Huasicancha would receive many of the improvement projects denied it by the government because of its confrontation over the recuperation campaign. In 1966 a number of these people took office in the municipality.[29] The invasion campaign against the hacienda continued under the direction of the community authorities led by the personero but improvements within the village were the mandate of the alcalde (the mayor).

This was the first time that people with no extensive networks developed through past livestock husbandry had a hand in the direction of Huasicancha's affairs. The mayor himself was drawn from the village. He was a longtime member of APRA. Most of his council came from the Huancayo migrants and a junior member of the council came from Lima: Eulogio Ramos (see chap. 5). Ironically, this openly APRA leadership in the village provoked the government to come forward with aid projects to Huasicancha to diffuse both APRA representatives and the hardline land invaders; a drinking water system was put in with public taps placed throughout the village, an agricultural secondary school was established (in the abandoned civil guard post) to serve the surrounding villages as well as Huasicancha; and a bridge was built to make Huancayo more directly accessible to the villagers (and the villagers more directly accessible to the army). A cooperative was initiated for the purchase of agricultural inputs and consumer items, and there was even discussion of Huasicancha instituting a colonization scheme in the jungle on the opposite side of the Mantaro Valley. Despite APRA and FENCAP's role, however, plaques on the finished works make reference only to Belaunde's generosity.[30]

All these projects were completed with community labor, and from 1966 onwards there was a revitalization of the community faena both for municipal works and in the cultivation of the communal fields. Migrants tried to organize the demands of their urban domestic enterprises so that at least one or other of the adults could get back to the community once or twice a year. Even so the ability to turn renewed interest in the village into real investment into its economy was, once more, unevenly distributed. Those with links through household confederations began to strengthen those links, but those without them were frustrated by their inability to find capital or credit with which to increase their flocks and so lay claim to the pasture which was, by now, coming increasingly under Huasicanchino control. Meanwhile they watched as de la Cruz and his colleagues were replaced by a younger group of village ex-migrants often, like Urbano (chap. 5), recently returned from Cercapuquio.

Strategy and Tactics

The strategy and tactics of the land invasion campaign itself were by now well established. The strategy was to deplete the basic resources of the hacienda—pasture and sheep. As informants often noted later, "We ate the hacienda." Simply by persistently trespassing onto hacienda land with livestock, the basis of the Hacienda's land-use system was undermined. Normally flocks were circulated over extensive areas of pasture to allow one area to recuperate while another was being used. Perpetual trespassing on pasture being left to rest played havoc with this system. Trespassers' flocks were swollen too by rustling, and an opportunity was never lost to damage or kill hacienda animals where they could not be carried off.

Tactics made army surveillance and even patrols by the hacienda caporales who were familiar with the hazardous mountain terrain very difficult. Small groups of invaders entered the hacienda land at widely dispersed points with their livestock. Hacienda staff, called upon to patrol over 30,000 hectares of mountainous terrain, could not travel in sufficient numbers to take immediate action once invaders had been spotted. Rather, they had to return to their bases for reinforcements. More often than not, when they returned they found the invaders gone.

The civil guard and army were even less successful. The fact that rural unrest was widespread throughout the entire central Andes meant that no large contingent could be kept in the area for any length of time. Rather a varying number of men (depending on the perceived state of affairs in the area) were quartered either at the hacienda buildings or in a location where they could keep an eye on the Huasicanchino bridgehead, whence invasions occurred. But the job was boring and morale was often low. Villagers have endless accounts of their fraternizing with the soldiers, providing music and offering them cane alcohol and then leaving them incapacitated in the early hours of the morning as the villagers drove their animals onto the hacienda land. And when their impotence drove small contingents of soldiers to journey away from the hacienda in pursuit of trespassers, more often than not they were led deep into the high mountains and there abandoned by trespassers turned decoys.

In effect it was a war of attrition in which one side was continually diverted from getting on with its business while the other side was, by the very nature of its strategy, pursuing its daily livelihood: pasturing livestock. As a result a gradual decline in the morale of both the hacienda administration and the civil guard set in from the latter part of 1966. The relative conditions of the two disputing sides by the end of the following year is nicely captured by a subtle change that was taking place in the role of the personero: while he continued to control the invasion campaign by designating people to "enter" the hacienda in specific places, this no longer really meant a cat-and-mouse game with the hacienda caporales; rather, it meant the allotment of estancias and surrounding pasture to specific families who began to settle for that area and protect it not only from hacienda personnel but also from fellow villagers. The importance of the position of personero and his accompanying authorities for the distribution of means of production cannot be overestimated, and these positions were now energetically sought—and successfully gained—by the new independent farmers who were systematically accumulating flocks. A subtle change had occurred in the kind of political campaign Huasicancha was now engaged in.

Meanwhile for the owners of Hacienda Tucle the climate was changing.

While there remained government sympathy toward reasonably efficient public stock companies like the Ganadero del Centro that ran the neighboring Hacienda Laive, nationally famous for its cheese, the writing for haciendas like Tucle was fairly clearly on the wall. Agrarian reform was going to affect them to a greater or lesser extent, so the choice was no longer one in which the owner of Tucle could envisage the return of the hacienda to its old dominance of the area. Maria Luisa Chavez, moreover, was over ninety by this time. Having failed to make a deal with the Agrarian Reform authorities to sell Tucle to them, her son, Manuel Duarte, took a fulltime job with the Huancayo office of the Ministry of Agriculture. He continued to run Haciendas Tucle and Rio de la Virgen under the Tucle Livestock Company but ceased to invest any capital in equipment or stock.

Hobsbawm (1974: 141) suggests that Tucle's poor management was decisive in the outcome of this campaign: "Tucle, as its neighbouring estates were frequently forced to note, was somewhat deficient in diplomacy, legal acumen and good management." This may have been so, but it would be misleading to isolate this behavior from a context in which this hacienda had for over a century had to deal with perpetual peasant resistance. We have seen, time and again, that the ability of Hacienda Tucle to institute rational management practices was preempted by peasant resistance in a whole variety of forms. We have seen too what little success the administration had on the few occasions where it favored diplomacy over less subtle means. As for legal acumen, again it is worth noting the kind of opposition Tucle had in the Huasicanchinos. For the sake of the inspection made by the civil judge, children had been carefully trained in the misnaming of landmarks. On another occasion, determined to have the army removed from a spot where it could observe their use of one squatter site as a bridgehead for deep incursions into hacienda land, the Huasicanchinos acquired a number of army uniforms, dressed themselves as soldiers and, with the help of a migrant who was an ambulant photographer in Huancayo, managed to produce photographs for the Huancayo district judge of "soldiers" molesting village women. (The army were instructed to withdraw from the area.)

So consistently inconsistent were the Huasicanchinos if ever their lawyer could get them into a witness box for their civil case against Tucle that he ended up paying people he picked up off the street in Huancayo, so that he could then rely on them to give consistent statements. Julian Paucarchuco Samaniego, for example, whom Hobsbawm notes knew the village boundaries since his father had taught them to him when a child (1974: 142), is not to be found in any village records, nor are either of his family names to be found among Huasicanchinos. He seems most likely to have been one of those fabricated witnesses, the last resort of a lawyer defending a people who had a watertight case in law but no faith in the people who stood in judgment over them.

In any event by 1967 it was almost as though the positions of the two sides were reversing as Hacienda Tucle began to look increasingly decrepid and incapable of carrying out the changes necessary to make it into a capitalist enterprise, while the leadership of the Huasicanchino campaign began to fall into the hands of capitalist-oriented independent farmers like Urbano. As these people began to move into the offices of the community and the live-stock cooperative initiated by Tacunan (who died that year), so they faced the apristas who held the municipal positions and the consumer cooperative.

"La Reivindicación de Nuestras Tierras"

Riding on a wave of support both from villagers who were proud of the highly visible improvements they had brought with their office and from the "huasi" migrants who at last found that they had a voice in village affairs, these municipal authorities were nonetheless forced to stand by helpless as they watched the independent farmers and the more established household confederations establish themselves on pasture ever more abandoned by the hacienda. Then in 1968 the military, headed by General Juan Velasco, impa-tient with Belaunde's inability to defuse the growing political opposition both on the coast and in the mountains, took over power. They quickly made it illegal for apristas to hold political office of any kind. This considerably re-duced the influence of a group of Huasicanchinos who had never managed to attain much power in the community before.

It was therefore Urbano, one of the wealthiest of the younger farmers who, coming to the position of personero in 1968, conducted the final battle against Hacienda Tucle. It was essentially a legal battle by now to achieve recognition of the Huasicanchinos' de facto occupation of territory. Although the military government put into effect a land reform program involving the expropriation of the entire hacienda bloc (Laive-Ingahuasi, Antapongo, Tucle, and Rio de la Virgen) and its transformation into a state run cooperative (See Horton 1974; Smith 1976) the Huasicanchinos did not participate in that program, refusing to acknowledge that any expropriation was necessary since the land was theirs in the first place.

Although a legal settlement was made in July 1970, aspects of the final settlement were still being negotiated during fieldwork in 1972 when the campaign came to an end. Huasicancha as a legally recognized "peasant com-munity" under the military government (which had thereby replaced the "In-dian Communities") now had legal possession of some 38,000 hectares of land that had once been controlled by Haciendas Tucle and Rio de la Virgen.[31] The judge who delivered the final verdict often sat with me in the cold ar-chives of the Huancayo Juzgado de Tierra, as I went through the evidence of the case. He confirmed that his task was made easier as Huasicancha's effective control over the area in the highlands became more and more estab-

lished. As he saw it, their legal claim was impossible to dispute. The problem
his predecessors had, so he argued, was that they had to make a ruling that
would be put into effect and thus appear to establish the power of the law.
Legal decisions innocent of the prevailing balance of power over possession
of pastures could only serve to make manifest the irrelevance of the law in
such cases.

The final decision is long and detailed. I select from it, the most interesting
points:

—It reviews the past cases, remarking that Hacienda Tucle attempted
to slow down the proceedings;

—The Constitutions of 1920 and 1933 were designed to protect Indian
lands; a land sale by Huasicancha to Tucle in 1933 was therefore entirely illegal. "It is also known that large properties in the sierra were
consolidated in the latter part of the last century and the beginning of
this, with enormous damage to communal properties, this not being
legalized in any way by the state";

—It compares the legitimacy of Huasicancha's documents with the
weakness of Maria Luisa's, contrasting the will of 1887, in which Bernarda Pielago laid claim to 12,000 hectares, with the 1905 land registration in which 103,000 hectares were claimed, referring to this as an
example of the aggressions committed against Huasicancha. Indeed
Maria Luisa has not presented a single legal document that served as a
title deed;

—Huasicancha's documents can be clearly verified by reference to an
ocular inspection in which all the ancient landmarks can be located;

—It attacks the behavior of the previous courts;

—And defends the land occupations as justifiable under the circumstances;

—The 1948–1949 sale of land to Huasicancha in return for the digging
of a ditch was entirely illegal insofar as the property was not Hacienda
Tucle's to sell;

—All previous sentences are null and void, especially 23 September
1966 and 1 March 1968;

—No costs.

Conclusion

What we are observing among the Huasicanchinos between 1958 and 1972
is not a mobilization that resulted from the solidarity of a group having iden-
tically shared perceptions (of property, of politics, of community, of class,

etc.) but a mobilization that expressed itself simultaneously as a struggle against an identifiable enemy and at the same time as a discourse between participants holding partial perceptions that interacted to create a perpetual momentum *generated by the political activity itself*. In chapter 6 I have attempted to demonstrate how heterogeneity in the developmental trajectory of differing kinds of domestic enterprises gave rise to the pursuit of differing interests, but there were also factors in the social reproduction of those enterprises that served to obscure those differences. Once the land invasions began to pick up momentum after 1963 the very existence of the campaign, its persistent presence in the daily discussion of every Huasicanchino, provided an opportunity for the working out of many of these untested differences of perception among Huasicanchinos, while at the same time keeping them tied together like two not entirely compatible Siamese twins, over their shared desire for the security represented by control over land.

There were men who took authoritative roles during this period, and in many cases their names are remembered: Sabino, Martín, Elias Tacunan, Elias Yaurivilca, Demetrio, Urbano, and others. But the fact that the list is so long for such a relatively short period and for such a small number of people casts doubt on the suggestion that leadership was decisive. Over this, scholars, the army, and the hacienda administration alike have made the same mistake. Urbano accused the hacendado in court in 1968 of having tried to bribe Demetrio with ten thousand soles, and when this kind of thing failed, leaders were imprisoned. Confusion followed temporarily but the campaign continued, as it had after the capture of Laimes the century before. But the Huasicanchinos themselves were not averse to dispensing with leaders when it was convenient to do so.

Rather than pay attention to the tactical skill of particular leaders, therefore, I have attempted to draw on the knowledge we have gained from the previous chapters to follow the expression of different interests over the course of the campaign, showing how the interaction among them gave the campaign its particular character, one in which its direction was perpetually negotiated through a heated discourse taking place during a very intense experience. I have tried to avoid presenting this as an inevitable trend in which—with hindsight—we have no difficulty in dispensing with the detailed experience between beginning and end to conclude easily that we are witnessing a progression from "peasant" struggle to the struggle of a "disguised proletariat" or of emerging simple commodity producers. It should by now be clear that I am reluctant to describe the Huasicanchinos with any label that deprives them of the heterogeneity that I believe has provided them with the motivation for perpetual discussion, a discussion which, in turn, has contributed to the vividness of their memories of actually participating in these events that have had such a major effect on their present. And what they remember at first is a generalized struggle and possibly the name of one surrogate hero or another.

But what each person remembers once he or she discusses his or her account with fellow Huasicanchinos, is the relationship of where each one stood vis-à-vis others in the specific developments that I have tried to present here in such detail. For this reason the reconstruction of this political mobilization by any one person serves to situate that person as a Huasicanchino both with respect to other Huasicanchinos and with respect to the world beyond the familiar faces of old neighbors. As such it provides an essential element—the element of experience—that must be placed alongside our understanding of the kind of enterprise each Huasicanchino relies on to generate a livelihood.

8

Class Consciousness
and Culture

One would expect people to remember the past and imagine the future. But in fact when discoursing or writing about history, they imagine it in terms of their own experience, and when trying to gauge the future they cite supposed analogies from the past: till, by a double process of repetition, they imagine the past and remember the future.

—Lewis Namier *Conflicts*

This study of one small group of rebellious peasants and their migrant kin serves as a critique on the one hand of the grandiose claims made by sweeping studies of class formation and revolution seeking conclusions of a very general nature and, on the other, the claims of those who make much of the microscopic description of cultures, whose ultimate purpose is to render the human condition relative such that exotic peoples starve differently, feel pain differently, die differently, and hence live differently from "us." The study suggests that far too much about the specificity of history and locality is lost in macroscopic studies of rural rebellion that endeavor to assert that this or that type of peasant, proletarian, or even social structure is best suited to rebellion or revolution. Conversely, it suggests too that studies of the minutiae of a people's culture not firmly situated within the context of economic and political relations of exploitation and domination, at regional, national, and international levels simply obscure the essential elements of struggle and resistance inherent in cultural production.[1]

Ninety-nine times out of a hundred a speech given in Huancayo by a junior minister, a general, or a campaigning politician would have to be sifted through very carefully indeed to find anything of immediate relevance to Huasicanchinos. It would certainly not be through verbal statements that Huasicanchinos would expect to have revealed to them the realities of the state, nor would they assume that the state took verbal expressions on their part very seriously. So the relevance of the state is certainly not made manifest through verbal statements—in either direction. People go through the motions of making an application to the appropriate ministries for grading the road to the village or recognition of an ambulant syndicate in Lima, but it is other forms of pressure, another kind of political language, which they know makes the most sense. And they know too that the real presence of the state will not be in the coming to fruition of some grand new development scheme announced at a political rally but in the interpretations put on a restrictive aspect of the law by some petty bureaucrat.

This experience of the Huasicanchinos is surely not atypical for the vast majority of poor people in the Third World. True there are always striking cases where some segment or other of the population is to be radically affected by a particular aspect of government policy, and this provides no difficulty for political analysis. It is not hard to study how the scrapping of a favorable trade agreement for the sale of the nation's sugar or coffee, for example, affects sugar or coffee workers. But for most of the people most of the time, political expression cannot be understood in such nicely confined terms without concluding that people have no politics at all, a conclusion that impoverishes the notion of politics as much as our understanding of these people.

And far from this being just the temporary condition of a rather frustrating period of fieldwork over a couple of years, when bureaucrats seemed especially slothful and corrupt, this reality reaches back into the recordable past. It is within this context that political consciousness must be assessed. So instead of assessing its development by bemoaning the sheer cynicism and doggedness of people whose entire lives are spent in this reality, its positive dimensions must be captured. For we are talking here of a space within which a social world is put together if not despite hegemonic definitions of reality, at least in a context where such definitions are shattered into tiny fragments of broken glass, fragments that are sharp, distorting, and dangerous to the touch. Under such circumstances the role of local dialogue in negotiating the interpretation of these fragments in order to assess their immediate or long-term relevance to the peasantry is sufficiently important to render suspect assertions about the political potential of the poor that fail to take this exercise of negotiated interpretation into account. Without such a dimension, "consciousness" becomes a static *tableau vivant* with no significant creative dynamism, just the possibility of adjusting a figure here or there to reorder the composition of the picture, nothing more.

Aware of the limitations of this perception of consciousness, social and cultural anthropologists have preferred the notion of culture, but they have not thereby found greater precision. Indeed anthropologists have been so defensive about this delicate term that they have kept it isolated in a hothouse, carefully watering it and adjusting its position in the shade, always cautious not to expose it too thoroughly to the winds of a greater historical and geographical reality. As a result, studies of culture tend to be bereft of the critical features of class relations that cannot be neglected in any contemporary social formation. The failure to integrate cultural studies with class analysis has meant first that anthropologists have only rarely addressed the question of the relationship between the inherent developmental tendencies of certain kinds of social relationships and their implications for consciousness, and second that they have found great difficulty in relating the local cultural distinctiveness of a group being studied within a larger nation-state to the particular class configuration of that nation-state. As a result we are deprived of the possibility of seeing cultural production *specifically* in terms of simultaneous interdependence and opposition, integration and autonomy at the level of the social formation, not just at the level of the local fieldsite.

> It is not possible to separate the problem of the connection between subjective experience on the one side and the objective structures on the other, between praxis and the social constitution of values, between perceptions and meanings, and between institutions from the problem of asymmetrical social relations, from questions of class formation, of the dialectic of historical change and of . . . processes of social, cultural and economic transformation. (Medick 1987: 97)

There have been moments when state policy has been of quite specific relevance to the Huasicanchinos. Although it is important to remember that those moments were precisely a response to local initiatives, it is nevertheless worth seeing how the Huasicanchinos in turn then responded to this spotlight of attention. The Huasicanchinos' immediate and daily grievances stemming from relationships with Hacienda Tucle in the early 1960s were met by official statements that a thoroughgoing land reform was about to go into effect, though little was said specifically about expropriation of the large haciendas. This gave rise to intense discussion among Huasicanchinos during which a wide range of possible interpretations of the prevailing situation were exercised. Eventually the Huasicanchinos made what might be called a forceful political statement: they occupied stretches of disputed land. Promises of reform if they removed themselves then gave rise to further interpretations of reality, and in the last section of the previous chapter we saw in some detail various manifestations of this heightened discourse among the Huasicanchinos. Eventually, however, they chose to stick with their own land reform in favor of promises of a state-run one, at some time in the indefinite future. This led to arrests, imprisonment, violence, and very real fear on their part: feelings no doubt as emotionally pregnant as a circumcision, face-scarring, or other manifestations of "cultural specificity." And these were feelings quite familiar to Huasicanchinos. Indeed they are experiences quite routinely expected by highland peasants in Peru and probably by poor rural people throughout the world.

Then, after the Huasicanchinos had thoroughly reduced the local hacienda and, again as a result of similar local initiatives elsewhere in the central Andes, a military government expropriated the entire bloc of haciendas in the region, and the question was raised of Huasicancha throwing in its land with the neighboring communities and joining the resulting cooperative, "SAIS Cahuide." Even though this production cooperative was the focus of much propaganda and there were reasonably convincing promises of development projects being carried out on the cooperative (while Huasicancha was now ostentatiously excluded from any small local improvement schemes), the community never seriously entertained the possibility of joining.

Most of the Huasicanchinos' political expression then should not be seen out of the context of these conditions, conditions in which state policy is generally negative or irrelevant. Their political action and what specific identity they derive from engagement in that action arise precisely from these conditions. Whichever way you look at it, therefore, whether as a political analyst seeking out the coefficients of political mobilization or as an anthropologist concerned with the production of culture, the very *specificity* of this situation matters. Insofar as what we are talking of here is very real, open, and at times bloody confrontation with the dominant power bloc, which has more or less support from the state from one time to another, it is patently ridiculous to suggest that such confrontation is irrelevant to class analysis because it is too local, too primordial or too "exceptional." Rigorous class analysis can only lose from such myopia. However, to suggest that Huasicanchino culture is comprehensible without regard to this much larger political reality is equally absurd. The production and reproduction of culture for *any* people in the modern world is an intensely political affair.

I have tried to get at this particular process in the previous chapters. In chapter 2 I suggested that for many years the social relations of production among the highland pastoralists were not thoroughly destroyed but built upon by those in power. The effect was to give an appearance of continuity to community institutions while in fact transforming them to serve new purposes. Then, in chapter 6, by reference to materials in the previous chapter, I showed why the preservation of certain particularistic relationships can serve a wide range of interests in diverse forms of domestic enterprise. While at one level it is taken for granted that customs and practices serve agreed-upon goals, at another, the heterogeneity of enterprises means that there is in fact a plasticity in meaning. So one reason why Huasicanchino political expression took the form it did was that key institutions remained in place while transformations in their meaning and practice occurred at first as a result of articulation with more dominant systems and then as a function of internal heterogeneity.

But reference only to the social and economic requirements for life to go on from day to day is not enough. I therefore suggested that incidents of political engagement should not be artificially separated from these social relations of production. In the case of Huasicancha, political mobilization has brought into play existing institutions to serve the purposes of the political struggle. This was the case for the subsistence techniques used by the montoneras, discussed in chapter 3; and it is revealed time and again in the land recuperation campaigns discussed in the previous chapter. The use of institutions in times of political struggle itself modifies the institutions, but it also gives a political dimension to the preservation of those institutions in subsequent periods of quiescence. Community institutions not only serve a daily livelihood function: they also become inseparable from the political identity and survival of the participants.

This provides a thoroughgoing link between the Huasicanchinos' livelihood and their political activity. There is another such link, too. For I have stressed not only that there is a slippage between the practice of an institution and what is accepted as its orthodox meaning but also that the heterogeneity of Huasicanchino enterprises has given people a variety of lenses through which they perceive what is the orthodox meaning of an institution. In the process of intensive political engagement a dialogue emerges over such matters and the more essential the institution is perceived to be for people's lives, the more thoroughly are they committed to this dialogue, and this gave form to Huasicancha's campaign. Then, because the campaign was articulated through this ongoing interaction both at the level of the meaning and that of the practice of institutions bound up with the "community," political engagement had the effect of modifying the idiom of community and at the same time investing it with contemporary relevance and vitality.

The Facets of Experience

Inasmuch as the struggle over land revolved around "the community of Huasicancha," it included groups as apparently different as destitute "peones" from the village and petty commodity producers resident in Lima. The question arises then, as to how this particular experience of political engagement relates to the Huasicanchinos' sense of themselves—their identity. I believe that this has to do with their experience but that the methods we use for studying experience predispose us to highlight certain elements of experience over others and that, unwittingly, "political peasants" collude in this exercise.

Thoughout the preceding pages I have treated the notion of experience very broadly, whether I was presenting the Huasicanchinos' shadowy and possibly hypothetical pre-Columbian past, their experience of work simultaneously in the community and on the haciendas, or their experience of guerrilla fighting against outsiders variously conceived. Moreover, through case material, I have shown the diversity of the Huasicanchinos' ordinary, daily round as it is today. And finally, I have described their contemporary, lived experience of political engagement. While these elements of experience are kept separate from one chapter to another, in essence no such separation is possible. Experience of the past suffuses the present; experience of political engagement draws attention to one element in the daily round and not another and so on.

What the evidence from the Huasicancha case suggests is that *structural determinants* of agency and the *conscious experience* those agents have as they engage in attempts to reestablish, maintain, or expand the conditions necessary for their livelihoods, are dialectically interconnected. To focus only on the way in which social relations once entered into, then ineluctibly unfold to give form to actors' subjectivity, would seem to miss a very important component of what was happening among the Huasicanchinos. Equally, to focus entirely on the Huasicanchinos' conscious experience of political struggle is to obscure the extent to which the struggle itself occurred as a result of unfolding contradictions of a structural kind, for example, between peasant enterprises in the process of commodification and a hacienda in the process of becoming a capitalist farm.

This study has continually shown how the unfolding of social relations structured in a certain way gave rise to tensions and inevitable contradictions. I have also stressed the importance of self-consciously felt and recorded historical experience too. Hence in chapters 4 and 5 I referred not only to the structural features of the Huasicanchinos' enterprises but also to their past experiences as herders, traders, and so on. But I have argued just as strongly that structural determinants hold no primacy in class formation over the agency of actors engaging in political struggle. Thus, in chapter 3, far from preceding our discussion of the uprising of the montonera decade with a discussion of prevailing social relations of production, I showed that community/hacienda social relations at the end of the last century must be understood by reference to the preconditions that lay in the experience of political struggle throughout the 1880s.

I have argued too, for a more hidden notion of experience, suggesting that relationships engaged in over the weeks and years have consequences that occur behind the backs of people in a way which actually contributes to their subjectivity as the agents of history. This was especially clear in the discussion of simple commodity production and community in chapter 6. But it underlies a proposition asserted throughout that agents negotiate the effective meaning of keywords referring to essential institutions. The notion that meanings are negotiated is not new to anthropology (see, for example, Bailey 1969) and has achieved renewed expression in the work of Marshall Sahlins (1985). But, rather than seeing this as an interesting cultural phenomenon *sui generis* I ground its occurrence among the Huasicanchinos in a materialistic interpretation of their reproduction vis-à-vis the overall society and economy.

In the recent past, this experience of slippage between the "proper meaning" of an institution and its actual institutionalized practice in any one instance has occurred for essentially two interconnected reasons. First, commodified social relations have not wiped away preexisting social relations but have been grafted onto them. Hence, as Huasicanchinos continue to use institutions of communal labor, the adoption of children, labor exchange, and so on, referring to each by its traditional name, the underlying logic of commodified relations undermines the older meanings. In doing so, it not only opens the way for a gap between orthodoxy and practice but also contributes to the sense of identity of the actors themselves. It reconstitutes them as agents.

Second, the Huasicanchino form of production is heterogeneous. Hence the areas of social reproduction affected by commodification—be they access to credit, mobilization of labor, or the constitution of land as property—vary from one enterprise to the next. So the way in which traditional notions of an institution are undermined in practice vary among Huasicanchinos.[2] The effect of confronting outsiders over access to the resources upon which all these institutions (however interpreted) are dependent, is to call attention to precisely these different resonances in meaning. Less than resolving the issue in a timeless fixity, however, political engagement for the Huasicanchinos served to intensify discourse that then itself gave to political engagement its own momentum.

Hence Huasicanchino history cannot be understood without stressing the heightened self-consciousness people acquire as they engage in political struggle. This is a view endorsed by E. P. Thompson (1968, 1978), but by excluding as it does the unintended and often immediately hidden consequences of social relations once entered into, this notion of experience is at once too narrow and too vague.[3] We therefore require both structural and expressive components of experience in the formation of identity. Yet, for Thompson, because structural tensions are themselves bereft of any dynamic impetus, the task of history is always left to the conscious agency of class actors:

> To put it bluntly: classes do not exist as separate entities, look around, find an enemy class, and then start to struggle. On the contrary, people find themselves in a society structured [*sic*] in determined ways, (crucially, but not exclusively, in productive relations), they experience exploitation (or the need to maintain power over those they exploit), they identify points of antagonistic interest, they commence to struggle around these issues and *in the process of struggling they discover themselves as classes*, they come to know this discovery as class-consciousness. *Class and class-consciousness are always the last, not the first, stage in the real historical process.* But if we employ a static category of class, or if we derive our concept from a prior theoretical model of structural totality, we will not suppose so: we will suppose that class is instantaneously present (derivative like a geometric projection, from production relations) and that *hence* classes struggle. (1978: 149)

Yet what for Thompson is the end product of an historical enquiry, for Brenner constitutes the *sine qua non* without which it is impossible to begin such an enquiry.

In a seminal article (1976) on the role of class conflict in social change in preindustrial Europe, Brenner develops his argument from an a priori structural view of class relationships:

> Class structure . . . has two analytically distinct, but historically unified, aspects. First, the relations of direct producers to one another, to their tools and to the land in the immediate process of production—what has been called the "labour process" or the "social forces of production." Second, the inherently conflictive relations of property—always guaranteed directly or indirectly, in the last analysis, by force—by which an unpaid-for part of the product is extracted from the direct producers—which might be called the "property relationship" or the "surplus-extraction relationship." (1976: 31)

These two elements of class relations are conventionally referred to as the "forces of production" and the "relations of production." The first element links people together within the process of production, and the second element, as Brenner stresses, locks them into conflictive relations.

For the purpose of clarifying my approach to the history of the Huasican-chinos, two points need to be stressed here. First, it is to be noted that both elements are necessary for the constitution of class relationships. *Any* conflictive relationship, however structurally inevitable it may be, is not thereby a class conflict, and *any* relationship that links people together in some shared experience is also not thereby *necessarily* a class experience. Secondly, Brenner places less stress on the fact that all these relationships—however much they may be the products of properties inherent in structure—are at some level or another *experienced relationships*, and while their underlying dynamism may have all kinds of historical significance, it is at this level of experience that they become of *sociological* interest.

Brenner then goes on to say,

> It is around the property or surplus-extraction relationship that one defines the fundamental classes in a society—the class(es) or direct producers on the one hand and the surplus-extracting, or ruling [*sic*], class(es) on the other. It would be my argument then that different class structures, specifically property relations or surplus extraction relations, once established, tend to impose rather strict limits and possibilities, indeed rather specific long-term patterns, on a society's economic development. (1976: 31)

It is the suggestion that class *structures*, already defined in terms bereft of the experience of actual political struggle, impose rather specific long-term patterns on development, which give to this position its structuralist character. It is a position which Thompson finds loaded with mystification, for while he is prepared to acknowledge that society is structured in determined ways, he is innocent of the notion of structural contradictions and the tensions that emerge from them.[4] Nevertheless, the evidence from this study suggests that certain social relations are so structured as to impose at least some developmental logic of their own.

After all, in chapter 6, I paused in the ethnographic narrative to bring together some of the threads of the Huasicanchinos' livelihood in order to show why the Huasicanchinos came together *as Huasicanchinos* prior to the political engagement of the 1960s, and I did so by arguing that this was explicable in terms of the structural requirements of certain of their forms of production. For all that, there was still something lacking: the contribution to their lives of the experience of political engagement itself, and yet the evidence from Huasicancha suggests that, through the centuries (as Thompson has suggested for other circumstances) political engagement has had its own history. And once they experience those tensions, which arise from the kind of contradictions Brenner describes, this history has given the Huasicanchinos the tools with which to bring their agency to bear, thus modifying (more or less radically) the determination of those contradictions.

I have tried in this book to interlace these two faces of experience without giving undue weight to the one or the other. Indeed, I have tried as best I could to dissolve the distinction between the one and the other. What often appears to be an especially newsworthy "political" act of resistance may best be seen as just one moment in a long trajectory in which livelihood and resistance are interwoven. So I have sought to provide both the stuff of daily life and the stuff of political action as one of a piece in the interrelations of people with one another.[5]

Though Thompson can be criticized then for the vagueness of his notion of experience (Anderson 1980: 16–58), we should be cautious about abandoning it altogether, for it captures something not quite embraced by anything else. Experience, for example, might be part of culture but it is not the same thing. It is hard to avoid the sense that there is something rather specific, rather ungeneralizable, about the Huasicanchino experience when, as one picks one's way along a hazardous mountain path illicitly to pasture sheep, one is given a gentle nudge and then a nod of the head toward a spot where the rocks are outlined against the sky, there to see the figure of a caporal on patrol. Or watching as an ambulant fruitseller in Lima upturns his barrow of fruit to be gathered up by passers-by rather than allow the arresting policeman to sell it off later. Or listening as three or four people share in the account of how *fulano de tal* (some person) was found in hiding, captured, and taken off to prison, liberally changing one "fact" for another with apparent indifference. These are matters equally of daily life and, in Tilly's useful expression, matters of contention: they are matters too that have the effect—intended or not—of asserting one thing and negating another. And once the specificity of the Huasicanchinos' experience becomes apparent so it becomes difficult to interpret the texture of their daily interactions and the way in which their domestic enterprises have developed without taking into account the constant presence of these very obvious and eminently describable experiences. Then again those more describable experiences themselves seem naked when taken out of the context of a more obvious and hence less visible kind of experience—the experience of the daily round of shepherding, weaving, trading, migrating once and then again . . . and so on.

And yet these are not all experiences of the same kind; experience is a multifaceted word, as we discover if we turn to the dictionary:

1. direct personal participation or observation [*sic*]; actual knowledge or contact: *experience of prison life*.
2. a particular [*sic*] incident, feeling etc., that a person has undergone: *an experience to remember*.
3. accumulated knowledge, especially of practical matters: *a man of experience*.
4. the impact made on an individual by the culture of a people, nation etc.: *the American experience*.
5. *Philosophy:* the totality of a person's perceptions, thoughts, memories and encounters.[6]

Though most studies of experience are probably aimed at the last of these, that is, the entry that embraces all the others, our difficulties are suggested by Item 1, which most closely preserves the Latin root (*experiri*: to prove) which "experience" shares with "experiment" (experience as a special form of observation). Item 2 takes the precise reverse position from experimental observation, being explicitly subjective. Though it is not my intention to enter into fine analytic exposition, far from encouraging me to disaggregate the term, the dictionary serves to reassure me that the multifaceted sense I had already accumulated of "experience" is not idiosyncratic but rather that the interconnectedness of these senses should be preserved.

Experience is not only something that happens in the past but something in which we participate from moment to moment. And experience is not only something to which we can consciously give form and describe, like a political confrontation on the pampa, but also the daily affairs that are so taken for granted that they escape our notice and thus elude description. As the various disciplines have attempted to study, and then talk about, experience, however, they have faced methodological problems that have had the effect of laying theoretical emphasis on one of these dimensions over the others.

For example, when conflict occurs between groups it gives rise to the negotiation of meanings within groups. Thus in the previous chapter we saw contentiousness provoking heightened political discourse (cf., Jones 1983: 90–178; Foster 1985) that itself created a momentum of its own. It seems to me that this was an especially intense period of cultural production. Yet this dimension of political engagement is lost as that experience becomes translated into accounts appropriate to the task of relating "what happened" in the past. Insofar as they become narratable history, events that were essentially incomplete, uncertain as to their outcome and unclear in the role played by participants, must conform to the requirements of narrative while not belying what can patently be seen to have happened. Hence, as accounts gain a closer approximation to narrative, so the role of participants becomes clearer, the outcome more certain, and the event itself more complete. Not only is there a tendency for hermetic closure to occur such that an account becomes *the* account and thence "the facts," but in conforming to the structures of narrative, disproportionate emphasis is placed on central characters (leaders) and the unity and homogeneity of followers.

In contrast, however, to the closure of this kind of narrative account, offered in response to inquiries from the visiting historian, vivid accounts of past events were themselves part of the heightened critical discourse taking place during political engagement. And here the deepened commitment participants have in how such accounts are interpreted gives rise to the ongoing and hence perpetually incomplete and negotiable nature of cultural production, while nevertheless restraining interpretations within the confines of very real conditions, testable in the outcome of political strategy.

Living with the Huasicanchinos during quite intense moments (or soon thereafter) convinces me of this; I find it hard, however, to reproduce the myriad facets of cultural production thus engendered within the exercise of political praxis. By referring to just one idea, that of landed property, I will try nevertheless to convey both the very definite limits and also the more immediately apparent dynamic properties inherent in the discourse which arises *within* a group of people engaged in a political engagement *against* others. In the case of the Huasicanchinos it is clear that, over the course of time, engagement in political struggles and interaction with changing economic conditions have together led to the reformulation of key institutions and hence the meaning of words used to talk about those institutions. But insofar as that engagement has not been uniformly shared by all, so the reformulations have varied and the role of manipulation through discourse, in contributing to further reformulation, becomes manifest. At the end of the day this entire set of activities becomes as much the precondition of the social relations of petty production as it is the result.[7]

The Role of Structure, Political Engagement and Discourse: an Example

The political conflict that arose between Hacienda Tucle and the Huasican-chinos reflected a major structural contradiction of the kind referred to by Brenner for preindustrial Europe. Once that conflict arose, however, height-ened discourse *within* the ranks of the Huasicanchinos occurred as a result of the variety of Huasicanchino units of production, and this complexity of social relations often prevented the logical unfolding inherent in any one set of re-lations when taken on its own (in chap. 6, the case of commodification was more thoroughly discussed). Moreover, once Huasicanchinos addressed themselves to the demands of the political struggle, this too, worked against emerging internal contradictions.

Nevertheless we cannot deny the power of unfolding internal contradic-tions. Despite the Huasicanchinos' perpetual manipulations of the bounds of the domestic sphere, of the use of kin, of community sentiment and so on, the contradiction between the property form necessary for simple commodity production on the one hand and the peasant economy on the other was funda-mental. Whereas community property involves the right to a flow of income from a specific resource and is contingent on certain social performances, limited and fragmented between holders, all of whom have rights in the same physical good, commodified property is confined to one owner and not tied to social performance. Simple commodity production requires this latter idea of absolute property at least in some of its material goods and can be far more rationalized where this can be extended to possession of livestock and—most crucial of all—land.

Of course, what precipitated land invasions against Hacienda Tucle were the administrator's attempts to restrict access to clearly delimited areas of ter-ritory and to convert "rights of entry" into wages, i.e., a move toward abso-lute property. Much of the confusion that followed in subsequent efforts to find settlements arose, not because the Huasicanchinos uniformly opposed this view of property, but because many of the better-off Huasicanchinos were already practicing such forms of possession. Moreover the essence of *these* people's conflict with Tucle derived from their growing realization that they could only establish such property rights of their own once Tucle was reduced or eliminated. For this reason simple commodity producers showed a keen interest in the direction of the land recuperation campaign that extended itself to their seeking leadership positions. Meanwhile the "proper" (i.e., "tradi-tional") use of the concept of property served political purposes both in terms of internal cohesion and the external presentation of the Huasicancha case.

Contradictions in these two forms of property, therefore, expressed themselves in Huasicancha through heightened discourse revolving around property and periodic crises when the clarity of the contradiction was forced to the fore. Such crisis invariably took the form of a turnover in the official leadership of the campaign. This was especially clear in the dismissal of both Tacunan as personero and the more established migrants who were his associates. Conversely, where such clarity was avoided in favor of more generalized and undefined references to possession, independent farmers were able to secure and retain political offices as representatives of the group as a whole, as was the case for Urbano at the end of the campaign.

But if the development of absolute forms of property among Huasicanchinos had the effect of making various independent farmers interested in the direction of the campaign, the continuation of contingent and fragmented property had the effect of giving widely dispersed participants an interest in the struggle through their confederation links back to the village. For the confederations of households were initially emergent from just such forms of property. And it was, after all, the existence of these confederations, spanning Huancayo, La Oroya, and Lima that most directly kept migrant ex-residents interested in land and livestock in and around Huasicancha.

It will be recalled that quite complex interrelationships of ownership were common among confederations of households. A shop assistant in Huancayo might also be a "*socio*" (partner) in a pig farm in Lima, a truck in Huancayo, and a marketstall in La Oroya. The more thoroughly livestock were interspersed across a variety of flocks shepherded by different households, the more healthy the confederation was said to be. These various practices had a significant effect on the definition of the domestic sphere: confederations themselves were seen by participants as a modified version of an institution in which one household was dispersed widely over terrain to gain full advantage of the vertical ecology. Therefore, if the contemporary versions of the confederations rarely reflect perfectly this ideal, they nevertheless benefit from a common understanding of what I can only refer to as "the proper usage" of what the institution "ought to be like"—a resonance from a commonly understood experience of the past.

And yet, even in the past, it was rarely households per se that stretched across the complementary zones of the ecology but a community of households (see chap. 2). These households, moreover, in the course of time, came to specialize in the agriculture of specific zones. What is more, the past also provides evidence of local leaders, going back to the days of the curacas, using the lack of precision between family and community to gain access to community labor for the benefit of their own households: the sphere of "all my kin" was strategically manipulated. And this manipulation was made possible by the contingent and fragmented nature of property.

A "special advantage" through reducing labor costs can be had then, for some households, by reducing reciprocal obligations (drawing *in* the family) while at the same time increasing the reciprocal rights due one (extending the net of "those who love me"). In the past this has been most effectively done through the use of political office within the community. And this not too far into the distant past. For one thing the fetishization of character and skill that predated commodity fetishism meant that those with skill and knowledge were obliged to put it at the disposal of the community.[8] They did this by taking office, and they were repaid by the community's obligations to them.

More recently successful independent farmers and urban petty commodity producers have been placed in positions of authority for similar reasons and accepted the task for similar purposes. But their special advantage results from their skill in privatizing certain elements of the production unit while continuing to take advantage of the dispersed forms of property and labor deriving from the community. The most striking combination of these is live-stock and land. Because Huasicancha's pasture is common property it is available to all, contingent only on community membership. Once livestock are systematically raised through careful breeding and use of medications etc., then they become a source of continual accumulation restricted only by the amount of land available. But as long as such systematic accumulation takes place through the extended system of the confederations and the various com-plex ties between the members of a highland estancia, as was the case for Grimaldo and Angelina (chap. 5), then the benefits of accumulation are to some extent dispersed. Moreover, insofar as the limitations on accumulation in this century have primarily been the result of limited land, the manifest hindrance comes from where it is controlled—in recent times not the com-munity but the hacienda.

With the paying of a wage to peones or the increased exploitation of the immediate domestic labor of the household, in lieu of these more extended ties, then accumulation is concentrated. And this was the tendency most prev-alent in the case of Urbano and Paulina (chap. 5). The area within which it is concentrated may vary in fact (e.g., to just the household head or just the adult couple) but ideologically it is restricted to a precisely delineated domes-tic sphere. Accumulated livestock take up ever larger amounts of pasture but do not benefit ever more extensive personnel. The comparative advantage of such a household does not therefore derive from a characteristic that can be put to the community's advantage—skill-knowledge—through being made available for the benefit of all, as in the past, but precisely from restricting the amount of capital to a defined sphere and, in the case of land, specifically at the expense of the amount of common good remaining available to others. This is a patently unresolvable fact: a contradiction to human resourcefulness. To dismiss it on the grounds that it is not clearly articulated in the discourse of locals is not just to blind oneself to an important element of social reality but to deny oneself the possibility of asking how it was continually obscured and why; whenever political and economic conjunctures forced a clarification it threatened a crisis in the political struggle against Tucle.

I have suggested in the previous section that this process can best be understood by recognizing the multifaceted resonances of keywords on the one hand and political conjunctures that serve to expose this variation on the other, giving rise to a heightened internal discourse. Even so, by referring here to the question of land, we see that it was not just the heightened discourse among Huasicanchinos that gave momentum to their political mobilization, but what that heightened discourse was about: the perpetual need for the land being held by the hacienda. Political discourse must be seen then as neither a superstructure enslaved by its appropriate economic base nor as the autonomous activity of somehow objectively-conscious subjects standing back from the conditions of their existence and coldly weighing "the facts at hand."

If the Huasicanchinos alone are far too small a group to call a class, we are nonetheless talking about the stuff from which classes emerge: from making statements (in a variety of "languages" from various forms of discourse, to making physical threats, to carrying them out)—against some, with others, and among themselves. Nevertheless if we dissociate the Huasicanchinos' political resistance from structural determinations, as Thompson would have it, then we find classes the moment we find struggles, and it becomes impossible to distinguish between alliances of temporary political convenience—popular fronts, if you like—and struggles that will do precisely what Thompson would have them do: crystallize—in my view through discourse—what is to be the class coming into formation.

Moreover, it is only through maintaining this linkage between the imperatives of social relations and consciously engaged-in political contention, that we are able to clarify a term which, in contemporary usage, has become confused. Thus when one talks of everyday forms of resistance, it is not always clear whether the resistance being referred to is the "irresistable force" type or the "immoveable object" type, a conscious act or an inherent capacity to withstand. A reference to "peasant resistance to capitalism," for example, may mean properties inherent in peasant social relations that make them resistant to capitalism (see Friedmann 1980 or Taussig 1982) or peasants' conscious acts of resistance, which, though not necessarily subjectively perceived as being directed against capitalism, can be interpreted as such (Hobsbawm 1959, 1984: 15–32; Wolf 1969; Scott and Kerkvliet 1973). I have not attempted to show simply that certain peasant enterprises have an inherent capacity deriving from their structure to resist capitalist social relations, nor to show simply that certain peasant attitudes encourage them to resist, rather I have shown precisely the way in which the one form of resistance is linked to the other.

James Scott (1986) is one of the few writers who has turned attention to forms of rural resistance that do not in themselves amount to major revolutionary transformations. Yet, it seems to me that because he does not link the structural determinants of social relations to the kind of conscious acts of resistance he focuses on—indeed in the absence of an especially rigorous notion of class at all—he is led towards a kind of Lewis Carroll riddle as to whether peasants say what they mean or mean what they say: can pilfering and sabotage be packaged together as forms of resistance if the one is selfish in intent and the other altruistic? This focus on the motivations of the individual peasant cut adrift from the wide variety of social relations in which he or she is embedded forces Scott to argue that acts performed in self-interest—such as deserting from the Tsarist army—can have just as great implications for resistance as those performed for group interest. Such a view not so much contradicts the views of Marx or Lenin as stops at the gates of their question, which was to try to ascertain the way in which individual interests might become those of an entire class and vice versa.

It almost seems as though Scott is abandoning the phenomenological element he ascribed to his earlier approach (1976) in favor of the peasant as strategizing individual, so that when he says "self-interest" we must read "individual self-interest" and what becomes something needing explanation is how selfishly motivated individuals, engaging in individual acts of defiance, can be the basis for more concerted resistance. The selfishly motivated individual seems to be incompatible with the unity and solidarity required of proper resistance. This is by no means a view confined to Scott (who anyway goes on to explain very well why this contradiction is only apparent, not real); it is one that is commonly held. And yet is a certain kind of self-confident individualism incompatible with solidarity in times of struggle? Interestingly, pressed by an outsider to explain, in retrospect, the success of their own campaign and the very few backsliders, Huasicanchinos will ascribe it to "unity" (*unión*), and hence appear to collude in an emphasis on the ability of a well-established collective will to overcome egoistic self-interest. And yet precisely what gave form to the political activity and created the momentum that carried it forward was that people were thoroughly engaged in asserting what they saw to be their self-interests and, moreover, felt a confidence in their own abilities to articulate those interests in the forum of open debate. What "community" existed among Huasicanchinos was of the kind described well by Sabean (1984: 29–30): "What is shared in community is not shared values or common understanding, so much as the fact that members of a community are engaged in the same argument, the same *raisonement,* the same *Rede,* the same discourse, in which alternative strategies, misunderstandings, conflicting goals and values are threshed out. . . . What makes community is the discourse." It is only in accounts retrospectively constructed that people reduce themselves to passive followers united in agreement behind a single-minded leader. At the time of political contention itself the link between individual and collective will is more dynamic, a process which Gramsci referred to as "the cultural aspect" of political struggle: "An historical act can only be performed by 'collective man,' and this presupposes the attainment of a 'cultural-social' unity through which a multiplicity of dispersed wills, with heterogeneous aims, are welded together with a single aim, on the basis of an equal and common conception of the world (1976: 348). This welding together of dispersed wills engaged in the same argument, in which strategies, misunderstandings and goals are threshed out, is the process of cultural production that I have tried to examine here, while grounding it in the imperatives of social relations.

Local Knowledge

I initially went to Peru to study an example of successful rural resistance in which outside influences, such as leadership and institutional support, were not present. I sought out a situation where resistance was actually taking place rather than one that had concluded some time in the past, and I set my sights on the Huasicanchinos. I felt that the intensive fieldwork associated with social anthropology could provide detailed material on the characteristics of rural resistance that was unavailable to studies conducted on a much larger scale or to historical studies dependent on accounts of past events.

Once having met Huasicanchinos in Huancayo and in Huasicancha itself, I found that there was no difficulty in getting them to talk to me about their resistance. Indeed it was hard to get them to talk of anything else. But I was struck especially by the thin line between getting by and total disaster. Their lives seemed to me so perpetually precarious. As I talked to them about this perception, I soon discovered that—surprised though they were by my interest—for them too this was a ceaseless preoccupation. Yet gathering data related to livelihood was far more difficult than acquiring material on the land invasions. So much was taken for granted. By contrast, aware of the disparities between us with respect to their beliefs about the hill spirits or the rituals surrounding curing practices, informants took very little for granted. But except for a few rather specific occasions, beliefs and rituals were of little interest to Huasicanchinos. What I have discussed in this book, then, is a product of my own initial interests as they were modified by my encounter with the Huasicanchinos. And this encounter provoked me to connect the characteristics of the Huasicanchinos' resistance to the way they made a living. But there are limitations to adding this very intimate and detailed evidence to broader studies.

I have wanted to learn something very specific about precisely what kind of "direct producers" they were who engaged in the land recuperation campaign and about their differing roles at particular stages of the campaign. I found that regardless of any "economic" differences, engagement in the political struggle itself carried people along and influenced their involvement. These issues are of some interest when compared to studies like Hobsbawm and Rude's (1973) of the Swing uprisings in Britain, Stedman Jones's essay (1983) on the Chartists, Eric Wolf's study (1969) of the role of peasants in twentieth-century revolutions, or Charles Tilly's (1986) study of "the contentious French." But the Huasicanchino campaigns were not the basis of a subsequent revolution. Indeed the guerrilla movements aiming at revolution in the central Andes in the 1960s were strikingly disconnected from these kinds of spontaneous local initiatives (Bejar 1970). Nor was their shared discourse as widespread as was the Chartists'. Indeed the extremely local referents in discourse are a notable feature of the Huasicanchino campaigns. And the absence of comparative data makes it hazardous to guess whether the Huasicanchino land invasions of the 1960s can exemplify the very widespread spontaneous insurgency in the central Andes of this period.[9]

What is striking, however, is how much we learn about participants in a long-sustained resistance campaign by attending to their specificity. It would be foolhardy to question the value of studies carried out at a much broader level (for example, Barrington Moore 1966; Wolf 1969; Skocpol 1979). But it is equally foolhardy to accept these broader studies without paying close attention to the evidence drawn from more detailed microscopic studies of such very widely divergent cases as say, LeRoy Ladurie's (1975) *Montaillou*, Warman's (1980) *We Come to Object*, Mintz's (1982) *The Anarchists of Casas Viejas*, or Sider's (1986) *Culture and Class in Anthropology and History*. Yet the kind of knowledge that emerges from this different sort of material means that much is lost when these cases are used for the purpose of broad generalization. Rather these latter studies would seem to confirm that we must seek out the origins of the class consciousness of the oppressed in locally specific forms of cultural identity.

In the case of Huasicancha, it is difficult to see how one could separate out those aspects of the local culture that are directly related to these people's opposition to a prevailing hegemony and those which are not. In this sense, it is quite reasonable in my view to refer to Huasicancha's culture as preeminently a "culture of opposition." It is striking for example how cultural production in Huasicancha contrasts with that described by Sider (1986) for Newfoundland. As long as we are careful not to see in all manifestations of cultural specificity expressions of real or potential opposition to the homogenizing effects of a dominant hegemony, then this observation provides a useful dimension to our understanding of the emergence of a politically significant class consciousness. While there is no doubt that the local nature of this culture of opposition prevents it from itself being an expression of consciousness of class, it seems obvious that the seeds for a more broadly based oppositional class consciousness are there and will inevitably influence any subsequent political participation. To this extent an understanding of the specificity of cultures of opposition is an essential part of class analysis, and it is to be emphasized that it is only attainable through attending to the details of historical and geographical variation, which are too easily lost in broader studies.

Notes

Introduction:
The World of the Huasicanchinos:

1. To avoid a rather cumbersome style, I refer to the period during which I did the major part of the fieldwork for this study—1972–1973—in the present tense. This is not quite the same as the anthropological convention known as "the ethnographic present" in which the present tense is used to refer to a rather longer period of time and is usually rather vaguely situated in terms of precise dates. A second period of fieldwork was carried out in 1981, but except for verifying information and substantiating material for the case studies in chapter 4, the findings of the second field trip are not referred to in this study.

2. Today the Huasicanchinos are predominantly sheep farmers, but they also have some cattle, llamas, and alpacas; pigs and poultry are usually confined to the area around the village. It is conventional to state animal ownership in terms of "units of sheep" in the following ratios:

Cattle and horses	10:1
Llamas and alapacas	6:1
Pigs and donkeys	3:1

3. In Huasicancha much of the character of the office of gobernador and his tenientes derives from a perception that it is a state-recognized version of a parallel institution, the *Campo de Vara* or *Varayoc* which is not officially recognized by authorities in Huancayo but nonetheless remains active in Huasicancha. Huasicancha is one of the last remaining communities to maintain this old institution in the central sierras (although it remains strong in Southern Peru). Identified by their silver-decorated walkingsticks (*varas*) the sixteen to twenty members compose a semireligious secret

fraternity whose main task today is the protection of the village from natural forces represented by the weather and by the hill spirit, *wamani*.

4. The development of these community cooperatives was by no means a major part of the government's agrarian reform program and was not pursued with any great singleness of purpose. Of far greater significance was the expropriation of the highland haciendas on both sides of the Mantaro Valley and their formation into a massive cooperative known as "SAIS Cahuide." Members of those communities bordering immediately on the ex-hacienda lands were given voting shares in this cooperative as were those working directly on the haciendas themselves. The community cooperatives were supposed to run in tandem with this larger cooperative. (See Smith 1976, Montoya et al 1974, Horton 1974, Roberts and Samaniego 1978, McClintock 1981.) By the time Cahuide came on stream, however, Huasicancha was well on the way to repossessing its own land and had no interest in membership in this cooperative.

1: Forms of Struggle

1. Lack of sensitivity about historical and local specificity makes global theories of underdevelopment and schematic theories of class analysis as unsubstantial as they are glamorous. In this such theorists share with many critics of Marx's historiography the false view that a global theory of history is an approach he followed, when in fact he continually returned to grapple with the specifics of particular political conditions: "Events strikingly analogous, but which take place in a different historical environment, lead to entirely different results. Studying each of these evolutions separately and then comparing them, it is easy to understand the key to understanding this phenomenon; but this understanding can never be attained by utilizing a universal master-key in the form of a general historico-philosophical theory" (Marx and Engels 1934: 254–255). For a sustained formulation of this view of Marx's historiography, see Sayer 1979, 1987.

2. By subjectivity I do not mean the "black box" of people's inner minds supposedly accessible through the rigors of hermeneutics, cognitive anthropology, or psychology. I use it, in contrast to a sense of being the objects of history, to refer to the particular form of the imposition of will to affect the outcome of history.

3. This is what I take Marx to mean by the famous passage from the *Preface* (1970: 21): "Just as one does not judge an individual by what he thinks about himself, so one cannot judge such a period of transformation by its consciousness, but, on the contrary, this consciousness must be explained from the contradiction of material life, from the conflict existing between the social forces of production and the relations of production." It is also reflected in his remark that if reality and appearance were one and the same thing, there would be no need for science.

4. It is not enough to deprive the word *resistance* of all its meaning by interpreting virtually every gesture of cultural distinction, delinquency, or being "on the fiddle" as "everyday forms of resistance." The Huasicanchinos acquired their cultural distinctiveness from forms of resistance far more explicit than that. What matters politically is how those experiences of real and spectacular resistance are kept alive through periods of repression and then become available and give form to a resurgence of explicit resistance at appropriate conjunctures. We know very little about this. In

Huasicancha jokes and stories served to keep the pot boiling. In other areas they act as a pressure valve to *divert* resistance. By trying to stress the quotidian nature of Huasicancha's resistance, therefore, I must hasten to distance myself from a literature that fails to distinguish between elements of culture that grow up "in resistance" (i.e., as a function of active resistance) and those whose practice has the effect of stressing difference, nothing more. To quarrel is one thing; to *beg* to differ quite another (cf., Scott 1985; Scott and Kerkvliet 1986). This issue is taken up in greater detail in chapter 8.

5. Sider (1986: 121) has captured this situation well by using Raymond Williams's (1977: 108–115) interpretation of Gramsci's (1976) notion of hegemony; Sider says, "Hegemony, as I define the term, is that aspect of culture that, usually in the face of struggle—or simple noncompliance—most directly seeks to unify work and appropriation, and *to extend appropriation beyond work* into neighbourhood, family, forms of consumption; in sum into daily life" [emphasis mine].

6. The reader should be warned, however, that this is perforce a very brief outline. I do not claim to deal exhaustively with the variety of issues discussed in this section.

7. The characteristics of commodities and [their influence on] social relations is taken up in more detail at the beginning of chapter 6.

8. Technically the term *exploitation* does not apply to either of these two cases, insofar as labor power is not paid a wage and hence surplus value cannot be calculated. I use the term rather broadly here.

9. Besides *ex machina* problems with the application of these concepts from political economy, there are difficulties inherent to the model itself. The argument suggests that response to competition leads the simple commodity producer to raise the organic composition of capital toward the real subsumption of labor and the extraction of relative surplus value. That is to say, surpluses are generated through techniques and machinery that increase the productivity of labor. For peasants the subsumption of labor is only formal, and whatever surpluses exist are generated by longer working hours. Strictly speaking, in a competitive environment of commodities generated through capitalist relations, it is hard to see how relative surplus value can be generated on the part of the simple commodity producer from one year to the next without ever greater increases in the organic composition of capital and hence expanded reproduction.

10. Armando Bartra (1979: 26) has suggested in this respect that peasant struggles to ensure access to land are analogous to proletarian demands for job security.

11. Models of peasant economy and simple commodity production that are based on a notion of the rationality of the form of production are generally seen to be based on "political economy." The term has come to be used to distinguish such studies from "economic" studies, which focus on the rationality of a decision-making actor. The political component of the former model is all too often absent, however, and I therefore retain the expression "economic" when referring to this interpretation of "political economy."

12. This rigid, nonnegotiable characteristic of hegemonic terms that gives them a kind of one-dimensionality is stressed by Marcuse (1969). The dynamic interface between the coin and currency of vital words among Huasicanchinos is in striking contrast to the rigid "fixing" of hegemonic words which Marcuse referred to in his essay

"Repressive Tolerance." There he pointed out the importance for social control of the citizenry tolerating these fixed meanings, deprived of all negotiation. A similar process was described more extensively and for a much longer historical period in the West by Michel Foucault (1965, 1970, 1979) when he distinguished between a kind of power that consists of limiting the citizenry through force and a kind of power whose goal is precisely not to limit or restrict but instead to seek control in order to maintain and increase the overall "productivity" of society. For Foucault, this latter form of power is expressed through the language of *norms* and emphasizes *technique*. Hence the development of fields of knowledge in the human sciences, for example, has the effect of bringing the people on whom they focus under greater control; indeed this is the purpose of knowledge and becomes the only justification for the continuance of a particular field. Observing chaotic or random data, organizing data, ordering information into certain categories, controlling external factors that impinge on data so to change them are all the stuff of knowledge and, as the words themselves make progressively clear—observing, organizing, ordering, and controlling—they all have to do with power. While Foucault wishes to stress the way in which these forms of power are de-centered and diffuse, which Marcuse would not agree to, the primary effect of Foucault's notion of power is to give rise to tolerance in Marcuse's sense: the collusion of the citizenry. I am suggesting that rebellion simultaneously negates both of Foucault's forms of power—the first in its external face, the second in its internal discourse.

2: Domination and Disguise

1. This payment to the community for the use of community institutions should not obscure the fact that others—landlords, merchants and so on—may be the ultimate beneficiaries of faenas, fiestas, and so on (cf., Wolf 1956). Insofar as peasant communities themselves pay costs for their social reproduction within a broader geographical circuit (the region or nation), then the importance of the shift in the circuit of social reproduction toward individuals referred to here has less to do with the broadening geographical space than in the way it bypasses the major role played by the community *as a whole* in social reproduction.

2. Equivalence is dependent upon the productivity of all households being much the same. See chapter 5.

3. Some writers prefer its more general meaning of being a poor person (see Samaniego 1974; see also Spalding 1984).

4. The most thorough classification of the Andean haciendas of this period was carried out by Baraona for Ecuador (1965). Juxtaposing the two variables—type of management and relations of production, Baraona proposed a set of possible hacienda types from centralized management/wage labor to ineffective management/traditional labor relations. In his discussion Baraona remarks on the tensions arising from the attempt by management to impose modern production relations and hence proceed toward capitalist farming, and the attempts by the peasantry to retain traditional production relations and hence restrain this tendency. This latter approximates conditions described here for Hacienda Tucle around 1960. (See also Mintz and Wolf 1957; Guerrero 1975; Hunt 1972.)

5. For a more general discussion of contemporary forms of *uyay, minka,* and *trueque* see G. Smith 1979*a,* 1979*c.*

6. See for example, Murra 1958, 1964, 1970, 1980; Wachtel 1973, 1977; Dalton 1981; Lumbreras 1970, 1980; Collier, Rosaldo, and Wirth 1982; Morris 1967; and Spalding 1984. The following discussion is based both on these writings and on material specifically related to the Huancas (Espinosa 1969, 1972; Samaniego 1974).

7. Local informants' knowledge of the details of their ancestors' lives under the Huancas may have little empirical validity of course, but this in no way diminishes it as a component of what it means "to be Huasicanchino."

8. See Patterson 1986: 84–85: "[Inca state policies] promoted an illusion of coherence, one that mimicked the kind of cohesion or connectedness provided by culture in kin-based societies." See also Patterson 1985.

9. "It was the mita which permitted production at Potosi alone to soar far beyond the contemporary total for all New Spain. . . . At Potosi the mita both created the first rapid boom and then subsidized continued production. The same was true at Huancavelica, *where Indians of the nearby districts, rather than working, paid a mita tax* which enabled the miners to meet their labour bills" (Brading and Cross 1972: 560 [emphasis mine]).

10. Cf., Stern, 1983: 27, 37. Wolf (1985: 147) comments: "At one point in time, a community might unite under a principal of its own against the encroachment of Spanish hacienda owners or entrepreneurs. At another time, that principal—*having become like an hacienda owner* or entrepreneur himself in his dealings with the people entrusted to him—might join the Spaniards or be accused of doing so by his followers" (emphasis mine).

11. The word *estancia* does not have the same meaning as in Argentina, where it refers to a large ranch. In Peru the word refers to the pasture controlled by the shepherd belonging to a particular family farm. *Cancha* refers to the small hut and corral where shepherds live and keep their sheep over night.

12. The ensuing data all come from these documents, unless otherwise stated. *CA* is used to refer to material drawn from these documents found in the community of Huasicancha.

13. Copies of this document in the Juzgado de Tierra in Huancayo give the date as 1607, but since names mentioned in it appear again in a 1717 document, it seems likely that the document had been changed, possibly to make the community's claims appear even more longstanding. In fact a copy of this document registered in 1902 refers to "the Viceroy of *the Republic* [sic]." This was corrected in 1968 by notarial amendment to read "de la Colonia?"

14. This incident coincided with the rebellion led by Tupac Amaru, the result of which was a further reduction in protection by the crown of the pueblos de los Indios.

15. Much has been written about the historical background of the Andean hacienda, its origins, transformations, and relations to the local peasantry. See especially, Wolf and Mintz 1957; Favre, Delavaud, and Matos Mar 1967; Lockhart 1969; Keith 1971; Kay 1974; Spalding 1975.

16. Hobsbawm's discussion of "social bandits" (1959, 1969*a*) offers other examples. Anthropological studies of pastoralists in general stress their independence from, and frequently uneasy relations with, the state. But the most colorful example comes

from Le Roy Ladurie's (1975) description of the shepherds of Montaillou, heretics and rebels, and travellers as far afield as Castellon de la Plana in Valencia.

17. That the hegemony of this idea of property was by no means established throughout the nineteenth century is illustrated by the fact that the Hacienda Runatullo of the Valladares family, when taken over by the Sociedad Gandera del Centro in 1910, was said to be, in terms of absolute property, "one million hectares more or less." Yet, never having lost a square foot of territory in the meanwhile, it was assessed in 1970 as being 105,741 hectares (Manrique 1978: 40).

18. For a similar suggestion with respect to early modern Germany, see David Sabean's discussion of *herrschaft* (1984: 20–27 and passim).

3: Growth of a Culture
of Opposition 1850–1947

1. This locating of the Huasicanchinos' struggles both vis a vis the nationally famous Indian rebellion of Tupac Amaru in the eighteenth century and through situating the community geographically within a self-consciously graded continuum of national institutions from the nation to the community, suggests that Huasicanchino class consciousness had developed well beyond that form of peasant consciousness Hobsbawm refers to when he notes that "The unit of their organized action is either the parish pump or the universe. There is no in between" (1984: 20).

2. The montoneros were guerrilla fighters recruited from the highland communities, who fought against both Chileans and collaborators. I use the terms montonera and *guerrillero* interchangeably.

3. The sources used for this period are various. Where especially relevant I refer to them specifically. Otherwise my references are to the community records in Huasicancha, some papers still remaining at the old Hacienda Tucle, the archives of the agrarian reform office in Lima, the office of the Juzgado de Tierra in Huancayo, and the Property Registry in Huancayo. The most frequently-used secondary sources were Basadre (1968–1970, vol. 8), Basadre et al (1979), Bonilla (1978), Espinoza (1969, 1979), Favre (1966, 1975), and the excellent work on the role of the guerrillas in the war with Chile by Nelson Manrique (1978, 1981). The initial stimulus for turning attention to this period however came from the oral accounts of the Huasicanchinos themselves.

4. *Comerciante* refers to a person generally involved in commerce. Most comerciantes were both merchants and independent farmers, and I therefore prefer to retain the Spanish word throughout.

5. If the character of the opponent is important in the development of a people's political consciousness, then it is worth noting that between 1846 and 1972—over 125 years—Tucle was owned by just two women, Bernarda Pielago and Maria-Luisa Chavez, both born poor and both resilient fighters.

6. Bonilla (1978: 118) sees this entire experience as the last of Peru's native rebellions. While he shares with me the belief that the experience of this rebellion was decisive for local peasants, his interpretation, based on the work of Henri Favre (1966, 1975) differs from mine and that of Nelson Manrique (1981) in a number of respects. While there is no space to argue each point of difference in turn, a number of issues

are of importance here. First, for Bonilla what we are seeing here is a race war. For him the valley figures I call comerciantes are, primarily *mestizos*, and the pastoralists primarily Indians, and the lines of conflict lie between whites and mestizos on the one hand and the Indian population on the other.

Favre (1975) plays down the role of patronage in the recruitment of the montoneras and stresses their very early radicalization against all property owners. He argues that as early as 1881 they occupied Hacienda Tucle and subsequently the neighboring Hacienda Rio de la Virgen, selling off the stock to buy arms. In this way other haciendas were subsequently similarly denuded, and the actions of the montoneras actually had the effect of driving property owners into seeking protection from the Chileans and hence hastened their collaboration (1966). For Bonilla, the fact that the Chilean occupying army "brought with it the spoliation of the peasantry" meant that "once in arms they naturally turned not only against the Chilean army but also against their more ancient and immediate oppressors" (1978: 111). The impression both authors give that "Indian" resistance turned immediately into uncontrollable fury directed at all property-owning whites and mestizos, is at variance with the view that the process of polarization took place over some years, in the course of the experience of contentiousness. For my part, with Manrique, I suggest that the period of montonera control of the highlands was as much as ten years (from 1882 to 1892), while Bonilla, contrasting the central highlands with other areas of Peru in which "as the Chileans retired from the country, the peasant rising grew in scale and intensity" (1978: 115), interprets the execution of the early leaders as a sign of the rebellion's demise in 1884. I argue below that, while this was the intention behind the executions, they did not have this effect. As elsewhere in Peru then, "the peasant rising grew in scale and intensity."

It would be surprising, of course, if the first hacienda (Tucle) to be occupied by the montoneras was that of their patron's cousin, though not so surprising that its stock was sold off to buy arms, since Caceres needed arms. Hacienda Rio de la Virgen could scarcely have been occupied by anybody in 1882, since it did not exist (Huancayo, Registro de Propiedad). As for the suggestion that the peasantry were the targets of Chilean extortion and that the Indians drove property owners into the arms of the Chileans, Bonilla shifts his language from Indians here to peasants, which is not quite consistent with the notion that peasant rebellions occurred only later. And yet it was largely the peasants of the valley floor who were so victimized. The highland peasants were nowhere nearly as heavily plundered by the Chileans as were the large haciendas. The actions of the peasants of Comas, to the north and east of the Mantaro Valley, who were the first to attack the Chilean army, suggest that one cause of peasant expropriation of hacienda livestock was the sight of Chileans driving it off before their very eyes. Finally, the earliest collaborators were those hacendados whose markets lay in Lima and their interests were in bringing stability to that market through an early peace and through dissuading the Chileans from extorting still more from their haciendas. Subsequently they were joined in their sentiments by most of the valley population, as Bonilla asserts.

7. Nemesio Raez writing in 1892 (Tello 1971) claimed that the montoneras pillaged, assassinated, and committed a thousand atrocities. Caceres, on the other hand, makes no mention of this (Manrique 1981: 306). Indeed, despite Caceres's observa-

tions that, "So monstrous were the accusations against them, and so difficult to believe, that I felt obliged to collect proof of their crimes" (Favre 1975: 65; and Bonilla 1978: 114). Yet even after attempts to collect such proof Laimes was never accused of these crimes with any specificity at his trial. It is surely significant though that at the time Raez was writing, Huancayo landlords were still trying to recuperate property from the highland guerrilleros.

8. Raez (Tello 1971) gives this exaggerated figure. By this date the guerrillas were concentrated on Colca and Huasicancha whose *total* population was roughly 8,000. Raez also claims that this massive force was repelled by a few cadets from a local college.

9. Laimes's occupation of Hacienda Antapongo is not recorded in his trial but, given its position, between Tucle and Laive, it must certainly have been requisitioned by the guerrillas. Unlike Bernarda Pielago or Juan Enrique Valladares (at the time of the trial of Laimes, a figure in Iglesias's Lima government) Giraldez was dead and therefore unable to speak for himself at Laimes's trial. The marginally greater crime— of having killed Giraldez—was therefore brought against Laimes despite Caceres's orders to execute colaboracionistas.

10. It should not be forgotten that the Chilean occupying troops had also plundered the highland haciendas (see note 4, above).

11. Antagonism between Moya and Huasicancha was to surface again in 1937 when Sabino Jacinto, a leader of Huasicancha's land recuperation campaign, was jailed as a revolutionary subversive on the evidence of two witnesses from Moya.

12. Presumably this comunero was the personero of Huasicancha. Since Indian communities were not recognized as holding property in common in 1884 this would have been a way of handing land to the village as a whole. I have not inspected other community archives, such as Colca's, to see if they received similar inducements.

13. When Priale became a senator, APRA was Peru's most powerful party of the left, though its support in Junin came chiefly from mine workers and small comerciantes (See Klaren 1970; Tullis 1970).

14. Hobsbawm (1974: 133), on Favre's evidence, records that Laimes is confused with the great Inca rebel Tupac Amaru and is reputed to have been executed by quartering. I have found no reference to this version among Huasicanchinos. The reference to Tupac Amaru may have been drawn from the trial notes. But Laimes's statement suggests that his impersonations of an Inca Emperor were at a time of drunken celebration. Annual fiestas in Huasicancha continue to contain the personality of Tupac Amaru as they do ample supplies of alcohol.

15. "F.H.T." refers to documents found at the hacienda buildings during fieldwork: Fundo de Hacienda Tucle.

16. Martinez-Alier (1973) suggests that huacchas could account for up to 75 percent of stock on the haciendas of the region.

17. Here is an example of a shepherd's agreement of the period:

I, Victor Yaranga Cahuana, formally agree with the administration of the Hacienda Tucle to the following terms:

1. I am authorized to enter [the hacienda land] on 15th February, accompanied by the following huacchas: 10 cattle, large and small, 50 sheep, 3 horses and 4 foals, 2 donkeys.

2. In virtue of which, provided that the numbers do not increase, the administration will receive them and give me tasks as it sees fit in the caring of its animals.

3. Understanding all parts of this document, I sign with my thumb. [Signed by both parties] (A.R.A., Lima)

18. In the previous chapter, for example, I made a distinction between hacendados who emerged from being village curacas and those Spaniards who received crown grants. See also, Favre et al (1967), Baraona (1965), Guerrero (1975), and Archetti and Stölen (1987).

19. I discount here Maria Luisa Chavez's claim to 103,000 hectares as merely absurd. There has never been a way of assessing precisely the hacienda's territory or the total area of land claimed by Huasicancha.

20. As the closest thing to a private army for the protection of the hacienda against 'invasion' by local peasants, caporales and mayordomos were never recruited from immediately neighboring villages. Ironically, it seems to have been Huasicancha's unruly reputation that made villagers attractive as caporales to haciendas: three infamous rebels, Jacinto, Tacunan, and Ramos were at times so employed.

21. Manuel Pielago was one of the very few of Huancayo's prominent businessmen to be a native of the region (most others were immigrants or Limeños). Apart from his interests in Hacienda Tucle he had interests in an egg business (1926), other cattle raising companies (1924 and 1935), a leather and shoe factory (1925), and flax mills (1942, 1946). See Roberts 1974*b*: 54.

4: Making a Livelihood

1. *Ex-residentes* is a term used by the Huasicanchinos themselves when referring to the migrants. It reflects both an expectation that migrants will eventually return and also that they continue to be regarded as members of the community and have the right to vote in community elections. I, therefore, prefer to retain this expression when referring to Huasicanchino out-migrants.

2. The names of main characters in case studies have been changed. In some instances, however, the person is sufficiently well known to make this practice confusing. Hence I have not changed the names of Elias Tacunan, Veliz Lizarraga, his one-time associate, and Elias Yaurivilca.

3. It will become clear from the case studies, however, that one must be very cautious about assigning any one occupation to a household or household head.

4. I have concentrated here on male migration. I have tried to give some idea of how migration in Huasicancha took off, which has meant focusing on the "first migrants," who were predominantly male. Later I shall deal with how this affected those who remained behind in the village. But of course women did migrate, and the reasons they did were very often so that their urban activities could supplement the income of the newly-set-up urban households.

5. The number of economic failures among these migrants is very high indeed. Perpetual good health is an essential prerequisite that is seldom attained so that most failures are associated with the onset of illness or an accident, and fear of bad health is proportionately high. Malnutrition among young children is very high. Unlike most

statistical information on the subject, village children suffer less from malnutrition than ex-resident children, and Huasicanchinos often cite this fact as a disincentive to migrate. It must be said here, that research on migrants was predominantly focused on their influence on Huasicancha's economy and politics. Insofar as the influence of these poor migrants was especially small, they received the least attention in the urban research.

5: Ghostly Figures Outside the Domain of Political Economy

1. Before doing so I must enter a caveat. It is of course absurd to disregard the importance of decision making and strategy, but often the use of case material gives these matters misleading prominence. The people we are talking of are like the crew of a small raft on a torrential river. While it would be foolish for the observer to dismiss the strategies by which individual crew members sought to stay afloat, it would be still more foolish to forget that it is the torrential river of the dominant economy that forces these decisions upon them and will carry some to a temporary safe haven and wreck others upon the rocks. Having said this, I hope it is clear from all I have said so far, and later in chapter 6, that I do not thereby dismiss as insignificant the dynamic potential of petty production as is the case for many world system theorists (see C. Smith 1985: 84).

2. Similar statements can be made about outlays on social occasions, the effects of which are to maintain the enterprise's position in a network of interpersonal ties that are crucial for its reproduction.

3. By 1981 a 75 percent inflation rate severely affected this practice. The unsavory nature of asking for a greater return of money than that which was borrowed meant that circulating capital simply dried up. Which of course severely affected the viability of enterprises.

4. Very few Huasicanchinos get formally married. To be *casada* (married) is to have built a *casa* (house).

5. Grimaldo's holding of 28 sheep has a rough value of $400 (U.S.). Angelina's claim on sheep is worth from $1400 to $2800, though of course these are not available to her at present, to use as liquid assets.

6. It was during a discussion of this predicament that Tomas likened himself to a fly caught in a web, quoted at the beginning of this chapter.

7. Agrarian Reform land in the area of Mala, where the plot was located, was expropriated because it was not in use, and the owners had let the irrigation system fall into disrepair. It was therefore sold for a nominal sum, but knowledge of the availability of this land had come to Tomas through *tintorillos*—in this case, shark lawyers—who gathered together suitable "peasants" to be reform beneficiaries and then charged them large legal fees. Tomas, therefore, in order to recover *any* part of the outlay had to sell the land illegally. As it transpired he regretted his decision because, as he said to me on a return to Lima in 1981, "The present government couldn't give a damn if the land is in use or not."

8. While there were of course major differences between land "invasions" in the sierras and those in Lima, not the least being that the former were virtually always

justified as recuperations of land stolen from communities in the past and the latter were openly referred to as invasions of land which was not being used and hence should be allowed as areas for constructing shelter, organizational lessons were nevertheless brought from the sierra to the barriadas for these invasions. It is not a coincidence that New Year's Eve had been chosen to initiate the invasion in Huasicancha in 1947–1948 and was chosen again in Lima in 1968–1969. And in the latter case the date was carefully chosen to maximize embarrassment to the government that was hosting an international meeting of the Andean Pact countries.

9. Replacement costs of capital equipment in an inflationary economy, especially where such equipment is imported from the West, are so astronomical that, except in conditions of systematic expanded reproduction, such equipment is always viewed as a onetime asset. In one case study revisited in 1981, for example, a new Datsun pickup had been bought at a cost of 185,000 soles ($4,000.00) in 1975. In 1981 the used pickup could be sold for 1.5 million soles ($3,500.00), but to replace it with an equivalent new model would have cost 3 million soles ($7,000.00).

10. I have used data gathered from other informants to check the degree to which this case material is representative. Though these figures should be regarded as deriving from this case, I have made slight modifications in line with the other data. What most frustrated informants when recording these figures was the way in which they failed to reflect the volatility of their operations.

11. $1.00 (U.S.) = 43 Soles (1973).

12. These goods are produced on order from clients within the village who provide Olivar (Eulogio's brother-in-law) with spun wool from their own animals, leaving him to weave and dye it.

13. There are obviously a number of extrahousehold ties with non-Huasicanchinos that I have not dealt with here, such as the nature of Eulogio's links to his suppliers at the wholesale market or with his retail customers. The same has been true throughout this view of the case studies. While much of the material in other chapters does locate Huasicanchinos within a broader set of social relations, here in the case studies I have tried to concentrate on the far less familiar field of the linkages petty producers have among themselves.

14. The effect clubs and sindicatos have in highlighting men's role in extrahousehold relations for the reproduction of the enterprise may simultaneously obscure the less formally institutionalized role of women's informal networks in these kinds of enterprises.

15. The cash value of this livestock would be somewhere between $7,500 (U.S.) and $9,000 (U.S.), depending on ability to hedge the market and the quality of the animals.

16. There is no record of Hacienda Tucle ever employing single men or women as pastores. Although the contract was made with an individual, the work could not be accomplished without the full complement of a domestic group.

17. The exact number of years is unclear as the entire arrangement was in dispute during fieldwork.

18. The point to be noted is the versatility of capital movements. Other similar enterprises have transferred capital too, though into other ventures in different sectors of the economy and with greater and lesser success. Those independent farmers who have remained inflexibly committed to livestock are forced ineluctibly into conflict

with the community as a whole, as their flocks expand still further onto the strictly finite amount of community pasture, just as before they had been forced into conflict with the hacienda. As a result their behavior becomes increasingly aggressive and anti-social (strictly speaking, anticommunal) and they lose thus the institutional benefits provided by being fully respected members of the community.

6: Commodification and Culture

1. Parts of the second and third sections of this chapter rely on extracts from an article previously published in the *Journal of Peasant Studies* (G. Smith 1985). I am grateful to the editors of that journal for permission to reproduce these extracts.

2. The best-known examples are the different conclusions about the process of polarization in peasant communities arrived at by Lenin (1974) on the one hand and Chayanov (1966) on the other. The point of argument had less to do with the fact that one classified the peasantry as thoroughly capitalist, while the other recognized a specific "peasant economy," but rather that the developmental chracteristics emerging from these two positions had far ranging economic and hence political implications for the future of the peasantry. More recent examples of the developmental implications of a particular form of production can be found in Bernstein's "simple commodity squeeze" (1979) and in Hedley's discussion of "independent commodity producers" (1976).

3. It is a *generalized* commodity market to which I refer here; Firth (1958), Wolf (1966), Nash (1967) and numerous others distinguish between various forms of market: sectional, local, circulating etc. For the market to have significance as a concept in political economy it is the perfect mobility of factors (commodities) which matters and it is their contact to this kind of market which makes the essential difference between peasantry and natural economy.

4. It should be emphasized that while my discussion here could well be described under Chevalier's definition (1983*b*: 92) "of capitalism as a polymorphous structure of variable relations of production," the conclusion he draws—that, inasmuch as goods need only the potential of being exchanged on the market to make them commodities, so the calculus of the market suffuses the entire production process, once any one item can be rendered in the commodity form—is very far from my own as stated here. According to this line of thought, there can be no such thing as partial commodification, because once one item has been exchanged on the market, any other has that potential and is hence also a commodity. For a less extreme and perhaps more useful formulation of this issue, see Lem 1987.

5. Writers who fear that the "moral" element in this kind of economy gives a romantic interpretation of the peasantry (see, for example, C. Smith 1984*a*) have emphasized that it is merchants, landlords, and/or the church who have had most to gain from community performance. I do not deny the existence of such parties, indeed the local hacendada performed a major role, intentionally or otherwise, in keeping alive Huasicancha's sense of community. But precisely which noncommunity members gain from the phenomenon I have described here, and work for its persistence, is irrelevant to the logic of the argument.

6. Discussion here is limited to noncommodified relations within the context of the institutions we find among the Huasicanchinos. We saw in the discussion of Long

and Roberts's work (chap. 1) that they argue that even the far more entrepreneurial farmers of the Mantaro Valley who reinvest surpluses into land and capital goods and hire wage labor, do not inevitably become simple commodity producers proper, but rely on family labor and regional networks for precisely the reasons I have described here (Long and Roberts 1978, 1984. See also Archetti and Stölen 1987, for highland Ecuador).

7. Evidence of the segmentation of the rural labor market as a result of "community sentiment" of this kind is demonstrated statistically for an area of West Bengal in Bardhan and Rudra (1986). For a circumstance where the employment of local labor by simple commodity producers means *higher* than average wages paid, see C. Smith (1984a).

8. Of course that original differential access to capital itself presupposes the introduction of a commodity of some kind to the community.

9. The nature of this "cheap labor pool" such as it is, can be clarified by situating it within the arguments of writers such as de Janvry (1982). If peasants subsidize the wages of workers in the large-scale capitalist sector by reducing the costs of reproduction in the noncommodified sphere, then the same holds for less pure forms of capitalism too. There are thus four possibilities: a) an employer can pay a wage that covers the reproduction costs of the laborer where the laborer purchases *all* items in the market; b) De Janvry and others suggest, however, that in the Third World, employers pay a wage that covers reproduction costs at a reduced rate because the laborer provides some of his/her needs from the noncommodified sector and hence does not have to account for profit; c) domestic enterprises in Huasicancha can reduce costs by exploiting unpaid domestic labor that is itself autoprovisioned; d) they can do so too by paying a wage to local laborers whose cost of reproduction derives from the noncommodified sector and is hence lower than (a). The point about using the "community" (and the "family") to retain labor within the locality is that it allows enterprises to employ labor at a wage even lower than (b).

10. The effect of this restructuring of the productive base had similar effects on cultural reformulation to those discussed by Clarke, Hall, Jefferson, and Roberts (1976): "The wider economic forces . . . *throw out of gear* a particular working-class complex: they dismantle a set of particular internal balances and stabilities. They reshape and restructure the productive basis, which forms the material and social conditions of life, the 'givens', around which a particular working-class culture developed. What [is] disturbed [is] a concrete set of relations, a network of knowledge, things, experiences—the *supports* of a class culture" (10–14).

11. The process occurred much earlier in the Mantaro Valley itself, of course. Referring to the northern end of the Valley in the 1930s, Mallon (1983: 305) notes a similar process to the one described here: "[E]ven if the outward form of communal relationships continued to look the same, their content was being profoundly altered."

7. The Land Recuperation Campaign, 1930 to the Present

1. It is important to note here that the montonera campaign of the Mantaro region discussed in chapter 3 was by no means the best reported or most significant "incident" of rural insurgency of the period. In all of the cases where I discuss Huasicancha ac-

1. I am authorized on 15 February 1943 to enter [the hacienda land] accompanied by the following huaccha animals:

   10 cattle large and small
   50 sheep
   3 horses & 4 goats
   2 donkeys

2. In virtue of which, provided the numbers do not increase, the Administration will accept them and give me tasks as it sees fit in the caring of animals.

3. Understanding all parts of this document, I mark with my thumb.

I, [Name] formally agree with the Administration of the Hacienda Tucle, to the following terms:

1. This contract has a duration of one year including Sundays.

2. In returning for the caring of animals the above named will receive 85 soles per month (200 soles in advance), plus be allowed huacchas as follows

   7 cattle
   2 horses
   2 donkeys

3. Dated 3 September 1953 and sealed by thumb mark.

22. The attempt to reinstall the Huasicancha Civil Guard is a much recounted story. Versions do not vary much from this one taken from my fieldnotes of May 1973:

Once the officers abandoned the post, they reported to their senior officer in Huancayo and we heard that he was to return with reinforcements to reinstall his men in the post. Some of the ex-residents living in Huancayo told the press about the whole event. So when the Lieutenant arrived one day with his men on horseback, there was a journalist with him too. We lined up some of the babies and small children in the village and then we listened very patiently while the officer addressed us, telling us that we were irresponsible "Indios" and that we needed the officers there so nobody would misbehave and to protect us. Then, when he had finished Don Angelino [the figure varies] stood up and said, "That is fine what you have said. We too don't want people misbehaving and acting irresponsibly. So, as long as the officer agrees about the children then of course that is fine with us here." The officer looked puzzled with this speech and a little uneasy. "Agree about the children? What does this mean, 'Agree about the children'?" And then we told him and we told the journalist, each woman having her own story, you see. And Don Angelino said, in a great spirit of compromise, "But if the guardia will take responsibility for these their illegitimate offspring, school them, feed them . . . then we welcome the officers back." And the lieutenant remounted his horse and went away and everybody went back to their daily business. And to this day there is no Civil Guard post here in Huasicancha. Now we have the *agropecuaria* school in that building.

The besieging of the post and the starving out of its occupants is never referred to in oral accounts. The officers seem to have just decided spontaneously to abandon their post. The data that refers to the siege is to be found in correspondence between the Civil Guard post in Huasicancha and the hacienda administrator (ARA).

23. The bypassing of the community is nicely captured in the difference between the two contracts for faena work, one in 1951, the other in 1962:

Hacienda Tucle 16 May 1951.

Celebrated on this date between Ing. Velarde of the Hacienda Tucle and Don S, Llacua of the Community of Huasicancha an agreement that this community will undertake the reaping of the barley fields at Rio de la Virgen and the transport of the produce to three threshings, faena to commence Monday, 21st of present month.

The hacienda agrees to pay at the termination of the job. 1600 soles (ca. U.S. $100.00], half a sack of coca, 10 packets of cigarettes and one meal at the end of the faena, or before if the participants so desire.

Being in complete agreement with the present contract the two parties sign as token of their commitment, [Signatures].

Hacienda Tucle, 21 April, 1962.

To: Señor Alcalde of Huasicancha

I request that you give assistance to the bearer of this letter, Señor A that he may recruit the help of the members of the munipality in the coming harvest. We will give 1 oz of coca and 2 cigarettes, plus 7 soles [U.S. 25 cents] per grown man to be paid at the end of the day's work, reaping and threshing. [Signed] Sub-Administrator (A.R.A.).

24. In this way pasaderos unwilling to work off their debt immediately could undertake to do labor service at a later date, the gobernador acting as guarantor on their behalf.

25. The role of the better-off pastoralists, some of whom, like Sabino Jacinto, had been figureheads in past campaigns, was affected by the hacienda administration's belief that they *mandan en la comunidad de Huasicancha* ("rule in the community of Huasicancha"), and therefore the hacienda administrators made arrangements personally advantageous to these pastoralists. Hence, though having radical views about the redistribution of pastures, these people, like their migrant colleagues, had their radical views compromised.

Nevertheless the hacienda was very limited in its ability to buy off these villagers once functional hacienda grazing land was reduced, for example by drought or by increased trespassing. These same people therefore began to dissociate themselves from both the hacienda and the migrant incumbents of office, both of whom were becoming embarrassing to them. But, despite their past roles in land struggles, because the individual deals they had made with the hacienda had threatened the community, they were not now, in 1963, apparently seen as suitable candidates for the leadership of the campaign.

26. To reproduce the responses to de la Cruz's visits to migrants in 1963 I rely on his report to the village meeting on his return (AC), the diary which he kept during that year and which he let me read, and interviews held with him and with migrants in Lima and Huancayo in 1973.

27. In retrospect, de la Cruz says that from the moment he left Huasicancha the idea had been to get the disgruntled Lima migrants participating once again in the campaign. He argues that, to this end, it had been his intention all along to have the migrants act as the delegates at the presidential palace and that he had only held out so as to appear to be making a concession (interview, Huasicancha, 1972).

28. The arrest of the elected authorities caught the Huasicanchinos by surprise and made them extraordinarily suspicious of any outsiders arriving from the direction of Huancayo. All adult males were afraid of being taken for "undesirable elements" and thus hid in nearby caves and other retreats when outsiders approached. This explains

the headline that appeared in Huancayo's newspaper at this time: "INCOMPREHENSIBLE COMMUNITY OF HUASICANCHA: LED BY WOMEN" [sic].

29. Tacunan and supporters of his FEDECOJ ran against these people but failed to get the support of the community. They did, nevertheless, set up a rival cooperative, this one involving members in the purchase of purebred sheep to be pastured on land specifically put aside for the cooperative.

30. One of the problems facing Belaunde in instituting rural reform was that there existed no government infrastructure capable of channeling development programs to the countryside. FAO therefore advocated the use of "politically reliable" federations for the transmission of assistance. Government assistance to reduce demands for expropriation took the form of proposing various cooperative structures and colonization schemes in the jungle (Petras and Laporte 1971; Bourque 1971). Both Tacunan's FEDECOJ and APRA's FENCAP received foreign aid funds as a result of this policy.

31. The actual area of the land is unknown and varies considerably according to different sources. The southern boundaries, falling back into the Province of Huancavelica, are entirely unmapped.

8: Class Consciousness and Culture

1. The concept of "a people" remains firmly entrenched in anthropological mythology, for it allows ethnographers to get on with the description of "a people's culture" without having to address the issue of the sociogenesis of difference.

2. Use of words like "undermine" and "negotiate" give the unintended impression that traditional institutions were at some point fixed. By juxtaposing contemporary with pre-Columbian social relations in chapter 2, I have shown that this was not so but rather that the appearance of fixity and permanence is nevertheless essential for any social practice to become "institutionalized."

3. Cf. Stuart Hall (1981), referring to both Williams and Thompson on this issue:

> Williams so totally absorbs "definitions of experience" into our "ways of living," and both into an indissoluble real material practice-in-general, as to obviate any distinction between "culture" and "not-culture". . . . This sense of cultural totality—of *the whole* historical process—over-rides any effort to keep the instances and elements distinct. . . . And since they [Thompson and Williams] constantly . . . read the other structures and relations downwards from the vantage point of how they are "lived," they are properly (even if not adequately or fully) characterized as "culturalist" in their emphasis . . . (26–27).
>
> The fact that "men" can become conscious of their conditions, organize to struggle against them and in fact transform them . . . must not be allowed to override the awareness of the fact that, in capitalist relations, men and women are placed and positioned in relations which constitute them as agents (30).

4. Those who have delighted in the discovery of Thompson's voluntarism and culturalism prefer to overlook this insistence on class structure.

5. This is the context within which Tilly (1986:4) also would like to place contentiousness:

> [P]eople act discontinuously: they put in considerable effort, then stop. If we concentrate on seditions, mutinies, riots and demonstrations, we neglect collective action for the pur-

poses of sociability . . . except when it spills over into contention. We likewise neglect routine ways of getting things done through workshops, churches, confraternities and other organizations, unless they become contentious. The study of contention will require us to pay some attention to these routine and self-centered forms of collective action; they form an important part of the context.

6. *Collins Dictionary of the English Language* (1985) London & Glasgow.

7. "I see cultural forms and ways of expression as historical motor forces. They are present as one moment that forms expectations, the ways of acting and their consequent historical event as much as in the "structuration" of the social world of class, authority, and of economic relations" (Medick 1987: 88–89).

8. I recognize here the idiosyncratic use of "fetishism," but I think it can be said that, in the period of the master craftsman, craft and skill were fetishized, for example, by the guilds; and many of the practices associated with the initiation rites of apprentices attest to this. In Huasicancha too I think, a certain mystification was associated with the possession and use of skill-knowledge and "fetishism" preserves that sense.

9. It is certainly strikingly different from the political mobilization in the La Convención Valley in Cuzco in the early 1960s (see Blanco 1972; Craig 1967; Hobsbawm 1969b; Neira 1964, 1968), or that of Andahuaylas in the 1970s (Sanchez 1981).

Glossary

[Note: In 1972–73 $ (U.S.) 1.00 = 43 Soles]

alcalde head of a municipality, appointed by Prefecture. *See also* varayoc below.

ambulante mobile street-vendor, on foot or tricycle.

anexo nucleated settlement in a distrito under the authority of a municipality.

A.P.R.A. (Aprista) Alianza Popular Revolucionaria de America (Popular Revolutionary Alliance of America). Member of, or sympathizer with same.

ayllu "A kin group with theoretical endogamy. . . . [which] owned a definite territory" (Rowe, 1946: 255).

"Any group whose members regard themselves as 'brothers' owing one another aid and support, in contrast to others outside the boundaries of the group" (Spalding, 1973: 583).

barriada shantytown. Those on the periphery of the city renamed pueblos jovenes by the government, after 1969.

barrio subdivision of the community.

cabo general lay term for junior-ranking noncommissioned officer.

cacique local headman recognized by Spanish colonial government.

campo de vara *see* varayoc, below.

cancha literally, corral. Used in text to refer to people with a past family background associated with pastoral farming.

caporal assistant foreman on a hacienda. Often doubled as member of hacienda defense force.

257

cargo	any office, political or civil-religious.
caudillo	political boss, usually deriving power from military sources.
chacra	arable plot.
chusco	mongrel, usually of sheep.
Civilistas	political party emerging after 1868 presidential elections, supporting a civilian president. Subsequently endorsed an early settlement of the war with Chile.
colectivo	a small bus or car used for public transport.
comerciante	merchant. In the Mantaro region often also having some farmland. Hence commercial farmers are also often referred to as such.
composición de tierras	colonial land registration, also involving the concentration of holdings and registration as individually owned property.
comunero	legitimately recognized member of the community, hence having a voice in the assembly.
contratos viales	government contracts recruiting labor gangs for road construction chiefly in 1920s and 1930s.
coralon	walled-in inner-city lot with huts for family dwellings.
cota	quota or head-tax administered to all community members to raise money for the land recuperation campaigns.
criollo	member of the Peruvian upper classes. Assumed to retain some Spanish blood.
curaca	senior member of an ayllu or subayllu.
distrito	area under jurisdiction of a municipality, including within it anexos.
encomienda	grant by Spanish crown, giving right of governance over a designated number of Indios. (The precise nature of the encomienda is in dispute. See for example Lockhart, 1969; Keith, 1971.)
estancia	refers variously to the hut and corral of a shepherd or the area of pasture over which she/he has usufruct.
faena	work team.
falda	skirt of land running down the side of a hill. Used in text to refer to the first reivindicación campaign of this century. *See also* pampa and puna.
fiesta	festival or fête.
fundo	the hacienda buildings; the farm[house].
gamonal	landlord and local boss.
guano	fertilizer "mined" from bird droppings on islands off the Peruvian coast.
hacienda	large farm or ranch run on traditional lines.

huaccha	literally orphan, hence, poor person. Animals belonging to same. Hence huacchilla, huacchillera/o.
huasi	literally, house. Used in text to refer to people with a past family background associated with petty trading, artisanal work, and some arable farming.
jornalero	day-laborer.
mayordomo	foreman on a hacienda. Also in charge of the hacienda defense force.
michipa	animals husbanded by shepherd in return for services or arable crops.
minka	reciprocal exchange of labor for goods.
mita	labor service owed to the Spanish crown by a male adult recognized as a member of an Indian community. Men without recognized membership did not owe this service.
montonera	guerrilla fighters recruited to fight for the army of resistance in the War of the Pacific.
pampa	flat or rolling pastoral plateau.
pasadero	one who "enters" hacienda land with animals for grazing purposes without hacendado's permission.
pastor	shepherd.
peon	one who works for another for pay other than reciprocal exchange.
personero	head of the community. Subsequently replaced by "Presidente de la Comunidad" and voted into office by the community assembly.
puna	high mountain grazing land.
reparto de mercancias	colonial laws obliging Indian community to engage in trade.
taita	any older male relative.
taller	workshop.
tramites	procedures for going through bureaucratic channels.
uyay	reciprocal labor exchange.
varayoc	vara = staff; yoc = bearer. Hence staff bearer. Traditional system of Indian government instituted by the Spanish, having alcaldes, tenientes, etc. Though officially unrecognized today and all but obsolete in the Mantaro region, retained in Huasicancha.

Bibliography

Agee, James, and Walker Evans. 1966. *Let us now praise famous men*. New York: Ballantyne Books.

Alberti, Giorgio, and Enrique Mayer, eds. 1974. *Reciprocidad e intercambio en los Andes Peruanos*. Lima: Instituto de Estudios Peruanos.

Alberti, Giorgio, and Sanchez Rodrigo. 1974. *Poder y conflicto social en el Valle del Mantaro*. Lima: Instituto de Estudios Peruanos.

Alegria, Ciro. 1973. *Broad and alien is the world*. London: Merlin.

Anderson, Perry. 1980. *Arguments within English Marxism*. London: Verso.

Archetti, Eduardo, and K. A. Stölen. 1987. "Rural bourgeoisie and peasantry in the highlands of Ecuador." In E. P. Archetti, P. Cammack, and B. Roberts, eds. *Sociology of "developing societies" : Latin America*. Basingstoke: Macmillan Education.

Archivo de la Reforma Agraria. Lima [Archives of the Agrarian Reform. Lima].

Archivo de la Comunidad de Huasicancha [Community of Huasicancha Archives].

Archivo del Juzgado de Tierra. Huancayo [Archives of the land claims judge, Huancayo].

Aston, T. H., and G. H. Philpin, eds. 1986. *The Brenner debate*. London: Past and Present Publications.

Assadourian, C. S. 1982. *El sistema de la economía colonial: mercado interno, regiones y espacio económico*. Lima: Instituto de Estudios Peruanos.

Baraona, R. 1965. "Una tipologia de haciendas en la sierra ecuatoriana." In Delgado, Oscar, ed. *Reformas agrarias en America Latina*. Mexico: Siglo XXI.

Bardhan, P., and A. Rudra. 1986. "Labour mobility and the boundaries of the village moral economy." *Journal of Peasant Studies* 13, no. 3.

Bartra, Armando. 1979. *La explotación del trabajo campesino por el capital*. Mexico: Ed. Mecehual.

261

Bartra, Roger, 1974 [1976]. *Estructura agraria y clases sociales en Mexico*. Mexico: Serie Popular Era. UNAM.

Basadre, Jorge. 1968–1970. *Historia de la republica del Peru*. 17 Vol. 6th ed. Lima: Editorial Universitaria.

Basadre, Jorge, et al. 1879. *Reflexiones en torno a la guerra de 1879*. Lima: Centro de Investigaciones y Capacitación. Editorial Fco Campodónico.

Baudin, Louis. 1928. *L'empire socialiste des Inka*. Travaux et memoires de L'Institut d'Ethnologie. Vol. 5. Paris: L'Université de Paris.

Bejar, Hector. 1970. *Peru 1965: Notes on a guerrilla experience*. New York: Monthly Review Press.

Bernstein, Henry. 1979. "African Peasantries: a theoretical framework." *Journal of Peasant Studies* 6, no. 4.

Blanco, Hugo. 1972. *Land or death*. New York: Pathfinder Press.

Bloch, Marc. 1974: *Feudal society*. 2 vol. Chicago: University of Chicago Press.

Bois, Guy. 1984. *The crisis of feudalism*. Cambridge: Cambridge University Press.

Bonilla, Heraclio. 1974. *Guano y burguesia en el Peru*. Lima: Instituto de Estudios Peruanos.

———. 1978. "The War of the Pacific and the national and colonial problem in Peru." In *Past and Present*, no. 81: 92–118.

Bourque, Susan. 1971. "Cholification and the campesino." Latin American Studies Program. *Dissertation Series*, no. 21. Ithaca: Cornell University.

Brading, D. A., and H. E. Cross. 1972. "Colonial silver mining: Mexico and Peru." *Hispanic American Historical Review* 52, no. 4.

Brass, Tom. 1986. "*Cargos* and conflicts: the fiesta system and capitalist development in eastern Peru." *Journal of Peasant Studies* 13, no. 3.

Brenner, Robert. 1976. "Agrarian class structure and economic development in pre-industrial Europe." *Past and Present*, no. 70.

Burawoy, Michael. 1985. *The politics of production*. London: Verso.

Caballero, José Maria. 1984. "Agriculture and the peasantry under industrialization pressures: lessons from the Peruvian experience." *Latin American Research Review*, no. 2: 3–41.

Caceres, Andres Avelino. 1973. *La guerra de 79: sus campañas*. Lima: Editorial Milla Bartres.

Castro Pozo, H. 1969. *Del ayllu al cooperativismo socialista*. Lima: Mejía Baca.

Chayanov, A. V. 1966. "Peasant farm organization." In Daniel Thorner, B. Kerblay, and R. Smith, eds. *A. V. Chayanov on the theory of peasant economy*. Homeward, Ill.: American Economic Association.

Chevalier, François. 1970. "Official *Indigenismo* in Peru in 1920: origins, significance and socio-economic scope." In Magnus Morner, ed. *Race and class in Latin America*. New York: Columbia University Press.

Chevalier, Jacques. 1983*a*. "There is nothing simple about simple commodity production." *Journal of Peasant Studies* 10, no. 4.

———. 1983*b*. *Civilization and the stolen gift*. Toronto: Toronto University Press.

Clarke, John, Stuart Hall, Tony Jefferson, and Brian Roberts. 1976. "Sub-cultures, cultures and class." In Hall and Jefferson, eds. *Resistance through rituals: youth sub-cultures in post-war Britain*. London: Hutchinson.

Cobo, Bernabé. 1956. *Historia del nuevo mundo [1653]*. Madrid: Biblioteca de Autores Españoles XCI, XCII.

Collier, David. 1971. "Squatter settlement formation and the politics of co-optation in Peru." Ph.D. Dissertation. University of Chicago.

Collier, George, Renato Rosaldo, and J. D. Wirth, eds. 1982. *The Inca and Aztec states 1400–1800: Anthropology and History*. New York: Academic Press.

Collins, Jane. 1986. "The household and relations of production in Southern Peru." *Comparative Studies in Society and History* 28, no. 4.

Connell, John, Biplap Dasgupta, David Laishley, and Michael Lipton. 1974. "Migration from rural areas: the evidence from village studies." *Discussion Paper*, no. 36. Institute of Development Studies. Sussex.

Cotler, Julio. 1979. "La crisis política (1930–1968)." In *Nueva historia general del Peru: un compendio*. Lima: Mosca Azul.

Cotler, Julio, and Felipe Portocarrero. 1969. "Peru: peasant organizations." In E. Landsberger, ed. *Latin American peasant movements*. Ithaca: Cornell University Press.

Crummett, M. de los Angeles. 1987. "Class, household structure and the peasantry: An empirical approach." *Journal of Peasant Studies* 14, no. 3.

Dalton, George. 1981. Debate between Augé, Chretien, Duby, Dalton, Godelier, Meillassoux, Murra, and Wachtel. In *Research in Economic Anthropology*, no. 4.

Deere, Carmen Diana. 1986. "The Peasantry in political economy: Trends of the 1980's." Mimeo. Department of Economics, University of Massachusetts.

Deere, Carmen Diana, and Alain de Janvry. 1981. "Demographic and social differentiation among northern Peruvian peasants." *Journal of Peasant Studies* 8, no. 3.

Deere, Carmen Diana, and Magdalena León de Leal. 1981. "Peasant production, proletarianization, and the sexual division of labour in the Andes." *Signs*, 7, no. 2.

Ennew, Judith, Paul Hirst, and Keith Tribe. 1977. "'Peasantry' as an economic category." *Journal of Peasant Studies*, 4, no. 4.

Espinosa Soriano, Waldemar. 1969. *Lurinhuaila de Huajra: un ayllu y curacazgo Huanca*. Huancayo: Casa de la Cultura de Junin.

———. 1972. "Los Huancas aliados de la conquista." *Anales Cientificos*. Huancayo: Universidad del Centro.

———. 1973. *Enciclopedia departmental de Junin*. Huancayo: Editorial Chipoco Tovar.

Favre, Henri. 1966. "La evolución y la situación de las haciendas en la región de Huancavelica: Peru." Mimeo. Lima: Instituto de Estudios Peruanos.

———. 1975. "Remarques sur la lutte des classes au Perou pendant la guerre du Pacifique." *Litterature et societé au Perou du XIVème à nos jours*. Grenoble: Université de Grenoble.

Favre, H., C. Delavaud, and J. Matos Mar, eds. 1967. *La hacienda en el Peru*. Lima: Instituto de Estudios Peruanos.

Firth, Raymond. 1958. *Elements of social organization*. Boston: Beacon Press.

Food and Agricultural Organization. 1969. "Mission to evaluate technical assistance requirements for agrarian reform in Peru." Mimeo. Regional Office for Latin America. Santiago.

Foster, John. 1985. "The declassing of language." *New Left Review*, no. 150.

Foucault, Michel. 1965. *Madness and civilization: a history of insanity in the age of reason*. Toronto: New American Library.

————. 1970. *The order of things: an archaeology of the human sciences*. London: Tavistock.

————. 1979. *The history of sexuality*. Vol. 1. London: Allen Lane.

Franklin, S. H. 1969. *The European peasantry: The final phase*. London: Methuen.

Friedmann, Harriet. 1978. "World market, state and family farm: Social bases of household production in the era of wage labour." *Comparative Studies in Society and History* 20, no. 4.

————. 1980. "Household production and the national economy: concepts for the analysis of agrarian formations." *Journal of Peasant Studies* 7, no. 2.

"Fundo de Hacienda Tucle. Fall 1972." Miscellaneous papers found at the abandoned hacienda building.

Galeski, Boguslaw. 1972. *Basic concepts of rural sociology*. Manchester: Manchester University Press.

Godelier, Maurice. 1977. *Perspectives in Marxist anthropology*. Cambridge: Cambridge University Press.

Golte, Jurgen. 1980. *La racionalidad de la organización Andina*. Lima: Instituto de Estudios Peruanos.

Gose, Peter. 1986. "Sacrifice and the commodity form in the Andes." *Man* 21, no. 2.

Gramsci, Antonio. 1976. *Selections from the prison notebooks*. Ed. and trans. Quintin Hoare and Geoffrey Nowell Smith. New York: International.

Guerrero, A. 1975. *La hacienda pre-capitalista y la clase terrateniente en America Latina y su inserción en el modo de producción capitalista: el caso Ecuatoriano*. Quito: Universidad Central.

Guillet, David. 1980. "Reciprocal labor and peripheral capitalism in the central Andes." *Ethnology* 19, no. 2.

Hall, Stuart. 1980. "Cultural Studies: Two Paradigms." In *Media, culture and society*, no. 2.

Handelman, Howard. 1975. *Struggle in the Andes: peasant mobilization in Peru*. Institute of Latin American Studies. Austin: University of Texas Press.

Harris, Olivia. 1981. "Households as natural units." In K. Young, C. Wolkowitz, and R. McCullagh, eds. *Of marriage and the market*. London: CSE Books.

————. 1982. "Households and their boundaries." *History Workshop*, no. 3.

Haya de la Torre, Victor. 1936. *El imperialismo y el Apra*. Lima: Amauta.

Hedley, Max. 1976. "Independent commodity production and the dynamics of tradition." *Canadian Review of Sociology and Anthropology* 13, no. 4.

Hindess, Barry, and Paul Hirst. 1975. *Pre-capitalist modes of production*. London: Routledge & Kegan Paul.

Hobsbawm, Eric. 1959. *Primitive rebels: studies in archaic forms of social movements in the 19th and 20th centuries*. Boston: Beacon Press.

————. 1969a. *Bandits*. New York: Delacorte Press.

————. 1969b. "A case of neo-feudalism: La Convención, Peru." *Journal of Latin American Studies* 1, no. 1.

————. 1973. "Peasants and politics." *Journal of Peasant Studies* 1, no. 1.

————. 1974. "Peasant land occupations." *Past and Present*, no. 62.

————. 1984. *Worlds of labour: further studies in the history of labour*. London:

Weidenfeld and Nicolson
Hobsbawm, Eric, and Terence Ranger, eds. 1983. *The invention of tradition*. Cambridge: Cambridge University Press.
Hobsbawm, Eric, and George Rudé. 1973. *Captain Swing*. Harmondsworth: Penguin.
Horton, David. 1974. *Land reform and reform enterprises in Peru*. Vols. I and II. Land Tenure Center. University of Wisconsin.
Huizer, Gerritt. 1972. "Land invasion as a non-violent strategy of peasant rebellion: some cases from Latin America." *Journal of Peace Research*, no. 2.
———. 1973. *Peasant rebellion in Latin America*. Harmondsworth: Penguin.
Hunt, Shane. 1972. "The economics of haciendas and plantations in Latin America." Discussion Paper, no. 29. (Oct). Mimeo. Princeton. Woodrow Wilson School.
Janvry, Alain de. 1982. *The agrarian question in Latin America*. Baltimore: Johns Hopkins University Press.
Johnson, Richard. 1979. "Three problematics: elements of a theory of working-class culture." In Clarke, Critcher, and Johnson, eds. *Working class culture*. London: Hutchinson.
Jones, Gareth Stedman. 1983. *Languages of class: studies in English working class history 1832–1982*. Cambridge: Cambridge University Press.
Kahn, Joel. 1975. "Economic scale and the cycle of petty commodity production in west Sumatra." In Maurice Bloch, ed. *Marxist analyses and Social Anthropology*. London: Malaby Press.
———. 1980. *Miñangkabau social formations: Indonesian peasants and the world-economy*. Cambridge: Cambridge University Press.
———. 1985. "Peasant ideologies in the Third World." *Annual Review of Anthropology*, no. 14.
Kay, Cristobal. 1974. "Comparative development of the European manorial system and the Latin American hacienda system." *Journal of Peasant Studies* 2, no. 1.
Keith, R. J. 1971. "Encomienda and hacienda in Spanish America: a structural analysis." *Hispanic American Historical Review* 51, no. 3.
Kerblay, Basile. 1971. "Chayanov and the theory of the peasantry as a specific type of economy." In Teodor Shanin, ed. *Peasants and peasant societies*. Harmondsworth. Penguin.
Klaiber, J. L. 1977. *Religion and revolution in Peru 1824–1976*. Notre Dame: University of Notre Dame Press.
Klarén, Peter. 1973. *Modernization, dislocation and aprismo: origins of the Peruvian Aprista party, 1870–1932*. Austin: University of Texas Press.
Kroeber, Alfred. 1948 [1923]. *Anthropology*. New York: Harcourt, Brace.
Laite, Julian. 1978. "Processes of industrial and social change in highland Peru." In Long and Roberts, eds. *Peasant cooperation and capitalist expansion in Peru*. Institute of Latin American Studies. Austin: University of Texas Press.
———. 1981. *Industrial development and migrant labour in Peru*. Manchester: Manchester University Press.
Lehmann, David, ed. 1982, *Ecology and economy in the Andes*. Cambridge: Cambridge University Press.
———. 1986. "After Lenin and Chyanov: new paths of agrarian capitalism." *Journal of Development Economics*, no. 11.
Lem, Winnie. 1988. "Household production and reproduction in Languedoc, France:

social relations among the wine-growers of Murviel-lés-Beziers." *Journal of Peasant Studies* 14, no. 4.

Lenin, V. I. 1974. *The Development of capitalism in Russia: the process of the formation of a home market for large-scale industry.* Moscow: Progress.

LeRoy Ladurie, Emmanuel. 1975. *Montaillou: village occitan de 1294 à 1324.* Paris: Gallimard.

Lockhart, James. 1969. "Encomienda and hacienda: the evolution of the great estate in the Spanish Indies" *Hispanic American Historical Review* 49, no. 3.

Long, Norman. 1979. "Multiple enterprise in the central highlands of Peru." In S. M. Greenfield et al., eds. *Entrepreneurs in Cultural Context.* Albuquerque: University of New Mexico Press.

Long, Norman, and Bryan Roberts, eds. 1978. *Peasant cooperation and capitalist expansion in Peru.* Institute of Latin American Studies. Austin: University of Texas Press.

———. 1984. *Miners, peasants and entrepreneurs: regional development in the central highlands of Peru.* Cambridge Latin American Studies Series. no. 48. Cambridge: Cambridge University Press.

Long, Norman, and Rodrigo Sanchez. 1978. "Peasant and entrepreneurial coalitions: the case of the Matahuasi cooperative." in Long, Norman and Bryan Roberts. Eds. *Peasant cooperation and capitalist expansion in Peru.* Institute of Latin American Studies. Austin: University of Texas Press.

Lumbreras, L. G. 1970. *De los origenes del estado en el Peru.* Lima: Editorial Milla Bartres.

———. 1980. "El Peru pre-hispánico." In *Nueva historia general del Peru: un compendio.* Lima: Mosca Azul.

McClintock, Cynthia. 1981. *Peasant cooperatives and political change in Peru.* Princeton: Princeton University Press.

MacEwen Scott, Alison. 1979. "Who are the self-employed." in R. Bromley and C. Gerry, eds. *Casual work and poverty in Third World cities.* Chichester: John Wiley and Sons.

Mallon, Florencia. 1983. *The defense of community in Peru's central highlands: peasant struggle and capitalist transition, 1860–1940.* Princeton: Princeton University Press.

———. 1986. "Gender and class in the transition to capitalism: household and mode of production in central Peru." *Latin American Perspectives* 13, no. 1.

Mangin, William. 1970. *Peasants in cities.* Boston: Houghton Mifflin.

Manrique, Nelson. 1978. *El desarrollo del mercado interior en la Sierra Central 1830–1910.* Series Andes Centrales. no. 6, La Molina.

———. 1981. *Las guerrilleras indígenas en la guerra con Chile.* Centro de Investigación y Capacitación. Lima: Editorial Ital Peru.

Marcuse, Herbert. 1969. "Repressive Tolerance." In H. Marcuse, B. Moore, and K. Wolff. *A critique of pure tolerance.* Boston: Beacon.

Mariategui, José Carlos. 1928. *Siete ensayos de interpretación de la realidad Peruana.* Lima: Amauta.

Martinez-Alier, Juan. 1973. *Los huacchilleros del Peru.* Lima. Instituto de Estudios Peruanos.

—————. 1977. *Haciendas, plantations and collective farms: agrarian class societies—Cuba and Peru*. London: Frank Cass.

Marx, Karl. 1964. *Economic and philosophical manuscripts*. In T. B. Bottomore, ed. *Karl Marx: Early Writings*. New York: McGraw-Hill.

—————. 1968. *Selected essays*. Ed. H. Stenning. London and New York.

—————. 1970. *Contribution to the critique of political economy*. Moscow: Progress.

—————. 1972. *Manifesto of the Communist Party*. Moscow: Progress.

—————. 1973. *Grundrisse: foundations of the critique of political economy*. Harmondsworth: Penguin.

—————. 1976. *Capital*. Vol. I. Harmondsworth: Pelican.

—————. 1981. *Capital*. Vol. III. Harmondsworth: Pelican.

Marx, Karl, and Frederick Engles. 1970. *The German Ideology*. Part I with selections from parts II and III, together with Marx's "Introduction to a critique of political economy." Ed. C. J. Arthur. London: Lawrence and Wishart.

Matos Mar, Jose. 1961. "Migration and urbanization: the barriadas of Lima." In P. Hauser, ed. *Urbanization in Latin America*. Liége: Unesco.

Medick, Hans. 1987. "'Missionaries in the row boat'? Ethnological ways of knowing as a challenge to social history." *Comparative Studies in Society and History* 19, no. 1.

Miller, Rory. 1974. "Railways and economic development in central Peru, 1890–1930." In R. Miller et al., eds. *Social and economic change in modern Peru*. Centre for Latin American Studies. University of Liverpool. Monograph Series, no. 6.

Mingione, Enzo. 1983. "Informalization, restructuring and the survival strategies of the working class." *International Journal of Urban and Rural Research* 7, no. 3.

Mintz, Jerome. 1982. *The anarchists of Casas Viejas*. Chicago: University of Chicago Press.

Mintz, Sidney. 1973. "A note on the definition of peasantries." *Journal of Peasant Studies* 1, no. 1.

Mitchell, B. 1962. *Abstract of British historical statistics*. Cambridge: Cambridge University Press.

Mitchell, B., and H. G. Jones. 1971. *Second abstract of British historical statistics*. Cambridge: Cambridge University Press.

Montoya, Rodrigo et al. 1974. *La SAIS "Cahuide" y sus contradicciones*. Lima: San Marcos.

Moore, Barrington, Jr. 1966. *The social origins of dictatorship and democracy*. Boston: Beacon.

Moore, Sally Falk. 1958. *Power and property in Inca Peru*. New York: Columbia University Press.

Moreno de Caceres, A. 1974. *Recuerdos de la campaña de la Breña*. Lima.

Morris, Craig. 1967. "The technology and organization of highland Inca food storage." Ph.D. Dissertation. University of Chicago.

Muratorio, Blanca. 1987. *Rucuyaya Alonso y la historia social y económica del Alto Napo 1850–1950*. Quito: Editorial Abya-Yala.

Murra, John. 1958. "On Inca political structure." In Y. F. Ray, *Systems of political control and bureaucracy in human societies*. Proceedings of the American Ethnological Association.

————. 1964. "Una apreciación etnológica de la visita." In Diez de San Miguel. *Visita hecha a la provincia de Chucuito*. Lima: Instituto de Estudios Peruanos.

————. 1970. "Current research and prospects in Andean ethnohistory." *Latin American Research Review* 5, no. 2.

————. 1980. "The economic organization of the Inka state." *Research in Economic Anthropology*. Supplement I. Greenwich: JAI Press.

Nash, Manning. 1967. "Indian economies." In *Handbook of Middle American Indians* 6: 87–101. *Social Anthropology*. Austin: University of Texas Press.

Neira, Hugo. 1964. *Cuzco, tierra y muerte*. Lima: Populibros.

————. 1968. *Los Andes, tierra o muerte*. Santiago: Editorial ZYX.

Oficina de Apoyo Juridico (O.A.J.). *Archivo de los expedientes de reconocimiento de comunidades*. Lima.

Paige, Jeffrey. 1975. *Agrarian revolution: social movements and export agriculture in the underdeveloped world*. New York: Free Press.

Patterson, Thomas. 1985. "Exploitation and class formation in the Inca state." *Culture* 5, no. 1.

————. 1986. "Ideology, class formation and resistance in the Inca state." *Critique of Anthropology*. 6, no. 1.

Pearse, Frank. 1976. *The Latin American peasant*. London: Frank Cass.

Petras, James, and Robert Laporte. 1971. *Cultivating revolution: the United States and agrarian reform in Latin America*. New York: Random House.

Piel, Jean. 1970. "The place of the peasantry in the national life of Peru in the nineteenth century." *Past and Present*, no. 46.

Redfield, Robert. 1941. *The Folk Culture of Yucatan*. Chicago: University of Chicago Press.

————. 1947. "The Folk Society." *The American Journal of Sociology* 52, no. 4.

Registro de Propiedad, Huancayo (Records of the Registry of Properties, Huancayo).

Reyna, Ernesto. 1929. *El Amauta Atusparia*. Lima: [Publisher Unknown].

Roberts, Bryan. 1973. *Organizing strangers: poor families in Guatemala City*. Austin: University of Texas Press.

————. 1974a. "Migración urbana: Peru." *Etnica*, no. 6 (Barcelona).

————. 1974b. "The social history of a provincial town: Huancayo 1890–1972." Mimeo. Department of Sociology. University of Manchester.

Roberts, Bryan, and C. Samaniego. 1978. "The evolution of pastoral villages and the significance of agrarian reform in the highlands of Peru." In Norman Long and Bryan Roberts, eds. *Peasant cooperation and capitalist expansion in Peru*. Institute of Latin American Studies. Austin: University of Texas Press.

Roseberry, William. 1983. *Coffee and capitalism in the Venezuelan Andes*. Austin: University of Texas Press.

————. 1986. "The ideology of domestic production." In Jonathon Barker and Gavin Smith, eds. *Rethinking petty commodity production*. Special Issue. *Labour, Capital and Society* 19, no. 1.

Rowe, John. 1946. "Inca culture at the time of the Spanish conquest." *Handbook of South American Indians*, Vol. II. Washington.

Rubin, I. I. 1928 [1975]. *Essays on Marx's Theory of Value*. Montreal: Black Rose.

Sabean, David. 1984. *Power in the blood: Popular culture and village discourse in*

early modern Germany. London and New York: Cambridge University Press.
Sahlins, Marshall. 1968. *Tribes*. Englewood Cliffs, N.J., Prentice-Hall.
———. 1972. *Stone age economics*. Chicago: Aldine.
———. 1985. *Islands of history*. Chicago: University of Chicago Press.
Samaniego, Carlos. 1974. "Location, social differentiation and peasant movements in the Central Sierra of Peru." Ph.D. Dissertation. University of Manchester.
———. 1978. "Peasant movements at the turn of the century and the rise of the independent farmer." In Norman Long and Bryan Roberts, eds. *Peasant cooperation and capitalist expansion in Peru*. Institute of Latin American Studies. Austin: University of Texas Press.
Samaniego Cordova, F. de J. 1972. *Los héroes de Sicaya*. Huancayo: Casa de Cultura de Junin.
Sanchez, Rodrigo. 1981. *Toma de tierras y conciencia política campesina: las lecciones de Andhuaylas*. Lima: Instituto de Estudios Peruanos.
Schneider, Jane. 1987. "The Anthropology of textiles." *Annual Review of Anthropology*, no. 16.
Scott, James. 1976. *The moral economy of the peasant*. New Haven: Yale University Press.
———. 1985. *Weapons of the weak: everyday forms of peasant resistance*. New Haven: Yale University Press.
———. 1986. "Everyday forms of resistance." In Scott and Kerkvliet, eds. *Everyday forms of resistance in South-East Asia*. Special Issue. *Journal of Peasant Studies* 13, no. 2.
Scott, James, and J. T. Kerkvliet. 1973. "The politics of survival: peasant responses to 'progress' in Southeast Asia." *The Journal of Asian Studies* 22, no. 1.
Scott, James, and J. T. Kerkvliet, eds. 1986. *Everyday forms of resistance in South-East Asia*. Special Issue. *Journal of Peasant Studies* 13, no. 2.
Shanin, Teodor. 1972. *The awkward class*. Oxford: Oxford University Press.
———. 1973. "The nature and logic of the peasant economy." *Journal of Peasant Studies* 1, no. 1.
———. 1979. "Defining peasants: conceptualizations and deconceptualizations old and new in a marxist debate." *Peasant Studies* 8, no. 4.
Sider, Gerald. 1986. *Culture and class in anthropology and history*. Cambridge: Cambridge University Press.
Skocpol, Theda. 1979. *States and social revolutions*. Cambridge: Cambridge University Press.
———. 1982. "What makes peasants revolutionary?" In R. P. Weller and S. E. Guggenheim, eds. *Power and Protest in the Countryside*. Durham: Duke University Press.
Smith, Carol. 1984*a*. "Forms of production in practice: fresh approaches in simple commodity production" *Journal of Peasant Studies* 11, no. 4 (July).
———. 1984*b*. "Does a commodity economy enrich the few while ruining the masses? Differentiation among petty commodity producers in Guatemala." *Journal of Peasant Studies* 11, no. 3.
———. 1985. "Local history in global context: social and economic transitions in western Guatemala" *Comparative Studies in Society and History* 26, no. 2.

————. 1986. "Reconstructing the elements of petty commodity production." In Alison McEwen Scott, ed. *Rethinking petty commodity production*. Special Issue. *Social Analysis*, no. 20.

Smith, Gavin. 1975. "The Account of Don Victor." *Journal of Peasant Studies*. 2, no. 3.

————. 1976. "Peasant response to cooperativization under agrarian reform in the communities of the Peruvian sierra." In J. Nash, J. Dandler, and N. Hopkins, eds. *Popular Participation in Social Change*. The Hague: Mouton.

————. 1977. "Contemporary peasant folk history: some preliminary observations." *Bulletin of the Society for Latin American Studies* 3, no. 3.

————. 1979*a*. "Socio-economic differentiation and the social relations of production among petty commodity producers in Central Peru 1880–1970." *Journal of Peasant Studies* 6, no. 3.

————. 1979*b*. "The use of class analysis in social anthropology." In Gavin Smith and David Turner, eds. *Challenging Anthropology: a Critical Introduction to Social and Cultural Anthropology*. Toronto: McGraw-Hill, Ryerson.

————. 1979*c*. "Small-scale farmers in peripheral capitalism: the Huasicanchinos of Central Peru." In Gavin Smith and David Turner, eds. *Challenging Anthropology: a Critical Introduction to Social and Cultural Anthropology*. Toronto: McGraw-Hill, Ryerson.

————. 1984. "Confederations of households: extended domestic enterprises in city and country." In Long and Roberts, 1984: *Miners, peasants and entrepreneurs: regional development in the central highlands of Peru*. Cambridge Latin American Studies Series. no. 48. Cambridge: Cambridge University Press.

————. 1985*a*. "Reflections on the social relations of simple commodity production." *Journal of Peasant Studies* 13, no. 1.

————. 1985*b*. "The fox and the rooster: the culture of opposition in highland Peru." *This Magazine* 19, no. 1.

————. 1986. "The long memory of a forgotten people: the struggle of Peru's highland peasants." *Canadian Dimension* 19, no. 5.

————. 1989. "Negotiating neighbours: livelihood and domestic politics in central Peru and the Pais Valenciano (Spain)." In Jane Collins and M. E. Gimenez, eds. *Work Without Wages*. New York: State University of New York Press.

Smith, Gavin, and Pedro Cano. 1978. "Some factors contributing to peasant land invasions: the case of Huasicancha, Peru." In Norman Long and Bryan Roberts, eds. *Peasant cooperation and capitalist expansion in Peru*. Institute of Latin American Studies. Austin: University of Texas Press.

Spalding, Karen. 1973. "*Kurakas* and commerce: a chapter in the evolution of Andean society." *Hispanic American Historical Review* 53, no. 4.

————. 1975. "Hacienda-village relations in Andean society to 1830." *Latin American Perspectives* 2, no. 1.

————. 1984. *Huarochiri, an Andean society under Inca and Spanish rule*. Stanford: Stanford University Press.

Stein, William. 1976. "Town and country in revolt: fragments from the province of Carhuaz on the Atushparia uprising of 1885 (Callejon de Huayla)." *Actes du XLIIème congrès international des Americanistes*. Vol. 3. Paris: Fondation Singer-Polignac.

Stern, Steve. 1983. "The struggle for solidarity: class, culture and community in highland Indian America." *Radical History Review*, no. 27.

Taussig, Michael. 1980. *The devil and commodity fetishism in South America*. Chapel Hill: University of North Carolina Press.

———. 1982. "Peasant economies and the capitalist development of agriculture in the Cauca Valley, Colombia." In John Harriss, ed. *Rural development: theories of peasant economies and agrarian change*. London: Hutchinson University Library.

Tello Devotto, R. 1971. *Historia de la provincia de Huancayo*. Huancayo: Casa de la Cultura de Junin.

Thompson, Edward. 1961. "The long revolution. Part 1" [Review article]. *New Left Review*, no. 9.

———. 1968. *The making of the English working class*. Harmondsworth: Penguin.

———. 1978. "Eighteenth-century English society: class struggle without class?" *Social History*, no. 3.

Thorner, Daniel. 1966. "Introduction" to *A. Y. Chayanov on the theory of peasant economy*. Homeward: Ill.: American Economic Association.

Thorp, Rosemary, and Geoff Bertram. 1978. *Peru 1890–1970: Growth and Policy in an Open Economy* London: Macmillan.

Tilly, Charles. 1986. *The Contentious French*. Cambridge, Mass.: Belknap, Harvard University Press.

Tullis, F. Lamond. 1971. *Lord and Peasant in Peru*. Cambridge, Mass.: Harvard University Press.

Turner, John 1972*a*. "The re-education of a professional." In Turner and Fichter, eds. *Freedom to Build: Dweller control of the housing process*. London: Collier-MacMillan.

———. 1972*b*. "Housing as a verb." In Turner and Fichter, eds. *Freedom to Build: Dweller control of the housing process*. London: Collier-Macmillan.

"U.S. Department of Commerce." *Historical Statistics of the United States: Colonial Times to the Present*.

Ulyanovsky, R., and V. Pavlov. 1973. *Asian Dilemma*. Moscow: Progress.

Vargas Llosa, Mario. 1983. "The story of a massacre" *Granta*, 11.

Vergopoulos, Kostas. 1978. "Capitalism and peasant productivity." *Journal of Peasant Studies* 5, no. 4.

Wachtel, Nathan. 1973. *Sociedad e Ideología: ensayos de historia y antropología andinas*. Lima: Instituto de Estudios Peruanos.

———. 1977. *The Vision of the Vanquished*. Hassocks, Sussex: Harvester Press.

Walton, John. 1984. *Reluctant rebels: comparative studies in revolution and underdevelopment*. New York: Columbia University Press.

Warman, Arturo. 1980. *We come to object: the peasants of Morelos and the national state*. Trans. Stephen K. Ault. Baltimore: Johns Hopkins University Press.

Weber, Max. 1949. *The methodology of the social sciences*. Ed. and trans. Edward A. Shils and Henry A. Finch. Glencoe, Ill.: Free Press.

Werlich, D. P. 1978. *Peru: A short history*. Carbondale: Southern Illinois University Press.

Williams, Raymond. 1961. *The long revolution*. London: Chatto and Windus.

———. 1976. *Keywords: A vocabulary of culture and society*. London: Fontana, Croom Helm.

———. 1977. *Marxism and literature*. Oxford: Oxford University Press.

Wilson, Fiona. 1982. "Property and ideology: a regional oligarchy in the central Andes in the 19th century." In D. Lehmann, ed. *Economy and ecology in the Andes*. Cambridge: Cambridge University Press.

Wolf, Eric. 1955. "Types of Latin American peasantry: A preliminary discussion." *American Anthropologist* 57, no. 2.

———. [1956] 1971. "Aspects of group relations in a complex society: Mexico." In Teodor Shanin, ed. *Peasants and Peasant Societies*. Harmondsworth: Penguin. [originally in *American Anthropologist* 58, no. 6].

———. 1966. *Peasants*. Englewood Cliffs, N.J.: Prentice-Hall.

———. 1969. *Peasant wars of the twentieth century*. New York: Harper & Row.

Wolf, Eric, and E. Hansen. 1967. *The human condition in Latin America*. New York: Oxford University Press.

Wolf, Eric, and Sidney Mintz. 1957. "Haciendas and plantations in Middle America and the Antilles." *Social and Economic Studies* 6, no. 3.

Young, Kate. 1978. "Modes of appropriation and the sexual division of labour: A case from Oaxaca, Mexico." In A. Kuhn and A. Wolpe, eds. *Feminism and materialism*. London: Routledge and Kegan Paul.

Zonabend, Françoise. 1984. *The enduring memory: time and history in a French village*. Trans. Anthony Forster. Manchester: Manchester University Press.

Index

Acobambilla, 36, 54, 89, 145, 147, 189
Agee, J., xi, xii
Agency, 16, 17, 223, 224
Agrarian reform. *See* Land reform
Agriculturalist. *See* Arable farmer
Agriculture, 62, 72, 85, 88–89, 94; commercial, 48, 64, 65, 88, 197, 198
Alberti, 23, 36
Alcalde, 6–7, 210
Alegría, Ciro, 177
Allegiance, 70
Ambulantes, 9, 13, 99, 100, 105–107 passim, 117, 122, 123, 124, 125–126, 128, 129, 133, 135, 134, 137, 138, 139–140, 226
Anderson, P., 24, 226
Antapongo, Hacienda, 2, 3, 5, 51, 52, 64, 73, 74, 78, 92, 172, 178, 179, 182, 186
Apoalaya (family), 47, 48, 51, 55
Appropriation, 239 n. 5
APRA party (Alianza Popular Revolucionaria de America), 76, 98, 103, 120, 136, 174, 175, 176, 181–182, 183, 185, 187, 193, 197, 205, 210, 211, 214
Arable farmer, 14, 58; farming, 9, 54, 85, 97, 103, 111, 128, 131, 134, 144; land, 26, 31–35 passim, 37, 39, 48, 54
Army, 26, 65, 74, 82, 170, 171, 175, 182, 189, 193, 204, 205, 210, 212, 213
Assadourian, 49
Aston, T. H., 24
Astucuri (family), 51, 54

Atusparia rebellion, 78
Autonomy, ideology of, 32, 33
Ayacucho, 4, 54, 68, 70, 78, 175
Ayllu, 39–47 passim, 52–53, 62, 64

Bailey, xii, 223
Balan, xiii
Bandits, 241 n. 16; banditry, 13, 102
Barona, 95
Barriadas (shantytowns), xiii, 9, 26, 93, 105–108 passim, 121–122, 124, 196; compared to *coralones,* 106; involvement in land invasions, 108; land, 129–130
Barter. See *Trueque*
Bartra, R., 20, 21
Basadre, 56
Baudin, L., 40
Bejar, H., 210, 235
Bernstein, H., 20, 21, 248 n. 2
Bertram, 90, 91
Bloch, M., 46
Bois, Guy, 159
Bonilla, H., 56, 57, 61, 68, 242–243 n. 6
Bourque, S., 199
Brading, D. A., 50
Brenner, R., 24, 225, 226, 229
Burawoy, M., 14

Caceres, General, 60–77 passim
Cacique, 48, 49, 50
Campo de vara. See Varayoc

ket, 85, 91, 93, 152; in mines, 50; service, 53, 55, 57, 97, 195; units, 22, 33
Labor process, 13, 14, 24, 84, 160, 162, 165, 166
Ladourie, L., 235
Laimes, Jaime, 63, 68–69, 72, 74, 75, 76, 181, 242 n. 16, 244 n. 7, 244 n. 9, 244 n. 14
Laite, J., 21, 91
Laive, Laive-Ingahuasi, Hacienda, 2, 5, 13, 51, 52, 55, 56, 61, 64, 65, 66, 69, 72–73, 74, 75, 92, 179, 186, 197
Land, 14, 24, 26, 31–34, 38–45 passim; claims to, 49, 151, 185 (see also *Reivindicación de tierras*); legal title or deed to, 20, 34, 49, 50, 56, 78, 80, 136, 147, 171, 172, 184, 189, 192, 214–215. *See also* Common land; Household land
Land reform, 130, 202, 203, 205, 208, 209, 213, 214, 220, 246 n. 7
La Oroya, 13, 98, 100, 134, 187
Laporte, 210
Leadership, 27, 76, 177, 193. See also *Reivindicación de tierras*, leaders of
Leal, Leon de, 23
Legal claim, 51, 57, 203–204; settlement recognition, 51
Legal land registry, 172
Lehmann, D., 19, 36
Lenin, V., 19, 20, 233, 238 n. 1, 248 n. 2
Lévi-Strauss, C., xi
Lima, receiving area for migrants, 4, 9, 93, 99, 100, 105, 119–143 passim, 187, 197, 201, 203
Livelihood, 11, 18–23 passim, 28, 33, 60, 103, 104–109 passim, 163, 167, 168, 193, 212, 217, 222, 234; daily struggle for, 13, 17, 122, 159, 170, 226. *See also* Domestic enterprise
Long, N., xii, 4, 21, 22, 23, 107, 174
Lumbreras, L. G., 42, 45

MacEwen, S., 22, 266
Mallon, F., 4, 21, 22, 23, 24, 56
Mangin, W., 122
Manrique, N., 50, 56, 62, 64, 69, 70, 71, 75, 76, 242–243 n. 6
Mantaro Valley, Region, xii, 2, 4, 5, 21–23 passim, 36, 38, 47, 48, 49, 50, 53, 56, 57, 61, 72, 76, 91; commercialization of, 50, 51, 65, 67, 77, 88, 89, 131, 174, 196
Marcuse, H., 27, 239–240 n. 12
Markets, 20, 36, 53, 90, 156, 158, 248 n. 3
Marketstall operators, owners, 13–14, 26, 36, 98, 100, 105–107 passim, 121, 129, 197
Marmanillo (family), 51, 55

Márquez, Gabriel García, 11
Martinez-Alier, J., xii, 95
Marx, 16, 29, 81, 112, 117, 155, 158, 160, 161, 162, 233, 238 n. 1, 238 n. 2, 238 n. 3
Matos Mar, José, 122
Mayer, 36
Meaning, 16, 26, 28, 30, 113, 159, 168, 194, 220, 221, 222, 224, 228, 239–240 n. 12
Means of production, 20
Medick, H., 18, 220
Memory, 26, 59, 76, 155
Michipa, 35, 37, 86, 87, 89, 92, 185
Migrants, migration, 1, 9, 13, 77, 93, 96–111 passim, 121, 133, 134, 142, 147, 150, 184, 186–187, 196, 206. *See also* Cancha; Exresidents; Huasi
Military. *See* Army
Miller, R., 91
Mingione, E., 163
Minka, 35, 89
Mintz, J., 235
Miraflores campaign, 68, 69
Mita, 49, 50, 53, 55, 241 n. 9
Mitchell, B., 90
Mitmaq, 43, 44, 47
Montoneras, 60, 67–77 passim, 80, 82, 170, 179, 222, 243 n. 7
Moore, B., 235
Moore, S. F., 38, 45
Moreno de Caceres, 66
Morris, C., 44, 46, 47
Movimiento Comunal del Centro, 197, 198
Multioccupational enterprise, 9, 94, 107, 110, 121–127 (case study), 129, 132, 142
Muratorio, B., 27
Murra, J., 36, 38, 39, 41, 42, 44, 45, 46, 49

Namier, L., 218
Narrative, 27, 59, 170, 177, 228
Nash, M., 248 n. 3
Negotiation (of meaning), 26, 28, 156, 168, 216, 219, 220, 223, 228
Networks, 14, 22–23, 115, 129, 133, 144, 196, 206, 247 n. 14

Organization of production, 31, 32, 83, 88, 106, 159, 163, 165
Ownership: absolute, 229, 230; conception of, 40, 79, 80, 172, 214, 229; de facto (claim by occupation), 1, 49, 57, 137, 141, 172, 178, 179, 180, 210, 214; by legal title or deed, 8, 49, 50, 56, 80, 171, 172; of pasture, claims to, 57, 62, 78, 80, 83, 86; private property, 8, 55, 78, 83, 184

Designer: U.C. Press Staff
Compositor: Prestige Typography
Text: 10/12 Times Roman
Display: Helvetica
Printer: Edwards Bros., Inc.
Binder: Edwards Bros., Inc.